DAILY DEVOTIONS
FOR A HEALTHY
LIFESTYLE

DAILY DEVOTIONS FOR A HEALTHY LIFESTYLE

Scripture Readings, Prayer,
Nutritional Information

Wayne E. Billon, Ph.D., RDN, LDN

Ordering Information:

For orders and inquiries, please contact:
1-888-404-1388
www.goldtouchpress.com
book.orders@goldtouchpress.com

Printed in the United States of America

ACKNOWLEDGMENTS

I would like to express my deepest appreciation to my lovely wife, Cathy, for her encouragement and help with this book. Writing a book takes a considerable amount of time away from normal family life. It takes a special wife to not only tolerate such an endeavor but to be an encouragement through the process.

I would also like to thank two special members of my church family that edited my book, Abigail Christopher and Madeleine Hagan. Thank you so much for your work and the speed in which you completed it. I will be ever grateful to you.

Last but the most important I thank the Holy Spirit for the inspiration to write such a book. The idea grew from a simple devotional to one that a included a prayer, and finally one that included the nutritional notes. I give the praise and thanks to my Lord for the Holy Spirit's guidance.

A DAILY DEVOTION FOR ANYONE WHO WANTS TO MAKE LIFESTYLE CHANGES TO BE HEALTHIER PHYSICALLY AS WELL AS SPIRITUALLY

HOW TO USE THIS BOOK

It has been decades since I started writing this devotional. I was teaching nutrition in college at the time, but I did not devote full time to it until I retired almost two years ago. I have a Ph.D. in Nutrition, and I am a registered dietitian. I have taught nutrition in college for thirty-three years, have consulted in five different areas of dietetics while teaching, and have practiced for six years as a nutrition support team dietitian in a large teaching hospital. I have been a born-again Christian for thirty-nine years, have been a lay teacher in several churches, and have taught classes on dieting for Christians. I have counseled many on weight reduction and I am well aware of the problems they face. It seemed reasonable to me to write a book that would combine my two areas of interest and expertise to encourage those who are trying to develop a healthier lifestyle while introducing them to the basics of nutrition. That is the purpose of this book. It is primarily intended for born-again Christians who believe in God's Word and trust in Him for strength to change to a healthier lifestyle. I say primarily because you do not have to be a believer to read this devotional. A healthier lifestyle includes those who are trying to lose weight but also those who may be fighting a disease state, like diabetes or elevated cholesterol. It also includes those who may be trying to gain weight, overcome an eating disorder, or just wants to be a healthier person. All of these conditions require proper eating, exercise, sleep, and relaxing. However, this devotional can be useful for anyone who is on a diet or not.

Each day has a scripture reference with a brief encouragement based on the scripture, a short prayer, and an instruction to basic nutrition facts with simple advice for those trying to eat healthier. It is not intended to be a diet book or advise you on a specific diet plan, but to give general information on the basics of nutritional facts while providing scriptural encouragement for you to improve your lifestyle. For specific dietary advice, you should consult a registered dietitian.

Each day the nutritional information builds on the previous day's knowledge. Because of this, the devotional does not start with January 1 but begins with day one and goes through day 365. This numbering system enables you to start the nutrition information from the beginning without starting in the middle of a nutrition section. It also allows you to begin the devotional anytime without waiting for the first of the month. Even though you could start this devotional on any day, it will be divided up into twelve sections with a different theme in each section.

It is essential that you understand this devotional is intended primarily for believers in Jesus Christ because it is designed to encourage you to call on your faith in Him. Of course, this devotional can be used by anyone and will inspire anyone. If you are not a believer, not to worry, I can help you with that. The first thirty-one days will have the theme *"Who am I in Christ?"* John 3:16 tells us that *For God so loved the world, that He gave*

His only begotten Son, that whoever believes in Him shall not perish, but have eternal life.[1] When you first received Jesus as your Lord and Savior, your initial belief was based on this scripture. In case that has been some time ago, you can renew or rededicate yourself to the Lord at any time. The last page of this book will help you with a prayer for salvation or rededication.

This devotional is intended to help you be victorious in any healthy life-change program. The encouragement comes from the Bible and describes God's love for us; this devotional will show you that God loves you and will never leave you. He wants you to be healthy, to succeed, and to be a witness for Him. His Word is extremely encouraging to us in every lifestyle that we are engaged. We have to continually remind ourselves of that in everything we do, whether it be dieting, exercising, performing in our workplace, relating to our family or friends, etc. Without God's love and guidance, we are nothing. To obtain the most out of this devotional, we need to understand that fact. Therefore, as you begin your program, remind yourself what it means to have been saved and who you are in Christ. The first month of this devotional describes who you are in Christ because knowing this will show you that you are more than a conqueror and that you can do all things through Christ who strengthens you.

Remember that the last page of this book will help you with a prayer for salvation or rededication.

---

1   Unless otherwise stated, all scripture quotations are from the NEW AMERICAN STANDARD BIBLE®, Copyright © 1960, 1962, 1963, 1968, 1971, 1972, 1973, 1975, 1977, 1995 by The Lockman Foundation. Used by permission. (www.Lockman.org)

Day 1
I Am a Believer

For God so loved the world, that He gave His only begotten Son, that whoever believes in Him shall not perish, but have eternal life. (John 3:16)

As born-again Christians, all of our daily activities should have Jesus in the center. He should be in the center of our homes, workplaces, hobbies, churches, and any extracurricular activities, including lifestyle changes. Everything we do should be Christ-centered. We get so tangled up with everyday routines that frequently we forget to submit everything we do to Jesus. Sometimes we need to stop and remind ourselves not just who we are as Christians, but what that means as who we are in Christ. This knowledge sets us apart from the daily, worldly, and secular routines. Therefore, start this first day of your new regimen by reminding yourself that you are a born-again believer and you are not of this world. You are in the world, and you have to participate in worldly activities, but as a child of God, you are not part of the world. As a believer, you are a child of God and you have an inner strength that enables you to be successful if you call on Jesus and walk in His light. Be bold and courageous. Determine with an act of your will that you can do this! If you trust in Jesus for help, you will not be doing this alone. Remember who you are in Christ and proceed with confidence.

Dear Father God, thank You for sending Your Son to die for me. I thank You that You love me that much, and knowing how much You love me, I know that You want me to succeed in everything that I do. I know that You love me no matter how much weight I lose or gain, but I know that You want me to succeed with my healthy lifestyle program. You want me to take the necessary steps to be healthy while trusting in You for guidance and strength. By an act of my will, I choose to be successful with Your help. I ask that You give me the strength and courage to stick with a new health plan for my life, and I pray that You allow me to become more efficient as a witness for You. In Jesus's name, I ask. Amen.

Nutrition Thought for the Day.
Always set realistic goals for losing weight or gaining weight. Expect fantastic results, but begin with realistic goals while believing strength and guidance come from the Holy Spirit and watch your realistic goals turn into excellent results. If you are trying to lose weight, know that ideal weight loss is one to two pounds per week. I know, you want to lose weight faster than that, but it took you a long time to gain weight and it would not be realistic to believe the weight will disappear overnight. If you lose one pound a week, that is fifty-two pounds a year and a lot of weight. Take one day at a time. If you are trying to gain weight, the proper exercise routine is essential. You will not gain muscle quickly, and you want to avoid gaining weight as fat. Weigh once a week at the same time and with the same clothes each time to be consistent. It is not advisable to weigh every day because weight comes off (or goes on) too slowly and you will get discouraged. Remember, if you are very overweight, slightly overweight, or at your ideal body weight, Jesus loves you just the same. His love for you is never based on your appearance. Even if you have not been saved, He still loves you for He died for you. Always remember this and use this fact as your starting point for your new program for a healthy lifestyle.

Day 2
Spirit, Soul, Body

> Now may the God of peace Himself sanctify you entirely; and may your spirit and soul and body be preserved complete, without blame at the coming of our Lord Jesus Christ. (1 Thessalonians 5:23)

Many Christians do not realize this scripture is true. We are a spirit, we live in a body, and we have a mind or soul (the seat of our emotions, intellect, and will). First Thessalonians 5:23 explains that. We know that when we die our bodies go into the grave and return to the dust from which they were formed, but our spirits go on to heaven or Hades, according to the way we lived our lives on the earth. Our minds move on with our spirits. When we were saved, our bodies did not change, and our minds did not change. The Bible tells us that when we are saved, we are new creatures (2 Corinthians 5:17). So what is new? What changes is our spirit. Our spirit is covered with the robe of righteousness, and when God our Father looks down, He sees the righteousness of Jesus. Ephesians 1:14 says our spirits are marked with a seal by the Holy Spirit, and that seal will forever be there. If we could see into the spirit world, we would be able to determine who is saved and who is not by the seal on our spirits. The seal by the Holy Spirit is part of who we are in Christ, a marked spirit set apart for eternal glory. This should be very encouraging for you and can remind you each day who you are in Christ. You have been claimed by the Holy Spirit and Jesus is in your heart. He promises guidance and wisdom. You are not trying a new healthy lifestyle alone, but you have the Trinity on your side. Knowing this, you can be bold and courageous. Keep reminding yourself of who you are in Christ. Make up your mind, by an act of your will to succeed with your new regimen.

Oh, there will be days when you get off your routine. Your spirit does not change when that happens. God does not fall off the throne or love you any less. Anything you do that is not pleasing in His sight has already been forgiven. If you fail in your daily routine, your biggest enemy is yourself. Forgive yourself and move on. Set your sights on a better tomorrow. Being knocked down is not being defeated. Being knocked down and staying down is being defeated. Get up, knowing your Father does not see your failures, but your righteous spirit sealed by the Holy Spirit. Not your righteousness, but the righteousness you have based on what Jesus did for you.

> Father God, thank You for saving me. Thank You that You love me no matter how many times I disappoint You and You will always be with me, even when I fail. By the power of Your Holy Spirit, continue to remind me who I am in Your Son. I know that with Your strength I can be successful. I am a child of God. I want to love You more each day and to be a witness for You. Strengthen me and help me in my daily walk. In Jesus's mighty name, I pray. Amen.

Nutrition Thought for the Day.
The more of a creature of habit you become concerning your lifestyle, the easier it will be for you to lose weight. Consistency is essential. I know it is not always possible, but if you can eat at the same time each day, your body will adjust to eating at that time, and you will get in sync, so to speak. It will be easier to lose weight or to gain weight if you eat at the same time each day.

WAYNE E. BILLON, PH.D., RDN, LDN

Day 3
I Am Made in God's Image

God created man in His own image, in the image of God He created him; male and female He created them. (Genesis 1:27)

This scripture tells us that we are created in God's image. How does God look? If we could see Him, would we see a striking resemblance? No. God is a Spirit. He lives in the spirit world and is a three-part being, Father, Son, and Holy Spirit. We are also a three-part being in that we live in a body, we have a mind, and we are a spirit. The thing that we have in common with God is our spirit being. When God created us in His image, He created our spirit to be similar to His Spirit. We cannot see into the spirit world but when we go to heaven we will have our new spirit bodies, and we will be able to see everyone in the spirit form. I know this sounds strange, but we know that we will not have corruptible bodies in heaven but incorruptible bodies in a spirit form.

What does this have to do with a healthy lifestyle? When we begin each day, we can wake up with the confidence that we are created in the image of God, and that as born-again believers we are children of God and we know that God loves His children. When we go about our daily routine, we can go with the understanding that, even though we may be overweight or underweight, we are created in God's image, and God's image is not something to scoff. We can, therefore, walk tall, and hold our head high with confidence knowing that our God is walking with His creation. This should encourage us and help us to face each challenge of the day knowing that with God's help we can overcome anything the world throws at us. Remind yourself of this every morning when you wake up and several times during the day to encourage yourself as to who you are in Christ—made in His image!

> Dear Father, I know that I have been created in Your image. I am indeed Your creation, and You are with me every step that I take. I know my physical appearance is not important to You, but my spirit is. I also know that my spirit is marked with a seal by Your Holy Spirit. I know You will go with me everywhere I go and that You will help me accomplish every task that I undertake. It is my desire, an act of my will, that I am a good representation of Your love. As I walk through my day, help me to remember how true this is and show me Your lovingkindness. Thank You for accepting me the way I look right now. I thank You in the name of Jesus. Amen.

Nutrition Thought for the Day.

Remember that it is important to eat three meals a day and not skip meals. This is also part of being consistent each day. If you only eat lunch one day, and the next day you eat breakfast and lunch, and the third day you eat breakfast, lunch, and dinner, this is inconsistency. Breakfast is important. If you spread out what you eat over three meals, and maybe a balanced snack or two, you can actually eat more food in a day and not gain weight then if you ate one or two very large meals a day. On the other hand, if you are trying to achieve weight gain and you are not accustomed to eating three meals a day, the new routine may help you gain weight. Timing is crucial.

Day 4
I Am Sealed by the Holy Spirit

In Him, you also, after listening to the message of truth, the gospel of your salvation—having also believed, you were sealed in Him with the Holy Spirit of promise, who is given as a pledge of our inheritance, with a view to the redemption of *God's own* possession, to the praise of His glory. (Ephesians 1:13)

When you were saved, your spirit was sealed with an indelible mark by the Holy Spirit. Note that this scripture also says that this was given as a pledge of your inheritance. The part of the scripture that says *with a view to the redemption of God's own possession* is not understood by many. It is stated in the New International Version (NIV) as such: "who is a deposit guaranteeing our inheritance until the full redemption of those who are God's possession." This is perhaps a little easier to understand, but whatever version you read, this scripture means that, upon salvation, you were sealed with the Holy Spirit with a forever-mark as a promise of your inheritance that you will receive with full redemption upon Jesus's return.

When you enter heaven, you will understand the full meaning of your redemption obtained for you on the cross. When you get discouraged and think that you can no longer make it, or if you feel like you cannot accomplish your purpose, you can encourage yourself with God's Word that says you have been marked with a seal until the day of redemption. It is a promise that God cannot break. Be encouraged in your daily walk knowing that this time on earth is only temporary. Even though you may be overweight or underweight, a healthy eater or a junk food junkie, God still loves you, and He is always with you. He wants you to be healthy, and He wants you to do the things in the natural that would help you to be healthy. Do not be discouraged. Claim this scripture and walk through the day with your head held high knowing that you have a tremendous reward coming with your redemption.

Dear Father God, I know that my spirit has been sealed by the power of the Holy Spirit and that I have a glorious redemption waiting for me. I know that in the meantime You will not leave me nor forsake me. I ask for You to continually remind me of Your love and Your redemptive power. I know that You will help me to get through this healthy lifestyle regimen so that I can be healthier and be a better witness for You. I thank You in the name of Jesus. Amen.

Nutrition Thought for the Day.

Did you know that eating before you go to bed can have detrimental effects on your body? Your body's metabolism slows down during sleep. Food that was ingested a few hours before sleep is not needed and is converted to fat. This is not good if you are trying to lose weight. As part of your consistent daily routine, try to set a time, at least three hours before you go to bed, and let that be the last time you eat for the day. Everyone's schedule is different but try for at least two hours, if not three or four.

WAYNE E. BILLON, PH.D., RDN, LDN

Day 5
God Sees my Heart

God *sees* not as man sees, for man looks at the outward appearance, but the LORD looks at the heart. (1 Samuel 16:7b)

When God looks down at us, He looks at our spirits and not our outward appearance. Our spirits are made in His image and sealed by the Holy Spirit. Because of this, when He looks at our spirits He sees the righteousness of Jesus Christ if we are born- again Christians. He does not look at our physical appearance and make some stupid judgmental statement like "he/she is too big, too overweight" or "he/she is too skinny, too pale" or anything that takes into consideration our physical appearance. He looks at our hearts. This scripture means that when He looks at our spirits He sees the real us and He sees that we have accepted Jesus as our Savior and Lord. This pleases and honors Him because that is why He sent His Son to the earth as a man.

Yes, it is important for us to be healthy and to make every attempt to live a healthy life. That is also God's desire for us. However, if our physical appearance is not pleasing to everyone around us, or is not even pleasing to ourselves when we look in the mirror, it does not affect our relationship with our God one iota. It only affects our relationship with those around us, and then only if we let it. We should not be moved by how other people see us or even by how we see ourselves. The only thing that matters is how God sees us when He looks down upon us. He sees our spirits, born-again spirits that make us children of God. He sees us as someone made in His very own image. Therefore, do not be moved by peoples' judgment of your physical appearance, but be moved by how God sees you. This fact should touch you, and it should give you encouragement and confidence that your almighty Creator sees you as His child and know that He will never leave you and `He will always be with you.

Dear Father God, I thank You again that I am created in Your image. I know that peoples' judgment of my appearance is of no consequence. I will not be discouraged by my weight or my looks, but instead, I will be encouraged that I am a child of God and that I am created in Your image. I know that when You look upon me, You do not see me as I see myself or as anyone else sees me, but You see me as I am, as Your child created in Your image. I thank You for who I am in Jesus Christ, and it is in His name that I pray. Amen.

Nutrition Thought for the Day.

You should eat your more substantial meal when your energy level for the day is at its highest. For example, some of us are morning people, some of us have higher energy levels in the afternoon, and some of us are evening people. If your mornings are slow and sluggish, your most important meal should not be breakfast. If your highest activity is in the afternoon, your most significant meal should be at lunch. If you slow down after the evening meal and just sit around the house looking at the TV, you do not want to make the evening meal your largest meal, even though that tends to be our American custom. Remember, you should not eat just before you go to bed. Most of us skip breakfast or have a light breakfast, a moderate lunch, and a large dinner. Depending on your activity and energy levels during the day, most of us should have a modest breakfast, a larger lunch, and a smaller dinner.

Day 6
You Chose Me

"You did not choose Me, but I chose you, and appointed you that you would go and bear fruit and *that* your fruit would remain, so that whatever you ask of the Father in My name He may give to you." (John 15:16)

Many times we lose sight of the fact that when Jesus hung on the cross, He saw all the sins that were ever committed and would ever be committed, including all of your sins. It is because of sin that He died. He knew that you would fail Him from time to time and He knew if you would or would not have a health problem, even a weight problem. Those things did not make any difference to Him. He died for your sins that you could be with Him eternally in heaven. He saw the problems and mistakes you would make in the future and, in spite of all of your insecurities, failings, and sins, He chose to die for you anyway. Even if He knew you would not accept Him, He chose to die for you. There is no greater love than that. So when you go through your day, and you feel miserable for one reason or another, you should stop and remind yourself that you are not just another creature walking around on this earth. You are special.

You have been chosen by your God to live eternally with Him in heaven. It does not matter how you feel, it does not matter what you look like, nor does it matter what you think about yourself. You need to know that, in Jesus Christ, you are one of God's chosen ones. Because of what Jesus did, you will have eternal life with Him; and you know what, your weight will not be a problem, nor will it prevent you from receiving His love, unless you let it. You are God's chosen, and He is with you and will never forsake you. You can accomplish a new healthy lifestyle knowing that God is with you and loves you no matter what you do. Do not be discouraged if you mess up with your program. Always be trying to do your best, stick to your regimen, and remember that if something happens you fail, you are still God's chosen and He still loves you.

Dear Father God, I know that You have chosen me to receive Your salvation. You knew all of my shortcomings and all of the times I would fail You in my entire life, yet You chose to die for me anyway. Your love is truly beyond my comprehension but I accept it. Help me to walk in Your love today and to see myself as You see me—as a child of God and as one who can do all things through Christ who strengthens me. In Jesus's name, I pray. Amen.

Nutrition Thought for the Day.

Your new lifestyle program should start with proper food choices, but before you can understand what to choose, you need to have a basic understanding of what happens when you eat. The first principle to discuss is your blood glucose level. If a doctor tells you your blood sugar is too high, he is referring to your glucose level in the blood. If your level is high and stays high, this is what is called diabetes. If your blood sugar level drops too low, you get weak and shaky. So what is glucose? Glucose comes from simple sugars and starch, compounds that are called carbohydrates. Diets low in ample carbohydrates can cause you to be weak and shaky. As your blood glucose level drops, this sends signals to your brain which sends signals to your stomach, and you begin to feel hungry. It is important to keep your blood sugar in the normal range.

Day 7
God's Promises Are True

For as many as are the promises of God, in Him they are yes; therefore also through Him is our Amen to the glory of God through us. (2 Corinthians1:20)

This scripture says that all the promises of God, through Jesus, are yes and amen. This means that all promises of God receive a yes. His promises are real. He cannot break them or change them because that is His nature. Note that it also says, "the promises of God, in Him." The *in Him* refers to in Jesus's name. The promises are real because of what Jesus did for us. "Amen" means, yes, I agree. Therefore when God promises something in His Word, and you say "Amen" to it, you agree that God's promises are real and they are for you. You have to decide in your mind if you believe God's Word or not. If you do, then you also have to choose to live by God's promises.

As a believer, you state that you believe God's Word. Thus, everything in this devotional so far you must believe is true. Know that God's promises are yes and amen. So when His Word says you are one of God's children, that He loves you, and that He will never leave you, then all these statements are true, and all you have to do is say Amen to them and move on. Be encouraged that God's Word is true and that God cannot lie. Be encouraged that He is with you and will never forsake you. Be encouraged that you can do all things through Christ who strengthens you (Philippians 4:13). Who you are in Christ means that all of God's promises are available for you. Remind yourself this day of all the good things God has done for you and all the promises He has given you for the future. Walk on with the determination that you can be successful with your new healthy lifestyle regimen.

Dear Father, I believe that Your Word is true and Your promises are real. Today I choose to say yes and amen to them. I look forward to seeing Your Word fulfilled in my life. I choose to believe Your promises. I know that I am a child of God and I can do all things through Christ who strengthens me (Philippians 4:13). I know I can conquer any addiction and be a healthier person for the greater glory of God, and I will be successful with my new healthy lifestyle regimen with Your help. I make this confession in the name of Jesus. Amen.

Nutrition Thought for the Day.

As your blood sugar drops, you become hungry. When you get hungry, you eat food, and this involves chewing. Chewing is something we take for granted but is actually very important. Some people gulp their food down very quickly, some are very slow picky eaters, and some are anywhere in between. The more you chew, the smaller the food particles are going to be and the faster they will be digested and absorbed. The more you chew, the longer it will take you to eat. As your food is digested and absorbed, your blood glucose level rises. When your blood sugar rises to normal or above, you begin to feel full. You want this to happen while food is still on your plate. This is when you need to exercise willpower and push yourself away from the table. If you can do this when you feel full, you will be able to eat less and this will help you to lose weight. If you are trying to gain weight, it will help prevent you from overeating and increasing fat. In either case, it will help you digest your food better, and that means more of the nutrients, vitamins, minerals, and antioxidants will be absorbed.

Day 8
Faith to Move Mountains

And He said to them, "Because of the littleness of your faith; for truly I say to you, if you have faith the size of a mustard seed, you will say to this mountain, 'Move from here to there,' and it will move, and nothing will be impossible to you." (Matthew 17:20)

I cannot prove the promises of God are true. I can give you examples of promises I have seen fulfilled in the lives of faithful Christians, and I know you have seen many also, but I cannot prove to you that they are true. In fact, I cannot prove anything to you about the Bible. I can give you example after example of things that I have seen happen based on biblical truths, but I cannot prove, nor can you, that if you received Jesus as your Savior and Lord, you would enter into the Kingdom of heaven after this life is over. Salvation and everything else after salvation are based on faith. So how much faith does it take? Look at the scripture above. Jesus says that if you have faith the size of a mustard seed you can speak to a mountain and move it. A mustard seed is a tiny seed, the size of a pinhead. No question about it, you have been given that much faith. You used it to receive salvation, and you need to continue to use it throughout your life in everything you do. The more you use your faith, the stronger it gets.

Right now your mountain is your weight, whether it be too little or too much. If you believe that Jesus is your Savior and Lord, and you believe that He is in your heart, then your faith is bigger than a mustard seed and strong enough for you to speak to your mountain. Your mountain is any obstacle that is trying to block you from losing weight (or gaining weight. Tell your mountain that it cannot stop you any longer because you have authority over temptations and any obstacles that try to block you. Exercise your faith as you exercise your body and command these obstacles to be gone from you. Believe everything the Bible says about you, and that is you can overcome—you will overcome—and be a healthier happier person.

Dear Father God, I now understand that You have given me sufficient faith to move the mountains in my life. My mountain is my weight and every obstacle that stands in my way, trying to block me from achieving my weight loss/gain and exercise goal. I receive the faith that You have given me, and I speak to my mountain and command it to be removed from my life! I am a child of God, and I choose to believe that Your Word is true and that Your promises are real for me, including my faith. I declare this to be true in the name of Jesus. Amen.

Nutrition Thought for the Day.
As your blood glucose levels drop, you become hungry. If you eat so fast and fill your stomach with a significant amount of food, more than you need, you will still be hungry because the food has not yet been absorbed and your blood glucose levels are still low. Thus, you go back for seconds and eat even. Once the food is digested and absorbed, you start to feel very full. This is when you sit in a big relaxing chair, moan and groan saying, "Oh, I ate too much." If you chew longer and eat slower, you will digest your food faster and your blood sugar will go up before you finish eating your first serving. If at that point you stopped eating, you will not overindulge. A key here is not to overload your plate.

Day 9
Faith vs. Doubt

And Jesus answered and said to them, "Truly I say to you, if you have faith and do not doubt, you will not only do what was done to the fig tree, but even if you say to this mountain, 'Be taken up and cast into the sea,' it will happen." (Matthew 21:21)

This is another scripture concerned with faith, but it never hurts to see too many examples of faith. In this story, in the book of Matthew, Jesus and His disciples were passing a fig tree from a short distance away. Jesus saw that the fig tree had leaves on it and He assumed that it also had figs. When He approached the tree He found that it had no figs, so He cursed the tree, and it withered. When His disciples saw what happened to the fig tree, and how quickly it happened, they were amazed. Jesus used this opportunity to teach them what they could do if they just used their faith. He told them they could also do that to the fig tree and they could even move a mountain.

The moving of the mountain was an illustrative example. The mountain could be different things for different people. If you are on a diet and trying to lose or gain weight, then your mountain right now is being overweight or underweight. You can speak to your mountain to help you to lose/gain weight. That does not mean that the weight will disappear or increase overnight. Several things can cause one to have an unhealthy weight including the metabolism you have through genetics or a secondary effect of some disease, but most people are carrying extra weight as a result of overeating and not exercising enough. Others are underweight because of an illness or an eating disorder. Whatever is causing your weight problem, be it medication, overeating, under eating, or a lack of exercise, any of those could be your mountain. Most of the conditions you can control by diet and exercise. You can speak to those problems directly and by an act of your will decide you are going to make positive, healthy changes. Start to exercise your faith so that you can fulfill what is stated in Matthew 21:21.

Dear Father God, I thank You that You gave me a measure of faith that is sufficient for me to conquer anything that blocks the path to my goal, and that goal is a healthy lifestyle. By an act of my will I, refuse to let my appearance or my desire for food rule over me. Instead, I speak to those desires and command them to be gone in the name of Jesus. And I speak to inactivity, unhealthy eating, and yes, even laziness, to be gone from my life in the name of Jesus. I choose to complete my new regimen in a healthy matter so that I may obtain a healthier status and use my experiences for Your praise and glory. I make these statements in the mighty name of Jesus. Amen.

Nutrition Thought for the Day.

An important note about dieting for someone that is pregnant: If you happen to be pregnant, you need to note that this is not a time for you to try to lose weight. For registered dietitians, the rule of thumb is to never put a pregnant woman on a weight reduction diet. At times there will be exceptions but generally speaking, if you are pregnant you do not want to go on a weight reduction diet without advice from your physician and a registered dietitian.

Day 10
You Are a Child of God

For you are all sons of God through faith in Christ Jesus. (Galatians 3:26)

This scripture relates to who we are in Christ as sons of God (sons refers to humanity and also includes daughters). Many scriptures tell us over and over that we are coheirs with Christ and sons of God. This fact, like the others, is based on faith but it is another scripture to encourage us as to who we are in Christ. Stop and meditate for a minute and think about what this says. Think of all of heaven and all of creation, everything that God has. Think of His riches and His grace, and then think that all of this is part of your inheritance. Yes, you are to share it with many others at the end of this age, but there is so much to share that you will still have more than you can ever imagine. God loves you so much that He calls you one of His children.

Do not be confused; God is not a sexist when He says "sons," He is referring to humanity and it means we are all children of His inheritance and it does not matter if we are male or female. You are coheir with Jesus Christ for the Kingdom of God. How awesome is that? Your God is an awesome God, and He loves you that much! You should be significantly encouraged. Go about your day knowing you have a great inheritance—and you know what? You will receive that inheritance regardless of your physical appearance. That does not suggest that you should not worry about your appearance from a health standpoint, but God loves you just as you are! Continue with your resolve to be healthy but remember that God loves you just the way you are.

> Father God, it is so awesome that You love me so much that You actually call me Your child. By the power of Your Holy Spirit help me to understand how real that fact is. As I meditate on the meaning of being a child of God, make it clear to me so that I can walk with my head held high and with the utmost confidence that I am coheir with Jesus Christ. You are an awesome God, and You love me so much just the way I am, no matter what my weight is or how much weight I lose or gain. I know I should try to be healthy, but I know that You will love me no matter what. I thank You in Jesus's name. Amen.

Nutrition Thought for the Day.

You probably have heard some mention of diabetes and blood sugar in the news and on TV. Blood sugar is the amount of glucose that is circulating in your blood. Glucose is a simple sugar also known as a monosaccharide. It is found in table sugar, fruits, some vegetables, and starch. To be absorbed, it must be released from whatever it is bound to, be that another sugar or some other compound. It is from glucose that we derive most of our energy. If glucose is low, we are slow, sluggish, and will feel weak and shaky. We will also begin to feel hungry when our blood sugar drops. However, if we are compulsive overeaters, we may still be hungry when blood sugar is high. If we have diabetes, we can still be starving when blood sugar is very high. If you have any of the symptoms mentioned above or have diabetes in your immediate family, you should have your blood sugar checked. Many times you can find screenings for blood sugar at drugstores and supermarkets. Take advantage of such opportunities. Controlling your blood sugar is an important step in preventing excessive weight gain and controlling/preventing diabetes.

Day 11
You Are a Child of God II

The Spirit Himself testifies with our spirit that we are children of God, and if children, heirs also, heirs of God and fellow heirs with Christ, if indeed we suffer with *Him* so that we may also be glorified with *Him*. (Romans 8:16–17)

Like yesterday, this devotion is also entitled You Are a Child of God because it is one of the scriptures that cements, so to speak, the fact that we are coheirs with Christ. It tells us that the Holy Spirit Himself testifies with our spirit that we are children of God. That means your spirit knows you are a child of God. You have to accept in your mind, through faith, that you are a child of God and your body will have to line up with that fact. The scripture also tells us that as a child of God, you are an heir and coheir with Christ. The last part tells you that you will suffer with Him.

As a Christian you can expect to be persecuted. In some parts of the world that is quite evident today. As an overweight or an underweight person, I am sure you have also experienced persecution or criticism. Growing up I was very skinny and I was teased about it constantly. They used to tell me that I could go in a pool hall, hold up a cue stick, and hide behind it. Like me, your persecution may have nothing to do with the fact that you are a Christian, but when you are persecuted for whatever reason, remember that as a child of God your time here is only temporary. You have a great inheritance waiting for you. Do not let persecution get you down. Do not be discouraged. God is on your side, therefore who can be against you? You are victorious. Continue in your healthy lifestyle program, and wait patiently for your inheritance while letting persecution roll off you like water off a duck's back.

Lord Jesus, I realize how much persecution and suffering You went through for me. I may be persecuted and criticized because of my weight or my general appearance, but my persecution is nothing compared to what You endured. Any persecution I receive is only temporary, and it will in no way separate me from Your love nor will it prevent me from my inheritance. I thank You that I am a child of God, chosen by You until the day of redemption. Remind me each day, by the power of Your Holy Spirit who I am in Christ, and I thank You again for my awesome inheritance. I thank You in the name of Jesus, Amen.

Nutrition Thought for the Day.

Carbohydrates consist of three different groups. One group is the simple sugars or monosaccharides. Mono means one; saccharide means sweet. These are glucose, fructose, and galactose. Disaccharides are also considered simple sugars. As the name suggests, disaccharides are two monosaccharides linked together. These are sucrose, lactose, and maltose. Sucrose is table sugar and is made up of one glucose and one fructose. Lactose is milk sugar and is made up of one glucose and one galactose. Maltose is malt sugar and is made up of two units of glucose. Disaccharides cannot be absorbed until they have been converted to monosaccharides. Once absorbed, all the sugars go directly to the liver. Galactose and much of the fructose are converted to glucose by the liver and allowed to go into the bloodstream. Some fructose and glucose are utilized in the liver for energy or are stored as a compound called glycogen.

Day 12
You Are a Child of God III

So that being justified by His grace we would be made heirs according to *the* hope of eternal life. (Titus 3:7)

This is the third day with the same title to strengthen further your conviction that you are a child of God. This scripture has another statement that we have not mentioned as of yet, and that is being justified by His grace. It is important to point out that you are a child of God not based on anything you have done, but based on what Jesus did for you. He chose you and you did not choose Him. The Bible tells us that it is by grace we have been saved. People try to define grace with several different catchy phrases, but basically it is unmerited favor, with emphasis on unmerited. God pours out His grace on you in an abundant fashion even though you do not deserve it. Yes, you are a child of God, and you are justified to be such, but your justification comes purely from what Jesus did for you. It has nothing to do with how good you are, how much of the Bible you read each day, or how much you pray each day. And as previously mentioned, it certainly has nothing to do with the way you look or if you mess up on your new healthy lifestyle program. No matter what you do, God's grace is still there in an abundant fashion. Be encouraged knowing that God's abundant grace is poured out on you in everything you do and that you are a child of God.

> Dear Father God, I thank You for the abundant grace that You pour out on me consistently even though I do not always do what I should, keep my promises to You, or faithfully follow my new healthy lifestyle program. I know that I do not deserve Your grace, but You pour it out on me anyway as a result of what Jesus did for me. I realize it does not mean I can do anything I want and still stand before You sinless, but I can be forgiven for anything I do because of Your grace. While that is true, the purpose of Your grace is to help me be an overcomer and be successful in all I do even though I do not deserve it. Thank You for never leaving me. I am indeed a child of God. In the name of Jesus, I pray. Amen.

Nutrition Thought for the Day.

Starch is long chains of glucose linked together and is also broken down in the intestines to individual units of glucose and absorbed as such. This is true if it is wheat starch, cornstarch, or any other kind of starch. The third classification of carbohydrate is fiber—yes fiber is a carbohydrate. It is long chains of glucose hooked together like starch, but we cannot digest it in our intestines. Most digestion and absorption takes place in the small intestines. The pancreas and the walls of the small intestines secrete enzymes that digest carbohydrates. Enzymes are compounds that cause a chemical reaction to take place or speed up a reaction but are not changed by the reaction. Enzymes are specific for what they react on. For example, sucrose is the disaccharide made up of one unit of glucose and one unit of fructose. To be absorbed, sucrose must be broken down into its individual units. This is done by the enzyme sucrose which will not react with any other sugar or compound except sucrose. It breaks sucrose down to glucose and fructose. Our primary source of energy in our body is glucose. All carbohydrates, when digested and used for energy, produce four calories per gram.

Day 13
Led by God's Spirit

For all who are being led by the Spirit of God, these are sons of God. (Romans 8:14)

It is imperative you understand that when you were saved, you became a child of God and coheir with Christ. This is absolutely amazing and awesome and is something you should spend some time meditating on and not just reading about in the scriptures. This is a fact that you have to get down into your spirit. Once you realize how much God loves you, and that He considers you as one of His children, you can walk with greater confidence in His love and guidance. When you know who you are in Christ and that you really are a child of God, you will be more prone to want to follow His Word and do what pleases Him. God still loves you if you are overweight, your normal weight, or you are underweight. However, He wants you to be healthy for your own good so that you can complete the mission He gave you in what is known as the Great Commission (Mark 16:15–18).

You should be doing everything you can to be healthy, not only for your own good and the good of your families but also for the glory of God and for spreading His Word. It is not just preachers or ordained people who have been given this Great Commission, but it has been given to all of us. We need to be a witness for our God wherever we are, to our family, to our coworkers, and to our neighbors. Thus, with each passing day be encouraged that you are a child of God and that Your Father God is with you. By the power of His Holy Spirit, He will help you to be successful in your healthy lifestyle program if you trust Him and have faith in Him.

> Dear Father, I am still amazed by Your awesome gift of eternal life that Jesus earned for me. I did not earn salvation based on my merit, but on what He did for me by dying on the cross. As a result of His merit, not only am I granted eternal life with You, but I am also Your child. I have the Holy Spirit guiding me and encouraging me. I know that I can do all things through Christ if I trust and obey. Remind me each day who I am in Christ and that by Your help, I can be successful with my healthy lifestyle program. I declare Jesus's name. Amen.

Nutrition Thought for the Day.

To have the energy to do our daily tasks, we must have sufficient carbohydrates in our diet. Complex carbohydrates (starch) are digested slower than the simple sugars, and this raises our blood glucose gradually. This slower digestion is a good thing. This provides us with energy without causing our pancreas to secrete too much insulin at one time. If our blood sugar rises too fast, like after we eat something that is very high in sugar, the pancreas overreacts and secretes too much insulin. This causes our blood sugar to drop rapidly and gives us a weak and shaky feeling. Because of this, it is not good to eat simple sugars on an empty stomach. We want to eat complex carbohydrates at every meal to help promote a slow rise in blood sugar. Avoid sugar as much as possible for it is also considered to be empty calories. This means that sugar provides us with only calories and no other nutrients such as vitamins, minerals, protein, fat, fiber, or antioxidants. It is glucose that causes our blood sugar to rise too quickly and serves no practical purpose for someone that is dieting.

Day 14
You Have a Right to Be a Child of God

But as many as received Him, to them He gave the right to become children of God, *even* to those who believe in His name. (John 1:12)

All you have to do to accomplish what this scripture says is to receive and believe in His name. Being saved, or being born again, is accepting Him. As a born-again Christian, you have already accomplished that fact. Remember, by believing in His name, you believe everything that His Word tells you. This includes all the encouraging statements that have been made so far in this devotional, such as being more than conquerors, being overcomers, and being called to spread God's Word to all the world. It also means that He will never leave you nor forsake you and that by the power of His Holy Spirit you can do all things through Christ who strengthens you (Philippians 4:13). So once more, be encouraged this day that you are a child of God, that is who you are in Christ. You can accomplish this healthy lifestyle program and be victorious for Christ. Do not be discouraged. You are loved by your Father God and He wants you to be successful. Walk on, head held high, and be victorious for not only yourself but also for Him.

Dear Father God, I thank You again for receiving me as Your child and for always being with me. I know I am successful in Your eyes because I have received Jesus as my Savior and Lord. I know I am more than an overcomer by Your Word and I am encouraged to know that I can complete my healthy lifestyle program with success. I thank You for being with me and for Your guidance. In Jesus's name, I pray. Amen.

Nutrition Thought for the Day.

There are several ways to slow down the absorption of glucose from our intestines besides taking in less sugar and more complex carbohydrates. One has already been mentioned on day eight of this devotional; it is something as simple as chewing food very slowly. We should take one average size bite (not a huge bite) and chew it very thoroughly until it is just about liquefied in our mouths before swallowing. This accomplishes a couple of things. First, it breaks the food down into smaller particles. When the smaller particles empty into the stomach from the esophagus, they increase the concentration of particles in the stomach. This causes the stomach to draw in water from the stomach wall to lower the concentration of particles per volume of fluid. While this is happening, the muscles surrounding the stomach wall are contracting and mixing the food. The stomach will not allow the food to move on to the small intestines until this is accomplished. This slows down emptying time of the stomach to some degree. Also, by chewing our food more slowly, it takes us longer to eat. This simple fact means that food is not introduced into the small intestines as fast and thus is not absorbed as quickly. This contributes to a steady rise in blood sugar. Concentrate on chewing your food very, very well and eating slower.

Day 15
Led by God's Spirit II

Do you not know that you are a temple of God and *that* the Spirit of God dwells in you? (1 Corinthians 3:16)

Or do you not know that your body is a temple of the Holy Spirit who is in you, whom you have from God, and that you are not your own? (1 Corinthians 6:19)

Your body is a temple of the Holy Spirit and He lives in you if you are saved. This begins a whole new set of ideas and is another remarkable fact about your God. You may not always feel like a temple. You may not always act like a temple. However, the Bible is not based on feelings. It is based on facts—every Word of it is true. If you are a born-again Christian, you believe that to be true. Therefore, you house the Holy Spirit in your body whether you understand it or believe it or not. Here is something to seriously spend time meditating. No matter how you see yourself, no matter what you have done right or wrong this day, no matter how well you maintained your healthy lifestyle program yesterday, God sees you as worthy enough to make you His temple. How awesome is that! Your God loves you so much that He chooses to abide in your body with His Holy Spirit. You do not have to beg or plead with God to send you His Spirit; He is already with you. You are one of His chosen people, a child of God, more than a conqueror. Meditate on this and decide to walk out His Word, not by your feelings or your image of yourself, but by His image of you.

Dear Father God, You are indeed an awesome God. Help me to see myself as You see me, as a vessel that is worthy of housing the Holy Spirit. I am not worthy on my account, but I am worthy because of what Jesus has done for me on the cross. Help me to be ever mindful of that fact and help me to be a living, walking example of Your love. In Jesus's name, I pray. Amen.

Nutrition Thought for the Day.

The total amount of carbohydrates you should ingest each day will vary depending on your weight, the amount of muscle you have, your activity, and the genetic factors controlling your metabolism. Generally speaking, most textbooks say that you should have at least 100 grams of carbohydrates per day. So, how much are 100 grams? A regular slice of white bread is about fifteen grams of carbohydrate. One half-cup of a starchy vegetable (like potatoes, winter squash, or pasta) is also fifteen grams of carbohydrate. A half of a cup of green-yellow vegetables (as in the cabbage family, tomatoes, eggplants, greens) is about five grams of carbohydrate. A glass (eight ounces) of milk contains eight grams of carbohydrate. This will give you some idea of what can add up to be 100 grams. If you have more muscle than the average person your size, or you are doing more exercise than the average person your size, you will need more than 100 grams of carbohydrate.

When I was teaching, I always advised my students to encourage people to get at least 150 grams of carbohydrate per day to be on the safe side. Many other things go into a balanced diet besides the carbohydrate-containing foods and eventually, we will cover all of them. Fiber is not a digestible carbohydrate, and fat and protein do not contain any carbohydrate.

Day 16
You Are Expensive

For you have been bought with a price: therefore glorify God in your body. (1 Corinthians 6:20)

Something you should already know, you are very valuable to our God. He paid a great price for you, the price was the death of His Son; and not just death, but a horrible, cruel, and excruciating death. This scripture tells us that since we have been bought for such a high price, we should honor God with our body. We can do this in several ways. First, we can thank God daily for what Jesus did for us, and we can sing praises to Him. We can also honor God by not abusing our bodies through illicit sex, illegal drugs, and yes, compulsive behaviors like extreme overeating, starving ourselves, and laziness. God designed our bodies to work with an extreme amount of precision and dependability. We override our bodies' abilities when we do not treat our bodies healthily. When we do this, we are dishonoring the body for which Jesus died. Maybe you have never looked at your body in this way. If not, you should now. In either case, spend some time in this devotional meditating on how you are glorifying God with your body and how you are dishonoring God with your body.

Resolve to change. You have already made one resolution to make at least one change. Hence you are on a new healthy lifestyle program that includes diet and exercise. You have taken a step in the right direction to complete this task. Do not give up! Do not be discouraged! Realize that as you follow a safe and healthy weight loss/gain program (that includes exercise), you are glorifying God with your body. Continue to do this but remember that on days when you may fail to maintain your goal, Jesus still loves you. You did not sin, but if it makes you feel better, just ask for forgiveness and start anew.

Dear Father God, I resolve this day not to dishonor you with my body by my unhealthy habits. I also resolve to continue with my healthy lifestyle program so that I can lose weight and increase my endurance, thus becoming healthier. In this way, I will be honoring you with my body. When I start to go astray from my healthy lifestyle plan, please gently remind me by the power of Your Holy Spirit and light my path so that I may follow after Your Holy Spirit's lead and increase my health and stamina. In Jesus's name, I pray. Amen.

Nutrition Thought for the Day.

No meal should be pure carbohydrate but should be a balance of the essential nutrients. The essential nutrients besides carbohydrate include fat, protein, vitamins, minerals, and water. Yes, fat is an essential nutrient, we just do not want to over eat or eat the wrong kind. Fiber, as mentioned, is also very important in our diet but is not listed as one of the essential nutrients because it is a carbohydrate, so it is hidden in this classification. To review, remember that fiber is a long strand of glucose linked together just as a long strand of starch is glucose linked together. However, fiber is connected with a different type of link, and the enzymes that break down starch will not digest fiber.

Day 17
You Have Been Washed

…but you were washed, but you were sanctified, but you were justified in the name of the Lord Jesus Christ and in the Spirit of our God. (1 Corinthians 6:11)

In the verses just before 1 Corinthians 6:11, Paul admonished the Corinthians for the many things that they were doing wrong. He told them about the evil deeds of the unrighteous that would prevent them from inheriting the Kingdom of God. These deeds included fornicators, idolaters, adulterers, effeminate, and homosexuals. Then in 1 Corinthians 6:11 He states that some of them participated in such things, but they were washed, sanctified, and justified in the name of the Lord Jesus. This is another powerful scripture that tells us how much we have been delivered from by the blood of Jesus. Whatever you may have done, even all the things mentioned in 1 Corinthians 6 that were an abomination in God's sight, you have been delivered from, sanctified, justified, and set apart. Because of your salvation, the sins of the past no longer have a hold on you—unless you allow it. The devil does not want you to succeed in anything that you do, particularly in things that would glorify God. By now you should be realizing who you are in Christ and be developing a desire to glorify Him with your body, including being successful with your lifestyle program. The devil tells you to look at your past and see all the times you messed up and all the things you did wrong, that you will never be successful, and you cannot complete this new healthy lifestyle. However, you can quote this scripture to him and remind him (for he already knows it) and yourself that you have been washed, sanctified, and justified by the blood of the Lamb. You are more than an overcomer and, by the power of the Holy Spirit, success can and will be yours as you glorify God with your body.

Dear Father, I know that the devil does not want me to be successful in anything that I do for You or to improve my own life. However, I know that the blood of Jesus has restored me to be in perfect union with You. I know I have been washed, sanctified, and justified to be in Your presence and to spend eternity with You. I also understand that this is not based on anything I did, but is based on what Jesus did for me. Thank You, Jesus, for washing me with Your blood and justifying and sanctifying me so that I may spend eternity with You. I know I can and will be successful with my new program with Your help and I thank You and praise You for it. I declare this Lord in Your precious name. Amen.

Nutrition Thought for the Day.
The two types of fiber are soluble fiber and insoluble fiber. Soluble fiber does not dissolve as sugar dissolves in water, but it forms a gel-like substance that attaches to bile in the small intestines. The liver makes bile from cholesterol and stores it in the gallbladder until fat is introduced into the small intestines. Through chemical signals in the blood, the presence of fat in the intestines causes the gallbladder to release the bile into the small intestines to emulsify fat. The bile is then reabsorbed into the blood at the end of the small intestines and is recycled back to the gallbladder. Soluble fiber binds with some of the bile and prevents it from being reabsorbed and thus being recycled. The liver then has to make new bile from more cholesterol. In this way, a diet that is high in soluble fiber can possibly help to lower cholesterol.

Day 18
We Are New Creatures

> Therefore if anyone is in Christ, *he is* a new creature; the old things passed away; behold, new things have come. (2 Corinthians 5:17)

A new Christian may not fully understand this scripture. You should know that being "in Christ" means being born again. You should also know that when you were born again, you may not have been able to see a change. You know that your body did not look any different and your mind was the same, so what changed? It was your spirit. You have a new spirit that is covered with the robe of righteousness. The old things passed away, behold, new things have come (2 Corinthians 5:17). What does that mean? You still have the old temptations you always had, so what passed away and what is new? After your salvation experience, you have a choice of returning to the old way and doing things the way you always did or accepting that you are a new creature by choosing to act like one. This means avoiding the things that tempted you in the past and, instead of looking at distracting TV programs, you could spend time reading God's Word. It is like an alcoholic that gets saved and delivered from alcohol then decides to go back to bars to try to get his friends saved. We all know that will not work. While his intentions are admirable, he will eventually end up drinking and getting back in the same old rut. So, what does this have to do with you?

You are a new creature, and you are venturing out into a new realm of a healthy lifestyle. You need to do all you can to renew your mind by studying God's Word, staying in Christian fellowship, and avoiding your old pastimes that were distractions. Surround yourself with people that will encourage you in your new lifestyle, that is, encourage you to stick to your healthy program. If you hang out with people that over eat or under eat continuously, and have a diet mainly of junk food, you will have a hard time sticking to your routine. It may require that you avoid some old friends. This may not be easy, but it is essential for your success. In all cases remember that Jesus is with you and He will see you through this. You are more than a conqueror.

> Dear Father, help me in my new regimen by leading me to like-minded believers that will encourage me to be successful. Help me to avoid those that would lead me back to my old ways of overeating and under-exercising. I do not want to offend anyone, but at the same time, I want to glorify You in my body by living healthy and eating healthy. I know that You will help me with this and I put my trust in You. In Jesus's name, I pray. Amen.

Nutrition Thought for the Day.

The other type of fiber mentioned was insoluble fiber. This fiber does not form a gel-like substance. However, it absorbs water and causes the digestive tract to expand. This is good because it increases movement through the digestive tract and prevents waste products from staying in the large intestines too long. If waste products remain in the large intestines for an extended period, the trillions of bacteria that live in the large intestines could digest them. The longer the material stays in the large intestines, the longer the bacteria have to digest it, and possibly produce carcinogenic (cancer producing) substances. By moving this material out faster, it could possibly prevent some intestinal cancers.

Day 19
Age Does Not Matter

Let no one look down on your youthfulness, but *rather* in speech, conduct, love, faith *and* purity, show yourself an example of those who believe. (1 Timothy 4:12)

In this letter, Paul was talking to Timothy and encouraging him because he was young. He said that youth did not matter, but the way he presented himself was the important thing to consider. Maybe you are not young, and you say, "this does not pertain to me." The point of this scripture is that your age, whether it is your chronological age or your spiritual age, does not dictate who you are in Christ, nor should it prevent you from being an example to those around you. What is important is all of the characteristics mentioned in this scripture, including your speech (the words you say and the way you say them), your conduct, the love you have for others, your faith, and your purity should be beyond reproach. This is important so that, as a born-again believer, you can show yourself as an example. It does not matter if you are elderly, middle age, young, or very young—be a witness to all of those around you and help them to grow in the Lord.

Lord Jesus, I thank You that You are ageless and in eternity there is no record of time. Too often I let age and my time as a Christian dictate my actions. You do not see me as young or old, but as one of Your children that Jesus died for and, regardless of my chronological age or my spiritual age, You want me to be Your witness to everyone around me. Help me to remember that I can be an effective witness for You. I know that with Your help and the Holy Spirit's guidance I can do this! Thank You that You have given to me the faith sufficient to be successful. Amen.

Nutrition Thought for the Day.

A common disease of the large intestines is diverticulosis, which are little out-pouches that form in the large intestines. The large intestines are wrapped with muscle fibers that go around the intestines circularly and longitudinally. It is believed that these muscle fibers can become weak and small pockets of the intestines can pop out between the muscle fibers. If digested food is trapped in these pouches, it can cause inflammation, become infected, and cause pain. Having these pouches is called diverticulosis. Once they are infected, it is called diverticulitis. They can rupture and require surgery. It is also believed that a diet high in insoluble fiber will cause the intestines to expand and thus strengthen these muscle fibers by reason of use and could help prevent these out pouches from forming.

Day 20
Never Be Thirsty

But whoever drinks of the water that I will give him shall never thirst; but the water that I will give him will become in him a well of water springing up to eternal life. (John 4:14)

This scripture tells you that if you drink the living water that Jesus gives you, that is, His Word you will never thirst. You will not need anything else; His Word is sufficient for you. But this scripture means more than that; it also says you will become a well of water yourself, even to eternal life. And how will this be? We are called to be a light to the world, to spread God's Word to all peoples. In your everyday life, as you encounter fellow workers, friends, family, and maybe fellow dieters, you are to profess who you are in Christ and proclaim God's Word to them. You can do this by being a witness concerning your new healthy lifestyle. With every successful milestone, each goal you meet, give the glory to your Lord and Savior. Let your peers know that the success you are obtaining is not based on just your strength, but on the guidance, encouragement, and peace you are receiving from God's Word. Let them know that you are a child of God and that you are relying on His strength to see you through your diet and exercise program. Do not be obnoxious about your faith by beating them over the head with the Bible or telling them about God's Word every five minutes. From time to time, gently remind them that you are relying on God's help for strength and endurance. Say you have a goal to lose five pounds in a month and you accomplish that goal, or you reached the weight gain goal you set. You can relate that to your peers by saying that you achieved another milestone by God's help and give glory to Him. Be careful not to judge or put anyone down that did not reach their weekly or monthly goal. Instead, encourage them with God's Word and show them how it is working for you. Be a light in a dark world.

Father God, I want to be a witness for You and let Your light shine through me. Give me the courage and wisdom to say the right thing to encourage others around me. Present me with opportunities to be a witness and give me the presence of mind to know an opportunity from an offensive situation. I know that when the opportunity comes, You will provide me with constructive and uplifting words to say. I thank You for dying for me and for giving me sufficient faith and wisdom to be Your witness. I pray in the mighty name of Jesus. Amen.

Nutrition Thought for the Day.

There are trillions of bacteria that live in our large intestines. A vast majority is beneficial if we are healthy. They thrive on the food material that we do not digest in our small intestines, especially fiber. As they digest these minute particles of food and fiber, they produce organic acids that can be utilized for energy by the cells that line the large intestines. This helps keep these cells healthy, which is very important to our health. The organic acids also maintain the pH of the large intestines in a low range. This is good because some harmful species of bacteria, like E.coli and others, cannot thrive in a low pH. Thus, this helps to prevent some intestinal.

Day 21
We Are His Workmanship

For we are His workmanship, created in Christ Jesus for good works, which God prepared beforehand so that we would walk in them. (Ephesians 2:10)

Another description of who you are in Christ is illustrated in today's scripture. You are His workmanship created for His glory. It says that you were created in Jesus Christ for good works. Yesterday it was pointed out that you should be a witness for Jesus by being an encourager with your peers and family. This also shows that you were created to do good works, but also it could include random acts of kindness. No matter how bleak it may look for you, there are many people in this world that are severely hurting. The homeless and veterans are some of the most overlooked. While you are trying to eat less to lose weight, why not take some of the food that you regularly eat, and give it to those who need food. This would indeed be good works. Without being obnoxious about it, let those around you know that you are doing these good works for the greater glory and not just for helping humanity, as good as that is.

The scripture also says that Jesus prepared these opportunities for you beforehand so that you could walk in them. You know that Jesus knew the direction you would be taking in your life. Some situations may come up that you think are coincidental, but they may be situations that were prepared for you to have an opportunity to do good works. As you follow your new healthy lifestyle, keep in mind that your abundance of food is not something that is available to all people. If you are dieting today, you may become hungry because you are not eating as much as you usually do. When you realize you are hungry, take a timeout and pray for those who are really hungry today, not because they are dieting, but because they just do not have enough food.

Father God, I want to take a moment to realize how blessed I am. A lack of food is not something that is a problem for me. Instead, I have an abundance of food, more than I need while others in my city, perhaps in my neighborhood, are going hungry. Thank You for the many blessings You have given me. Help me be aware of the people around me that are not as fortunate and show me opportunities to help those that have greater needs than I so I can be the person You called me to be. I know that I am Your workmanship and that I was created to glorify Your name. By the power of Your Holy Spirit, help me to be aware of my overindulgence when there are people around me that are being underfed. I thank You in the name of Jesus. Amen.

Nutrition Thought for the Day.

There are other advantages to a high-fiber diet, particularly when you are trying to lose weight. Fiber absorbs water and swells in our G.I. tract. This gives us a feeling of fullness. If we can control the compulsion to overeat, and push ourselves away from the table when we feel full, this can deter weight gain. A high-fiber diet can help us in that regard. A problem that confronts many people when they are dieting is constipation. High-fiber, with ample water, will also help prevent constipation. A key here is that we need to be sure to take in lots of water, particularly if we are in ingesting a fiber supplement. The old rule of thumb of eight glasses of water a day may not be enough. Water itself can add to the feeling of fullness. If our added fiber comes from fruits and vegetables, then this is also increasing our intake of the other nutrients that are found in fruits and vegetables (vitamins, minerals, and antioxidants).

Day 22
God Is Love

The one who does not love does not know God, for God is love. (1 John 4:8)

The Old Testament is based on law. The New Testament is based on grace. The Old Testament says, "an eye for an eye and a tooth for a tooth" (Exodus 21:24). The New Testament replaces revenge with love. Jesus summed up all the commandments with a new statement in John 13:34: "A new commandment I give to you, that you love one another, even as I have loved you, that you also love one another." This is a powerful statement. Note that Jesus clearly says, "a new commandment I give to you." This is not a suggestion that He makes or something that would be nice to follow but is a command and the command is that we love one another as He loves us. He loved you so much that He died for you. Are you ready to die for your fellow man? Yesterday's devotion suggested that you go about doing good works out of love. That was a prelude to today's lesson. Today's scripture says that the one who does not love does not know God, for God Is Love. You can show love for your fellow man in many ways. This includes all the people that you come in contact with each day, but I want to suggest that you especially try to reach those that are also trying to lose or gain weight. Since you are dieting, you probably know several other people that are doing likewise. They may not be at the same spiritual place you are, and perhaps they could benefit from some appropriate spiritual enlightenment and encouragement. This is a place where you can shine. Share the encouragement that you are receiving with them. Never be judgmental of their diet, their progress, or lack thereof. Let them see who you are in Christ by your words, actions, and love.

> Father God, help me to be ever mindful of who I am in Christ and of my call that You have given me in Your Word. Give me words to say to encourage those around me, especially those that are also trying to lose or gain weight. Lead me to people that I can witness to for Your sake. If I am more successful on my healthy lifestyle program than one of my peers, instead of bringing that up and possibly make them feel discouraged, remind me to encourage them and to lift them up instead of putting them down. I want to be Your servant in everything that I do. Thank You for giving me the opportunity to use my new healthy program as a means of ministering to others. In the name of Jesus, I pray. Amen.

Nutrition Thought for the Day.

So far I have mentioned several advantages to a high-fiber diet that include helping in the prevention of heart disease, cancer, constipation, nourishment for the cells lining the large intestines, control of the bacterial population in the large intestines, and may present a feeling of fullness. However, there are also some side effects that are not beneficial. High-fiber in the diet bonds with some minerals and renders them partially unavailable. High-fiber can bind with calcium, phosphorus, iron, copper, and zinc. This does not mean we should reduce the fiber in our diets, but that we should make sure we are getting adequate minerals in our diet. One way to accomplish that is by increasing our intake of fruits and vegetables to at least five servings a day. By obtaining our fiber from a variety of fruits and vegetables, we will also be adding a variety of vitamins and minerals to our diet at the same time.

Day 23
Have Jesus's Attitude

Have this attitude in yourselves which was also in Christ Jesus, who, although He existed in the form of God, did not regard equality with God a thing to be grasped, but emptied Himself, taking the form of a bond-servant, and being made in the likeness of men. (Philippians 2:5–7)

To help us understand who we are in Christ, it is important to realize that Jesus, by His own free will, became a man; that is He grew as a human in every detail, just as we are human. His Spirit was the Spirit of the Son of God, but His body was in every way the same as our body. As a man, He was tempted in every way that we are tempted (Hebrews 4:15), but He never sinned. He knows what it is like to be tempted from the standpoint of the devil tempting a man. You are perhaps frequently tempted to go off your diet. I do not believe Jesus had a weight problem and had to diet, however, He did fast for forty days in the wilderness (Matthew 4:1). How would you like to go for forty days with no food? Do you think you might be tempted to eat?

See the analogy here, Jesus knows what it is like to go without food. He can understand the temptations that you receive as a result of trying to eat healthily. He received strength from His Father God, the same place from where you receive your strength. Know that you can call on Jesus at any time to help you with your diet, and He will know exactly what you are going through, not just as God that knows all things, but as a man that had to control His desire for food. Today's scripture tells us to take on the attitude Jesus had. I know that sounds like a tall order, but remember He walked the face of the earth as a man and not as God. He is your answer to a successful, healthy lifestyle. Call on Him and trust Him to see you through your trials.

Note: A forty-day total fast is not recommended for anyone today. Referring to the fast that Jesus completed is not at all suggesting that you do the same.

Lord Jesus, it amazes me to realize that You walked the face of earth as a man and not as God. It also amazes me to know that You were tempted in every way that I am tempted—You even went on a forty day fast and completed it. You know what it is like to diet in a way that I will never experience. You know my struggles and my temptations. Help me so I may successfully complete my new healthy regimen. I know I will be doing this much longer than forty days, but I will not be fasting without food. I know I can do this with Your help. I thank You for helping me this day. I pray to the Father in Your name for strength. Amen.

Nutrition Thought for the Day.

So, how much fiber do we need every day? The RDAs say adult women need 25 grams/day and adult men need 38 grams/day. If you are not making a conscious effort to take in more fiber daily, and you are eating a typical American diet, you are probably taking in less than 10g a day. The recommendation to get 25g of fiber is to take in fiber in the form of fruits, vegetables, grains, and nuts. There is no fiber in milk, meat or fat. Most green-yellow vegetables have about two grams of fiber in a one-half cup serving. Starchy vegetables have about three grams of fiber in a one-half cup serving. For other starches, you need to read the label. For example, a slice of bread could have from one gram to five grams of fiber, depending upon the kind of bread and size of the slice. The label will give you this information. If a serving has at least three grams of fiber, it is considered a fair serving of fiber. Anything less is poor.

Day 24
No Condemnation

Therefore there is now no condemnation for those who are in Christ Jesus. (Romans 8:1)

There is no condemnation for those who are in Christ Jesus—none. If you are a born-again Christian, all of your sins, past and future, have been covered by the blood of Jesus; so there can be no condemnation for you. Does this mean that you can go on sinning as you please? Paul was asked this very question too, and his answer was, "May it never be!" This does not give us a license to sin. Once we realize who we are in Christ, this will help us not want to sin again. However, being human we know will sin again but, as soon as we do, we can ask for forgiveness, and our sins are already accounted for and are forgiven. Going off your healthy lifestyle program is not a sin. Eating that extra serving, or that last piece a cake, is not a sin. However, if you are earnest about following your new program, it may seem like a grave sin to you. The devil will take advantage of that opportunity to put you down. Thoughts may come into your head, "Oh! What have I done? I have messed up again. I just cannot stick to this healthy plan. It is too much for me." Those thoughts may come into your head in the first person as spelled out here, but they are really coming from the devil speaking to you in the first person. You may be discouraged with this demonic technique in areas other than dieting. This could cause you to believe you cannot complete your task. However, you are depending on Jesus's opinion of you and not the devil's opinion of you. When this happens, remember that there is no condemnation for those who are in Christ Jesus. Yes, when Paul wrote this he was referring to much more significant problems then going off of a diet plan, but the principle still applies to whatever brings condemnation to you. You can complete this new plan! Remember from where you receive your strength.

Lord Jesus, I thank You again for dying for me and forgiving me of all my sins—past, present, and future. I thank You that I am not condemned for my actions even though I may try to condemn myself. I know that You forgive me for every wrong doing I commit, whether it is a grave mistake or just going off my diet. I know that I can accomplish this new program with your help. I ask Your Holy Spirit to remind me of who I am in Christ, including that there is no condemnation for those who are in Christ. I thank You for Your love, forgiveness, and guidance. I pray in Your name Jesus. Amen.

Nutrition Thought for the Day.
While fruit juice is a fruit, it does not provide you with the same nutrients as a piece of fruit. It will not have the fiber that a piece of fruit has, and fruit juice is high in natural sugars. One half-cup of grape juice provides more sugar than a half-cup of soda. It has more nutrients than soda, but it still has a lot of calories. Fresh fruit is a better choice. Fiber and antioxidants in fruit are found in the peelings. So when you eat fruit, such as an apple, wash it thoroughly and eat the peeling. Eat a variety of fruits and vegetables and not the same ones everyday. Include more salads in your diet. This not only increases fiber, but also gives you a variety of vitamins, minerals, and antioxidants while giving you

a feeling of fullness. Do not add a lot of high-fat salad dressing or meats and cheeses. This adds a lot more calories. Have salad dressing on the side and dip a fork into the dressing to give you the taste without consuming a large quantity. Using low-calorie or fat-free salad dressing is also good.

Day 25
Only Boast in the Lord

But by His doing you are in Christ Jesus, who became to us wisdom from God, and righteousness and sanctification, and redemption, so that, just as it is written, "LET HIM WHO BOASTS, BOAST IN THE LORD." (1 Corinthians 1:30)

A reminder that you are in Jesus, not based on what you have done, but on what He did for you. Note the scripture starts out saying, "But by His doing you are in Christ Jesus." Also, note that the *His* is capitalized and refers to God. It is by His doing that you can say you are in Christ Jesus. The scripture tells you that Jesus became "wisdom from God and righteousness and sanctification and redemption." All of that is passed on to you as you are in Christ Jesus. Every good spiritual gift and blessing that you have is because of what He did for you and not based on anything you did. You should never boast about your accomplishments. Instead, you should give glory to God and boast of the accomplishments you have achieved because of Him who is in you and works through you. When you brag about anything you have accomplished, brag on it as an accomplishment completed by the power that works within you and give the glory to God. In your daily walk boast as if you are boasting on the Lord. Saturate yourself with knowledge and information of who you are in Christ and this will help you to be successful in everything that you do. You can, and will, make great accomplishments this day if you trust in God and follow His Word.

Thank You, Jesus, that all of my accomplishments are a result of Your gifts. You have laid the foundation for me to follow and have provided me with wisdom, sanctification, and redemption through Your blood. When I do anything that is worth any merit, remind me of where my strength comes from so that I may boast on You for giving me the grace and the power to be successful. Help me be Your witness and be a reflection of You in everything that I do. I look forward to seeing the good things that are going to happen to me today so that I can pass the glory on to You. I pray in your name, Jesus. Amen.

Nutrition Thought for the Day.

I am sure you have seen advertisements for probiotics. What are probiotics? I mentioned that there are trillions of bacteria living in your large intestines and they produce desirable effects. It is wise for us to keep a healthy bacterial population in our large intestines. If you have ever taken broad-spectrum antibiotics, you may have ended up with diarrhea as a side effect. This happens because the antibiotic also kills the good bacteria in the intestines and it is the bacteria that live in your large intestines that cause you to have solid stools. Some people ingest strains of good bacteria to help keep the bacteria in the large intestines healthy. These are probiotics which are live cultures and are added to some foods. If you eat yogurt, check the label to see that it has live cultures. Buttermilk could be another source of live cultures. There are many capsules on the market that contain billions of live cultures to help populate your G.I. tract with good bacteria. To make sure these bacteria have food to eat, we feed them fiber and chains of fructose that is found in fruit. These are called prebiotics. It would be good to include foods in your diet that have probiotics along with fruit, vegetables, and grains to help maintain a healthy G.I. tract.

Day 26
The Mystery of His Will

He made known to us the mystery of His will, according to His kind intention which He purposed in Him. (Ephesians 1:9)

The first four pronouns in this sentence referring to He/His are speaking of God the Father. The last pronoun, Him, refers to Jesus. God's Word makes us aware of the ministry of His will, and He purposed His will to happen through Jesus. And what is the purpose of His will? In the scriptures preceding this one, Paul speaks of how we have been blessed with every spiritual blessing through Christ. He says that we were chosen before the foundation of the world that we would be holy and blameless before Him. It also means that He predestined us for adoption as sons through Jesus Christ. And finally, Paul says that through Jesus we have redemption through His blood and forgiveness of all of our trespasses according to the riches of His grace.

You have been redeemed by the blood of Jesus, you have been forgiven of all of your sins, and you have become an heir of God, coheir with Christ. All of this is part of His divine will for you. Not mentioned here, but also a part of His will, is that you worship Him and give Him glory by being His witnesses. As you go about your daily routines, it is extremely comforting to know that God has chosen you before the beginning of time and has blessed you with every spiritual blessing. I know, sometimes you do not feel like you are blessed, especially when you realize how overweight or underweight you are. It does not matter how you feel. What matters is what God's Word says, and it says He has made His will known to you and His will is that you be blessed with every spiritual blessing. Be at peace with this and do not be discouraged.

Father God, I continue to thank You that You have chosen me and blessed me with every spiritual blessing. I thank You that Your Word clearly makes Your will known for my life. I know that You have nothing but good plans for me. I know that I am blessed, redeemed, and forgiven by the blood of Jesus. Knowing how much You love me gives me the strength to complete every task that lies before me. I ask for You to remind me each day of my blessings and to help me remind those around me how much You love them also. I know I can finish this healthy lifestyle program and I will finish it with Your help. I thank You in the name of Jesus, my Savior, and Lord. Amen.

Nutrition Thought for the Day.

Fructose was mentioned earlier as a monosaccharide. Fructose is the sweetest sugar of all the monosaccharides and disaccharides. In the early 1970s, fructose started to be added to corn syrup to make it sweeter. Industry began using fructose in drinks and foods. This is called high-fructose corn syrup or HFCS. Corn syrup is 100% glucose, but HFCS is close to 50–50 glucose and fructose. There are several reasons why they added fructose to corn syrup. It is sweeter, so less total sugar may be used to sweeten a drink. Fructose also increases the capacity to retain moisture, enhance flavor and lowers the food's freezing point. However, it is metabolized in the body differently than glucose and recent research indicates that it may cause additional fat deposits in the body, particularly in the abdominal region. Fatty deposits in the abdominal region cause more health problems than fat deposited elsewhere in the body. This is part of what is known as metabolic syndrome and leads to insulin insensitivity, which could lead to diabetes. Fructose is under scrutiny now because of its questionable harmful effects, so much so that you can find labels on certain foods that say "fructose free". It would be wise to avoid foods that contain added fructose.

Day 27
Be Strong and Courageous

"Have I not commanded you? Be strong and courageous! Do not tremble or be dismayed, for the LORD your God is with you wherever you go." (Joshua 1:9)

When Joshua took over Moses's role in the desert, God commanded Joshua to be strong and courageous. He promised him that He would be with him wherever he would go. Be strong and courageous is stated thirteen times in the Old Testament in the New American Standard Bible. If God tells us something thirteen times, you know it must be important and something He wants us to know. Be strong and courageous!

If this was true in the Old Testament to be stated thirteen times, how much more would this be true in the New Testament after what Christ did for us? God's grace is poured out in greater abundance on us in the New Testament than in the Old Testament. We also have God's promise in the New Testament that He will never leave us nor forsake us (Matthew 28:20, Hebrews 13:5). Granted, when God told this to the inhabitants of the Old Testament, He was speaking about them being bold and courageous in their physical battles of war. You are trying to follow a healthy regimen through diet and exercise. Is this not a battle? Is this not sometimes a very tough thing to accomplish? Of course, it is. This is true for all of us, whether you are overweight or underweight. In all circumstances, you need to remember that God is with you and He will never forsake you. In all things you should be strong and courageous!

Father God, continue to remind me that You are forever with me wherever I may go and whatever I do. When You told Your people in the Old Testament to be strong and courageous, You were not only speaking to them, but to all Your people in all ages of time. Sometimes I do not feel strong or courageous. Instead, I sometimes feel weak and fearful. When those times come upon me, by the power of Your Holy Spirit, remind me of Your Word, be strong and courageous! When I am weak in my flesh, I am strong in You. Thank You for giving me strength and delivering me from fear. In Jesus's name, I pray. Amen.

Nutrition Thought for the Day.
At this point, I will begin the first part of a several part discussion of food labels. The first thing I want to mention is the ingredient list on a food label. Every label has a list of ingredients. The ingredients are listed on the label in the greatest quantity found in the product to the least quantity. In other words, the ingredient listed first is in the greatest quantity in the container, and the ingredient listed last is in the least quantity in the container. That does not tell you how much is actually there, but it does give you some vital information. When it comes to carbohydrates, if the carbohydrate is a starch or starch-like substance, the label will tell you if it has been enriched or if it is whole-grain. Many years ago before we became civilized, farmers grew their own grains, ground them up to flour, and made their own bread. As we became advanced in technology, farmers begin grinding the grains up in a mill and producing flour that is known as refined flour. This was well liked by consumers because it produced a finer flour with a softer texture and stayed fresh longer. However, the refinement process removed the brand and germ from the grain and left a flour that consisted of only the endosperm. This resulted in a loss of fiber and nutrients to be discussed tomorrow.

Day 28
His Lovingkindness Endures Forever

Who gives food to all flesh, for His lovingkindness is everlasting. Give thanks to the God of heaven, for His lovingkindness is everlasting. (Psalm 136:25–26)

Not only is God with you in everything you do and everywhere you go, but His lovingkindness is everlasting. He is not just with you for the sake of being with you, but He is with you because He loves you more than you can imagine. I know there are times when none of us feels like we are being surrounded by His lovingkindness, but you know what, He is there with us. He promised this in His Word and He cannot lie. Your God loves you and His lovingkindness surrounds you everywhere you go in everything you do. If you are not aware of it, it is because you are not in the right frame of mind to receive what He has to offer.

Each day, you need to make sure that you are humble and are open to whatever He has for you that day because He only has good things for you. If something bad seems to come your way, it is not because God does not love you. There is a devil and he tries to confuse you and beat you down, but your God is stronger than the devil. Be strong and courageous! No matter what comes your way remember that God's lovingkindness is with you and He loves you and will never leave you. As His Word says, "you give food to all flesh." God gives you food through His Word.

Father, I thank You that You love me so much that You sent Your only begotten Son to suffer and die for me because of my sins. I thank You that Your lovingkindness is with me everywhere I go and that You will never leave me. When days come that I am not aware of Your lovingkindness, remind me of who I am in Christ, that You are with me, and that Your lovingkindness surrounds me. I am never alone. You are always with me and will help me in all that I do. Help me to be successful with my diet and exercise program so that I can be a healthier person and a better example of one of Your children. I thank You, Father, in the name of Jesus. Amen.

Nutrition Thought for the Day.

The milling of grains produces flour without the brand and germ portions of the grain resulting in less fiber and a loss of nutrients. Those nutrients consist of various vitamins and minerals. Years ago, people that were dependent on this process used flour as a significant portion of their nutrition and ended up with vitamin deficiencies. Scientists figured out why that was happening and in the early 1940s began to enrich the processed grains. The grains were enriched with thiamin (vitamin B1), riboflavin (vitamin B2), niacin (vitamin B3), and iron. Over the years it was determined that most women of childbearing age were deficient in folic acid, a vitamin necessary for the proper development of a fetus, among many other things. It was decided that since most people eat some processed grain that it would be good to add folic acid to the list of vitamins and iron above. In 1998 folic acid was added to this process. Under the ingredient section of a food label, it will tell you if the grains in the food are whole grains or have been enriched and it will tell you what the enrichment included. Whole grains are not processed and do not need to be enriched.

Day 29
Jesus Is the Living Bread

I am the living bread that came down out of heaven; if anyone eats of this bread, he will live forever; and the bread also which I will give for the life of the world is My flesh. (John 6:51)

The end of yesterday's devotion stated: "you give food to all flesh." This was a quote from yesterday's scripture found in Psalm 136:25–26. Many people that heard Jesus speak the verse in John 6:51 were perplexed. They did not know how they could eat His flesh. Jesus was using a metaphor and was not referring to His flesh per se. Instead, He was referring to Himself. When Jesus said, "if anyone eats of this bread, he will live forever; and the bread also which I give for the life of the world is My flesh." He was merely saying that He gives Himself for the world.

He did this by His death. If you unite yourself to Him in faith, then you become one with Him, and you receive Him into your heart. You receive His Word by faith and walk with Him by faith. By accepting Him in this way you are taking Him into your life and since He is referring to Himself as His flesh, you are, metaphorically speaking, taking of His flesh because you are receiving Him and His Word into your heart. This is a compelling verse, and it should help you understand how much God is with you and how much He loves you. When things are getting tough, and you have a hard time completing your daily task, you should take note that when you received Him, it was like receiving His physical self within you, just as if you were to partake of His flesh. He is part of you! This should help you be strong and courageous and accomplish the day's tasks.

Lord Jesus, once again I am in awe of Your love for me and that You are actually in my spirit and are a part of me. This is more than my finite mind can comprehend, but I receive it on faith. It is by faith that I walk with You. I know that You have given me the faith I need to be an overcomer but sometimes I do not feel like an overcomer. Help me when I begin to feel weak and remind me that You are in me and You are for me. I will walk out this day with boldness because of the strength You give me. I declare this in Your powerful name. Amen.

Nutrition Thought for the Day.

So, what carbohydrate products are considered processed and are enriched? All processed flours, wheat, rye, barley, cornstarch, and anything made from these flours. This will include all bread, cakes, cookies, crackers, pastries, pasta, corn chips, and anything else that is made from processed flour. This also includes even unhealthy things like high fat and high-sugar foods that we usually call junk foods. The amount of nutrients added back to enriched flours is more than would have been found in the unprocessed grain. This has dramatically diminished nutritional deficiencies in our country. Since the addition of folic acid, spina bifida, a disease of the spinal column, has been decreased by about 70%. This disease is caused by a deficiency of folic acid during the very beginning of pregnancy.

Day 30
Rejoice in Your Undertakings

There also you and your households shall eat before the LORD your God, and rejoice in all your undertakings in which the LORD your God has blessed you. (Deuteronomy 12:7)

It may seem to you like this scripture does not fit here, but I chose it because of the devotional scriptures we used the last two days. In the verses before this scripture, God told His people to rid themselves of their sinful habits and bring sacrifices to Him. Then He gave the scripture, Deuteronomy 12:7, where He told the people that they and their households should eat before the Lord their God. What does this mean?

Unlike the Old Testament, you do not have to bring burnt sacrifices to God to receive forgiveness. Jesus was the last and ultimate sacrifice. In the Old Testament, after the priests went through the rituals of offering animal sacrifices to God for the sins of the people, they could then come before the Lord and eat in His presence. In the scriptures reviewed the last couple of days, you saw that Jesus is the bread of life and when you receive Him in faith, it is as if you are at the same place the Jews were in the Old Testament when animal sacrifices for their sins was completed. The sacrifice for your sins is finished, and you can bask in God's presence and receive His Word as food for your life. This day, instead of asking God for more, why don't you give Him praise and thanks for what He has already done for you and, by faith, walk in His presence.

Lord Jesus, I thank You for what You have done for me, and I give all praise, honor, and glory to You this day. You are worthy of all praise, and I am forever grateful for all that I have in You and for all that I am in You. Receive everything I do this day as a praise offering before Your throne. I am not worthy of all that You have done for me and have given me. I give it all back to You for Your praise and glory. In Your name Jesus, I pray. Amen.

Nutrition Thought for the Day.

There is a push today to include more whole grains in our diets. Whole grains increase the amount of fiber, trace minerals, vitamins, and antioxidants. They also provide more protein, calcium, magnesium, and potassium than processed foods. Research has presented evidence that a diet with a variety of whole grains may be helpful in reducing the risk of heart disease, some types of cancer, type 2 diabetes and, something that should be a great interest to you, may also help in weight management. Remember that a high-fiber diet gives you a feeling of fullness and it may help you to eat less. Also, whole grains are digested more slowly than processed grains and helps to control a spike in blood glucose. The 2010 Dietary Guidelines for Americans recommends that we consume at least half of all grains as whole grains. We should reduce our refined grains and replace them with whole grains. A serving of whole grains is considered to be equivalent to three ounces. Included in the classification of whole grains are whole wheat, whole oats, oatmeal, whole-grain cornmeal, popcorn, brown rice, wild rice, whole-grain barley, triticale, buckwheat, bulgur wheat, millet, quinoa, and sorghum. There is another group of grains that are becoming more and more popular today called ancient grains. These include amaranth, farro, and spelt.

Day 31
For His Glory

Whether, then, you eat or drink or whatever you do, do all to the glory of God.
(1 Corinthians 10:31)

Whatever you do, do it for the glory of God. When Paul presented this scripture, he was in discussion with the Corinthians about whether or not they should eat meat sacrificed to idols. His bottom line was if you eat or drink, or whatever you do, do it for the glory of God. This should be your theme for your daily walk whether you are trying to diet or not, but it can apply here to your new healthy lifestyle regimen. You are going through this healthy lifestyle program so that you can be healthy, but you are doing it for more than that. The healthier you are, the stronger you are, and the more you can use your body and your strength for God's glory.

If you feel that temptation is leading you to break your healthy lifestyle routine, remind yourself that what you are doing is for God's glory and not just for your own satisfaction of losing or gaining weight. Give God the glory for every temptation you overcome and for every pound you lose. Never forget that you are living your life for His glory and that your body is His body and the temple of the Holy Spirit. Be encouraged by your faith in His presence.

Father God, I want to give You all the glory for everything that I accomplish. Every accomplishment I make, and every temptation I overcome, is because of Your strength in me, and I offer my victory to You for Your glory. Remind me each day that I live for Your glory. It is not me that overcomes, but it is You who is in me that overcomes. Therefore, everything that I do to overcome is glory for You. In the name of Jesus, be glorified. Amen.

Nutrition Thought for the Day.

There is one more observation about the ingredients label I want to share. As previously stated, the item listed first is in the container in the greatest quantity, the item listed next in the next greatest quantity, and so forth. You do not know the amount, but you know the proportions. For example, if you had a can of tomatoes, what would you expect to see first on the ingredients label? Most people, by far, would say tomatoes. That is certainly logical, but that is not the case. The typical ingredient list for a can of tomatoes would be water, tomatoes, and salt. This means there is more water in the can than anything else and there are more tomatoes in the can than salt. You do not know how much salt is in the can from the ingredient list, but you know salt is in the can in the least quantity of the three ingredients listed. Next, we will start to look at determining how much of each ingredient is in a container.

Day 32
Be Disciplined

But have nothing to do with worldly fables fit only for old women. On the other hand, discipline yourself for the purpose of godliness; for bodily discipline is only of little profit, but godliness is profitable for all things, since it holds promise for the present life and *also* for the *life* to come. (1 Timothy 4:7–8)

In this chapter of Paul's letter to Timothy, Paul was instructing Timothy how to deal with some errors and inconsistencies that were taking place in the church as a result of deceitful spirits. He told him not to have anything to do with deceitful spirits or doctrines of demons (1 Timothy 4:1–5). In verse seven he told Timothy to discipline himself for godliness, but he points out that discipline is only of little profit while godliness is profitable for all ages.

To be successful at what you are doing requires a lot of discipline. It will require discipline in the amount of food you eat and the food choices you make; it will also require discipline for you to stick with an exercise program. The exercise program will be of some value to you in several ways. One, it will help you to lose fat and gain muscle. Two, the exercise portion will be helpful in many ways that just weight change alone will not accomplish, such as strengthening your heart and lowering your blood pressure. More glucose and fat will be utilized because of the exercise, and your muscle cells will become more sensitive to insulin. There are many other benefits of the exercise program, and it can only be completed with discipline.

So, in your case, discipline is a good thing but keep in mind that it is better for you to discipline yourself also for godliness. This will not only help you with your new healthy lifestyle program but with everything else you do in life. This day, as you complete your program, remember that you are not only helping your body now but you are also preparing yourself for the life to come.

Dear Father God, help me this day to discipline myself not only concerning my diet and exercise program but also relating to everything I do in my life, particularly as it pertains to godliness. Help me to spend more time talking to You in prayer and studying Your Word. I do not want to be legalistic about time spent in Your Word or in prayer, but the more time I spend in Your Word, the closer my walk will be with You and the greater success I will have in disciplining myself while on this earth. This I pray in Jesus's name. Amen.

Nutrition Thought for the Day.

So far I have discussed ingredients on the food label. Now I will look at how to read the carbohydrate information on a label. Food labels are essential and are something you must read if you are going to not only diet effectively but if you are going to eat healthy, whether you are on a diet or not. Concerning carbohydrates, when you read a label you will see a line that says **Total Carbohydrate** and next to that it will tell you how many grams of carbohydrates are in one serving. It will also tell you something about fiber. Sometimes it may say *dietary fiber*, *total fiber*, or *soluble fiber*. All fiber in a product should be considered dietary fiber, so this probably means total fiber. I say probably because there are no rules as to how this has to be stated.

Day 33
Present Your Bodies as a Living Sacrifice

Therefore I urge you, brethren, by the mercies of God, to present your bodies a living and holy sacrifice, acceptable to God, *which is* your spiritual service of worship. (Romans 12:1)

This is one of my favorite scriptures. In yesterday's devotion, I encouraged you to seek godliness. Along the same lines, this scripture encourages you to present your body as a living and a holy sacrifice, which would be a spiritual form of worship. You may say, "How can I present my body as a holy sacrifice? I am not holy!" No, you are not, not in your ability or power, but by the power of Jesus who died for you, you are holy based on what He did for you. Remember that you can only be holy based on His righteousness, not your own righteousness. When you look in the mirror, look at your body as belonging to the Lord. You may see yourself as being overweight or underweight, but when Jesus looks at you, He sees your spirit and does not judge you on how your body looks. So, when you look in the mirror, try to see yourself as Jesus sees you, and that is as someone who is covered with His robe of righteousness. That being said, you still want to be successful in your healthy lifestyle regimen so that you can present a body that is not lazy or gluttonous. You are completing your program not only for yourself but also for Jesus.

Dear Father God, every day I am learning more about who I am in Christ and about how You see me. Help me to see myself as You see me. I know that I am covered with Your robe of righteousness, and I am holy based on what You did for me. I do not always feel righteous so when I am weak, help me to shine with Your righteousness. In Your name Jesus, I pray. Amen

Nutrition Thought for the Day.

Some labels will break the fiber down to its components and list the amount of soluble fiber. Remember that fiber is classified as soluble or insoluble. If it says dietary fiber or total fiber and then says soluble fiber, you can subtract the soluble fiber from total fiber to determine how much insoluble fiber is in a serving. New labels have been proposed but may not give this additional information. The next line will be a new addition (if approved) and will tell you how much of the total sugar is added sugar. This can be very important to help you avoid added sugar. As previously mentioned, carbohydrates consists of starch (or complex carbohydrates), sugars, and fiber. The label will never list complex carbohydrates, but you can determine how much is there by adding total fiber and total sugar and subtracting it from the total carbohydrates. The remainder is starch. A new label law was supposed to be approved in the spring of 2017. That did not happen, and it has announced that it will not be until January of 2020.

Day 34
Do Not Conform to the World

And do not be conformed to this world. (Romans 12:2a)

One of the ways you can present your body as a living sacrifice is not to conform to the world's philosophies. In the Gospel of John, Jesus mentioned several times that He was not of this world, nor were His apostles of this world, even though they were in the world (John 15:19, John 17:14, John 17:16). The world is concerned with material things that choke out God's Word (Mark 4:19). If you conform to God's Word while attending a good Bible-believing church that teaches the uncompromised Word of God, you would not be conforming to the world.

What does that have to do with being healthy? Directly, it has nothing to do with diet or exercise; indirectly, everything. Your strength in completing your healthy lifestyle regimen does not come from you, but from Jesus in you. If you follow the world's advice, you end up lusting after the desires of the world, which include unhealthy foods, and you will not be successful in your program. That does not mean that everything in the world is wrong. You need to have discernment to know what are good choices concerning your diet and exercise and what are bad choices.

Some diet regimens taught are correct, but many of them are wrong. You cannot carry a registered dietitian around with you all the time to separate the good things from the bad, but you can take Jesus with you the all the time and look to the Holy Spirit to give you discernment, including when you should question dietary choices. You may hear a still small voice in you that tells you something is wrong. Do not ever give up on yourself. Keep looking to God for hope in directing you. If you doubt an aspect of your diet or exercise, by all means, consult someone who has training in those areas and trust in God to lead you to the right conclusion.

> Father God, the world is a confusing place to live in today. There are many who would deceive and cause physical harm for the sake of money. There are many recommendations for diet foods and for regimens to follow that are not in my best interests. Give me wisdom in making the correct choices for everything I do each day, not only for those things that pertain to my diet, exercise, or health. I trust in You and the power of Your Holy Spirit to give me direction. In Jesus's name, I pray. Amen.

Nutrition Thought for the Day.

From the information given on the label about the sugar component of carbohydrate, you cannot tell what kind of sugar is in the product. For example, the sugar that is listed on the label could be monosaccharides or disaccharides. That means it could be glucose, fructose, sucrose, honey, syrup, or one of several other classifications since none of those are starches but consist of either mono—and/or disaccharides. Since milk contains lactose and lactose is a disaccharide, this would also be included in the total sugar content but not in the added sugar content. The same is true for the sugar that is in fruit juice or fresh fruit. By looking at the list of ingredients, you can tell what sugars are in the product naturally and which are added. It will tell you if it is corn syrup, high fructose corn syrup, honey, sucrose, etc. All of these are added sugars and something you want to avoid.

Day 35
Be Transformed

But be transformed by the renewing of your mind, so that you may prove what the will of God is, that which is good and acceptable and perfect. (Romans 12:2b)

This second half of Romans 12:2 tells us how to be transformed, and that is by the renewing of your mind. You renew your mind by getting into God's Word and staying in fellowship with like-minded believers who can encourage you in your walk with the Lord. The more time you spend in God's Word, by reading the Bible, reading good books about the Bible, staying in fellowship, and praying, the more you will renew your mind.

Notice the last part of the scripture above. It says that once you do this, you will be able to prove (that is know) what God's will is—what is good and acceptable and perfect. The more you seek God, the clearer you will be able to hear what His Holy Spirit says to you. The less you seek God, the more you will depend upon the world for your direction, and it would be very difficult to hear from God under those conditions. Seek God with all your heart every day and be encouraged that you are doing the right thing. Continue to be diligent with your diet and exercise and, while you may not see an immediate difference, you will eventually see victory.

Heavenly Father, give me the endurance and the courage to continue after Your Word in everything I do every day. I know that if I continue to seek You, I will learn more about You. The more I learn about You, the better I will be able to hear that still small voice speak to my spirit. When I get discouraged, give me a word through the Bible, or through a person that crosses my path and encourage me for Your glory. In Jesus's name, I pray. Amen.

Nutrition Thought for the Day.
The top of the food label will tell you how many calories are in one serving. In reading about calories in other places, you may see them listed as kcals, which is the abbreviation for kilocalories. A kilo is a thousand, so a kilocalorie is a 1000 calories. A calorie is a very small quantity and is a measure of potential energy in the product. Since the calorie is so small in value, we often speak of calories as kilocalories. When you look at material telling you about the calories you should consume, you may see it listed as kilocalories. Just know that this is the same thing as the calories listed on the label. This is just a minor point for your information, so you do not get confused when reading different pieces of literature about diets.

Day 36
You Can Overcome the World

Who is the one who overcomes the world, but he who believes that Jesus is the Son of God? (1 John 5:5)

This scripture plainly says that whoever believes Jesus is the Son of God overcomes the world. If you are a born-again believer, then you are born of God, and this means that you can overcome the world. You may not feel like an overcomer, but you are if you are a born-again believer because the Bible says it is so. To believe the Bible, you have to accept this by your faith. We talked about faith last month and mentioned that the Scriptures tell us we have each been given a measure of faith that is suitable for moving the mountains in our lives. You can overcome the world by your faith; you have been given ample faith to do that as a believer. If you can overcome the world, you can overcome your weight problem, whether it is underweight or overweight. You must be encouraged by God's Word and not give up. Believe what the Scriptures say about you. I am not saying it is always easy to be an overcomer, but it is possible, or God's Word would not say it to be so.

Heavenly Father, I thank You for the encouragement that You give me in Your Word. I know that I am nothing without You. And I have seen in Your Word that You have given me the faith I need to be an overcomer. Continue to give me the guidance that I need to remember who I am in Christ and what authority You have given to me. I know that as I walk through this day, I will be successful if I trust in You. In Jesus's name, I pray. Amen.

Nutrition Thought for the Day.
I mentioned that absorption takes place in the small intestines; I also mentioned that the large intestine houses a large number of bacteria that is helpful to us for digestion and important to us for general good health. Bacterial populations do not normally live in the small intestines, only the large intestines. I also mentioned diverticulosis previously, and that occurs only in the large intestines and not in the small intestines. The function of the large intestines is to absorb water and electrolytes. As you know, a normal bowel movement consists of solid material. The material is made solid by the absorption of the water through the large intestines. With the absorption of water, electrolytes such as sodium (Na), potassium (K), chloride (Cl), and many other elements are also absorbed. Most heavy metals such as iron (Fe) are absorbed in the small intestines. Any disease that affects the large intestines is going to affect the absorption of water and electrolytes.

Day 37
You Are Free from the Law

For the law of the Spirit of life in Christ Jesus has set you free from the law of sin and of death. (Romans 8:2)

The Old Testament is based on law, and if you broke the law, there were severe consequences, some of which included being stoned to death. You are no longer under that law. That does not mean you do not have to obey the commandments, but it does mean that if you do not follow them to the letter, you do not have to be stoned to death. The New Testament is based on grace. Grace means that when you fail, you are covered by Jesus's righteousness based on what He did for you. Jesus died for every sin you ever committed or ever will commit. This does not necessarily mean there will not be consequences. When we sin we may have to make restitution to someone for what we did, but God does not abandon us, and we are not stoned for our fall.

While this is true in your spiritual life, it can also be true in your physical life. This is another note of encouragement for those times when you may get off your healthy lifestyle regimen. There may be consequences, like extra weight gain, but it is not a failure, just a setback. Know that you do not have to give up at that point. Instead, be more determined that you will do better with God's help and get up and move on, holding your head high, knowing that you are under God's grace.

Father, I know that Your grace is sufficient for me in everything that I do. I know that Your grace covers me. There are times when I do not do what I am supposed to concerning my spiritual life as well as my healthy lifestyle regimen. When that happens, remind me, that I am under Your grace and all I have to do is ask for Your forgiveness and continue to seek You with all my heart. I also understand that if I go off my diet program, You are not angry with me and You will not forsake me. Your grace is sufficient for me spiritually and physically! I am an overcomer! Thank You for Your grace in Jesus's name. Amen.

Nutrition Thought for the Day.

Two of the organs that are very important in digestion are the pancreas and the gallbladder. The pancreas has several functions, but in digestion its role includes the secretion of enzymes and pancreatic juice into the small intestines. Some of the enzymes are necessary for starch digestion, disaccharide digestion, the digestion of protein, and the digestion of triglycerides (fats). When the ingested material comes from the stomach into the small intestines, it is very acidic because of the acid produced in the stomach. This acid also helps with digestion in the stomach. The stomach lining is so designed to be able to cope with the low pH of the stomach contents, but the lining of the small intestines is not capable of withstanding such strong acid. If the material coming from the stomach was not neutralized, the lining of the small intestines might be damaged, resulting in ulcers. The pancreatic juice is a bicarbonate solution that helps to neutralize the acid coming from the stomach by raising the pH and thus protecting the lining of the small intestines. Anything that affects the pancreas will affect digestion. Pancreatitis can be caused by viral infections, alcohol (even one episode of heavy binge drinking), trauma, and some disease states such as cystic fibrosis.

Day 38
Hope in Perseverance

We urge you, brethren, admonish the unruly, encourage the fainthearted, help the weak, be patient with everyone. (1 Thessalonians 5:14)

If you have been paying close attention to the devotions that you have read so far, and you have been staying in God's Word, you should be able to see some spiritual growth by this time. As mentioned to some extent last month, take what you have learned and use it to help others. It is really difficult to feel sorry for yourself and to be down on yourself when you see people around you that are as bad as, or worse off than you are. Helping others uplifts you, particularly if you can help them over a bump in the road that you have already overcome. Use the strength that you have obtained so far to help others in their diet/exercise programs, or in any situation they may be facing, and you will be pleasing to your God while helping yourself also. Examine yourself and see if you would call yourself a patient person. If not, what do you have to do to become more patient? Make a plan today to activate immediately a plan that would enable you to be more patient. You will find that you will be happier and experience peace.

Father, I may have concerns about my weight, but I am blessed that I am doing something about it by Your guidance and help. Many people around me have lots of problems, and not all have to do with their weight. Show me those around me that need an encouraging word and give me the wisdom and boldness to give them that word. Help me to be a light in a dark place. Guide me this day by the power of Your Holy Spirit to be a blessing to someone less fortunate than myself. In Jesus's name. Amen.

Nutrition Thought for the Day.

The gallbladder is a small sack-like container attached to the liver that stores bile. The bile is synthesized in the liver from cholesterol. It is transferred to the gallbladder to be stored until fat is included in a meal. The presence of fat entering the small intestines causes the secretion of a hormone in the small intestines that goes through the blood to the gallbladder. This hormone causes the gallbladder to contract and releases bile into the small intestines through what is known as the common bile duct.

Bile is not an enzyme and does not digest fat, but it is an emulsifying agent that coats droplets of fat and prevents them from coming together. This allows the enzymes that come from the pancreas to get to the droplets of fat much faster and digest them. Therefore, fat needs to be in the diet for the gallbladder to release bile. Without bile, much of the fat in the diet will not be digested and will pass on to the large intestines. The bacteria that live in the large intestines would then digest the fat. There is not enough of space here to discuss this entire process, but the bottom line is severe diarrhea. Thus bile is necessary for fat digestion.

Day 39
Set Your Mind on the Spiritual

For the mind set on the flesh is death, but the mind set on the Spirit is life and peace. (Romans 8:6)

When the scripture says, "the mind set on the flesh is death," it is talking about setting your mind on the lusts of the flesh or worldly things. When it says, "but the mind set on the Spirit is life and peace," it is talking about setting your mind on godly things. Worldly things include money, cars, clothes (any possessions), worldly fame, and yes, even food. If you set your mind on godly things such as God's Word, doing godly deeds, and trusting the Holy Spirit to guide you through your everyday experiences, you can expect to have a happier life and be at peace.

Do not get stressed out over anything, not even the big things. You could make your healthy lifestyle program a worldly thing and be very stressed out if you do not reach your daily goals. Yes, you should shoot for perfection but do not condemn yourself if you do not make it. Tomorrow will be a better day if you seek God's peace and guidance. You will have greater peace than if you set your mind on worldly things and try to complete your healthy lifestyle program on your own. Seek the Holy Spirit's guidance not only in your healthy lifestyle but also in everything that you do.

Father, I choose this day to set my mind on spiritual things and not on worldly things. I know that when this is done, I will have peace in my everyday walk and will be successful in my attempts for my healthy lifestyle program. I also know that if I try to accomplish this on my own, I will be unsuccessful. By the power of your Holy Spirit continue to give me the guidance to make the right choices this day. In Jesus's name. Amen.

Nutrition Thought for the Day.

What happens if the gallbladder is removed? The bile is stored in the common bile duct mentioned yesterday, and it is still released into the small intestines in the same way. Here is an important fact: if you do not have sufficient fat in your diet, as is the case with many who are on low-calorie diets to lose weight, the hormone that causes the gallbladder to contract and release the bile into the small intestines will not be available. This means that the bile will build up in the gallbladder. This can cause the bile to crystallize. The crystals will grow and turn into hard substances like rocks. This results in gallstones and can be quite painful and possibly cause the removal of the gallbladder. While fat is high in calories and should be reduced in weight reduction diets, it should not be eliminated. Fat is necessary for a healthy existence and should be included in the diet to prevent gallstones. Fat serves many other important purposes too. Gallstones are very common with people on low-calorie weight reduction diets, the amount of fat necessary in a diet will be discussed later.

Day 40
Seek Heavenly Food

Do not work for the food which perishes, but for the food which endures to eternal life, which the Son of Man will give to you, for on Him the Father, God, has set His seal. (John 6:27)

Earlier in this chapter by John, Jesus fed the five thousand after which He crossed the Sea of Galilee. When those who were fed realized He crossed the sea, they followed Him in boats. In John 6:26 the scripture tells us that they were seeking Him not so much because of the signs He performed, but because He fed them. Then in verse 27, He tells them to seek the food which endures to eternal life. The food He was referring to is the food we can receive from Him through His Word. Do not get caught up in the cares of this world and get consumed with dieting. Yes, you should be seeking after nutritious food, and this is very important to your health, but remember that during this time you need to be seeking the spiritual food of Jesus. Since you are reading this devotional, you are obviously doing that, but do not just depend on this devotional. Get into God's Word every day and find a good illustration of His Word that works for you.

Father, thank You for the guidance I receive every day from You. I am attempting to eat healthily and while I know, that is a good thing, help me that I do not get so hung up on choosing the right foods and following my healthy lifestyle that I overlook the food that You are offering me each day. The food I consume on this earth is good for a period, but I know the food that You offer is good for eternity. Help me always to remember that. In Jesus's name. Amen.

Nutrition Thought for the Day.

Fats are also called triglycerides, triglycerols, or fatty acids. They have several different classifications. When we talk about fats in our daily discussions, we are really referring to triglycerides which many are now calling triglycerols (same thing). Fatty acids are composed of one molecule of glycerol and either one, two, or three fatty acids attached to the glycerol. If one fatty acid is attached, it is called a monoglyceride. If two fatty acids are attached, it is called a diglyceride, and if three fatty acids are attached, it is called a triglyceride. Most of the fat that we take in our diet is in the triglyceride form.

Day 41
I Am Saved

"And I will give them one heart, and put a new spirit within them. And I will take the heart of stone out of their flesh and give them a heart of flesh, that they may walk in My statutes and keep My ordinances and do them. Then they will be My people, and I shall be their God." (Ezekiel 11:19–20)

God was telling His people through the prophet Ezekiel that one day He would put a new spirit within them and He would take away their heart of stone and give them a new heart. This happened to you when you received Jesus as your Savior and Lord. Be encouraged that God's Spirit is in you and you now have a heart that is after God Himself. You can choose to turn away from that fact but instead, be encouraged and remember that God's Spirit lives in you. You may not always feel like you have the Spirit of the living God in you as you walk through your day, but the fulfillment of God's Word is not based on feelings. If the Word says it, then it is true. If you are a born-again believer, the Holy Spirit is in you whether you feel like He is or not. As you continue with your healthy lifestyle program, continue with the knowledge that God is with you and guiding you. Be strong and courageous!

Dear Father God, I thank You for Your Holy Spirit that You gave me upon my salvation and for the new heart that You gave me. Continuously remind me of who I am in Christ and that Your Spirit lives in me. I am an overcomer, and I can do all things through Christ who strengthens me. I choose to receive the heart of flesh that You have given to me, and I choose to seek You to get closer to You each day. I thank You, in Jesus's name. Amen.

Nutrition Thought for the Day.

Fats can also be classified as short chain, medium chain, or long chain fatty acids. Fatty acids are chains of carbons connected to each other. The chain length is determined by the number of carbon atoms attached in a row. Each carbon atom makes four bonds. Carbon has a unique property that allows a carbon atom to connect to another carbon atom. If the letter C represents a carbon atom, then the following would be a chain of carbon atoms making up a fatty acid: C-C-C-C-C-C-C-COOH. Each dash (–) between the carbon atoms represents a bond. The last carbon in the chain is attached to the OOH. The first carbon has three open bonds. Each of those bonds, in all fatty acids, has a hydrogen attached (not shown here). Every other carbon in the chain can have two hydrogen atoms attached. This is organic chemistry and is difficult to explain without illustrations but for the sake of this discussion, just remember the bottom line.

Bottom line: Fatty acids are chains of carbon with various numbers of hydrogen atoms attached. The different lengths of the fatty acids give the fatty acid different properties. This is very important and will be explained as we progress.

Day 42
We Are God's People I

'I will give them a heart to know Me, for I am the LORD; and they will be My people, and I will be their God, for they will return to Me with their whole heart.' (Jeremiah 24:7)

Before this verse God's people were carried off as captives by Nebuchadnezzar and God told them that in time He would bring them back to their land, He would build them up, and He would not overthrow them again. In Jeremiah 24:7, He promised to give them a heart to know Him. The analogy with this scripture for today could be that prior to your salvation experience you were held captive by the world, your flesh, and the devil. Upon receiving Jesus as Savior and Lord, you were given a new heart, a heart after God Himself. It is now your choice to receive that heart and to follow Him. As He promised His people in the Old Testament, He now promises you in the New Testament that He will never leave you. If you are born again, be encouraged today that you have a new heart and that you can serve God with obedience to His Word. Knowing this to be true, you can receive spiritual strength through the Holy Spirit so that you can be successful with your healthy lifestyle program.

Dear Father, I thank You for the new heart You have given me upon my salvation. I choose to receive that heart and to seek after You with all my mind, body, and spirit. I know that the Holy Spirit is guiding me and that Jesus lives in my heart. I know that because they are biblical truths. I can be successful in my diet and exercise program by calling on that strength that is within me and by staying in line with Your Word. I thank You in Jesus's name. Amen.

Nutrition Thought for the Day.

Fatty acids are also classified as saturated, monounsaturated, and polyunsaturated. Saturated fatty acids have a hydrogen atom attached to every open bond on the carbon atoms. Thus, a saturated fatty acid is one that is saturated with hydrogen. In the following illustration, if every carbon atom had every available bond attached to hydrogen, it would be saturated with hydrogen and would be called a saturated fatty acid. The fatty acid in this illustration has eight carbons and would be a medium chain fatty acid: C-C-C-C-C-C-C-COOH. Fatty acids can be classified as short chain, medium chain, or long chain depending on the number of carbons in the chain. All chain lengths are important to us, but for the most part, the fatty acids we are concerned with that affect heart disease are long chain fatty acids. If this is too technical, remember the bottom line.

Bottom line: Avoid saturated fat – choose more monounsaturated and polyunsaturated fats.

Day 43
We Are God's People II

If Christ is in you, though the body is dead because of sin, yet the spirit is alive because of righteousness. (Romans 8:10)

In the book of Romans, God tells us that if Christ is in us (and as born-again Christians He is in us), then even if our body is dead because of sin—that means even if we have fallen and committed sin in a time of weakness—our spirit is still alive because of righteousness. Remember that this righteousness is not our righteousness but the righteousness of Jesus. Also, remember that when we are born again, the Holy Spirit marks our spirit with a permanent seal that distinguishes us as people who have received Jesus Christ as Savior and Lord. Sin cannot stop you from being righteous in the eyes of God if you turn from the sin, confess it, and move on in God's Word.

While this is undoubtedly true in the spiritual, the same is true in your diet/exercise regimen. In the physical it is true also in that if you go off your program, you are not condemned. Instead, forgive yourself and pick up where you left off. Do not ever give up because of one set back. One of our hardest tasks is to forgive ourselves for the mistakes we make, whether it be spiritual mistakes or physical mistakes. Do not be ashamed to admit that you made a mistake and do not let mistakes keep you from your goal. Be bold and courageous!

Dear Father, I know that I have the righteousness of Jesus, not based on what I have done, but on what He did for me. I know that if I sin, I have an advocate in Jesus that I can turn to for forgiveness and that I am not condemned. Likewise, I know that if I fail for a time in my healthy lifestyle, I have an advocate in the Holy Spirit to comfort me and encourage me without condemning me. Finally, I also know that if I have a bad diet day, it is not the end of the program for me. All I have to do is resolve that I am going to pick up where I left off, ask the Holy Spirit for strength, and move on to complete my program successfully. I thank You that this is true, in Jesus's name. Amen.

Nutrition Thought for the Day.
A monounsaturated fatty acid has one double bond. That means that between two carbons there is a double bond instead of the normal single bond. In the following illustration, you will see two dashes between two of the carbons: C-C-C-C=C-C-C-COOH. This represents a double bond and counts for two of the four bonds a carbon can make. Since carbon can only make four bonds, and the double bond takes up two bonds, the two carbons involved in the double bond can now attach to just two additional hydrogens instead of four. Thus it is not as saturated and since it has one double bond and it is called a monounsaturated fatty acid. This has significant health implications. A polyunsaturated fatty acid has more than one double bond; it could have two, three, or four and still be called a polyunsaturated fatty acid. This also has health implications that will be discussed later. Remember the bottom line from yesterday.

Day 44
Let's All Praise the Lord

Both young men and virgins; old men and children. Let them praise the name of the LORD, for His name alone is exalted; His glory is above earth and heaven. (Psalm 148:12–13)

Spend another day just giving praise and thanks to the Lord your God. This Psalm tells us that we all, young or old, virgins or not, men and women, should praise the name of our Lord. Think back on what you have accomplished since you have been on this healthy lifestyle program, even if that has been small accomplishments, you are moving in the right direction.

Continue with your program and do not give up. Be strong and courageous! The Lord, your God, is with you and will never leave you. Give praise to the Lord today in everything you do. At the beginning of the day make a decision that today is going to be a day of appreciation for your God. Ask the Holy Spirit to remind you this day that everything you say and do is to be done for the glory of God; then it will be easier for your actions today to be in line with God's Word.

Dear Father God, Lord Jesus, I want to offer this day as a living sacrifice for You. Holy Spirit, as today moves on remind me of anything I start to say or do that is not of You. I declare that You are worthy of all praise, honor, and glory. I give praise to You, and I thank You for the accomplishments that I have made thus far, and I give all credit for my achievements to You. May Your name be exalted forever. I praise You this day, in Jesus's name. Amen.

Nutrition Thought for the Day.

Most of the fats important to us in nutrition are long chain fatty acids. Saturated fats are bad, polyunsaturated and monounsaturated are better. Saturated fats include the fat found in meats and dairy products. The fat of lamb is more saturated than beef fat, and beef is more saturated than pork fat. The fat of poultry and fish are predominately monounsaturated. Pork is close to being considered monounsaturated. This is why you see advertisements for pork as the other white meat, referring to the fact that it is close to poultry in its fat makeup. Coconut oil and palm oil are saturated vegetable oils and will be discussed later. Monounsaturated fats include olive oil and canola oil. Polyunsaturated oils are plant oils and include (from the most unsaturated to the least unsaturated) safflower oil, sunflower oil, corn oil, soybean oil, and cottonseed oil.

Bottom line: Eat less red meat, more chicken and fish, and more fruit and vegetables.

Day 45
God Creates Only Good Things

.....*men* who forbid marriage *and advocate* abstaining from foods which God has created to be gratefully shared in by those who believe and know the truth. For everything created by God is good, and nothing is to be rejected if it is received with gratitude; for it is sanctified by means of the word of God and prayer. (1 Timothy 4:3–5)

In1 Timothy 4:1, Paul is telling Timothy to be aware because in the latter days men will fall away from their faith and will pay attention to deceitful spirits and doctrines of demons. Picking up in verse three above, he tells him that men will "forbid marriage and advocate abstaining from foods which God has created to be gratefully shared in by those who believe and know the truth". Finally, he says, "that everything created by God is good and nothing is to be rejected if it is received with gratitude and sanctified by means of God's Word and prayer."

You are probably on a healthy lifestyle program that is telling you to avoid certain foods, such as certain fats and sweets. This is good and a healthy thing to do but do not come under condemnation by thinking that it is a sin to eat such foods. They are not necessarily good for you if consumed on a regular basis, but if on occasion you indulge in something that is not healthy for you, it is not a sin. Granted your body is the temple of the Holy Spirit and, because of that, you should want to treat it that way with healthy foods. However, do not come under condemnation for going off your diet. Remember that God still loves you.

> Dear Father God, I thank You for creating everything for a purpose, and if all things are used for their proper purpose, they are good. I know I need to eat healthy to be healthy and I resolve to do that. But if I do not completely follow my diet from time to time, I know that I am under no condemnation from You. I know that You love me and will never leave me regardless of what kind of diet I am following. I ask for wisdom from Your Holy Spirit to direct me to choose foods that are healthy for me, and I ask for Your strength so I can resist the foods that are not healthy for me. In Jesus's name, I pray. Amen.

Nutrition Thought for the Day.

Cholesterol is not fat but is a fat-like substance in that it is not soluble in water. If triglycerides and cholesterol were not attached to lipoproteins in the blood, they would clump together and cause blockages because the blood is water, and fats are not soluble in water. A lipoprotein consists of part lipid (which is fat) and part protein attached together. The lipid part of the compound attaches to cholesterol and triglycerides. The protein part of the molecule is soluble in water and carries the particles through the blood. The different lipoprotein carriers have an important significance in our health.

Bottom line: Since cholesterol is found in animal products, eat less animal products and more plant proteins that complement each other (to be discussed later).

Day 46
God Blesses Your Food

"But you shall serve the LORD your God, and He will bless your bread and your water; and I will remove sickness from your midst." (Exodus 23:25)

In the Old Testament God promised His people that if they obeyed His commands and followed Him, He would bless their food and water. While this is still true, God also gave us a brain to use in making wise decisions. In the New Testament, He also gives us direction through His Holy Spirit. Use this devotion in conjunction with yesterday's devotion in that you should make wise choices in the foods that you eat and not just eat anything saying, "It will be okay if I eat this. I know it is not good for me, but if I do everything right in God's Word, He will not allow anything to happen to me." God is definitely looking out for you but, as mentioned, He has given you a brain to use with wisdom. You would not jump off a ten-story building saying, "It is okay, I will not be hurt, I am following God's Word, and He will not allow me to be hurt." I am trying to help you understand that there is no condemnation if you go off your diet, and all food is good for the body to a degree, but not all food is entirely healthy to be eaten all the time. Ask for wisdom, study about foods on your own, and trust the Holy Spirit to guide you.

Father God, I know that You will bless the food and water that I consume when I dedicate it to You, and I thank You for it, but I also understand that some things could be very harmful to me. I know that I should not test You by just eating anything to fulfill my lust for food and expect You to make it right. I trust in Your Holy Spirit to give me wisdom and guidance so that I can make healthy choices and be a healthier person for Your glory. In Jesus's name, I pray. Amen.

Nutrition Thought for the Day.
You probably already know that cholesterol can be harmful. Cholesterol and triglycerides can become attached to the lining of blood vessels and cause a buildup known as atherosclerosis. However, you may not know that cholesterol is a required nutrient. It does not have an energy value, and it is not utilized for energy, but it is a precursor to the sex hormones, testosterone, and estrogen. It is also a precursor for vitamin D formation and, it is the primary constituent of bile. Cholesterol is also necessary for the structure of cell membranes and is present in every cell in our bodies. Cholesterol comes in our diet from animal products only. Cholesterol is not found in any plant products unless it has been added by the manufacturer. Cholesterol is synthesized in our body, for the most part in the liver, but also in the gastrointestinal tract and other places.

Bottom line: Some lean animal products can be healthy but your body can produce all the cholesterol it needs.

Day 47
Do Not Seek Sympathy

"Whenever you fast, do not put on a gloomy face as the hypocrites *do,* for they neglect their appearance so that they will be noticed by men when they are fasting. Truly I say to you, they have their reward in full." (Matthew 6:16)

Matthew gives us a little tidbit of knowledge here that may be useful in your everyday walk. It is obvious he is talking about people that are fasting for religious reasons and not trying to lose weight, but I believe the same principle applies to dieters/healthy eaters. Since you are not eating the same foods as people you associate with, you could become obnoxious and always bring up your healthy lifestyle program with the poor me attitude. Some people seek the sympathy of the people around them because they are dieting, but you should not do that. That is not helping you, nor is it helping them.

God sees what you are doing, and He knows your motives. That is all that matters. When you have the opportunity to point out that you are on a new healthy lifestyle program, and you depend on God's guidance for success, use your program as a testimony to Him. Be at peace with yourself as you diet and give the glory to God.

Father, once again I choose to give You the glory for any success that I make with this new healthy lifestyle program. It is good for me to be encouraged by my peers as I make progress but it is not good for me to seek their sympathy because I cannot eat all the foods they are eating. That could bring them under condemnation instead of my diet/exercise program bringing glory to You. I desire to lose weight and get healthy for myself and my family, but ultimately to give the glory to You. I thank You for helping me and reminding me of who I am in Christ, and that is a witness for You. In Jesus's name, I pray. Amen.

Nutrition Thought for the Day.

You have seen or heard, I am sure, advertisements that refer to bad cholesterol and the good cholesterol. There is no such thing as good and bad cholesterol. Cholesterol is cholesterol. What they are calling bad cholesterol is the lipoprotein that carries cholesterol to the peripheral tissues, which are the tissues away from the liver. This includes the linings of the blood vessels. That lipoprotein is called a low-density lipoprotein (LDL).

The lipoprotein that carries cholesterol back to the liver from the peripheral tissues to either be converted to bile, stored in the liver or to be excreted from the body through the liver is called high-density lipoprotein (HDL). The fact that HDL cholesterol is on the way to be excreted is why it is called good cholesterol. Obviously, you would want as much cholesterol as possible coming from the peripheral tissues to the liver, so there is less of a chance for cholesterol to be deposited in the blood vessels. Thus the ratio of LDL to HDL is very important.

Day 48
Do Everything for God's Glory

Whatever you do in word or deed, *do* all in the name of the Lord Jesus, giving thanks through Him to God the Father. (Colossians 3:17)

Everything we do should be done for the glory of God. Note that it says that whatever we do in word or deed we should do in Jesus's name so that, through Him, we can give thanks to God our Father. You are more likely to give glory to God for the accomplishments you make in areas that are important to you, especially the more significant, more apparent achievements. Smaller day to day accomplishments are more likely to be overlooked or taken for granted. You might notice a small accomplishment in weight loss (or gain) and, since it is so small, you do not think of it as being related to a godly act. You may give glory to yourself for such a small accomplishment.

With such small accomplishments with your new healthy lifestyle program, it will be easy to let everyone know how you are doing and brag. This is okay, and it will probably give you positive feedback as encouragement from some of your peers, but if you do this continuously, it may cause you to overlook God's hand in your daily life. Not only can it become obnoxious but you could gradually get very puffed up and lose your focus. After a while, you could become a stench to the people around you, especially those who are trying to lose weight and maybe are not as successful as you are. Be careful to give glory to God in word and deed. Be accountable for every word and deed and give the glory to God and not to yourself.

Father God, if I ever get off track and begin to be prideful about my accomplishments and take the glory for them instead of giving You the glory, then I ask You to lead me back in the right direction by the power of Your Holy Spirit. I want to be a reflection of Your glory and not absorb it for myself. I know that I cannot do anything of any merit on my own and I rely on You for all the accomplishments I make, not only in my healthy lifestyle program but in everything that I do. In Jesus's name, I pray. Amen.

Nutrition Thought for the Day.

The level of cholesterol in your body is not as important as the ratio of LDL to HDL. Most people have considerably more LDL than HDL. The more cholesterol you have in your body, the more LDL your body has to make to carry that cholesterol and the unhealthier that is. Triglycerides are also transported through the blood to the peripheral tissues by LDL. Thus the more triglycerides you have, the more LDL the body has to make. Triglycerides come from the diet as such, but they are also synthesized in the body when we have an excessive calorie intake. That excessive calorie intake can come from carbohydrate, fat, or protein.

Bottom line: If you are taking in more carbohydrate, fat, or protein than your body needs, you probably are making excessive LDL. This could be a health hazard.

Day 49
You Are a Crown of Beauty

You will also be a crown of beauty in the hand of the LORD, and a royal diadem in the hand of your God. (Isaiah 62:3)

Be encouraged as to who you are and how your God sees you. In this scripture, Isaiah was talking collectively about God's people in the Old Testament but if you follow His Word, this scripture carefully, you will see that it comes true for you. You are 'a crown of beauty in the hand of the Lord.' You are a royal diadem in the hand of Your God. No matter if it is the Old Testament or the New Testament if you are God's child, and, as a born-again believer, you are just that, then God sees you like a crown of beauty in His hand. It does not matter if you see yourself as a crown of beauty or not, you are what God's Word says about you.

I encourage you to see yourself as God sees you. He does not see you as someone who is struggling to keep a diet/exercise program. Instead, He sees you just as the Bible describes you and that description includes you being a crown of beauty to your God. Remember that and move on with your head held high as you serve your God on this earth.

Father God, I do not always see myself as a crown of beauty, particularly when I have a bad day and return to an unhealthy lifestyle. But I know that You see me as Your child—a crown of beauty in Your hand. If Your Word says this is true, then I say amen and let it be so. I know Your Word is true and You cannot lie but help me when I do not see myself as I should—as You see me. Give me the strength and endurance to complete this program and always remind me, by the power of Your Holy Spirit, who I am in Christ. In Jesus's name, I pray. Amen.

Nutrition Thought for the Day.

Substances that will increase LDL include excessive calories, whether they be from carbohydrate, fat, or protein. HDL can be increased with consistent significant aerobic exercise. Claims have been made for increasing HDL by the intake of various foods, but the research backing these claims is limited and inconsistent. Olive oil is one of the foods that may help increase HDL. Moderate alcohol intake can raise HDL, but alcohol should not be consumed for this reason because it can cause many other health problems such as high blood pressure, cirrhosis, cardiomyopathy, and cancer—not to mention alcoholism. Smoking reduces HDL. If you quit smoking, HDL tends to come back up.

Bottom line: Do not take in excessive calories, do not smoke, only drink alcohol in moderation or not at all, and get good, healthy exercise.

Note: You may not like these suggestions, but it is up to you if you want to be healthy and have a greater chance of living longer. The alternative is a greater chance of being plagued with numerous illnesses and perhaps die prematurely.

Day 50
God Is at Work in You

For it is God who is at work in you, both to will and to work for *His* good pleasure. (Philippians 2:13)

After reading yesterday's devotion, you still may not see yourself as a crown of beauty. One more thing to remember about that, since you have given your life to Jesus He is at work in you. But what does "both to will and to work for His good pleasure" mean? "To will" refers to God in you helping you to complete your efforts, that is, your tasks at hand. Simply said, He is at work in you to help you to desire to complete your goal and to physically complete your goal—that is your will and your work effort. What a blessing that is! The work you are doing, not only concerning changing to a new healthy lifestyle but everything you are doing is being guided by God your Father. Be encouraged to know that you are not alone. Even though you may sometimes feel like you are alone, remember that God's Word is true and it says that He is with you and will never leave you.

Thank You Father God for being with me, even when I am not aware of it and when I am not thinking about Your presence. Even on those days that I wake up with the task of the day on my mind and do not give You the first acknowledgment of my love. Instead, I go about my busy self, trying to accomplish things on my own power. Even at those times You are with me and guiding me. I know that with Your help I will be successful in all that I do, not just starting a healthy lifestyle. I give thanks to You in the name of Jesus. Amen.

Nutrition Thought for the Day.

Saturated fat is bad for us because it promotes cholesterol absorption in the intestines and once the saturated fat is absorbed, it promotes cholesterol synthesis in the liver and causes an increase in LDL. Saturated fat may also be involved in causing inflammation in the blood vessels. For atherosclerosis to begin in our blood vessels, inflammation has to take place first. This will be discussed later with heart disease.

Monounsaturated fats may help with slightly reducing cholesterol absorption and may slightly increase HDL production. Polyunsaturated fats probably do not affect absorption and likely do not play a significant role in cholesterol synthesis, but they do not have an unhealthy effect. They are believed to be beneficial. If I had to choose between monounsaturated fat (such as olive oil or Canola oil) and polyunsaturated fat (such as safflower oil, sunflower oil, corn oil, soybean oil, or cottonseed oil), I would choose olive oil. If the choice is between saturated fat and monounsaturated, choose monounsaturated. If it is between saturated fat and polyunsaturated, choose polyunsaturated fat.

Day 51
Do Not Grumble

Do all things without grumbling or disputing. (Philippians 2:14)

We are instructed not to grumble or dispute God. Knowing that God is in you, helping you with your desires and with your efforts, you should then move on through your day praising Him for helping you. The best way to do that is to complete your tasks, whatever they may be—however difficult they may be—without grumbling, complaining, or disputing things with your peers and family. Even though you may be trying your best to follow God's Word, you know that everything will not always go the way you want or expect. Do not complain and do not blame God; praise Him in the hard times as well as the good times. This will give glory to God; grumbling will not. Being an obedient and willing servant and trying with all your heart to complete the task set before you, will give glory to your God. This is true even if you are not always successful. God is not asking you to be great or to be number one in everything you do. He is asking for your effort and your attitude while completing your tasks. Be reminded of this today and approach everything that lies ahead of you with confidence, love, and obedience.

Lord Jesus, thank You for reminding me that if I am to be Your loving servant, that I must take each day in stride in obedience to Your Word and without grumbling or disputing. By the power of Your Holy Spirit, continue to remind me of who I am in You and give me the grace to become the person that You have created me to be. I once again remind myself that when You look at me, You do not see a person that is overweight. Instead, You see a crown of beauty. Amen.

Nutrition Thought for the Day.

Another fat that is in the news a lot today is *trans* fats. Two possible bonds can be made between the carbons of fatty acids, *trans* and *cis* bonds. *Cis* bonds are the natural bonds that take place in nature. *Trans* bonds are found in nature sparingly, but most are man-made. The more double bonds a fat has, the more susceptible the fat is to oxygenation. In oxygenation, oxygen in the air reacts with the double bonds of fatty acids and breaks them. When this happens, the fat is changed and is no longer the same fat it was before oxygen reacted with it. This makes the fat rancid and undesirable. It also can cause harm to our bodies.

Bottom line: Read labels and avoid *trans* fats. The food label will list at least the amount of total fat, saturated fat, and *trans* fat. *Trans* fats should soon be banned from processed food.

Day 52
The Holy Spirit Is Your Teacher I

"But the Helper, the Holy Spirit, whom the Father will send in My name, He will teach you all things, and bring to your remembrance all that I said to you. (John 14:26)

The Holy Spirit is with you and will lead and guide you as promised in this scripture. Keep in mind that the scripture does not mean you will naturally know all things by asking the Holy Spirit a simple question and receiving a direct answer. He will answer your request but only if you seek Him and study His Word. He may not answer you immediately and He may not answer you in a way that you are expecting. As you get closer to Him, you will learn how to hear His voice.

The scripture says that He will bring to your remembrance all that Jesus said in His Word. He cannot bring something to your remembrance if you did not know it to start with. If you seek God with all your heart and study His Word on a regular basis, then when you need to know something He will remind you of what you have already studied. You probably will not hear an audible voice telling you what you need to know, but when you are trying to make a decision, you will feel inner peace, knowing what you should do, and may very well be reminded of some scripture that will confirm your decision. This is the Holy Spirit guiding you and directing you. Do not expect to hear this clearly the first day you decide to follow the Holy Spirit's advice. It does take time and devotion on your part to listen to the Holy Spirit speaking to you. The ability to hear God's voice happens slowly as you study God's Word and speak to Him in prayer. Any relationship takes time to develop.

Father God, I know that You sent the Holy Spirit to me in the name of Jesus. I know that I must seek You on a regular basis and study Your Word on my own. As I seek You, I expect to be guided by Your Holy Spirit with that still small voice that speaks to me in my spirit. I thank You for Your Holy Spirit, and I look forward to the guidance that You will provide for me. I especially look forward to the success I will obtain through my healthy lifestyle program by Your guidance. In Jesus's name, I pray. Amen.

Nutrition Thought for the Day.

When manufacturers make cookies, they want the cookies to have a long shelf life. They want the cookies to stay fresh in your kitchen cabinet for a long time. If the cookies are made with polyunsaturated fatty acids, they would be more susceptible to oxygenation and rancidity because of a large number of double bonds. Double bonds are more accessible for the oxygen in the air to break (oxygenation). This would, of course, affect the sale of the cookies. They would prefer to make the cookies out of saturated fats which are less susceptible to oxygenation because they do not have any double bonds. The popular teaching is to avoid saturated fats, so manufacturers convert polyunsaturated fats into saturated fats without explaining what they are doing. They do this by heating polyunsaturated oils in large vats under pressure and bubbling hydrogen gas through them. This breaks the double bonds and saturates them with hydrogen, but the bond that is made in this process is a *trans* bond instead of the *cis* bond that was there from the start.

Day 53
The Holy Spirit Is Your Teacher II

But when He, the Spirit of truth, comes, He will guide you into all the truth."
(John 16:13a)

The Scriptures also confirm the fact that the Holy Spirit is your teacher and your guide. Many other scriptures outline the fact that the Holy Spirit is your teacher, comforter, and guide who will direct you in your time of need. While this is true, you need to study God's Word so that you can clearly understand what the Spirit is telling you. You also need to use wisdom so that you can make wise decisions to determine if it is the Holy Spirit who is speaking to you or if it is your flesh, the world, or the devil that is speaking to you. If you are not walking closely to God, it is sometimes difficult to tell the difference. The Bible tells you to ask for the spiritual gifts (1 Corinthians 14:1 and 1 Corinthians 14:12). Among the spiritual gifts referred to in these scriptures is included the gift of discernment. It is good to ask God for this gift so that you may have a greater ability to discern between the Holy Spirit, the world, the flesh, and the devil. With each passing day, attempt to get closer to God by reading His Word and talking to Him in prayer.

Father God, help me each day to organize my time that I can spend more time in Your Word. Help me to realize that I must not only read Your Word, but I must also spend time meditating on Your Word, and being still and quiet so that I can hear Your Holy Spirit speak to me in that still, small voice. I want to get closer and closer to You with each passing day. Time management is something that I ask Your Holy Spirit to help me with so that I may accomplish these goals. In Jesus's name, I pray. Amen.

Nutrition Thought for the Day.
It was mentioned earlier that saturated fats might cause more cholesterol to be absorbed in the small intestines and, once absorbed, it may cause more cholesterol to be synthesized by the liver. It seems that *trans* fats have an even more significant effect on both of these functions. Also, before atherosclerosis can form in our blood vessels inflammation forms in the walls of the blood vessel. Many things can cause inflammation, some of which we probably do not know of yet, but one of the greater causes of inflammation is believed to be *trans* fatty acids.

Bottom line: Avoid *trans* fats.

Day 54
The Holy Spirit Is Your Teacher III

"Do not fear, for I have redeemed you; I have called you by name; you are Mine!" (Isaiah 43:1b)

In this Old Testament scripture, God is talking to His people Israel, and He is telling them not to fear for He has redeemed them and He calls them by name. He declares they are His. This is before Jesus came to the earth. If this was true in the Old Testament, how much more is it true today after Jesus came, suffered, and died for your sins? His blood redeems you and you are now a child of God and coheir with Jesus. Considering all of this you should be more resistant to fear than the people of the Old Testament. Walk through this day with your head held high knowing that you are redeemed, and God calls you by name—He knows every hair on your head. You are His child, therefore walk without fear in whatever you do today. Be bold and courageous with your healthy lifestyle regimen and know that, while it is important, but it is not as important as the fact that you are redeemed! Be blessed and be thankful this day.

Thank You, Father God that You have redeemed me by the blood of Jesus. Thank You, Father, that I am Yours and that You have not given me a spirit of fear but a redeemed spirit that is full of Your power. As I walk through my busy day, I know that You walk with me, but remind me of these facts when the cares of the world close in on me and my concerns with my healthy lifestyle regimen try to get the best of me. I will not fear, for You are with me. In Jesus's name, I pray. Amen.

Nutrition Thought for the Day.

Since *trans* fats tend to increase cholesterol in the blood, this increases the need for the LDL carrier and causes LDL, the so-called bad cholesterol, to rise. It has also been reported to decrease the good cholesterol, HDL. All of this increases the risk of heart disease and stroke. Also, *trans* fats have been associated with an increase in obesity and the risk of type 2 diabetes. In summary, *trans* fats can possibly increase the absorption and production of cholesterol, increase LDL, decrease HDL, increase the possibility of inflammation in blood vessels, increase obesity, raise the likelihood of type 2 diabetes, and increase the risk of heart disease and stroke. Is this enough reason to read labels and avoid *trans* fats?

Day 55
Avoid Jealousy and Strife

For where jealousy and selfish ambition exist, there is disorder and every evil thing. (James 3:16)

If you want to open a door for the devil to get into your life, then just allow jealousy and selfish ambition in your day. The King James Version says, "Where envying and strife *is*, there *is* confusion and every evil work." All of us are susceptible to envy, jealousy, selfish ambition, or strife. We all have to be aware of these faults throughout our daily lives. You probably know several other people who are on a diet/exercise program and some of them may be doing better on their program than you are doing on yours. This opens the door to envy or jealousy. As soon as you see a crack in the door, slam it shut. Do not let the devil get a foothold in your life as to envy and strife. Be at peace knowing that you are the redeemed, a child of God, and that is the only thing that is important. If someone else is doing better on their program than you are on yours, give them praise and encouragement and move on.

Lord Jesus, I know that envy and strife is an open door to the devil to get into my mind. I resolve not to be envious or jealous of anyone else's success, but I will encourage them in their accomplishments so that I can be a better witness for You while closing the door to jealousy. I also resolve to close the door to any form of strife or selfish ambition that would cause me to walk out from under Your protection. Confusion has no place in my life, and I rebuke it in the name of Jesus. I am thankful that the Holy Spirit is my encourager and will guide me in everything that I do. I thank You, Lord Jesus, for what You have done for me. Amen.

Nutrition Thought for the Day.

Because *trans* fats are known to be such a problem, they will soon be banned from being added to foods (may already be banned by the time you read this), yet they may still be around for a while. Several years ago food manufacturers were required to include information on the food label to let you know if *trans* fats were in their food products. Look on the label under fats and look for a title *trans* fat, and it will tell you the number of grams of *trans* fats in the product. Most labels will say zero grams but here is the trick, they are not required to list how much *trans* fat is in the product unless there is 0.5grams or more. That means if there are 0.4grams of *trans* fat in the product, the manufacturer can officially list it as 0 grams of *trans* fat.

Day 56
Do Not Allow Yourself to Be Arrogant

Knowledge makes arrogant, but love edifies. (1 Corinthians 8:1b)

This is the second part of verse one of 1 Corinthians 8 and deals with another area that can allow strife to creep into your life. Yesterday's devotion addressed being envious; today's addresses being arrogant. If someone believes he is smarter or better than someone else, it can set the stage for arrogance. The New International Version says, "knowledge puffs up." Instead of yesterday's scenario that could cause envy if someone who is on a healthy program and they are doing much better than you are, the opposite of that scenario could cause arrogance. That is, suppose you are doing much better on your program than some of your peers. This would create an opportunity for you to be puffed up or arrogant and brag about your accomplishments. This would not be acting like a child of God, and it would not present a very good witness. Instead, do as the scripture says and let love edify. Show them love and encouragement to be a good witness and to help them to overcome the obstacles that are preventing them from being successful. Regardless of how others treat you, as hard as it may be, make an effort to always treat them with love and respect in the name of Jesus.

Lord Jesus, another trait I always want to avoid is that of arrogance. I know that arrogance or a know it all attitude is not of You and will not be a good witness for me. I resolve to put forth an extreme effort to be loving and encouraging to those that I meet, regardless of how they may treat me. If I am better at something than they are, I resolve to encourage them and, if possible, with a loving spirit, show them how they may be able to be better at their diet or whatever it is they are trying to accomplish. I declare this in the name of Jesus. Amen.

Nutrition Thought for the Day.

How many grams of *trans* fats are harmful? It is considered that one gram of *trans* fat can cause the problems listed a few days ago. This is not very much, approximately one-fifth of a teaspoon. Remember, the amount listed on the label is per serving. If the product has five-tenths of a gram (0.5) of *trans* fat per serving, and you eat two servings, you already have one gram from one food item for that day. Many foods have some *trans* fats in them, even if it is only one-tenth (0.1) or two tenths (0.2) of a gram per serving. It would not be hard to get one gram of *trans* fat in a day if you are not careful. How can you be careful? This will be tomorrow's topic.

Day 57
Let Jesus Flow from You

"He who believes in Me, as the Scripture said, 'From his innermost being will flow rivers of living water.'" (John 7:38)

John 7:38 says, that if you know Jesus, living waters will flow from your innermost being. This is a way to overcome the potential problems mentioned in the last two devotions, and that is the problems of envy, strife, and arrogance. If you can remember who you are in Christ as you walk through your daily routines, then you can be an encouragement and an up-lifter to those around you when they are going through trials or hardships. You have to allow the love of Jesus to flow out of you and into those around you. This is being a new creature in Christ and not conforming to the ways of the world. This is not always as easy to do as it may sound, but it is your call, and you know that God's grace for you is sufficient. Be bold and courageous in all that you do and be an encourager for Christ.

Lord Jesus, You are the light of the world, and that light has been given to me by what You did for me on the cross. Help me to be ever mindful of the light that is in me and to be ever willing to let that light shine and to let Your living waters flow from me to those that are around me. I want to be an encourager for You and lead the people in my circle of influence to You. I cannot do that on my own but only by letting You be apparent through me. I resolve to be ever mindful of the abilities I have through You so that I can be a light to those that are around me. In Your name, Jesus, I pray. Amen.

Nutrition Thought for the Day.

While the food label may say zero grams of *trans* fat, it could still have up to four-tenths (0.4) of a gram. To find out if there is any *trans* fat in the product at all, look at the ingredients label. When it mentions the kind of fat in the product, the label will tell you if it is corn oil, coconut oil, soybean oil, etc. As long as it names the oil and does not mention anything about how the oil is processed, you are okay. If it includes partially hydrogenated corn oil or any other kind of oil, it means it was processed, as mentioned in an earlier devotion. That would result in some *trans* fat being in the product. You do not know how much *trans* fat is there, but there is at least one-tenth (0.1) of a gram of *trans* fat up to four-tenths (0.4) of a gram. The best thing to do is to avoid any food that has partially hydrogenated oil if at all possible.

Day 58
Sow Seeds in Joy

Those who sow in tears shall reap with joyful shouting. (Psalm 126:5)

In this Psalm, God's people are praising Him for the things He did for them when they were brought out of captivity. The next verse of this Psalm says, "Those who go out weeping, carrying seed to sow, will return with songs of joy, carrying sheaves with them." They knew that even if they sow seed while weeping when the seed matures to a fruit-bearing plant, they were returning joyfully with a great harvest. If your attempts to encourage those around you are not apparently producing fruit at the time you sow your seed of God's Word, do not be concerned or discouraged. There is always seedtime and harvest. Before you can reap a harvest, you have to sow seed. Sometimes it takes a while for a harvest to become ripe for the picking. In time, that seed will produce fruit, and you will have joy when you see the fruit of your labors—and that fruit will be people coming to know Jesus Christ as Savior and Lord. So, when you let the living waters from Jesus flow through you, you are sowing seed, and in due time you will reap a joyful harvest. Do not be discouraged! Be bold and courageous!

Lord Jesus, I know that even when I allow Your living waters to flow out of me, they do not always seem to be received by those around me, but I also know that in due time those living waters will produce fruit. Your Word says that it will not return unto You void but will accomplish the purpose for which You sent it (Isaiah 55:11). I will not be discouraged if I witness for You and it is not received well, for I know that whenever I speak Your Word to someone, I am planting a seed and in due time that seed will bear fruit for You. I thank You that this is true in Your name, Jesus. Amen.

Nutrition Thought for the Day.

Foods that are usually high in *trans* fats include, not only the foods that have *trans* fats added to them, but any food that has been fried at high temperatures like doughnuts and French fries. Foods that have *trans* fats added include almost all foods that the manufacturer wants to have a long shelf life. For the most part, baked goods such as pie crusts, pastries, cakes, cookies, crackers, etc. This includes snack crackers like peanut butter crackers, cheese crackers, and any of the numerously available snack cakes. You must read the ingredients label and look for hydrogenated or partially hydrogenated fats to determine if the product contains *trans* fats.

Day 59
Maintain Your Focus

If the ruler's temper rises against you, do not abandon your position, because composure allays great offenses. (Ecclesiastes 10:4)

If you are in a situation where your boss or someone else that is over you finds fault with you, do not abandon your position in Christ and say something stupid that would cause you to be in greater trouble. Instead, maintain your composure and show love in the situation. The scripture above says that this allays great offenses. "Allays" means to reduce, diminish, relieve, or alleviate great offenses. By being loving in bad situations, you can often win your boss over to your side instead of creating a wall and making things worse. Again, I know this is easier said than done, but by reminding ourselves each day who we are in Christ, and by resolving that we are going to follow His Word, we can make great accomplishments while being a witness for Him. You can do the same thing if you receive criticism from someone about your weight or your healthy lifestyle program. The only judgment you need to be concerned with is Jesus's judgment of you. All other judgments are worthless. Keep your eyes on Jesus and reflect His love.

Father God, when I am accused of something I did not do or if I am the object of someone's anger, help me to be a shining light for You. I know that if I suffer persecution for Your sake, my reward in heaven will be even greater. It may be that I am the object of ridicule for some reason other than the fact that I am a Christian, but if I am not rude or belligerent in my response and show love instead, I am receiving ridicule for Your sake. Lord Jesus, I ask that my enemies be made Your footstool and that You give me grace and the words to say in times of stress by the power of Your Holy Spirit. Father, I know that You will help me to be strong in such circumstances and I put my trust entirely in Your hands. In Jesus's name, I pray. Amen.

Nutrition Thought for the Day.
The Food and Drug Administration gave the food industry until 2018 to entirely eliminate *trans* fats from the food supply, but we still must be diligent about reading food labels to see how much *trans* fat is in the foods we are eating because at the time of this writing, summer of 2019, *trans* fat information is still on labels. So, this sounds like good news, right? Do not be so quick to make such a judgment because food manufacturers have found a substitute for *trans* fats that preliminary research shows to be worse. The new product is called interesterified fat. Interesterification produces products that do not exist naturally. They are reportedly already in many of the foods we eat. They are high in stearic acid, which is the fatty acid that is high in beef and can be atherogenic, that is, it can cause atherosclerosis. They can be used in all the foods that previously used *trans* fats.

Bottom line: Read the label.

Day 60
Overcome by Your Faith I

For whatever is born of God overcomes the world; and this is the victory that has overcome the world—our faith. (1 John 5:4)

The devotions for the next 30 days will be concerned with building your faith. "For whatever is born of God overcomes the world...." If you are a born-again Christian, then you are born of God, and that makes you a world overcomer. And how are you a world overcomer? The next part of the scripture tells you that you overcome the world by your faith. You may not feel like your faith is strong enough to overcome the world, but you have been given faith that is sufficient for that purpose. You do not start working on your faith by believing for a million dollars if you have a hard time believing for a dollar. Build your faith gradually by believing in God for the small things; like instead of believing to lose fifty pounds, start believing to lose one to two pounds per week, or believe to gain weight gradually if weight gain is your goal. As your faith grows, your victories will increase and get even more significant. The point to remember is that you are a world overcomer because the Bible says so. Keep repeating that to get it into your spirit and then walk it out. I know this is easier said than done, but practice your faith every chance you get and watch it grow!

Father, if Your Word says that I am an overcomer, then I choose to believe it by an act of my will. I do not always feel like an overcomer, but if Your Word says it, I will believe it. Remind me as necessary that I am a world overcomer and give me the grace to walk out that belief. I know that the faith You have given me is sufficient for me to accomplish Your will for my life. Continue to encourage me so that I can become the person You created me to be. In Jesus's name, I pray. Amen.

Nutrition Thought for the Day.

Fat digestion is more complicated than carbohydrate or protein digestion. Carbohydrate digestion starts in the mouth (to a very small percentage) by an enzyme that is found in saliva. Carbohydrate digestion stops in the stomach and restarts in the small intestines with enzymes from the pancreas and the walls of the small intestines. Fat digestion in adults does not start until the small intestines. The stomachs of infants can digest the butterfat in milk, but this is not of much use to adults. Remember that fats come into the body mainly in the form of triglycerides; these could be as triglycerides with long chain fatty acids, medium chain fatty acids, or short chain fatty acids. A small amount of free fatty acids is also found in foods. Medium chain triglycerides, short-chain triglycerides, and free fatty acids can be absorbed directly into the bloodstream without the need for enzymes or bile.

WAYNE E. BILLON, PH.D., RDN, LDN

Day 61
Overcome with Your Faith II

Fight the good fight of faith; take hold of the eternal life to which you were called, and you made the good confession in the presence of many witnesses. (1 Timothy 6:12)

If, after reading yesterday's devotion, you still do not feel like a world overcomer, be mindful that you can be an overcomer of all things by faith. Understand that the world is overcome by faith and has already been overcome by Jesus as He declared in John 16:33. Yes, you will always have trials and tribulations, but fight the good fight of faith and walk in the faith of Jesus. When God created you He had in mind for you to be an overcomer and to walk in faith until it was time to go to the new eternal life to which you are called. In John 16:33, Jesus was talking to His disciples when He told them to beware because they were going to have trials in this world, but He told them to take courage because He had already overcome the world. The same words Jesus gave to His disciples, He intended for you to have today. You can overcome by receiving what Jesus said and fighting the good fight of faith. Jesus's words are alive and intended for you. Be at peace today knowing that you really are an overcomer and you have been called to eternal life with Jesus. Remember that Jesus would not ask you to do something that was impossible for you to do.

Lord Jesus, thank You for overcoming the world for me. Thank You for giving me Your peace in this world and for reminding me that You have already overcome the world. I understand that You have called me to eternal life with You. You have defeated sin and Satan, all I have to do is rely on Your Word and walk out Your Word in faith. Thank You for Your victory, and I look forward to seeing myself complete my undertakings victoriously, including my healthy lifestyle, as I walk out Your Word in faith. In Your name, Jesus, I pray. Amen.

Nutrition Thought for the Day.

Long chain triglycerides need to be digested to free fatty acids and glycerol by means of an enzyme called lipase. This occurs in the small intestines with the enzyme lipase that comes from the pancreas. The presence of fat in the small intestines is detected by sensory cells in the intestines. These send a signal to the pancreas and cause the pancreas to secrete pancreatic lipase into the small intestines through the pancreatic duct. At the same time, sensory devices detect the presence of fat and secrete the hormone cholecystokinin into the bloodstream. As the blood passes through the walls of the gallbladder, cholecystokinin causes the gallbladder to contract, forcing the bile in the gallbladder down what is known as the common bile duct. The bile enters into the small intestines at the same place the pancreatic enzymes enter. Again, if this too technical for you, just remember the bottom line.

Bottom line: Fat digestion is a process that takes place in the small intestines with the help of the pancreas and the gallbladder. The pancreas, gallbladder, and small intestines must be functioning normally for effective fat digestion. Too much fat in the diet can cause a problem with the normal digestion of fat.

Day 62
Jesus Is Faithful

But the Lord is faithful, and He will strengthen and protect you from the evil *one.* (2 Thessalonians 3:3)

Yes, we will have trials and tribulations in this world, and at times they may seem overbearing; however remember this scripture and the truth it reveals—the Lord is faithful, and He will strengthen us and protect us from the evil one! This does not mean that every day will be rosy and without any cares, but it does mean that when the trials and tribulations come, your Lord is faithful and He will provide the strength you need to overcome. Once again, I say be strong and courageous! You are a world overcomer by your faith in Jesus. The trials, tribulations, and discouragement that you may face when you do not lose the amount of weight that you want to will just strengthen your faith if you keep your eyes on Jesus. Trials always make us stronger when we come out the other side. The key is not to give up, but keep your eyes on Jesus and continue to fight the good fight of faith.

Lord, help me keep my eyes on You at all times but especially when the trials and tribulations come. I particularly pray for those trials and tribulations that have to do with my healthy lifestyle program. I know that I will be successful with this program with Your help and I choose, by an act of my will, not to be discouraged. I thank You for protecting me from the evil one and for guiding me down the straight and narrow path. In Your name, Jesus, I pray. Amen.

Nutrition Thought for the Day.
Pancreatic lipase digests fat by breaking off the fatty acids from the glycerol and allowing them to be absorbed. Bile from the gallbladder helps to emulsify fats. Bile does not digest fats but helps to emulsify them. If fats were allowed to enter the small intestines without bile, they would clump together since fats are not soluble in water and are hydrophobic. That means they will come together as one large molecule when in water. You have seen this if you ever washed dishes that were coated with oil. A bunch of small oil droplets will float on top of the dishwater. If you allow them to stay there for a while, you will find that you no longer have several small droplets of oil, but one large blob of oil since the oil (which is fat) tries to come together because of their insolubility in water. The same thing would happen in the small intestines if something were not done to separate them (some of this was discussed day 39 if you need a refresher).

Day 63
No Temptation Can Overtake You

No temptation has overtaken you but such as is common to man; and God is faithful, who will not allow you to be tempted beyond what you are able, but with the temptation will provide the way of escape also, so that you will be able to endure it. (1 Corinthians 10:13)

This excellent scripture is worth meditating on when you are experiencing trials and tribulations. It should strengthen your faith to know that any trial or temptation that the devil comes at you with is not anything new—his tactics are centuries old. I do not want to give the devil more credit than he deserves, but he can tempt you at your weakest moment and he knows what temptations are most effective against you. However, be strengthened in your faith to know that when you are tempted, no matter how strong it may seem, God will not allow you to be tempted beyond what you can bear. He will provide an escape from the temptation.

It may be in the form of reminding you of a scripture, a previous time when you overcame such a temptation or a word of encouragement from someone that does not even know what you are facing. In any case, He will provide a way out for you. Set your faith on believing that and look to Him for your way out when temptations come. If you are turning from God's Word for whatever reason, or you are enjoying the temptation, you will have difficulty recognizing the escape the Lord is making available for you. He will not hit you over the head with the Bible to get your attention, so you have to be alert to hear His voice. In any case, rest assured that He is there with you through the temptation.

Father God, thank You that You want me to be successful and You will provide the means for me to overcome any temptation that comes my way. I have faith in Your Word that You will provide a way for me to be victorious in all temptations if only I will look to You for that escape route. Thank You for loving me so much and for providing a means for me to be victorious. In Jesus's name, I pray. Amen.

Nutrition Thought for the Day.

Bile is an emulsifying agent that helps to keep fats separated. Bile does this by putting a light coating around the fat droplets. This coating prevents the fat droplets from coming together by causing them to repel each other as they get close to each other; these coated droplets are called micelles, which enables the enzymes to digest fat faster. If this were not to take place, there would be large clumps of fat in the small intestines. Enzymes would have to digest the outer layer, the next layer, and the next layer, and so forth until all of the fat was digested, like peeling off the layers of an onion. This would be inefficient and would take much longer than if there were numerous small droplets of fat they could all be digested at the same time.

Day 64
God Is Not Your Tempter

Let no one say when he is tempted, "I am being tempted by God"; for God cannot be tempted by evil, and He Himself does not tempt anyone. (James 1:13)

I think it is important to point out that God is not the one who tempts you. Many people do not know this or do not believe this, but it is true. There are those who think that when they go through trials and temptations, it is God who is causing the temptations to test them. That is definitely not the case. This scripture clearly says that God does not tempt you; however, He can use the temptations that the devil throws at you to teach you something—but the temptation comes from the devil. Temptations make you stronger if you rely on the Holy Spirit to see you through them. The next time you are tempted do not say, "God is tempting me for a reason." It is not God who is tempting you, it is the devil, but look to God to give you a way out from the temptation, and you will be stronger in your faith as a result of it.

Father God, thank You that You are not the tempter and You do not tempt me to test me. I know that You will take advantage of the temptations the devil comes at me with to teach me something and to make me stronger. I thank You for that and ask that, by the power of Your Holy Spirit, You give me the wisdom to turn to You in a time of temptation to show the devil and the world that I am a world overcomer by Your grace. In Jesus's name, I pray. Amen.

Nutrition Thought for the Day.
This is a review of the function of the gallbladder. In the event the gallbladder is removed, the liver still makes bile, but instead of the bile being stored in the gallbladder, it is stored in the common bile duct that comes from the liver. When fat enters the intestines, the presence of fat is picked up by sensory cells in the small intestines and this causes the secretion of the hormone cholecystokinin, which then travels through the blood to the common bile duct and causes it to contract, just as it would the gallbladder if it were present. The bile is then emptied into the small intestines. Theoretically, if a person had their gallbladder removed, they should not have to go on a low-fat diet for the sake of not having enough bile to help digest fat.

WAYNE E. BILLON, PH.D., RDN, LDN

Day 65
Take Every Thought Captive

We are destroying speculations and every lofty thing raised up against the knowledge of God, and *we are* taking every thought captive to the obedience of Christ. (2 Corinthians 10:5)

This scripture clearly shows that God's Word promises that you can control your thought life. It declares that you have the power to destroy speculations and every lofty thing that rises against the knowledge of God and gives you the ability to take every thought captive and make it obedient to Christ. This means that when thoughts of defeat, in any area of your life, comes into your head, you can take authority over those thoughts and refuse to pay attention to them. This is not going to happen automatically just because you are a born-again Christian and read God's Word every day. Also, note that it does not say this will be easy, you have to actively take the authority over your thought life and choose to think of the promises in God's Word.

The more you study God's Word and the more you learn about Him, the stronger you get in controlling your thought life. This is not a casual power—instead, it is one that comes with determination, resolve, and a closer walk with your God. Just like in anything else in life, the more you practice, the better you get. The more you read God's Word and practice taking authority over your thought life, the more efficient you become. This is extremely important because every battle that you encounter in your Christian walk takes place first in your mind. Every sin, or outburst of anger or evil plot begins with a thought. You cannot stop such thoughts from coming, but you do not have to entertain them when they arrive. It is absolutely essential that you be aware of this scripture so that you understand you can take authority over your thought life.

> Father God, I am so glad to see that Your Word gives me the authority to control my thought life. I know I cannot turn this off and on like a light bulb, and that I will have to fellowship with You frequently through prayer, meditation, and Your Word to gain control of my thought life. I know that if I accomplish those tasks, I will become more efficient in controlling my thought life. I resolve to take control of my thought life by the power of Your Holy Spirit. I thank You in Jesus's name. Amen.

Nutrition Thought for the Day.

To be absorbed, long-chain triglycerides have to be broken down to at least a monoglyceride and two fatty acids. Medium chain triglycerides and short chain triglycerides can be absorbed directly across the intestinal wall without being digested and without the need for carriers. Medium chain and short chain fatty acids are absorbed directly into the bloodstream and go straight to the liver from the small intestines. There they may be utilized for energy or be incorporated into other compounds. Long chain triglycerides require a different mechanism.

Day 66
Help Me with My Unbelief

And Jesus said to him, "'If You can?' All things are possible to him who believes." (Mark 9:23)

In Mark chapter 9, a man brought his son to Jesus and asked Him to heal the boy possessed of a demon. The demon caused the boy to roll around on the ground and foam from the mouth. Jesus asked the man how long the boy had been like that. The boy's father told Him since childhood and asked, "But if You can do anything, take pity on us and help us!" Jesus's response was Mark 9:23, "'If You can?' All things are possible to him who believes." By the man asking "If You can," he was expressing some degree of doubt, not knowing if Jesus could cast demons out of everyone. Jesus told him that all things are possible to him who believes and, this believing He referred to, comes from faith. The man responded, "I do believe; help my unbelief." You can believe in something miraculous, but your faith may be hindered by a degree of unbelief. It is possible to have unbelief at the same time you are operating in faith. If you choose to overcome this unbelief and make an active decision to only believe, you can start to build your faith stronger. In this case, the man's belief was strong enough, and Jesus delivered the boy from the demon. Do you struggle with unbelief? If so, give it to the Lord and choose to increase your faith this day and only believe.

Father God, I believe Your Word is true, and I choose to act on Your Word in faith but I know there are times that doubt tries to enter into my mind. This is another case when I have to take those thoughts captive and rebuild them in Your name. As the man in the scripture, I believe but help me with my unbelief. By the power of Your Holy Spirit continue to give me wisdom and direction so that I can strengthen my faith and overcome any obstacle in my way, not only in a diet and exercise program but also in everything that I do. In Jesus's name, I pray. Amen.

Nutrition Thought for the Day.
Once the long chain triglycerides are broken down into fatty acids and glycerol, they are absorbed into the intestinal wall and are reassembled into triglycerides (the free fatty acids are reattached to glycerol). At this point, they cannot go directly into the bloodstream like the medium and short chain fatty acids because they would tend to clump together, just like it was discussed for the small intestines. The blood is water, and these triglycerides are still hydrophobic and tend to clump together. Instead, the intestinal wall assembles them into a large compound called a chylomicron, to be discussed tomorrow.

Day 67
Only Believe

But when Jesus heard *this*, He answered him, "Do not be afraid *any longer*; only believe, and she will be made well." (Luke 8:50)

In Luke 8, an official of the synagogue named Jarius came to Jesus and asked Him to please come to his house to heal his only daughter who was dying. While he was still speaking to Jesus, someone from his house came to him and said, "Your daughter has died; do not trouble the Teacher anymore." Jesus's response was, "Do not be afraid any longer; only believe and she will be made well." Jesus went home with the man and raised the little girl from the dead. His response, "only believe," was all the man needed to hear. When you believe, you can still leave room for unbelief as in yesterday's scripture. That is why Jesus told Jarius to "only believe." As in yesterday's devotion, this is what Jesus was telling the man with the demon-possessed boy. All things are possible for those who believe! I am not saying this is easy, but you can build your faith to come to the point that you only believe. Believe in the faith of Jesus that is in you and believe in yourself. Take on this day with the attitude of only believing and be successful in all that you do.

Father God, the statement, "only believe," is easier said than done, but I know that Your Word is true and I can rebuke fear as Jairus did. While it is possible, I do not expect my faith to blossom to such a degree that I can control every thought and have absolutely no fear by just reading one or two of Your scriptures. However, I choose to believe Your Word and to begin practicing my faith in the smallest of areas in my life until I can come to a point to practice the faith demonstrated by Jesus in the New Testament. I thank You for Your grace and wisdom for me to accomplish this feat. In Jesus's name, I pray. Amen.

Nutrition Thought for the Day.

Chylomicrons are composed of part lipid and part protein just like the lipoprotein carriers discussed with HDL and LDL. The lipid part attaches to the triglycerides and the protein part, being soluble in water, carries the compound through the bloodstream. Chylomicrons are also arranged so that if they come into contact with each other, their protein components will repel each other, as the opposite ends of a magnet repel each other, preventing them from ever coming together and causing a blockage. Chylomicrons contain other compounds besides triglycerides such as cholesterol, phospholipids, and some free fatty acids.

Day 68
It Is Impossible to Please Him without Faith

And without faith it is impossible to please *Him,* for he who comes to God must believe that He is and *that* He is a rewarder of those who seek Him. (Hebrews 11:6)

When you first read this scripture, your heart may feel heavy because the thought will probably run through your mind, "Oh no, is my faith strong enough to please Him?" As a young Christian, this thought entered my head, and I questioned my faith; I now know better. Faith is at the very essence of Christianity. It is by faith that you are saved. It is by faith that you are filled with the Holy Spirit. It is by faith that your sins are forgiven. I could go on and on, but I think you should get the point. Are you saved? Are your sins forgiven? Yes, they are if you asked Jesus to be your Lord and Savior. The fact that these things are true demonstrates that you have enough faith to please Him because you have already done so by your actions. You believe that God exists and that He is everything His Word says about Him. You are speaking to Him every day and seeking Him with all your heart. Believe His Word and make an act of your will to only believe. Therefore you have ample faith and you can expect Him to reward you, this should be a very comforting thought. As you go through your day, you know that your God is a rewarder of those who seek Him, and that includes you! As you have been taught, only believe and live each day expecting your reward as you seek Him.

Father God, I thank You that You reward those who seek You and I thank You that You have given me sufficient faith to receive Your salvation and to be successful in all that I do. I know that on my own I can do nothing. But I also know that by Your Spirit I can do all things through Christ who strengthens me. I want to seek You more and more each day, and I ask that by the power of Your Holy Spirit You give me the wisdom and grace to experience an ever-increasing growth in my love for You. In Jesus's name, I pray. Amen.

Nutrition Thought for the Day.
Chylomicrons do not go into the bloodstream right away. Everything that is absorbed through the small intestines goes directly to the portal vein which is delivered directly to the liver; chylomicrons are an exception. If chylomicrons were allowed to go directly to the liver, they are such large compounds of lipid or lipid-like material (compared to the other compounds in the blood) that they would be a huge lipid load for the liver and would be overwhelming. Instead chylomicrons travel through the lymphatic system and are gradually transported to the liver. An explanation will follow tomorrow.

WAYNE E. BILLON, PH.D., RDN, LDN

Day 69
Ask for Wisdom

But if any of you lacks wisdom, let him ask of God, who gives to all generously and without reproach, and it will be given to him. But he must ask in faith without any doubting, for the one who doubts is like the surf of the sea, driven and tossed by the wind. For that man ought not to expect that he will receive anything from the Lord, *being* a double-minded man, unstable in all his ways. (James 1:5–8)

This scripture is even tougher on doubters than those previously discussed. It calls a doubter one who is tossed back and forth like waves of the sea. If you want wisdom, you should ask for it. However, it is pointed out here when you ask for wisdom you must do so with faith. This is not as big a challenge as it may sound. Remember that you already have the faith to be saved and you know that you will be rewarded for seeking God with your faith. That same faith is all you need when you ask for wisdom. When you ask, believe that you will receive. Do not pray and ask for wisdom and follow up your prayer by saying something like, "Well, I hope that prayer works." This is not expressing faith. When you pray and ask for wisdom, believe in your heart that you will receive wisdom and do not doubt. If doubt tries to come in, recall the scripture that tells you that you have control over your thought life, take control over the doubt, and cast it out in Jesus's name (see 2 Corinthians 10:5).

However, keep in mind that you probably will not receive some big announcement saying "Here is the answer to your question." The wisdom will come but it may not be immediately, and it may be that still small voice that you hear in your spirit. Listen for it and when God speaks, you will know it.

Father God, pieces of the faith puzzle are beginning to fit together for me now. I know from Your scriptures that I can have control over my thought life. I also know that when I ask for wisdom or anything else, I need to ask in faith, not doubting. I know that I have sufficient faith to receive what I ask for if I only believe and do not doubt. If doubt comes, I can control my thought life and cast the doubt out. I know that Your Word says this and I believe it! By the power of Your Holy Spirit, continue to give me the strength and direction to recall the Scriptures and put them into practice in my everyday life. I thank You in Jesus's name. Amen.

Nutrition Thought for the Day.

The lymphatic system is a series of vessels that run through the body but are not attached to the heart as blood vessels are. Lymph material is a relatively thick milky white substance that contains lymphocytes and white blood cells for fighting infections. These vessels are found throughout the body and periodically are attached to lymph nodes. The material in these vessels is moved through the vessel by muscle contractions and one-way valves that close off and prevent backflow. Chylomicrons move through the lymphatic system until they reach a lymph vessel in the thoracic cavity (in the chest) that is attached to a blood vessel. At this point, the lymphatic material is allowed to empty into the circulatory system slowly.

Day 70
Do Not Fear the Devil

Be of sober *spirit,* be on the alert. Your adversary, the devil, prowls around like a roaring lion, seeking someone to devour. But resist him, firm in *your* faith, knowing that the same experiences of suffering are being accomplished by your brethren who are in the world. (1 Peter 5:8–9)

This is an interesting scripture, and it is frequently misunderstood. It says to be on the alert for your adversary the devil which is good advice. Then Peter goes on to say that he prowls around "like a roaring lion after his prey." However, note that he prowls "like a roaring lion" because all he can do is roar. Jesus's sinless life, death, and resurrection defeated the devil and pulled his teeth. He cannot devour you; he can only roar to scare you. His greatest weapons are doubt and fear; if he can get a toe in the door with doubt, then he can bring in fear with it. Do not doubt God's Word and do not fear the devil. Know that your God is with you and will never forsake you. In John 16:33, Jesus tells us that in this world we will have trouble but to take heart because He has already overcome the world. In so doing, He overcame the devil and defeated him along with doubt and fear. Be strong and courageous! Do not fear the devil!

Thank You, Jesus, that You have already defeated the devil for me. Thank You that while he may tempt me and roar to scare me, I know that he has been defeated. I am free in You! I have authority over the devil, and I can proceed with my daily activities and be successful with my healthy lifestyle program without fear that the devil will block me in any way. I realize that this is because of what You have done for me and not because of anything that I have done. Without You I am nothing. Remind me throughout this day that I am the victorious one. In Your name, Jesus, I pray. Amen.

Nutrition Thought for the Day.
Once in the circulatory system, the chylomicrons circulate toward the liver. Along the way they can be temporarily attached to the walls of the blood vessels and, with the help of the enzyme lipase, some of the triglycerides and cholesterol are removed from the chylomicrons to be utilized by the cells in the walls of the blood vessels. Even though excessive cholesterol and triglycerides can cause blockages in the blood vessels, cholesterol and triglycerides are required nutrients by all the blood vessels. The chylomicron remnants break free, return to the circulatory system, and eventually end up in the liver but much smaller than if they went straight to the liver from the small intestines.

Day 71
Faith Comes by Hearing the Word of Christ

So faith *comes* from hearing, and hearing by the word of Christ. (Romans 10:17)

Want to increase your faith? This is one way to do that—by hearing the Words of Christ. Decades ago, as a young Christian, I was taught that whenever I read God's Word, to read it aloud, loud enough for my ears to hear it. Knowledge comes into your brain through several gates. When you see something, it is an open door through your eye gate into your brain. When you say something, it is an action that affirms to your brain what you believe. When you hear something, the sound enters your brain through your ear gate. So when you read the Word aloud, you are using three different means of establishing the Word in your brain. You see it, you hear it, and by speaking, you are affirming that you believe it. This scripture does not mean that you should just have to hear God's Word as being taught to you by someone else reading it, but you can hear God's Word as you speak it aloud. If you do this continuously, and you particularly do this with the scriptures that are faith builders, you will build your faith. This is one of the many reasons why it is important to read God's Word every day.

> Lord Jesus, I know that Your Word is powerful and produces results. I resolve by an act of my will to read Your Word on a regular basis as often as I can. I also resolve that, when possible, to read Your Word aloud so that my ears can hear it. I know that in this way I will be entering the power of Your Word into my mind as efficiently as possible. I expect to see my faith grow because I believe Your Word is true. In Your name Jesus, I pray. Amen.

Nutrition Thought for the Day.
The liver breaks down chylomicron remnants and removes the cholesterol to either reattach it to LDL and send it out to peripheral tissues or send it to the gallbladder. The triglycerides can also be attached to LDL and be sent out to peripheral tissues (tissues away from the liver) or can be utilized for energy in the liver. An excessive intake of fat in the diet will result in excessive amounts of chylomicrons. It will be necessary for the liver to make more LDL to transport the triglycerides and cholesterol that were on the chylomicrons to peripheral tissues. Depending on some factors, this could be inducive to cardiovascular disease. Calories come from the macronutrients we eat. Remember that macronutrients are carbohydrate, fat, and protein.

Bottom line: If this is too much physiology for you, just remember the more excessive your total calorie intake is, and the more excessive amounts of fat you ingest, the greater the chances of getting fatty deposits in your arteries.

Day 72
We Have the Righteousness of Christ

For in it *the* righteousness of God is revealed from faith to faith; as it is written, "but the righteous *man* shall live by faith." (Romans 1:17)

In Romans 1:16, Paul tells the Romans that he is not ashamed of the Gospel because it is the power of God for salvation to everyone who believes. He continues in verse 17 to say that the Gospel reveals the righteousness of God from faith to faith. This means that faith springs forth from the Gospel and when you receive that faith, it leads to additional faith. Remember, faith comes by hearing and hearing the Word of God (Romans 10:17). In other words, as your faith increases, more faith can be built on top of your existing faith. When you realize your faith is real, your confidence in God's Word will increase. The more your confidence increases, the more you exercise your faith.

Paul then says that the righteous man shall live by faith. You are righteous, but not because of what you have done, but your righteousness springs from what Jesus did for you. When you receive righteousness by faith, it enables your faith to grow even more and get stronger. Your strength comes from your faith in God's Word. This gives you strength to fulfill your everyday tasks, including your healthy lifestyle program. Be encouraged; you have the faith to complete your program and anything else you attempt with success in Jesus's name.

Lord Jesus, I know that my righteousness does not come from my good works but from the completed work on the cross that You did for me. I receive that righteousness on faith in Your Word and I believe that my faith will continue to grow as long as I stay connected to You by the power of the Holy Spirit. As I walk through this day I choose, by an act of my will, to receive Your righteousness and to walk out my day in faith in Your Word. In Your name Jesus, I pray. Amen.

Nutrition Thought for the Day.

What is our fat requirement? The total fat requirement varies from individual to individual depending upon size, muscle mass, and daily activity. I mentioned carbohydrate requirement in an earlier devotion. I said that most textbooks indicate we need at least 100g of carbohydrate a day to prevent hypoglycemia (low blood sugar) and ketosis (high levels of ketones in the blood). I also said that I like to see at least 150g of carbohydrate per day to be on the safe side. However, that also depends on how much activity a person does during a day, how much muscle they have, and several other factors. When we get to protein, we will see our protein requirement is based on muscle mass. The fat requirement is calculated a bit differently than protein and carbohydrate.

Day 73
We Walk by Faith

For we walk by faith, not by sight—(2 Corinthians 5:7)

Earlier in this chapter, Paul talked about the trials and tribulations you will have in this life and how you may yearn to be with the Lord in the next life. That being true, you still have to walk out your existence here even when things look bleak. You accomplish that by walking by faith, that is, your faith in God's Word. You do not walk out your life based on the circumstances and trials and tribulations around you, but you walk out your life based on faith in God's Word. Your healthy lifestyle program could be a source of trials and tribulations for you but remember that you are walking this out by the inner strength you have from faith in God's Word. Do not depend on your own power to be successful but depend on His power. Do not be discouraged by circumstances but be encouraged by faith in God's Word.

> Father, I thank You that You give me the strength to walk out my daily existence based on faith in Your Word. I will not be moved by the circumstances around me, whether good or bad. I choose to rely on Your Word for my strength to see me through whatever circumstances life may throw at me. I know that any troubles I have are not the result of You causing those troubles to test me. Troubles come from the world, the devil, or my own flesh. I ask You for discernment to know when I am being attacked or when I am just stupid. Give me the wisdom to know the difference. I know that I will be successful in all that I do and I thank You for Your guidance. In Jesus's name, I pray. Amen.

Nutrition Thought for the Day.

Usually, we determine the amount of fat in our diet as a percentage. For example, a typical diet would contain somewhere between 45% and 55% of total calories from carbohydrate, 15 to 20% of total calories from protein, and 20 to 30% of total calories from fat. The exact percentages depend on some factors such as if a person is trying to lose, gain, or maintain weight and the activity level of the person. You can see that there are many variables from individual to individual and there is no way I can give a direct recommendation without knowing the variables. Concerning fat, most average healthy diets should contain around thirty percent of the calories from fat. If someone is trying to lose weight, that percentage could be less—down to 25% or perhaps 20% of the calories from fat. If they are trying to gain weight, particularly muscle, the diet would contain more protein and carbohydrate and maybe less fat—25% to 30%. Again, this would depend on the person's size, activity level, etc. You need to consult a registered dietitian for help in determining your nutrient requirements.

Day 74
Our Justification Is Not in the Law

Now that no one is justified by the Law before God is evident; for, "the righteous man shall live by faith." (Galatians 3:11)

The Old Testament is based on law; the New Testament is based on grace. In the Old Testament, animal sacrifice was necessary for people to be forgiven of their sins. In the New Testament, Jesus became the Lamb of God, and the sacrifice of His life took place for the forgiveness of our sins for once and for all, for all of mankind. In the Old Testament, people were justified by animal sacrifices. Today, we are justified by Jesus's sacrifice. This change is based on faith. It is by faith that you receive what Jesus did for you and that gives you what we call salvation. Everything you do is based on faith. By receiving Jesus as your Savior and Lord, you become righteous, not based on what you did or did not do, but based on what Jesus did for you. Walk out this day knowing that you are the righteousness of God. You may not feel like the righteousness of God, but that is the way He sees you. See yourself as God sees you and see each other as God does, as someone His Son died for, whether they accept that or not.

Father, I am so glad that I am not judged based on my righteousness but on the robe of righteousness that covers me that I received from Jesus. I cannot be justified under the law because it is impossible for me to keep the law. Jesus kept the law to the letter for me when He walked on the face of the earth. He did not sin one time. Instead, He took on all the sins of the world that were ever committed and that ever will be committed. He took away my sins, and in place of them, He gave me the robe of His righteousness. Thank You, Jesus, that I am righteous in Your sight because of what You did for me. Help me to walk out this day knowing that I am walking in righteousness and that every temptation, be it a spiritual or a physical temptation trying to cause me to go off my healthy lifestyle program, I can control it by faith in Your Word. In Your name, Jesus, I pray. Amen.

Nutrition Thought for the Day.
There are differences of opinions today as to whether a weight reduction diet should be low fat or low carbohydrate. The old standard was low fat, higher carbohydrate, and moderate protein. This low fat we are talking about is about 30% of total calories from fat. However, low is relative. For example, typical deep South diets that include a lot of fried foods and gravies would have an average fat intake of as much as 50% of the total calories. A diet that contains no more than 30% of the total calories from fat would be extremely low fat for that person. So it depends on what your normal diet is like to determine the best diet for you to be on for weight reduction. A registered dietitian can help you with this decision.

Day 75
God Does Not Play Favorites

But now apart from the Law *the* righteousness of God has been manifested, being witnessed by the Law and the Prophets, even *the* righteousness of God through faith in Jesus Christ for all those who believe; for there is no distinction. (Romans 3:21–22)

In Romans 3, Paul tells us that we cannot be justified by the law but, apart from the law, the righteousness of God has been manifested through faith in Jesus Christ. He ends Romans 3:22 by saying, "there is no distinction." What Paul is saying is that anyone who receives Jesus as Savior and Lord receives His righteousness. You may not feel like you are righteous, but if you received Jesus as your Savior and Lord, then you are covered with the robe of righteousness based on what He did for you. It has nothing to do with your worthiness because there is no way any of us can be worthy of all that He did for us. He chose to die for you because of His love for you. Walk out this day realizing how much Jesus loves you! Also realize that as His righteousness, no matter what trials befall you this day, or how many times you may go off your healthy lifestyle program, you are still the righteousness of Jesus! That is an awesome biblical fact. Walk with confidence knowing who you are in Christ.

Lord Jesus, thank You that You do not show favorites. Thank You that, as my Savior and Lord, I am not judged based on my worthiness but based on my acceptance of what You did for me on the cross. I know that I have Your righteousness Jesus, even though I am utterly unworthy. You are an awesome God and with each passing day I want to get to know You better, and I will be ever seeking to get closer to You. In Your name, Jesus, I pray. Amen.

Nutrition Thought for the Day.

Some people think that the lower the fat in their diet, the easier it is to lose weight, regardless of how much carbohydrate or protein is in the diet. That is not always true. For example, there was one study that placed two groups of people on the same caloric intake. The caloric intake should have been low enough for the people to lose weight. One group consumed a diet with 35% of the total calories come from fat and the other group consumed a diet with 25% of the calories come from fat.

The group with the diet with 35% of the calories coming from fat lost more weight than did the group with the diet with 25% of the calories coming from fat. This did not happen because of the percent of fat per se, but because of the palatability of the diet. Those on the diet that contained 25% of the calories coming from fat found the diet so unpalatable that they went off their diet and went back to eating their usual eating style and thus gained weight. The people on the diet with 35% calories from fat found the diet more satisfying, stayed with the diet, and lost weight. Thus there are many different ways to evaluate diets.

Day 76
Do Not Think More Highly of Yourself than You Ought

> For through the grace given to me I say to everyone among you not to think more highly of himself than he ought to think; but to think so as to have sound judgment, as God has allotted to each a measure of faith. (Romans 12:3)

Romans 12:1–3 is one of my favorite quotes in the Bible. In Romans 12:1–2 Paul tells us not to be conformed to the patterns of this world but to be transformed by the renewing of our minds so that we may be able to prove what the will of God is, that is, what is good and acceptable and perfect. Then, in today's devotion, he tells us that even though we should not conform to this world, we should not think more highly of ourselves than we ought. If you have peers that are not saved, you should not think of yourself more highly than they are because they have not received Jesus as Savior and Lord. Each of us has been allotted a measure of faith, and if you are saved, then you have used your faith wisely to receive Jesus. But you should also use sound judgment and not look down on those around you that are not saved. Instead, reach out to them and share the love of Jesus with them to try to bring them into God's Kingdom.

This is true in a spiritual sense, but we can also make a comparison in the physical sense. If you are doing well on your healthy lifestyle program m and you have peers that are not doing as well, do not think of yourself as better than them, but reach out to them to try and help them to do better. Use your faith in a spiritual sense as well as in the physical sense in all circumstances.

> Lord Jesus, give me the wisdom to see those around me that are lost and are not as fortunate as I am, and give me the compassion to reach out to them to help them spiritually and physically. Holy Spirit, give me direction and guidance and lead me to those people that are hurting whether it be because they do not know You or they are having trials in their life similar to mine while trying to eat more healthy. Help me to be ever mindful of the things I say and do and remember that even the small things can make a big difference in seeing someone else receive salvation. In Your name, Jesus, I pray. Amen.

Nutrition Thought for the Day.
Generally speaking, a diet with around 30% of the calories coming from fat, 20% of the calories coming from protein, and 50% of the calories coming from carbohydrate would be appropriate for most people. As mentioned, this will vary depending on activity level, muscle mass, and if the person is trying to lose, gain, or maintain weight. Muscle requires more calories to be maintained then does fat. The more muscle a person has, the more calories they need. Exercise burns calories and builds muscle. The more exercise a person does, the more calories they require. If they were trying to lose weight, then the caloric intake would need to be adjusted. The best way to determine your caloric need is to have a metabolic and anthropometric assessment completed by a registered dietitian.

Day 77
Do Not Pass Judgment on Those Who Have Weak Faith I

Now accept the one who is weak in faith, *but* not for *the purpose of* passing judgment on his opinions. One person has faith that he may eat all things, but he who is weak eats vegetables *only*. (Romans 14:1–2)

In Paul's time, there was some controversy concerning the type of foods people should eat even as this exists today. There was a question as to whether or not it was lawful to eat meat sacrificed to idols. There was also a question if they should eat only vegetables. In Romans 14, Paul was telling the people not to pass judgment on each other based on what they eat or do not eat. This was more of a spiritual concern in those days then a health concern as it is today, but the principle applies.

Do not pass judgment on people because they do not eat the way you do. You may be of the opinion that your healthy lifestyle program is the best one around. Others may not see it that way and may have a diet that has significant contrasting elements to your diet. Do not judge them on this basis. If you have been in contact with a registered dietitian, and you know for a fact that they are eating something that is harmful, do not lord it over them but advise them to see a registered dietitian so they can learn for themselves. Remember, you are God's witness, and you will not win people to the Lord by condemning them. Romans 12:21 says, "Do not be overcome by evil, but overcome evil with good." This is not to say that everyone who is following a different diet then you are doing evil, but the principle applies that if they are lost and you are trying to win them over, arguing over a diet will not help. Be open to those with opinions that differ from yours but be ever mindful of ways to bring them into God's Kingdom.

> Lord Jesus, I know that there are many different opinions in this world about the best way to eat and to lose weight. A diet that works for me may not work for everyone else. Help me to be open to the opinions of others but not to be moved by their opinions when they concern Your Word. Give me wisdom on how to use my daily experiences (healthy lifestyle program) to be a witness to others without being overbearing to them. Thank You, Jesus, that You died for all mankind and helped me to see those around me as You see them—and that is, as someone for whom You died. You love us all no matter how overweight or underweight we are and the diet we follow certainly does not affect Your love for us. Help me to be aware of this every day. In Your name, Jesus, I pray. Amen.

Nutrition Thought for the Day.

Concerning the previous discussions on the amount of fat in the diet, you may ask does this include all types of fat? No, it does not. Some fatty acids are called essential fatty acids (EFA). These fatty acids are essential because they are necessary for the synthesis of some very important compounds in our bodies and the EFAs cannot be synthesized in the body; therefore, they have to come into the body from the food we eat. Only a small percentage of these EFAs is necessary for a healthy body and can be obtained easily through the healthy fats in our diet. If someone were to go on a deficient fat diet for an extended period, they could develop EFA deficiency but, in a developed country, this would be highly unusual.

Day 78
Do Not Pass Judgment on Those Who Have Weak Faith II

The one who eats is not to regard with contempt the one who does not eat, and the one who does not eat is not to judge the one who eats, for God has accepted him. (Romans 14:3)

This was intended for the people that lived in the time of Paul that had different beliefs about what foods they could eat and could not eat. This adds to yesterday's devotion, and you can apply this same principle today in a different sense in that if someone does not follow the same diet you do, it certainly does not mean that person is spiritually incorrect. It does not even have to refer to a diet per se; maybe they just have strange eating habits compared to your eating habits. In actuality, they may be physically incorrect and unhealthy, but it is not your place to be the food police and correct them. This will run the risk of creating a wall between you and them instead of showing love to break down barriers. You will not bring your peers into the Kingdom by building walls. Instead, build bridges and help them to improve their diets. The last part of the scripture reiterates that God accepts you no matter what kind of a diet you are following. You should always remember that and walk as if you are seeing your fellow dieters, coworkers, friends, and family as God sees them.

Thank You, Jesus, for accepting us all, no matter what we eat or how we look. I know that You love all of us equally, even though we may not love You back with the same intensity or maybe not at all. Help me to be ever aware of those around me that do not know You so that I may be especially cautious to show them love to win their respect for You. This is true for those that I may be dieting with, my peers, friends, and family. I want to be the best witness I can be for You. In Your name, Jesus, I pray. Amen.

Nutrition Thought for the Day.
Calories come from the macronutrients we eat. Remember that macronutrients are carbohydrates, fats, and proteins. Every gram of carbohydrate and protein we eat provides our bodies with four calories. Fat provides us with nine calories per gram. Another source of calories is alcohol; one gram of pure alcohol provides us with seven calories. These numbers are not exact, that is not every gram of carbohydrate produces precisely four calories; however, four is the average number used in all nutrition discussions. Vitamins, minerals, and water are calorie free.

Day 79
Do Not Pass Judgment on Those Who Have Weak Faith III

One person regards one day above another, another regards every day *alike*. Each person must be fully convinced in his own mind. He who observes the day, observes it for the Lord, and he who eats, does so for the Lord, for he gives thanks to God; and he who eats not, for the Lord he does not eat, and gives thanks to God. (Romans 14:5–6)

Most of Romans 14 is concerned with observations and beliefs about eating certain foods. This had more spiritual meaning for the Romans than a physical meaning, but I believe the principles developed in this chapter can be applied to today. Paul points out that different people have different practices concerning certain days as special and concerning the eating, or not eating, of certain foods. Basically what Paul is telling you in today's scripture is that whatever you do, you should do it for the glory of the Lord. Whether it is the way you look at certain days, or whether it is the way you look at eating or not eating certain foods, all of your actions should be for the glory of the Lord, and you should be giving thanks to Him on all occasions. This is saying that you should make Jesus the center of your life and everything you do should revolve around Him. If you can remember that fact and apply that to your everyday life, it will not matter what those around you eat or what observances those around you do from day to day. You need to continue to see them as Christ sees them and be as perfect a witness to them for Christ. Put Jesus first and lead others to Him and your day will go well.

Lord Jesus, by an act of my will, I choose to make You the center of my life. Everything I do each day I want to do for Your glory and always give thanks to You for every possession, ability, and gift that I have because I know that every good thing comes from You. I want to be ever mindful to avoid being judgmental of those around me and, to the best of my ability, witness to them for Your sake. Continue to give me the wisdom and guidance that I may carry out this plan for You. In Your name, Jesus, I pray. Amen.

Nutrition Thought for the Day.

A question you may be asking yourself at this time is, How do we know how many calories we should be taking in? This will depend upon so many variables that it is difficult to give a simple formula that will fit all situations—in fact, there is no simple formula. For example, your caloric requirement will depend on your gender, your age, your height, your weight, your body composition (how much muscle versus fat you have), your exercise level, your metabolism (determined in part by genetics), if you have any active disease states, your sleep patterns, and possibly medications that you are taking. It also depends on how much, what, when, and how you eat (that is whether you are a fast or a slow eater or somewhere in between).

Day 80
Know the Difference between Clean and Unclean

I know and am convinced in the Lord Jesus that nothing is unclean in itself; but to him who thinks anything to be unclean, to him it is unclean. (Romans 14:14)

This scripture brings up an important factor to consider. Paul is telling us that if something is not a sin according to God's Word, but someone believes it is a sin and does it anyway—thus thinking that they are sinning—then for them it is actually a sin. If you have peers that refuse to eat a particular food on a specific day (some denominations or religious affiliations have such beliefs), it would be best for you not to argue with them or try to get them to change their ways. They would see this as you trying to get them to sin and it will not go well for your relationship. Instead, plant seeds of truth and water them with God's Word when the opportunity presents itself, and in time you or someone else may reap a harvest in their lives. From this scripture, you can see that Paul did not consider any food to be unclean but remember that Paul was talking about being spiritually clean. That does not mean that every food available to be eaten is physically good for you. Foods that are high in sodium (salt), sugar, and fat may be on the spiritually clean list but not on the list of foods that are physically good for you.

Lord Jesus, give me the wisdom to know what to say, when to say it, and how to say it to my peers when they are doing something that is not by Your Word. Some sow, some water, and some reap a harvest. I would love to be the reaper but if I am being called to be the sower, so be it, I will accept that. All I ask is for the wisdom to know the difference between planting a seed and destroying a relationship. In Your name, Jesus, I pray. Amen.

Nutrition Thought for the Day.

There are general formulas that people use to determine their caloric requirement, but none of the formulas take into consideration all of the variables mentioned yesterday. If I were to list the formulas, many of you would find some of them very complicated and if you selected one that was not right for you, and you calculated your caloric requirement according to that formula, the results may be very bad by providing you with entirely too many calories or not enough calories. This would result in frustration and possibly cause you to stop dieting. In reality, the best thing to do is to talk to a registered dietitian and let them make a complete evaluation to help you choose the right amount of food and the right kind of food. The ideal situation is to have an individualized meal plan to meet your particular needs.

Day 81
Walk According to Love

For if because of food your brother is hurt, you are no longer walking according to love. Do not destroy with your food him for whom Christ died. (Romans 14:15)

This scripture could be taken in one of two ways. One, if you are doing something that is entirely correct according to God's Word, but one of your peers sees you as sinning, and it is leading your peer astray, then you are no longer walking according to love. Does this mean that you can only do those things that your peers see as correct, even though scripturally speaking they are wrong? No, you do not. Either you can make an effort to complete your actions in the absence of your peers, or if the timing is right, you can gently inform them of the scriptural truth. Romans 14:21, to be covered in a few days, will address that.

Second, if your peer is doing something that is not scripturally wrong but is unnecessary and you correct him, you may no longer walk according to love if what he is doing is not harmful. On the other hand, if your peer is doing something that is harmful, and you do not correct him in love, you may not be walking in love. If you have a good rapport and your peer is easy to approach, talk to him in love. Sometimes these situations can be very tricky and can be so subtly overlooked that they can cause problems without you ever realizing something is wrong. Be ever mindful of your words and your actions that they do not cause your brother to sin or to feel convicted instead of loved.

Lord Jesus, I continue to ask for direction and wisdom so that I can recognize when I am saying or doing something, no matter how small it may be, that will cause my brother to stumble. I know there will sometimes be a fine line between what is right and wrong, and it may be easy for me to cross that line without realizing it. I want to be a witness for You in all circumstances, but I need the guidance of the Holy Spirit so that I do not fall into a trap to cause my brother, who You died for, to be led astray. In Your name, Jesus, I pray. Amen.

Nutrition Thought for the Day.

If you knew your caloric requirement, the general rule of thumb is to take in 500 calories less a day then your requirement to lose one pound of fat a week. The way this number was arrived at is as follows: if one pound of fat were burned to completion in an apparatus called a bomb calorimeter (a machine that burns food under controlled conditions and measures the total amount of calories released), it would burn approximately 3500 calories. Dividing 3500 by seven (seven days in a week) would amount to 500 calories per day. However, this is assuming all the other variables I have mentioned would not have an effect on this—which is never true. On paper, this looks good, but in actual practice, it does not always work. The converse of this is also a rule of thumb, that is, if you take in 500 calories more a day, then you need you should gain one pound of fat a week, but that does not work for everyone either.

Day 82
Know the Kingdom of God

For the kingdom of God is not eating and drinking, but righteousness and peace and joy in the Holy Spirit. (Romans 14:17)

Today's scripture brings us back to reality, and that is, "What is the Kingdom of God about?" We know, as born-again Christians, we are the righteousness of Jesus Christ and possess the fruit of the Holy Spirit that includes peace and joy. These are available to you as a born-again Christian and should be evident in your everyday life. People around you should be able to look at you and tell that something is different—that difference being the love of Jesus. Do not get wound up very tight about some things that, while they may be important in everyday life to a degree, do not matter in the overall scheme of eternity. Remember who you are in Christ, remember your goals for yourself in your healthy lifestyle program, and remember that in accomplishing those goals you want to be a witness for Christ. You do not want to be identified as a Christian for demonstrating worldly characteristics at the expense of destroying the peace and joy of those around you.

Father God, I know that the Kingdom of God is about righteousness, peace, and joy. I want to demonstrate these and all the fruits of the Holy Spirit to all of those that I contact. I know that will not always be easy and I know that there will be trials and tribulations to distract me. I know I can depend on You to make me aware of the times when I may not be so joyful or peaceful to be around. Help me to be ever mindful of how others see me so that I can be an expression of You to let others see You in me. In the name of Jesus, I ask. Amen.

Nutrition Thought for the Day.

The first thing you should do in any weight reduction program is to keep very accurate records. If you are following some organized diet, you should have been taught this from the very beginning. You need to be writing down everything you eat as well as how much you eat. Everything should be included, even those things you may take for granted. For instance, if you have a cup of coffee, did you add any sugar—how much? Did you add any milk/cream—how much? If you have a slice of toast, did you put anything on it— margarine/jelly—how much? You get the point. You have to account for everything that goes into your body and the amount consumed. You also want to keep accurate records of the time of day. It is also very important to keep track of the non-caloric things that you eat, particularly fluids. You want to record how much water you take in, diet soda, unsweetened tea, black coffee, etc.

Day 83
Do Not Cause Your Brother to Stumble

It is good not to eat meat or to drink wine, or *to do anything* by which your brother stumbles. (Romans 14:21)

Where do we draw the line with what we can do that is scripturally legal but may not be legal to some of our peers or brothers in Christ? In Romans 14 Paul discusses the sinfulness of eating and drinking certain foods. Among the major items of that day were meat and wine. Many believed that it was sacrilegious to eat meat that was offered to idols. This requires some explanation in that people brought animals to the Levitical priest to be sacrificed to God for their sins. It was perfectly legal for the priests to keep some of the meat for themselves. The priest of the false god Baal would also sacrifice animals to Baal on behalf of the worshipers of Baal. They would also keep some of the meat. You can imagine that at the end of the day, without refrigeration, they each had large amounts of meat. The priests of Baal would sell the extra meat on the market.

Paul's stand on this was that if they believed the idol was a real god, and because of that the meat was sacred, it would be wrong to eat the meat. If they did not believe Baal was anything more than a carved piece of wood or stone, and they thought they were just getting a good price on a piece of meat, it was okay to eat the meat. However, if a brother saw them buying meat sacrificed to Baal, and the brother was under the impression they were buying it because it was sacred, it would be wrong to buy the meat and mislead their brother. So Paul says that before you lead someone else into sin, it is better not to eat meat, wine, or anything else.

This should not present much of a problem to us today but it could in relation to drinking alcohol. If someone believes it is wrong to drink alcohol, and you believe it is okay on occasion, and someone sees you buying alcohol, it could cause him or her to pass judgment on you which would give them an opportunity to commit a judgmental sin. The same could be said for cigarettes. Be careful not to cause your brother to sin because of something that you do even if it is scripturally legal.

Father God, I do not want to knowingly cause anyone around me to sin because of my actions. I do not always know what those around me consider to be scripturally wrong so I depend on You and the power of Your Holy Spirit in me to give me guidance and wisdom to let me know when I may be doing something that others would consider sinful or scripturally incorrect. It is my heart's desire to always serve You and be a witness for You. I thank You in advance that You will keep me from leading anyone astray. In the name of Jesus, I ask. Amen.

Nutrition Thought for the Day.

Water is essential to maintain proper hydration and keeping the kidneys functioning. Reasons that may not be so obvious include the fact water will help fill you up at a meal and promote satiety. Ample water is necessary for expanding fiber in the intestines and preventing constipation. A very low-calorie diet will make toxins as a result of metabolism and water will flush these toxins from your body. The old rule of thumb is eight glasses of water a day. Actually, this is probably not enough for everyone. Here again, the correct amount depends on your body surface area, exercise level, room temperature and outdoor temperature, humidity, and other factors.

Day 84
Your Faith Is Your Conviction

The faith which you have, have as your own conviction before God. Happy is he who does not condemn himself in what he approves. But he who doubts is condemned if he eats, because *his eating is* not from faith; and whatever is not from faith is sin. (Romans 14:22–23)

Paul continues to tell us that whatever we do in this life we should do by faith. If you understand God's Word and you are following His Word, then there is no reason for you to condemn yourself. You should be happy that you are blossoming in God's grace. On the other hand, if you doubt that you are acting in righteousness according to God's Word, and you do it anyway, then you are not performing in faith. Paul tells us that anything we do that is not from faith is sin. This was mentioned previously in that if you believe something is wrong, even though in actuality it is not wrong according to God's Word, and you proceed with what you think is wrong, you are sinning just as much as if it really was something that was forbidden. You may need to read this twice to understand it fully and get it down into your spirit, but the bottom line is, if you have a question about the scriptural lawfulness of any act or procedure, before proceeding with it seek God's wisdom and make sure that you are acting appropriately. This will give you confidence or, as the scripture says, make you happy because you are doing right. It will also let you shine as a witness.

Father God, I continue to ask that You give me the grace to know when my faith is weak and causing me to do something that is not appropriate in Your sight. I only want to be a witness for You in everything that I do. In this healthy lifestyle program that I am completing, I want to be successful for my health but also so that I can give You the glory for the victory. I know I can do nothing on my own and everything I accomplish is because of your faithfulness. In Jesus's name, I pray. Amen.

Nutrition Thought for the Day.

Another rule of thumb is to never go below 1200 calories per day without the supervision of a physician or a registered dietitian. It is difficult to get in all of the nutrients you need with less than 1200 calories per day unless you know what you are doing. With no disrespect or criticism meant for physicians, it is a fact that most physicians are not adequately trained in nutrition to counsel people on diet and weight reduction to the degree of efficiency that they need to be. Some physicians may be able to do this if a focus of their practice is weight reduction and they have studied this beyond medical school. However, most medical schools only offer one course in nutrition, if that, which is not enough to cover all the aspects of diet and disease, diet and health, and diet and exercise, etc. The registered dietitian (that is someone with RD or RDN after their name) has to go through a rigorous program censored by the Academy of Nutrition and Dietetics (AND), an intense internship program upon graduation, pass a rigorous test, and continue to maintain their registration with continuing education hours after beginning practice. This is not to say that the registered dietitian has all the answers, but it is less likely that you would receive false information from someone that has been so adequately trained for this purpose.

Day 85
Accept One Another for the Glory of God

Therefore, accept one another, just as Christ also accepted us to the glory of God. (Romans 15:7)

This will complete our look at Romans during which we studied faith as it relates to our daily lives. Paul's message in this short verse is to accept one another just as Christ has also accepted us, and we should do this for the glory of God. I know this has been mentioned in the past, but repetition is an excellent form of teaching. We all need to be constantly reminded of who we are in Christ and you need to constantly see yourself as Jesus sees you.

In like manner, you need to see all those around you as Jesus sees them too. Whenever Jesus looks down at you, no matter who you are by way of religious affiliation, gender, race, or any other means by which we can classify ourselves—including being overweight or underweight—and even saints or sinners, Jesus sees us all the same—as someone for whom He died. Even that person who you may have to work with every day that makes it obvious to everyone that he or she does not believe in God and walks down a dark path, Jesus still loves that person. It is your place to accept someone like that because Jesus accepts everyone and thus, you also accept everyone for the glory of God. That does not mean that you should hang out with them, go out to eat with them, etc. but you should not condemn them. In a subtle and peaceful way you need to continue to be a witness to such people in all circumstances.

Father God, I know that You love all of mankind because You sent Your only begotten Son to die for all of us. Even those that have committed very heinous crimes are still precious in Your site. You hate the sin, but you still love the sinner. It is not always easy for me to see people in that light but I know it is what I should do for Your glory. I will continue to make this attempt in my daily walk and ask again for Your Holy Spirit to give me direction and guidance each day. In Jesus's name, I pray. Amen.

Nutrition Thought for the Day.

Be aware that not everyone that calls himself or herself a nutritionist is necessarily knowledgeable in the specifics that they should be to counsel people on diet and weight control. In most states, it is against the law to practice nutrition without a license. There is more than one way to get a license in some states, but in all states, if you are a registered dietitian, all you have to do is apply to receive your license (and of course, pay a fee). Some people call themselves personal nutritionist who are not registered dietitians (some are). These individuals may be very well qualified to counsel people on nutrition, but they may not. Make sure you are talking to someone that can give you correct information about nutrition.

Day 86
Do Not Be a Doubter I

But he must ask in faith without any doubting, for the one who doubts is like the surf of the sea, driven and tossed by the wind. (James 1:6)

When you ask your Father God for something, you must ask in faith without doubting. The scripture says that he who doubts is like the surf of the sea driven and tossed back and forth by the wind. When you pray and ask God for something, then you should expect your prayers to be answered. If after you pray you say something like, "Well, I hope that works," then you are not asking in faith. This is doubting, and you are like the waves of the sea being tossed back and forth. The last several devotions have shown us that to accomplish God's will we must have faith. If you are not used to walking in faith, do not start by asking for extensive changes; instead start small and build your faith by exercising it on a regular basis just as you build muscles by exercising them on a daily basis. As an example, suppose you were 50 pounds overweight and you wanted to lose 50 pounds. You ask God to allow you to lose them in one month, is that realistic? No, it is not. Ask Him to help you lose one to two pounds per week and give you the grace to be satisfied with the gradual loss of weight. As you stick with your healthy lifestyle, you should lose more weight the longer you stay on the program, or gain more weight if that is your goal. This will encourage you and strengthen your faith so that you can complete your task.

Lord Jesus, Your Word says that I have been given a measure of faith. I know that measure of faith is enough for me to accomplish everything I need to do in this life, even though it does not always seem like it to me. I have the faith to be victorious, help me to rid myself of doubt. When doubt tries to come in, I ask for Your Holy Spirit to remind me that I am a victorious overcomer, and I have the faith that I need to be successful. In Jesus's name, I pray. Amen.

Nutrition Thought for the Day.

Before you start to keep records of your intake, be sure to weigh yourself to get a baseline weight. It is best to weigh yourself in the morning when you first get up and weigh yourself at the same time of day each time you weigh. It is also good not to weigh yourself every day because you will not see a significant change in your weight from one day to the next. That could be very discouraging to you. Weigh yourself once a week before eating anything. If you keep very accurate records of the amount of food you take in each day, add up your daily total caloric intake. After a week weigh yourself again. If you lost weight, you are probably on target. If you gain weight, reduce your calories by another 500 per day (if that does not bring you below 1200 calories) and weigh again in a week. If you weigh the same after one week, reduce your intake by another 500 calories (as long as you do not go below 1200 calories without the supervision of a registered dietitian) per day and weigh again the next week. If you keep your exercise constant and your calorie level constant, you can use these records to determine the calories you should be taking in each day once you determine your starting place. However, it is still very important that you show this data (including your food records of what you ate and how much) to a registered dietitian to make sure that you are getting ample nutrients.

WAYNE E. BILLON, PH.D., RDN, LDN

Day 87
Do Not Be a Doubter II

For that man ought not to expect that he will receive anything from the Lord, *being* a double-minded man, unstable in all his ways. (James 1:7–8)

James 1:6 continues where yesterday's scripture left off. If you continue in doubt and do not get control of it, you cannot expect to receive what you ask for because you do not ask in faith. James calls this person "double-minded" who is unstable in all his ways. If you are a strong doubter and you question if your prayers will be answered, you will likely question many of the decisions you make during the day. Choose small things to pray for and believe you will receive them. As you see your prayers answered for the small things, you will not only strengthen your faith, but you also strengthen your confidence in your ability to get things done.

This will help you in your physical life as well as in your spiritual life. You can overcome doubt by memorizing God's Word that says who you are in Christ. Positive thinking will not cause things to happen by itself, but it does help to be positive to overcome doubt. You are a world overcomer! Do not be discouraged! Continue with your program in faith that you will be successful and be willing to accept gradual steps towards success and not lose all the weight at once.

Lord Jesus, I am a world overcomer (1 John 5:4), I can do all things through Christ who strengthens me (Philippians 4:13), I have not been given a spirit of fear (2 Timothy 1:7), I have the mind of Christ (1 Corinthians 2:16), and I know that You will never leave me or forsake me (Matthew 28:20, Hebrews 13:5). Sometimes the trials and tribulations of the world seem to be more than what I can bear. I resolve to memorize Your scripture that tells me who I am in Christ and encourages me in everything that I do. When adversity gets its toughest, I ask for Your Holy Spirit to help me recall the Scriptures and to walk in faith and victory, without doubting. In Your name, Jesus, I pray. Amen.

Nutrition Thought for the Day.

The time of day you eat is important. To be consistent when you eat will help you in losing weight if it is possible for you to eat at the same time each day. If you skip one meal, it is not okay to say, "I did not get to eat lunch so I can eat twice as much at dinner." What happens, in this case, is you eat more than what you need at dinner and the excess goes to fat. The meal you missed at lunch does not cause you to burn off as much fat between lunch and dinner as you add with the extra food at dinner. The other very important thing to remember is not to eat before you go to sleep. During sleep your metabolism slows down, and you need fewer calories to maintain your body. Much of the food you eat before going to bed will turn into fat.

Day 88
Faith Can Move Mountains

But seeing the wind, he became frightened, and beginning to sink, he cried out, "Lord, save me!" Immediately Jesus stretched out his hand and took hold of him, and said to him, "You of little faith, why did you doubt?" (Matthew 14:30–31)

In this passage, the apostles were trying to row against the wind on the Sea of Galilee in the midst of a storm. Jesus came to them walking on the water. When they saw Him they were afraid and thought it was a ghost. Jesus spoke to them and told them to be at peace. Peter spoke out and said, "Lord, if it is You, command me to come to You on the water." Jesus told him to come. Peter stepped out of the boat and started walking on the water. Following this is verse 14. You can apply this scripture to your own life. Maybe you are facing some task that seems insurmountable, like the rough seas to the apostles, and, with the Lord's help, you decide to take on the task head on. Then the cares of the world around you mount up and your task seems to be insurmountable; you succumb to the pressure as Peter did when he saw the waves and the wind. Call out to the Lord to save you and He will lift you up as He did Peter. Do not give up. Your healthy lifestyle program is not insurmountable, nor is any other task you are facing. Call out to Lord and be victorious. The point of this lesson is that if you feel like your faith is too small, know that it is not. Your faith is ample to accomplish all the tasks that may come before you if only you believe. When the going gets rough, do not be discouraged but know that trials and tribulations should not be looked at as problems but as opportunities to strengthen your faith.

> Lord Jesus, I know that the faith I have been given is ample for me to accomplish the call that You put on my life. I know that You will not ask me to do something that You have not equipped me to do, but there are times when it seems to me that I am not equipped to accomplish the tasks before me. At those times remind me of who I am in Christ and that I have the faith to move mountains. I resolve to practice my faith and strengthen it by moving the smaller mountains first, and as my faith grows, I will be ready to take on bigger mountains. I know this is true and I declare it to be so in Your name, Jesus. Amen.

Nutrition Thought for the Day.
Protein is the third macronutrient that needs to be discussed. The list of functions of the other macronutrients (carbohydrate and fat) is small compared to the list of functions of protein. This is not to say that one macronutrient is more important than any of the other macronutrients. We have to balance all three to live. Example, carbohydrates are absolutely necessary for our energy production. Most of the energy our body expands comes from carbohydrates. There are a few places in the body where carbohydrate attaches to other compounds, but energy is by far the most important role of carbohydrates. Fat is also very important in energy production, but fat has several other roles such as the roles in lipoprotein formation (LDL and HDL are examples), some fatty acids are precursors for some very important hormones, and fats are part of cell membranes. This is by no means an exhaustive list of the functions of carbohydrates and fats, but it covers the most important functions.

Day 89
How Little Is Your Faith?

"But if God so clothes the grass of the field, which is *alive* today and tomorrow is thrown into the furnace, *will He* not much more *clothe* you? You of little faith! (Matthew 6:30)

Several places in the Scriptures Jesus asked His disciples this question, "How little is your faith?" In this scripture and the scriptures immediately preceding it, He tells them not to worry about material possessions such as what they will eat or drink, or what clothes they will wear. Earlier He told them that the lilies and grass of the field do not toil or spin, yet even Solomon was not clothed as good as they are. If God will do that for the grass and lilies of the field, how much more will He do it for you?

There is a small minority of people in this world that have so many worldly possessions that they do not have a need or desire for anything else. Most of us do not have that luxury, but we have considerable needs for housing, clothes, food, etc. God knows all of your needs before you even ask and He wants to fulfill your needs in abundance. There are times when you may question how you are going to pay a certain bill or complete a certain task that seems impossible. At those times remember this scripture and remember that God cares about your needs, and if you ask in faith, He will meet your needs.

Father God, we all have needs in this world and sometimes it seems like our needs outweigh our resources to fulfill those needs. I know that You want to grant me all of my needs and You want to see me live in abundance. Knowing that, there are still times when I worry about having my needs met. This is a place where I can practice my faith by putting my hope and trust in You, expecting You to meet all of my needs. I also know that I have to ask You in faith, without doubt, and expect to see my needs met. I thank You, Father, that You love me so much that You will provide for all of my needs. In Jesus's name, I pray. Amen.

Nutrition Thought for the Day.

The bulk of the proteins in our body is in the form of muscle, otherwise known as lean body mass (LBM). Other important functions of proteins include: enzymes, nothing happens in our bodies by way of metabolism without enzymes and enzymes are made of proteins. Hormones are absolutely necessary for life and are made of protein (an important example is insulin). The lipoproteins are part protein and are absolutely necessary for carrying lipids through our blood; there are other proteins in the blood that help us maintain what is known as oncotic pressure (this means the proteins in the blood, such as serum albumin, hold fluid in the blood and prevent edema). All compounds that fight infections are made of protein, such as white blood cells and antibodies. Proteins are important carriers for other things such as hemoglobin, the carrier oxygen through our bodies. The protein that is necessary for blood clotting is prothrombin. Proteins in the back of our eyes enable us to see. Our fingernails are made of protein and hair is made of protein. The list goes on and it is easy to see that protein is an extremely important component in our bodies and thus in our diet.

Day 90
How Little Is Your Faith? II

But Jesus, aware of this, said, "You men of little faith, why do you discuss among yourselves that you have no bread? (Matthew 16:8)

Again Jesus is asking His disciples, "How little is your faith?" Earlier in this chapter, Jesus and His disciples crossed the Sea of Galilee and when they arrived at the other side, Jesus warned them to watch out for the leaven of the Pharisees and Sadducees. They talked among themselves and thought that he was talking about the fact they forgot to bring any bread with them. Following this comes verse 8 when Jesus asked them about their little faith. In chapter 15 Jesus fed four thousand men plus women and children with seven loaves of bread and a few small fish. They just saw this miracle happen the day before and they were wondering what they were going to do now because they forgot to bring bread. Jesus is scolding them in a way by saying, "you men of little faith" because they just saw the miracle He performed in front of their eyes the day before and they had already forgotten His power to meet their needs.

This is another way of encouraging you in that, when you see a lack and you wonder how that is going to be fulfilled, remind yourself of the way Jesus fulfilled lack by miracles. To remind yourself of this you need to be familiar with the Scriptures. Thus a daily scripture reading program is necessary if we are going to know how to respond to troubling situations. The Bible is our survival handbook. Become very familiar with it and develop your faith by reading and meditating on the examples of faith in God's Word.

> Father God, Your Word is my survival guide and my plan for success. In order to know You better and find direction for my life, I need to renew my mind by reading and meditating on Your Word. Help me to be organized in my daily routine so that I will not need to find time, but make time for Your Word. You are all that I need to be successful, and I resolve to spend more time talking to You and meditating on Your Word. I declare this in Jesus's name. Amen.

Nutrition Thought for the Day.

Protein is classified in several different ways. First of all know that carbohydrates and fats are both composed of carbon (C), hydrogen (H), and oxygen (O). Protein is composed of the same three elements but has a fourth, nitrogen (N). The building blocks of carbohydrates were monosaccharides. The building blocks of fats were fatty acids. The building blocks of protein are amino acids. Each amino acid has the four elements mentioned above with nitrogen being included in at least one amino group (a chemical group that contains nitrogen). Two amino acids hooked together are called a dipeptide. Three amino acids hooked together are called a tripeptide. More than three amino acids hooked together are called a peptide. When multiple amino acids are linked together, they make proteins. There are other classifications as chain lengths increase, but they are not at all important for your diet or this discussion.

Day 91
We Are Cleansed

If we confess our sins, He is faithful and righteous to forgive us our sins and to cleanse us from all unrighteousness. (1 John 1:9)

There can be several different obstacles that block you from having strong faith. One of those obstacles could be a feeling of guilt or unforgiveness. Many times you know that you are forgiven because you know that God's Word promises you forgiveness, but you still manage to get down on yourself because of things that you may have done in the past. If you do not feel like you are righteous in God's eyes, then it may be difficult for you to have faith in something for which you are believing. Many scriptures can help you with that, but this scripture should be all that you need. It says that if you confess your sins, He (God the Father) is faithful and forgives your sins and cleanses you from all unrighteousness. A small but very keyword in this sentence is "all." This does not mean some unrighteousness, only the small not so significant sins, but **ALL** unrighteousness. That means every sin you have ever committed or ever thought about committing is forgiven. The next thing you should do is forgive yourself. If God forgives you, who are you to still hold something against yourself? Forgive yourself and move on with the resolve that you will not go back to that place again.

Father God, thank You for forgiving all my sins and for giving me the righteousness of Jesus Christ. No, I do not deserve it, but You give it to me anyway. There are times when I do not feel forgiven. If those times resurface in the future, remind me by the power of Your Holy Spirit that You are faithful and have forgiven me of all unrighteousness. I can walk through my day knowing that I am a loved, forgiven, child of God. I thank You, Father, in Jesus's name. Amen.

Nutrition Thought for the Day.

There are twenty different amino acids in our bodies that are important to us in nutrition. There are more than that in nature, but only twenty are important to our health. Each amino acid has the same basic structure with at least one amino group (NH2), at least one carboxyl group (COOH), a hydrogen (H), a carbon (C) at the center of the amino acid, and a side chain. The side chain is what makes each amino acid different from every other amino acid. That side chain could be something as simple as one more hydrogen. That would make the simplest amino acid known as glycine. The side chain could be what is called a methyl group (CH3) which would make the next simplest amino acid known as alanine. This is organic chemistry and probably is of no interest to you, but it is extremely important to the health of our body because side chains take place in various reactions and they are important in the overall chemical makeup of our bodies. If you cannot follow the chemistry do not be concerned. For right now, it is important to understand that proteins are made of amino acids. This will help you understand the rest of this section and soon you will see the purpose of this instruction.

Day 92
Our Sins Are Removed

As far as the east is from the west, so far has He removed our transgressions from us. (Psalm 103:12)

If you confess your sins, they are forgiven, and you are covered with Jesus's robe of righteousness. This verse tells you that your sins are more than just forgiven; they are not covered up or glazed over; they are removed! Not only that, they are removed from you as far as the east is from the west. If you had a straight line and the east was one way and the west was the other way, and they continue to go in opposite directions to infinity, then that is how far your sins are removed from you. The bottom line is your sins are gone. You have been completely forgiven so that when God the Father looks down, He does not see any mark, stain, or blemish of sin. They are completely removed. When you became a born-again Christian, you were made a new creature and you were set right with God. You do not have to be born again once more—you cannot be born again once more—since Jesus died only once for you, and He is not going to die again. But just as you were made a new creature at the time of your salvation, you are still that new creature. Your sins are gone! Be encouraged by this and do not walk with a burden on your shoulders but know that you can walk in peace and freedom in the love of Christ.

Wow! Father, I have just read that my sins have been removed from me as far as the east is from the west. It is as if they never existed. They have not been covered up or hidden, but You removed them from me forever. You are an awesome God, a loving God, and a forgiving God! I dedicate this day to Your love and Your faithfulness and I look forward to seeing how You will move in my life today. In Jesus's name, I pray. Amen.

Nutrition Thought for the Day.

Amino acids are classified according to what makes them different from each other. The difference is the side chain. For example, if the amino acid has an additional carboxyl group as a side chain, it becomes an acidic amino acid. If the amino acid has an additional amino group as a side chain, it becomes a basic amino acid. If the side chain contains sulfur, it can be called a sulfur-containing amino acid. Several other classifications could be given to amino acids, but an important thing to note is that the amino acid could be basic or acidic. One of the functions of amino acids in our blood is that they act as buffers to help maintain a constant pH value of our blood. Amino acids circulate in our blood as individual amino acids or possibly as dipeptides and tripeptides. For this to happen, proteins that we ingest must be digested in our small intestines to individual amino acids, dipeptides, or tripeptides. The healthy small intestine normally does not allow peptides longer than a tripeptide to be absorbed.

Day 93
Our Sins Are White as Snow

"Come now, and let us reason together," says the LORD, "Though your sins are as scarlet, they will be as white as snow; though they are red like crimson, they will be like wool." (Isaiah 1:18)

The Lord is talking to Isaiah and tells him that though your sins are scarlet, they will be white as snow. Though they are like crimson, they will be like wool. This is another way of saying that their sins (and your sins) will be invisible. They will not look like sins at all but are removed, and you are covered with the robe of righteousness that you received from Jesus Christ upon your salvation. Sin has no more control over you. Sin cannot master you unless you allow it to. You have been forgiven, and you should walk in forgiveness, and that is not only God's forgiveness but also your own forgiveness of yourself. You are a new creature this day. Receive it, live it, and profess it. If you have been messing up with your healthy lifestyle program, today is a new day. Cast off your past failures and move on without looking back.

By an act of my will, I choose to walk as a forgiven child of God! I choose not to take back the guilt and shame of sins that were committed yesterday, a year ago, or ten years ago. It does not matter how many sins I have committed or how many times I have committed them, I have confessed them to my Father God, and I am forgiven! I will wipe out my past diet/exercise failures, and I will start where I left off. Thank You, Father, for forgiving me in Jesus's name. Amen.

Nutrition Thought for the Day.

Amino acids are also classified as essential or nonessential. Some textbooks classify them as dispensable or indispensable. I do not like either of these classifications because all amino acids are important to our health whether they are classified as essential or nonessential. What the textbooks really mean is that the essential amino acids (or indispensable amino acids) cannot be synthesized in the body and have to come in through the diet. Nonessential amino acids (dispensable amino acids) can be synthesized in the body with the right components available and are thereby classified as nonessential. Another classification is conditionally essential. This means that under normal conditions certain amino acids can be synthesized in the body. However, under certain stressful conditions, as in certain disease states, some amino acids cannot be synthesized in the body fast enough to meet the body's needs and therefore must come into the body through the diet. While they are generally non-essential, this condition now causes them to be essential.

Day 94
Our Sins Are Not Remembered

"I, even I, am the one who wipes out your transgressions for My own sake, and I will not remember your sins. (Isaiah 43:25 and Hebrews 10:17)

This scripture for today is recorded in two places; one in the Old Testament and one in the New Testament. This is an awesome scripture because it carries the idea of forgiveness one-step further. God forgives your sins, removes them from you, and separates them from you as far as the east is from the west. This scripture adds the fact that He does this for His own sake and that He will not remember your sins. These are two significant additions. God the Father sent His only begotten Son to the earth as a man to die for you. That is an incredible statement in itself. The reason for doing that was so that your sins could be forgiven. If you confess your sins to your Father God, and He does not forgive them, He is nullifying the life, suffering, and death His Son had to endure. Imagine the grief you would go through if you made your only son go through the same humiliation, trials, and horrible death that Jesus suffered. Actually, it is not possible to suffer as much as Jesus did and be humiliated as much as Jesus since He was not just a son but the Son of God. Suppose you had the best reason in the world to cause your son to suffer so much, but after his death, you denied that reason. Maybe this viewpoint will help you see why forgiving your sins is such a big deal to your Father God. We will look at the second part of the scripture tomorrow.

> Father God, we often think about and talk about the suffering that Jesus did for us but seldom do we consider how much suffering You had to go through to watch Your only Son be persecuted to such a horrible degree and be killed. You did that so we could be forgiven of our sins! You are indeed an awesome God, and I thank You for what You and Jesus did for me. I thank You, Father, in Jesus's name. Amen.

Nutrition Thought for the Day.

Every protein in the body has its own unique structure. There is no rule as to how many amino acids need to be hooked together to make a protein. The smallest biologically active protein in the human body has only three amino acids. The mean or average number of amino acids in a protein in the human body is about 476. In addition to this, the sequence of amino acids in every protein is different. When you consider the vast range in the size of proteins and a total of twenty different amino acids, you can see that there is an indefinite number of proteins that can be synthesized. The length of the peptide chain and the arrangement of amino acids in that chain give each protein its distinctive characteristics. Every protein is different from every other protein.

WAYNE E. BILLON, PH.D., RDN, LDN

Day 95
Our Sins Are Not Remembered II

I, even I, am the one who wipes out your transgressions for My own sake, and I will not remember your sins. (Isaiah 43:25 and Hebrews 10:17)

The second part of the scripture adds another incredible fact, and that is God not only forgives you of your sins, removing them from you, but also chooses not to remember them. That is something that most of us have trouble wrapping our brains around because we cannot choose to forget something forever intentionally. I am sure you had someone do something to you in the past that was not right, and it really hurt you—but you forgave the person. You really did forgive them from your heart with Christian love. Have you forgotten that event? No you have not, and from time to time it will pop back up in your head, and you will have to say, "I rebuke that thought because I have forgiven him and I am not going back there again." That is not the way it happens with God. His mind is so superior to ours that He chooses to forget something totally and when He does, it is completely erased from His memory. You do not have that ability so it may be hard for you to understand how forgiven you really are. The Scriptures say that you are forgiven, your sins removed as far as the east is from the west, your slate is wiped entirely clean, and your sins are completely forgotten, never again to be remembered! What an awesome day this can be knowing that fact! You can do the same thing with your healthy lifestyle program. If you mess up, choose to forget it and move on.

Father God, it is so hard for me to know how to thank You for sending Your only begotten Son to die in my place for my sins and then to forgive me of my sins, remove them from me, and never again remember them. This is more than I can imagine or think, but I receive it because Your Word says it and I walk today in total forgiveness. I praise You, I glorify You, and I thank You with all my being. In Jesus's name, I pray. Amen.

Nutrition Thought for the Day.

The human body contains thousands of different enzymes, and one cell may contain from 200 to 3000 enzymes. Remember that virtually no metabolic process takes place in the body without enzymes and enzymes are made of amino acids and are thus proteins. Enzymes are necessary for us to digest our food, synthesize lipoproteins, synthesize all the proteins in our blood, synthesize muscle, enable us to see, synthesize antibodies, white blood cells, red blood cells—in short, everything our body needs. These enzymes are synthesized in our bodies from amino acids, some of which have to come into the body through the diet. Those that the body can synthesize, it does so by breaking down some unneeded amino acids that occur in the diet and rebuilds them into other amino acids. Knowing this, think about how important it is to have high-quality protein at every meal.

Day 96
Our Sins Are Not Remembered III

"For I will forgive their iniquity, and their sin I will remember no more." (Jeremiah 31:34b)

The second part of Jeremiah 31:34 says, I will forgive their iniquity (sin), and I will remember their sins no more. This is a repeat of what was said yesterday, but the Scriptures say that out of the mouth of two or three witnesses shall a matter be confirmed (Deuteronomy 19:15). God must have really thought that statement to be important because it is in the Bible five different times (Deuteronomy 19:15, Matthew 18:16, 2 Corinthians 13:1, 1 Timothy 5:19, and Hebrews 10:28). So this repetitive scripture is listed just in case you wanted to have a second witness to the fact that not only does He forgive your sins, but He chooses not to remember them anymore. Your God is a gracious God that loves you very much. It is essential that you spend some time meditating on how much God loves you. God's love and forgiveness is something that all of us tend to take for granted, and we should stop, put everything out of our heads, get in our quiet place, and meditate on how much God loves us. It will change your day!

Father God, help me to organize my day so that I can make time to meditate on how much You love me. If I can only get into my head the realization of everything that You did for me and how much You love me, it would be easier for me to serve You and follow Your Word. Help me to get to know You and the rest of the Trinity more intimately so that I can have a closer walk with You. In Jesus's name, I pray. Amen.

Nutrition Thought for the Day.

Enzymes are specific for the substances they react on. The material that is reacted on by an enzyme is called a substrate. The enzyme reacts with the substrate producing a product, but the reaction does not change the enzyme. After the reaction is complete, the product is released, and the enzyme reacts with another substrate of the same kind. For example, the disaccharide sucrose is made up of one molecule of glucose and one molecule of fructose. Sucrose cannot be absorbed through our small intestines and has to be digested to its individual components, fructose, and glucose. This is accomplished by the enzyme sucrose which reacts with sucrose; as a result of the reaction, glucose and fructose are released and can be absorbed in the small intestines. Sucrase is then released and can attach to another sucrose and start the reaction all over again. This reaction takes a millisecond to be performed.

Day 97
How Blessed We Are

How blessed is he whose transgression is forgiven, whose sin is covered! How blessed is the man to whom the LORD does not impute iniquity, and in whose spirit there is no deceit! (Psalm 32:1–2)

Start off this day by stopping a minute and meditating on the devotions for the last week as you think about what you read. Think about your status now as it stands in the eyes of your Father God. Your sins are completely forgiven, not just washed away but removed, separated as far as the east is from the west, and forgotten! You are a new creature in Christ! You are free of guilt and condemnation. Your future could not be brighter— and that is true no matter how much overweight or underweight you may be. Remember that your weight and your eating habits—while they may need to be improved—have nothing to do with how much your God loves you. You are indeed blessed because your transgressions are forgiven, and your sins are not just covered but are removed. When your Father God looks at your spirit, He sees the seal of the Holy Spirit, and He does not see any deceit at all. How blessed you are this day!

Thank You, Father, for blessing me beyond what I can imagine or think. Thank You that You love me no matter how much weight I lose or do not lose, gain or do not gain. There are no barriers, no roadblocks, nothing that can separate You from me. The only thing that can hinder me from getting closer to You is me. By not accepting everything that You have done for me, I can block my relationship with You. Help me to accept myself as well as You accept me. In Jesus's name, I pray. Amen.

Nutrition Thought for the Day.

Enzymes also are specific to environmental conditions. Enzymes are sensitive to heat and pH. If the environmental temperature of the enzyme (temperature of our bodies) is too hot, the enzyme will be destroyed. If it is too cold, the enzyme will be destroyed or, at best, will be inactive. If the pH is too high, the enzyme will be destroyed. If the pH is too low, the enzyme is destroyed. Thus the pH balance in our intestines and blood is crucial for the proper functioning and survival of our body. The proper temperature of our bodies is also critical for enzymes to function and for cells to survive.

Day 98
Return to Me

"I have wiped out your transgressions like a thick cloud and your sins like a heavy mist. Return to Me, for I have redeemed you." (Isaiah 44:22)

Okay, so you are forgiven and a new creature. What happens if you stumble again tomorrow and fall back into an old sin? I know this would be very discouraging, but it does not change the way your Father God sees you. You have to remember and believe that any sins of the future are also wiped out. Jesus died for all the sins that were committed before His walk on the earth and for all the sins that will ever be committed after His death and resurrection until His return. All you have to do is return to Him by turning your back to sin again, and for your own peace of mind, ask for forgiveness. You will be at the same place you started the very day you asked Jesus to be your Savior and Lord. Do not get back into self-condemnation! You have been delivered, and God has redeemed you. True, God was speaking to Isaiah in the Old Testament, but after all Jesus went through, how much more accurate is this verse for us today?

Thank You, Father, that no matter how many times I fall You are there to pick me up and set me back on a firm foundation without condemnation. I know how difficult it is for me to continue to forgive someone that has wronged me for the same wrong over and over again, but that is precisely what You do for me. I am constantly amazed by Your love, and I glorify You for it. I declare this in the name of Jesus. Amen.

Nutrition Thought for the Day.

Now I can explain in a little greater detail some of the notes on digestion that was previously covered. Carbohydrate digestion can begin to a small degree in the mouth with salivary amylase (an enzyme that digests long chains of starch into smaller chains). Carbohydrate digestion stops in the stomach because the pH of the stomach is too low (due to stomach acid) and salivary amylase is destroyed. Carbohydrate digestion continues in the small intestines with an enzyme from the pancreas called pancreatic amylase. The pancreas also secretes a bicarbonate solution (this is a base that neutralizes stomach acids) that raises the pH of the material coming from the stomach and allows pancreatic amylase to be active and to continue to break down carbohydrate. Enzymes secreted from the walls of the small intestines break down the disaccharides to monosaccharides. If you will remember we have three disaccharides that are important to us in nutrition; sucrase digests sucrose, maltase digests maltose, and lactase digests lactose.

Day 99
Jesus's Love Did Not Start at Salvation

When you were dead in your transgressions and the uncircumcision of your flesh, He made you alive together with Him, having forgiven us all our transgressions. (Colossians 2:13)

Before you asked Jesus to be your Savior and Lord, when you were lost in your sinful ways, He already loved you. He loved you from the beginning of time, and He knew what sins you would commit, when, and how many times. None of this made any difference to Him. He was always there for you, just waiting for you to recognize what He did and to receive it in your heart. You were dead in your sins, and you did not know it, but there was a divine plan to bring some laborer across your path to introduce you to God's Word. Yes, you had to say okay and ask Jesus to be your Savior and Lord, but it was not because of your doings that this happened. Instead, it was because of Jesus's love for you and His guidance over you even when you did not know Him!

Thank You, Jesus, that You loved me when I was still a sinner, and I did not even know You. I was lost in my own ways, and I did not even realize it, but You knew it and had already completed the plan for my salvation. Your Holy Spirit guided and directed me when I was lost and not even asking You for guidance. I thank You for all that You have done for me and my salvation. In Your name, Jesus, I pray. Amen.

Nutrition Thought for the Day.

Some people, due to a genetic predisposition, are not able to produce specific enzymes. The obvious example here would be lactase. This is the enzyme that digests lactose. Lactose is only found in milk (or substances that have milk added). If the person ingests milk, the milk will pass on to the large intestines undigested. The bacteria in the large intestines will digest the milk and produce gas. This will cause more water to come into the large intestines and produces bloating, gas, cramps, and diarrhea. This can be overcome by the person ingesting the enzyme lactase with the milk or ingesting milk with the lactose already digested. This type of milk can be found in some grocery stores. This is another good reason for reading the label.

Day 100
Abounding in Lovingkindness

But You are a God of forgiveness, gracious and compassionate, slow to anger and abounding in lovingkindness; and You did not forsake them. (Nehemiah 9:17c)

Several scriptures have emphasized how much God has forgiven you, but you should not forget a few of the attributes that He has that blesses you in addition to forgiveness. Your God is gracious and compassionate. How much more compassionate could someone be then what He did for you by sending His Son, His only begotten Son, to die for your sins? If someone continues to do wrong against you, it may take you a while, but you will forgive that person because of your Christian heritage. But in the process of such forgiveness, most of us would surely get angry with the person that did us wrong. Your God is slow to anger, and He does not get angry with you or give up on you. We do not ever have to worry about our God saying "Oh no! They did it again. What am I going to do with them?" That is not our God. Our God abounds in lovingkindness and compassion. Do not forget that and always be ready to return to Him with any problems that you have and you can fully expect Him to hear you and see you in your time of need. Remember that He is not judging you by how much weight you are losing or gaining.

Thank You, Father, that You abound in lovingkindness, compassion, forgiveness, and You are so gracious. I know that You do not get angry with me when I continue to miss the mark. My finite mind has a hard time understanding Your compassion and love for someone who continues to fall. When I also take into consideration that You do not only treat me that way, but You would do the same for every person on the face of this earth who receives Your Son as their Savior and Lord, that is beyond my comprehension! While Your Scriptures are wonderful, saying that You are gracious, compassionate, forgiving, and abound in lovingkindness, they do not even begin to describe Your love for us. You are an amazing God! I declare this in the name of Jesus. Amen.

Nutrition Thought for the Day.

Fat digestion begins in the stomach with infants when the infant ingests milk. At birth, an infant is not producing hydrochloric acid in its stomach, so the lipase produced in the stomach is not affected. As the infant grows, it begins to produce acid in its stomach, and this destroys the enzyme lipase. This is why the lipase produced in the stomach of adults is not very effective and does not contribute to digestion of fat to any extent. When ingested material passes into the small intestines, the pancreas produces an enzyme called pancreatic lipase which will also digest fat.

Day 101
Redeemed by His Grace

In Him we have redemption through His blood, the forgiveness of our trespasses, according to the riches of His grace. (Ephesians 1:7)

I mentioned that the Old Testament is based on law and the New Testament is based on grace. Today's scripture points out that you have redemption through the blood of Jesus and that redemption grants you forgiveness for all of your trespasses. The point is that all of this is a result of God's grace. Your forgiveness results from love. This is the Father's love for His only begotten Son and the Father's love for you; it is also Jesus's love for you. When Jesus died on the cross, He died for all mankind—not just the good guys—but all mankind. This includes those that brought about 9/11. This includes those who are leading ISIS today. Jesus's death covers all the sins that will ever be committed for the rest of this planet's existence as we know it. All this is the result of His grace. You are covered with grace even though you have done absolutely nothing to deserve it, and there is nothing you can do to earn it. It is God's love for you. Receive it and walk in God's forgiveness.

Thank You, Father, for Your grace that abounds to all mankind even though we have done absolutely nothing to deserve it, nor can we earn it, nor can we pay You back in any way. It is truly unconditional love that You have for us, a love that we can only think about but cannot fully comprehend. I thank You again for that love, and while I cannot pay You back for all that You have done and will do for me, I resolve to serve You with all my heart and to make every attempt to fulfill the call that You have placed on my life. I am not worthy of that call, but Your righteousness makes me worthy. Continue to guide me in that call by the power of Your Holy Spirit. In Jesus's name, I pray. Amen.

Nutrition Thought for the Day.

Protein digestion begins in the stomach with an enzyme called pepsin and with the action of hydrochloric acid. The hydrochloric acid does not digest protein but can cause the protein to unravel. Proteins are also classified by the arrangement of their protein strands. The protein strands could be arranged in sheets, pleated sheets, linear proteins, and other structures. These structures slow down the work of the enzymes because the enzymes cannot get to all parts of the protein at once. The hydrochloric acid causes the protein structure to unravel and allows enzymes to get to the protein easier. The low pH denatures protein as does heat. An example would be when you fry an egg. When you put the cold egg in a frying pan, the white is clear and liquid. The egg white is made of protein, and the heat causes it to denature. You see this happening before your very eyes as it solidifies and turns white. The pepsin in the stomach breaks long protein chains down to smaller chains. Pepsin happens to be an enzyme that works well in a low pH. It is important to know this because if you take meds to stop the production of stomach acid, you could affect protein digestion.

Day 102
We Need Not Offer Anything for Forgiveness

Now where there is forgiveness of these things, there is no longer *any* offering for sin. (Hebrews 10:18)

In the Old Testament man had to offer animal sacrifices to God for his sins continually. The animals were slaughtered on an altar, and the blood was sprinkled on the altar for the sins of those that were making the offering. This had to continue year after year. For those who have made Jesus Christ Savior and Lord of their lives, they need not offer anything else for the forgiveness of their sins. Jesus Christ took the place of the animal offerings on the altar of the Old Testament. His blood took the place of the animal blood that was sprinkled on the altar. His blood completely removes our sins from us. Jesus will not die again. There will never be another offering for your sins; it is finished. If after receiving salvation you sin again, you do not have to make another offering for your forgiveness. All you have to do is receive forgiveness from God because of His loving grace that He pours out on all mankind continuously. Today, walk in His forgiveness and grace!

Lord Jesus, You already completed the ultimate sacrifice for my sins, and no additional sacrifice will ever be needed. I am redeemed, forgiven, washed clean, separated from my sins, and I am free in You. I thank You for Your sacrifice, and I know that nothing else has to be done for my forgiveness. I glorify You this day for who You are and for what You have done for me. In Your name, Jesus, I pray. Amen.

Nutrition Thought for the Day.
When the ingested protein that has been denatured in the stomach reaches the small intestines, the pancreas secretes several enzymes, and the walls of the small intestines also secrete several enzymes, that continue breaking down protein to amino acids, dipeptides, and tripeptides. Some of the protein enzymes are very specific and will react on a bond between two specific amino acids and not break the protein chain anywhere else. The individual amino acids, dipeptides, and tripeptides are absorbed across the intestinal lining into the bloodstream and go directly to the liver where they are utilized to synthesize proteins, or they may be passed on into the blood to go to the other cells of the body. If we ingest an excess of protein, the amino group of the amino acids is broken off, and the rest of the amino acid is utilized to make fat. Remember that fat does not have nitrogen attached and the amino group of the amino acid has nitrogen so it has to be removed before fat can be synthesized.

WAYNE E. BILLON, PH.D., RDN, LDN

Day 103
Jesus Is Exalted

"He is the one whom God exalted to His right hand as a Prince and a Savior, to grant repentance to Israel, and forgiveness of sins." (Acts 5:31)

This scripture is, of course, referring to Jesus as a result of His life, death, and resurrection. After Jesus's successful mission, God the Father exalted Him to His right hand where He sits on the throne next to His Father. He sits there as your advocate and your intercessor, interceding for you constantly. The devil is your accuser and he is always accusing you of the sins that you have committed. However, they are of no account because your advocate is sitting on His throne in the presence of our Father God interceding for you continually. You can walk the face of this earth with confidence that even when you fall in your spiritual walk, you know that sitting at the right hand of your Father God you have an intercessor that has given His life for you and is constantly interceding for you. What a comforting thought! Do not be discouraged! Do not ever feel defeated! You are more than a conqueror, and you are the beloved heir to God's Kingdom, coheir with Jesus. Walk out this day in confidence with who you are in Christ.

> Lord Jesus, I know You are my advocate and that You intercede for me directly to my Father God twenty-four hours a day, seven days a week. No matter how many mistakes I make or how many things I do wrong, I know I can always come to You and that You wait for me with open arms to intercede for me and encourage me. You want me to come to You. It gives You great joy for me to call on Your name and ask for help. You do not like to see me in trouble or see me suffering in any way, but when I am in need of help, it gives You pleasure for me to come to You. Lord Jesus, I thank You so much for this love that You are pouring out all over me. In Your name, Jesus I pray. Amen.

Nutrition Thought for the Day.

The amino group that is removed from the excess amino acids contains the compound NH_2 which forms ammonia as a waste product. This ammonia is the same ammonia you use to clean silverware and your floors. Obviously, if this were allowed to build up in your blood, it would be toxic. Two of these NH_2 compounds are attached to a carbon, and the resulting compound is urea. Urea by itself is not toxic unless it builds up to very large amounts in the blood. The kidneys do not allow this to happen by excreting the urea out in the urine. If the kidneys fail, then urea builds up, and this becomes a problem. If the liver fails, then this also becomes a problem with ammonia buildup because the ammonia pathway that synthesizes urea is in the liver. This does not mean much to you now, but it will be important to you later on, especially as a dieter, if your diet is not balanced. Too low of a caloric intake can cause you to catabolize (breakdown to bare components) your own body proteins producing excessive urea and overworking the kidneys.

Day 104
Forgiveness Is Proclaimed

"Therefore let it be known to you, brethren, that through Him forgiveness of sins is proclaimed to you." (Acts 13:38)

Acts 13:38 is additional biblical proof proclaiming that through Jesus the forgiveness of your sins is proclaimed before God's throne. This has been emphasized to a great extent the last few weeks on purpose. By reading every day about the forgiveness of your sins as declared in so many scriptures, it will get down into your spirit to such a degree that you will have no doubt whatsoever about who you are in Christ. There are still several more scriptures that make this proclamation. It would be good for you to write the scriptures down on notecards or index cards so that you can memorize them and repeat them to yourself whenever necessary. If you let one day go by without acknowledging to your God and to yourself who you are in Christ, then it will be easy to let the second day go by without any acknowledgment, and the third, and so on. Eventually, you will be separated from your relationship with your Lord and God. This can happen sooner than you can imagine. That is one advantage to reading a devotion every day so that you can spend at least some time talking to your God and reminding yourself of who you are in Christ. Do not mind the repetition but use it so that you do not have to hesitate or think twice about calling on your God. Call on Him not only in a time of trouble but also give Him glory when things are going well for you. Continually trust Him to help you with your healthy lifestyle program.

> Lord Jesus, I want to be ever conscious of who You are in relation to myself and the advantages I have in my everyday walk by just keeping in contact with You. It is my intention that I always remind myself of who I am and what my goals are in You. I thank You again for proclaiming to my Father God the forgiveness for my sins and shortcomings. Holy Spirit continues to guide me and direct me in my everyday walk. I want to glorify You this day in everything that I do. In Your name, Jesus, I pray. Amen.

Nutrition Thought for the Day.

When evaluating how much protein a person should ingest, several factors need to be taken into consideration. A significant amount of protein may not be sufficient if the protein is of poor quality. It was mentioned earlier that there are nine essential amino acids (amino acids that the body cannot synthesize and they have to come into the body with the diet). For a dietary source of protein to be of high quality, it has to contain all of the nine essential amino acids, and they have to be in the right proportion. Secondly, if the protein is to be broken down and absorbed correctly, it has to be digestible. Based on these measures of protein quality, proteins are defined as complete or incomplete. There is another term that you may see called partially complete. A complete protein is one that has all the essential amino acids in the right proportion and is digestible. An incomplete protein is one that is completely missing in one or more of the essential amino acids. Partially complete is a gray area that some people define as a protein that has all of the essential amino acids but one may not be in the right proportion and will be depleted quickly in the body.

WAYNE E. BILLON, PH.D., RDN, LDN

Day 105
None Righteous

As it is written, "There is none righteous, not even one;" (Romans 3:10)

There is none that is righteous—no not even one since Adam and Eve. Paul's reference to none included all mankind, except Jesus of course. His reference also relates to everyone ever created not being righteous by man's standards—by our own abilities. In another place, he says that we have all sinned and fallen short of the glory of God (Romans 3:23). Every man and woman who walks the face of this earth needs a savior. We all have missed the mark at one point or another and will continue to do so until Jesus comes back for us. That does not mean that we are bad people, but that our flesh has a sin nature that we have to keep under control constantly. But, as mentioned, we can take heart and be encouraged because we have an advocate before our Father God that intercedes for us at all times. As a result of what Jesus has done for us, we are now righteous in Him. Yes, you should always remind yourself that you are not righteous by your own works, but you are righteous by what Jesus did for you.

> Thank You, Lord Jesus, for my robe of righteousness and for the blessed assuredness that I can spend an eternity in heaven with You where there will be no more pain, suffering, want, and yes—even no weight problems. I look forward to accomplishing on this earth what You have called me to do, but I also look forward to spending eternity with You in heaven. I thank You, Jesus, for assuring me of this blessed eternity. In Your name, I pray. Amen.

Nutrition Thought for the Day.

When amino acids are absorbed into the body and transported to the liver, the liver may utilize them to synthesize one of the numerous proteins that the liver makes. The liver is a vital organ. All the proteins circulating in our blood that were mentioned earlier to help maintain oncotic pressure are synthesized in the liver. Antibodies and immunoglobulins are synthesized in the liver. Many of the enzymes and hormones are synthesized in the liver. Protein carriers that are needed to carry iron and other minerals are synthesized in the liver. Some of the amino acids that are not needed by the liver pass out of the liver into the bloodstream where other organs and muscle absorb them. These organs utilize the amino acids to maintain the organ and complete any repair that is necessary. Muscles utilize the amino acids to make new muscle and to repair any damaged muscle.

Day 106
We Are United to Christ

For if we have become united with *Him* in the likeness of His death, certainly we shall also be *in the likeness* of His resurrection, knowing this, that our old self was crucified with *Him,* in order that our body of sin might be done away with, so that we would no longer be slaves to sin; for he who has died is freed from sin. (Romans 6:5–7)

Read this scripture carefully. It says if you have become united with Jesus in the likeness of His death (which you did when you received Jesus as your Savior and Lord), then you will also be united with Him in the likeness of His resurrection. Just as Jesus rose from the dead and ascended into heaven with a glorified body, so will you. Then it says that your old self (that sinful part of you before you were saved) was crucified with Him. When Jesus was nailed to the cross, all of your sins were nailed to the cross with Him. This did away with all of your sins so that you would no longer be a slave to sin, for he who has died (to sin) is freed from sin. Sin no longer has any hold over you. Does this mean that you will never sin again? No, you will, but because of Jesus's death, the sin has no more power over you unless you give it power. You have been forgiven, even the sins that you have not committed yet because Jesus died for ALL your sins, past, present, and future. If you choose to turn your back on this and continue to sin, then you could enslave yourself again, but you have the cleansing power of Jesus's blood to forgive you and give you strength to keep from returning to the old nature.

Father God, I thank You for Your mercy and grace that allows me to be united with Jesus's death on the cross so that I will also be united with Him in the resurrection. Once my time on this earth is complete, I will be resurrected from the dead and given a new heavenly body that will be spotless in Your site. I want to glorify and praise You once again for all that You have done for me. I can walk through this day knowing that I have an incredibly bright future because of Your love, mercy, and grace. I thank You in the name of Jesus. Amen.

Nutrition Thought for the Day.

A few items about cellular metabolism need to be understood to continue with the discussion on protein. Cells in our body do not last from the time they were created until the time our bodies die. Each cell type has a different lifespan. When it is time for a cell to die, enzymes inside that cell destroy the cell, and healthy cells will make a new one to take its place. For example, cells lining the small intestines have a rapid turnover in that they only live for about five days, die, and are sloughed off into the intestinal tract. Skin cells also have a short lifespan and are replaced about every two weeks. Liver cells live somewhere between 300 and 500 days. Red blood cells live for about a hundred and twenty days. Muscle cells may live between 10 and 16 years. For a new cell to be regenerated in the body, all of the raw materials necessary for making that cell must be present. That means all the vitamins, minerals, amino acids in the right proportions (essential and non-essential), lipids, and cholesterol must be available for the synthesis of cell membranes, etc.

Day 107
What God Has Said Will Come to Pass

God is not a man, that He should lie, nor a son of man, that He should repent; has He said, and will He not do it? Or has He spoken, and will He not make it good? (Numbers 23:19)

When you decided to receive Jesus as your Savior and Lord, there were a few other things that you chose to believe at that time. They are obvious and are necessary to receive Jesus as your Savior and Lord. You believe that the Bible is the infallible Word of God and you live by what you believe. Considering that, you understand that God cannot lie. It is against His nature to lie; it is not even possible. Sometimes this may cause some people a problem because as humans we find it very easy to lie and do not understand how someone cannot lie. But in God's case, it is so. And since God is God and not a man, He does not have to repent of anything He said—He never said anything wrong. What is written in His Word is what will take place. This includes everything this devotional has mentioned concerning salvation, righteousness, and forgiveness. You do not ever have to even think about considering doubting His Word. This day you are everything God's Word says you are and every promise in his Word is for you. Walk in confidence this day as a child of God.

Thank You, Father God, for Your Word because Your Word is truth and cannot be changed. You cannot lie. You are not sorry for anything You said nor should You be. Your Word is truth and everything You said will happen and must occur exactly the way You said it would. I receive Your Word as truth, and I set my body, mind, and soul on following Your Word. Thank You, Father, for Your mighty Word. In Jesus's name, I pray. Amen.

Nutrition Thought for the Day.

When a new protein is synthesized inside a cell, whether that protein is an enzyme, a hormone, or a new muscle fiber, it is made by following a specific DNA code for that protein. The code lists each of the amino acids in the proper sequence that is required to make the protein. Transfer RNA travels through the cell, finds the appropriate amino acid, and transports it to the code. The next amino acid is found and added to the first one. This sequence continues until all the amino acids required for that protein are added in sequence. If at any point during this process one of the necessary amino acids cannot be found, the synthesis stops and an enzyme inside the cell breaks up all the amino acids that were attached, and the process starts over again. If the protein that was being synthesized during this process happened to be one that fights infections, that protein is not synthesized. The way to make sure all the amino acids are present all the time is to eat a diet that is adequate in high-quality protein, so you are continuously supplying your body with the amino acids needed to maintain a healthy lifestyle. This is why this discussion on protein is so important.

Day 108
Hope Does Not Disappoint

And hope does not disappoint, because the love of God has been poured out within our hearts through the Holy Spirit who was given to us. For while we were still helpless, at the right time Christ died for the ungodly. (Romans 5:5–6)

The trust and hope that you put into God's Word will not disappoint you but will make you stronger. God has poured out His love within your heart through the power of His Holy Spirit whom He freely gave to you. The Holy Spirit lives in your heart and guides you each day. God's timing is perfect. Even though you may have been helpless for a number of years during your lifetime, God was right there the whole time. While Jesus may have died two thousand years ago, the timing of you realizing that He did that for you was perfect. You have a God that is never late, never has to repent, and will always freely love you. Hope does not disappoint. Do not let your hope to be successful in your healthy lifestyle program diminish. Hope for greatness as you realize the love your God has poured out over you and is still pouring out over you.

Thank You, Father God, that You are never late. Sometimes it seems to me that things could happen at a different speed or different time for my advantage, but I know that whatever happens to me You are always there with me and will never leave me. I know that my ways are not Your ways and I accept Your timing in my life because I know that You will never do anything to hurt me. Everything You do is for my good. I thank You, Father, in Jesus's name. Amen.

Nutrition Thought for the Day.

For proteins to be synthesized, energy is required. For every metabolic activity that takes place in our bodies energy is required. Where does that energy come from? Our primary source of energy is glucose (which is a carbohydrate). Fat can also be utilized to produce energy for muscle synthesis, but carbohydrate is the primary and preferred overall choice for energy. For muscle to be synthesized, a certain amount of energy is required. How much energy is required depends upon the amount of muscle you have and how fast synthesis is taking place—which will depend on the amount of activity a person does. If carbohydrate intake is too low, and there is not enough energy from carbohydrate for protein to be synthesized, the body has to make glucose. There are two sources for this. One, when we take in more carbohydrate then we need, we store some in muscle and our liver as a compound called glycogen. We can only store a limited amount of glycogen. During starvation, without adequate carbohydrate intake, we may store enough glycogen to last only a few hours or maybe a day or two depending on how much energy we are using.

WAYNE E. BILLON, PH.D., RDN, LDN

Day 109
You Are God's Possession

Do not fear, for I have redeemed you; I have called you by name; you are Mine! (Isaiah 43:1b)

This scripture was used for day 54, but from the standpoint of being redeemed. This time it will be discussed from the standpoint of do not fear. When a scripture says something like "do not fear," I hope you remember that is not a suggestion; it is a command. God, your Father, tells you not to fear. And why not? Because He has redeemed you and, if that is not enough, He calls you by name and says you are His. You are a child of God! I know you may hear that a lot in church and we all know that, but I do not think we really get that down into our spirit as we should. You are the possession of your God! He owns you; you belong to Him. Why should you fear anything? And of course, the answer is you should not! I know there are times when all of us lose sight of this and allow fear to creep into our minds. We need to take charge of those thoughts and cast them out because they are not of God, they are of the enemy. Our God loves us, redeemed us, calls us His own, and commands us not to fear.

Father God, You know my every thought, my every desire, and my every action. Many times those thoughts and desires are not holy and are not in complete line with Your Word. Nevertheless, in spite of everything that You know about me, You still claim me to be Your child. You are not ashamed of me. You will never abandon me. Instead, You have redeemed me, and You give me a command to not fear anything. You are an awesome God. I thank You for Your faithfulness and Your lovingkindness. In Jesus's name, I declare this. Amen.

Nutrition Thought for the Day.
If we run out of glycogen, where do we get the energy to continue with protein synthesis? Not only for the muscle that we are trying to build from exercise, but also for our everyday body functions and health? Everything requires energy, i.e., making antibodies, red blood cells, replenishing organ tissue, etc. We cannot make glucose from fat, but we can break down amino acids, remove the amino group, and use the carbon skeleton that remains to convert to glucose. So, in this case, we would have to break down some of the protein we took in for our muscles and convert it to glucose to have energy available to make more muscle. This is a very inefficient process and will not result in proper muscle synthesis or replenishment for the rest of our body tissues.

Day 110
You Are God's Possession II

But grow in the grace and knowledge of our Lord and Savior Jesus Christ. To Him *be* the glory, both now and to the day of eternity. Amen. (2 Peter 3:18)

Hopefully, by now you are getting the picture of how much your God loves you and how intent He is to forgive you for all your trespasses. Based on everything that has been discussed so far, your next step is to do as this scripture says—grow in the grace and knowledge of your Lord and Savior Jesus Christ. I have been a Christian for over forty years, and I am still learning things from God's Word. So growing in His knowledge is something that will be ongoing. Do not ever stop reading His Word and meditating on it.

The second part of the scripture says, "To Him be the glory, both now and to the day of eternity." Something else that most of us do not do enough is give glory to God. That is, to get on your knees and glorify His name or to raise your hands and glorify His name or however you choose to worship Him. In any case, we do not do that enough. God created you so that you could fellowship with Him. When you read His Word, you learn more about Him, but you do not necessarily glorify Him by just reading His Word. It is important that you take time to glorify your God. Give Him credit for all of your accomplishments. If you are successful with your healthy lifestyle program, give Him the glory.

> Father God, I want to glorify Your name in everything that I do. I do take You for granted sometimes and give others or myself around me the credit for something I accomplished when the credit should go to You. Forgive me for not glorifying and praising Your name more. You are worthy of all praise, honor, and glory as the scripture says, now and always! I exalt You, Father, in the name of Jesus. Amen.

Nutrition Thought for the Day.

Now you may understand why I like to say we should have at least 150g of carbohydrates a day so that we have enough energy for the protein to be used as protein. When we have enough carbohydrates for this to take place, we say that the carbohydrate is protein sparing. That means we are ingesting enough carbohydrates so that the protein in our diet can be utilized to synthesize new proteins and does not have to be used as energy. On any weight reduction diet, we do not want to use protein for energy. We want proteins to be used for all the functions previously mentioned. For that to happen, adequate calories have to be in the diet coming from carbohydrate and fat.

Day 111
I Will Give You Thanks Forevermore

That *my* soul may sing praise to You and not be silent. O LORD my God, I will give thanks to You forever. (Psalm 30:12)

Give praise to the Lord, oh I say again give praise to the Lord. As the author says in this Psalm, you should not let your soul be silent but be continuously giving praise to your God and to give Him thanks forever. There is no way you can ever praise your God or thank Him enough for what He has done for you. Take a minute to stop and think about how long an eternity is. It is overwhelming, isn't it? An eternity of peace and happiness without tears, without pain, without any strife or fear—that is what you have waiting for you. And the kicker on top of all that is you do not deserve one minute of it; none of us do. We receive it because of the mercy, grace, and love of our God. Can you praise Him enough for that? Can you thank Him enough for that? No, you cannot, none of us can, but you should thank Him and praise Him every day.

You may be thinking that you cannot go around constantly praising your God. You have work to do, people to talk to, and things you have to concentrate on. However, you can praise Him by letting your life be a sacrifice of praise and thanksgiving to your God. This may help remind you daily that everything you do should be for the glory of God. Even if you have a bad day or a bad week, or do not lose or gain as much weight as you desire, give Him thanks and praise anyway. As any parent receives pleasure when one of their children gives them honor, so much more so does your heavenly Father receive pleasure when you praise and honor Him.

> I praise and thank You, Father God, for granting me an eternity of joy, peace, and tranquility in a place that my mind cannot imagine. I look forward to living forever with You without strife, war, or rumors of war. No weather disasters, no mass shootings, no phone calls in the middle of the night—none of this will happen for an eternity! I do not know how to thank You for such a gift, but I want to try to glorify Your name by the way I live my life. I want to live my life as a reflection of Your love. Holy Spirit, give me direction and guidance to help me accomplish such a feat. In Jesus's name, I pray. Amen.

Nutrition Thought for the Day.

What are the sources of protein? Protein is found in most foods. Protein found in vegetables varies as to the amount and to the quality and this will be discussed in a few days. The highest quality protein is animal protein. All animal protein (beef, pork, lamb, poultry, eggs, fish, wild game, milk, cheese, and yogurt) is complete protein and contains all the essential amino acids in the right proportion. Animal protein is more digestible than plant protein. Eggs are also included in this list but the egg white is the most digestible animal protein. The egg white also has no fat, no cholesterol, and no carbohydrate, it is pure protein. Cholesterol is found in the yoke of the egg only. When proteins are classified according to the quality, the standard that they are compared to is the egg white.

Day 112
Nothing Will Separate Us from Our God

Who will bring a charge against God's elect? God is the one who justifies; who is the one who condemns? Christ Jesus is He who died, yes, rather who was raised, who is at the right hand of God, who also intercedes for us. Who will separate us from the love of Christ? Will tribulation, or distress, or persecution, or famine, or nakedness, or peril, or sword? (Romans 8:33–35)

There are so many amazing scriptures that encourage us like this one. Who will bring a charge against God's elect? Do you know that you are God's elect? Who is going to bring a charge against you when you are justified in the eyes of your God? Only God has the right to condemn and, instead of condemning you for the wrongful things you have done, He has decided to forgive you and elevate you to heavenly places. His only begotten Son came to this earth in total humility and died for your sins. He now sits at the right hand of your Father God and intercedes for you continually. So what can separate you from the love of God the Father and the love of His Son, Jesus Christ? No kind of tribulation, or any distress, or persecution, or famine, or nakedness, or peril, or sword will separate you from the love of your God. Be joyful this day and be thankful for the love that you are receiving from your God. Approach your healthy lifestyle program with new intensity knowing that even if you do not lose (or gain) all the weight you intended to lose (or gain) this week, you are still a winner!

No matter what I do on this earth, as long as Jesus Christ is my Savior and Lord (and He is), I am righteous in the eyes of my Father God and Jesus. It is not that I can do no wrong as a spoiled child, but that when I do mess up I am forgiven, and my God still loves me. What an awesome feeling I can have today knowing this to be a fact! I thank You, Father, for not allowing anything to come between You and me. You are an awesome God, and I am one blessed child! I thank You, Father, in the name of Jesus. Amen.

Nutrition Thought for the Day.

Generally speaking, plant proteins are of poorer quality than animal proteins. The one exception is soy protein. Most research indicates that well-processed soy protein isolates and soy protein concentrates are essentially equivalent to that of food proteins of animal origin. This does not mean eating the soybean itself will provide you with the same high-quality protein as the isolates or concentrates. Some soy-based infant formulas may need to be supplemented with the amino acid methionine. Animal proteins may be more digestible than the soy proteins. Beans and peas (legumes) are higher in protein than other vegetables, but the quality is not as good as animal protein. How do vegans get by if they do not eat any animal protein? They can have very healthy diets if they eat wisely and they choose good examples of protein complementation to be discussed tomorrow.

Day 113
You Turn My Mourning into Dancing

You have turned for me my mourning into dancing; You have loosed my sackcloth and girded me with gladness. (Psalm 30:11)

You indeed turn my mourning into dancing. Even on those mornings when I do not feel like dancing, I choose, by an act of my will to worship You and to praise You. Today we do not wear sackcloth and ashes anymore, but we still tend to put on a gloomy, sad face and perhaps even dress gloomy because we feel discouraged. I do not have to be like that anymore. You give me joy in the morning and all I have to do is receive it and put on my happy face. You make me happy! I choose to accept Your joy, and I want for my day to be glorious because of Your love. No matter what comes my way I choose to be joyful. Being joyful is a state of being, a decision I make, it is not an emotion. I thank You, Father, for the joy that You give me this day.

Dear Father God, there are days, I admit, I do not wake up feeling joyful. There are times when I do not want to face the chores that I have before me each day. Joy is not an emotion, it is a state of being, and I get to choose if I want to be joyous or not. You have given me the strength and ability to choose to be joyous. I can choose to be joyous, or I can choose to be sad. Because of Your love for me and Your grace, I choose this day to be joyful and to glorify Your name in the process. I thank You, Father, for my joy today, in Jesus's name. Amen.

Nutrition Thought for the Day.
Protein complementation is consuming two different foods at the same meal that complement each other concerning their protein content. For example, legumes (beans and peas) have a more substantial amount of protein per serving than other plants, but the protein is not complete protein because it lacks in one amino acid. Grains (rice, corn, oats, barley, wheat) are a decent source of protein, but they are not complete proteins because they also lack in an amino acid. The amino acids that are low in legumes are high in grains. The amino acids that are low in grains are high in legumes. So, if both legumes and grains are eaten at the same meal, you would have all the amino acids that you would obtain if animal products were eaten at that meal. The digestibility may not be quite as good as animal protein, but it would still be good protein. Examples are beans (legumes) and rice (grain); beans (legumes), and cornbread (grains).

Day 114
Our God Is Compassionate

Who is a God like You, who pardons iniquity and passes over the rebellious act of the remnant of His possession? He does not retain His anger forever, because He delights in unchanging love. He will again have compassion on us; He will tread our iniquities under foot. (Micah 7: 18–19a)

In the Old Testament, the people lived by the law, unlike the way we live by grace today that is granted in the New Testament by Jesus's life, death, and resurrection. When God's people would rebel against His law, the result was God's wrath on His people, but this verse says that God would eventually pardon the iniquity and pass over the rebellious acts of His people and that He did not retain His anger forever. His love never changes, and because of that love, He again had compassion on His people and trod their iniquities underfoot. Today we are under grace and not law. How much more would your Father God have compassion on you, one of His people, after what Jesus did for you? His love is still unchanging. I had a loving biological father but, if I did something to invoke his wrath, I received a penalty. Because I had seen the wrath of my father and the wrath of many other fathers demonstrated towards their children when they disobeyed, it is sometimes difficult for me to picture a father that would now never get angry with me no matter what I did. This is probably also true for you. That is the kind of father your Father God is. He is not happy with you when you are disobedient, but He does not show His wrath to you because of what Jesus did for you. As you go through your day today, know that even if you mess up, your God has an unchanging love for you. Amazing!

> Father God, I thank You for withholding Your wrath from me when I do something that does not please You. I know that You forgive me because of what Your Son did for me. I also know that this does not mean that I can go on about being disobedient and not have to worry about being forgiven. That is not the point of Your grace for us. The point is for me to realize how much You love me and how much Jesus did for me. Once that realization gets down into my spirit, I will not want to disobey Your Word and displease You in any way. When I do something that is wrong, I want to turn to repentance immediately and try harder to obey all Your precepts. In Jesus's name, I pray. Amen.

Nutrition Thought for the Day.

Before going any further, I want to discuss a fast and easy way we classify foods according to what we call the exchange lists. This is lists of foods that are separated into categories that have similar characteristics. For example, there is a dairy group, a starch group, a vegetable group, a meat group, a fruit group, and a fat group. Each group is a list of foods that belong to that group and the serving size for each food. Most foods in the group will have the same serving size, but some vary. The group also lists the average calories, protein, fat, carbohydrate, and fiber per serving. Free foods are also found on the list.

WAYNE E. BILLON, PH.D., RDN, LDN

Day 115
We Are Free from the Law of Sin and Death

For the law of the Spirit of life in Christ Jesus has set you free from the law of and of death. (Romans 8:2)

The Old Testament held the people responsible for the law, and the New Testament covers them under grace. The result of the law brought about death and God's wrath. The result of grace is forgiveness and God's compassion. All this is possible because of the life in the Spirit that you now have in Jesus Christ. You have been set free from the law of sin and death, and you are now under God's grace. Again, this does not mean that you are free to sin as you want. As Paul said when he was addressed about this, "may it never be" (Romans 6:2). You have a way out now through God's grace for the forgiveness of your sins because they have been accounted for by the blood of Jesus. Walk in freedom and grace this day. Do not let these daily devotions seem redundant to you because they repeat a lot of scriptural truths over and over. A great way to get the message of the cross down deep into your spirit is to say it over and over again from every angle.

Lord Jesus, I thank You for setting me free from the law of sin and death by Your life, death, and resurrection. I know that I am now under Your grace but that this does not mean I am free to be disobedient and then receive forgiveness for anything I do as a child that is never punished. Help me to fully understand all that You did for me so that I will have such a close walk with You I will not want to sin. I know that this is a huge task and I ask for Your Holy Spirit to guide me. I thank You, Jesus, and pray in Your Holy name. Amen.

Nutrition Thought for the Day.

If you check out the exchange lists, you will see that fruit does not have protein listed as part of its makeup. There is a trace of protein in a serving of fruit but not enough to count. The fat list, such as oils, butter, margarine, and the fat on a piece of meat, has zero grams of protein. Vegetables are divided up into starchy and green-yellow vegetables. Starchy vegetables are obvious and include all flours, grains, rice, potatoes, macaroni, bread, winter squash, cereals, peas, legumes (beans), and lentils. The green-yellow vegetables are everything else that is left such as, the cabbage family, all greens, green beans, eggplants, tomatoes, peppers, summer squash, cucumbers, onions, garlic, etc.

Day 116
My God Is Gracious and Compassionate

Light arises in the darkness for the upright; *He is* gracious and compassionate and righteous. (Psalm 112:4)

If you do a word study for the word gracious, you will find it mentioned numerous times in the Psalms. God is declared to be gracious over and over and over in the Scriptures. The same is true for compassionate. This verse spells that out and adds something new in that it says, "light arises in the darkness for the upright." When you are in a dark place, if that is due to sin in your life or sin from people that are around you or some trial and tribulation that you are going through, let God's light arise. He is with you and will never leave you. Call on Him when it is dark but also when everything is going well. He wants to hear from you daily in all circumstances. He loves to help you in everything you do, no matter how insignificant a task may seem to you. Walk in the light today and do not let darkness overtake you. Be encouraged!

Lord, I thank You that my days are brighter than ever and that darkness has no place in my life. You are gracious and compassionate and a righteous God that loves me very much. Your light will rise and shine no matter how dark things are. I receive Your light, and I look for it to guide my paths everywhere I go. Shine Your light in my heart and see if there is any darkness there. Shine Your light in my mind and see if there is any darkness there. By the power of Your Holy Spirit remove any darkness that you find in me. In Jesus's name, I pray. Amen.

Nutrition Thought for the Day.

Starchy vegetables vary as to how much carbohydrate they contain, but it is usually about 15 grams per ½ cup serving. Some starchy grains, such as rice, are about 15 grams of carbohydrate per 1/3 of a cup. One serving of a starchy vegetable usually has about 3 grams of protein. One serving of most green-yellow vegetables has about 5 grams of carbohydrate and about 2 grams of protein. I say about, because the exchange lists are not exact but are estimates. Green-yellow vegetables, when eaten raw as in salads, would have even less protein. Nuts and seeds are good sources of protein as far as quantity of protein is concerned. For example, there are about 21 grams of protein in 3 ounces of almonds and about 23 grams of protein in 3 ounces of sunflower seeds. The quality is not as good as animal protein.

Day 117
Jesus Is the Light

For with You is the fountain of life; in Your light we see light. (Psalm 36:9)

This Psalm tells us that Jesus is the fountain of life (see John 4:10, 14). We already know that because of Jesus's life, death, and resurrection we have new life. The Psalm also says that by Jesus's light we see light. Water and light are metaphors the Bible used to mean life. Jesus gave you a new life. When He walked the earth as a man, He shed light on the meaning of the Old Testament. His life and death on this earth gave you the ultimate example for you to follow in His light. His Word sheds light on everything. Thus He is your fountain of life and the light of your life. He gives you new life and then lights the path for you to follow to show you how to experience that new life on this earth, as well as an extraordinary life in eternity.

The more you commit to studying God's Word, the more light you will have in your life. As you complete the tasks of this day, try to identify what areas of your life need to be enlightened by Jesus's Word. Everything we do needs to be done in the light of God's Word. If you can be conscious of this fact all day long, it will help you to always be thinking of how God's Word will apply to your daily tasks. This may not be easy at first, but I think this is part of completing Romans 12:1–2, and that is—making yourself a living sacrifice. The more you try it, the better you will get.

Lord Jesus, You are the light of my life, and a fountain of life for me. By the power of Your Holy Spirit, I ask that You shed light on everything that I do this day. Help me to be ever mindful that Your Word will be a lamp unto my feet and will guide me in all things. The more conscious I am of that fact, the more careful I will be where I place my feet. This is a new practice for me, and I need Your help. I know that once I can accomplish having a greater dependence on Your Word in my daily walk, I will be more fulfilled and will be successful in everything that I do. I pray in Your name, Jesus. Amen.

Nutrition Thought for the Day.

The meat exchange list is divided into four sections: very lean meat, lean meat, medium-fat meat, and high-fat meat. The amount of protein per serving in each of these exchanges remains the same, but the amount of fat per serving increases accordingly from very lean meat to high-fat meat. No carbohydrates or fiber are found in meat. If you look up the internet address for the exchange list I posted a few days ago, you will see a list of how all of these meats are separated, and you will see a list of meat substitutes. One ounce of protein is considered one meat exchange and is 7 grams of protein. A typical serving of meat at a meal would be 3 to 4 ounces. The fat exchange lists may surprise you in that you may find some things listed that you did not consider to be fats. An example is 1/8 of a medium-size avocado is considered to be one fat exchange because the avocado has so much oil in it. The amount of food per fat exchange will vary because of the large variation in oil between foods. The exchange lists give you a lot more information and many useful tips. We use this to get a rough estimate of a number of calories, protein, carbohydrates, and fat we are ingesting in a day. This exchange list is not an exact science and is not intended to be.

Day 118
Present Yourself to God as a Workman

> Be diligent to present yourself approved to God as a workman who does not need to be ashamed, accurately handling the word of truth. (2 Timothy 2:15)

This should be our daily goal, to diligently present ourselves as workmen who do not need to be ashamed, accurately handling the Word of truth. If you follow the advice given in yesterday's devotion, you will be on the path to completing this task. The way to accomplish this is by letting God's Word be your shining light each day, with every step you take. If you continuously seek God with all your heart, read and meditate on His Word, you will be diligently presenting yourself before God and, as a born-again Christian, you will be approved by God as a workman and will not need to be ashamed. The more you study God's Word, the more you will accurately handle the Word of truth in your life, and the more you will be a witness to those around you. This will also bring about greater success in your healthy lifestyle program.

While this is a large task to accomplish, it is certainly doable if you can discipline yourself to try to stay in God's Word every day. Oh, there will be days when you will not stay in God's Word as you should, I know, because I have such days. We all do. But that does not mean you should give up and say, "I missed it today so if I miss tomorrow I may as well give up on this, I can't do it." If you find yourself thinking such thoughts, they are probably coming from the devil. They are definitely not from the Holy Spirit. No matter how many days you miss, do not give up but pick up where you left off and start anew. God still loves you, and He is still pulling for you.

> Father God, I want to be diligent in Your Word and show myself to be approved by You. It is a choice I will make every day. However, there are days when the world's trials and distractions come at me very hard, and I do not stay in Your Word as I should. Give me strength on those days to pick back up where I left off and not to be discouraged. No matter how many times I do not accomplish my goal, I will not give up. I resolve that I will discipline myself to such a degree that I will spend time reading, meditating, or listening to Your Word each day. I know that I am too weak to do this on my own and I trust that by the power of Your Holy Spirit I will accomplish this. In Jesus's name, I pray. Amen.

Nutrition Thought for the Day.

What is our protein requirement? There are two ways of calculating protein requirement. One is using the recommended dietary allowances. According to this method, it says that our protein requirement is about 0.8 grams of protein per day per kilogram of body weight. To determine kilograms, divide your weight in pounds by 2.2 (Example 170 pound man = 170/2.2 = 77 kilograms ---77 kilograms X .8 = 61.6 or 62 grams of protein/day). For athletes, the RDA recommendation is 1.2 to 1.5 grams per kilogram of body weight. Most athletes like to ingest more than that but research does not indicate an excess of protein in the diet will increase muscle mass. The other method for looking at your protein intake is as previously discussed as a percentage of total calories, i.e., the average person would take in around 20% of the calories from protein.

Day 119
Your Lord Will Sustain You

The LORD sustains all who fall and raises up all who are bowed down.
(Psalm 145:14)

Yes, from time to time you will not meet your goals and you will not finish the day feeling very diligent about accomplishing anything for the Lord. This will happen to all of us, do not be discouraged. No matter how many times you fall, as the scripture says, Your Lord will sustain you. As you continue to seek Him and to serve Him (or bow down to Him as this scripture suggests), He will raise you up. Remember something mentioned earlier, getting knocked down is not a failure; getting knocked down and refusing to get up is a failure. No matter how many times you may go off your healthy lifestyle regimen, or how many times you may not get into God's Word as you promised Him and yourself, you need to get up again and take up where you left off. When you do not meet your goals, the one who is disappointed is you! Does God want you to meet your goals? Of course He does, but He does not give up on you when you do not meet them. You are an overcomer. Do not be discouraged.

Thank You, Father God, that You never give up on me. No matter how many times I miss my mark that I set for myself, whether that is with my healthy lifestyle regimen, or my diligence in studying or meditating Your Word, You still see me as a winner! You see me as a child of God, and You will always see me that way because that is what I am. You will never give up on me; by the power of Your Holy Spirit help me to never give up on myself. In Jesus's name, I pray. Amen.

Nutrition Thought for the Day.

I want to emphasize one more time the importance of obtaining good quality protein each day, preferably at each meal. You now should be able to see the importance of protein in our diets and in maintaining healthy bodies. There is no little locker somewhere in your body that you store amino acids to use later on if you need them to build some particular enzyme or hormone. If you run out of amino acids while synthesizing a protein, that protein is not synthesized. Your body then has to break down some other proteins to get to the amino acids it needs to use for the protein you are building. In essence, you cannibalize your own body to stay alive.

This happens when you go on a starvation diet that does not have enough calories or enough protein. The other point here is that for protein in the diet to be used to make proteins in the body, adequate calories must be present. Those calories come from carbohydrate for the most part but also from fat. One thing not mentioned yet is that enzymes require cofactors to be active. Cofactors are either vitamins or minerals. Thus if you do not have ample vitamins and minerals in your diet, you cannot make the active enzymes that you need to synthesize proteins. A balanced diet is absolutely essential for a healthy body.

Day 120
Be Filled with the Fruit of Righteousness

And this I pray, that your love may abound still more and more in real knowledge and all discernment, so that you may approve the things that are excellent, in order to be sincere and blameless until the day of Christ; having been filled with the fruit of righteousness which *comes* through Jesus Christ, to the glory and praise of God. (Philippians 1:9–11)

Congratulations! After today you will have finished one more month of this healthy lifestyle program and devotional. The scripture for today summarizes everything so far, it would be good for you to read it over several times and let it be your devotion for today. It covers everything that has been mentioned of so far and it is my prayer for you. May your love abound more and more in real knowledge and discernment so that you may approve the things that are excellent. May you accomplish this so that you will be sincere and blameless until the day of Christ's return. You have been filled with the fruit of righteousness which comes through Jesus Christ when you received Him as Savior and Lord, and all of this you are doing, do for the glory and praise of your God.

Father, this prayer is a prayer of thanksgiving. I thank You that I am growing in knowledge and discernment about You and I will continue to grow. I want to be sincere and blameless in my walk with You until the day of Jesus's return to this earth. I know that I am filled with the fruit of righteousness that Jesus gave to me when I received Him as my Savior and Lord. I offer everything I do this day and for the rest of my being for Your glory and praise. I pray this in the mighty name of Jesus. Amen.

Nutrition Thought for the Day.

The program that you are on should include exercise. Exercise is different things to different people. The levels of intensity of exercise and the length of time you exercise are very important. The more you exercise the more strain you put on your muscles, and some damage is done. Your body repairs that damage and in the process makes the muscles a little bit stronger than they were before you exercised. That repair requires synthesis of protein. That protein comes from your diet. If you ever tried to build muscle and gain weight, you know that you do not build muscle overnight. It takes a while to develop and strengthen your muscles because it happens over time at a prolonged rate. Because of this, you do not need large amounts of protein.

If you are exercising hard, you just need a little more protein than you would typically take in for the extra repair. Do not go overboard with excessive amounts of protein since too much will be converted to fat—the very thing you are trying to lose. On any weight loss program, you want to lose fat and not muscle. To be sure you get this right, it is best to talk to a registered dietitian that has experience with exercise and weight loss.

WAYNE E. BILLON, PH.D., RDN, LDN

Day 121
Learn How to Resist the Devil

Submit therefore to God. Resist the devil and he will flee from you. (James 4:7)

During the past four months, you probably have undergone several different types of trials and tribulations. Many of them would have been just to consume an extra piece of pie, an extra snack, or something similar. Events happening to keep you from exercising properly were probably not infrequent. Some trials may have been distractions at work or at home that caused you to think about eating as a way of relieving your stress. Some of these may have just been life happening, and some may have been purposely brought about by the devil to get you to give up on your healthy lifestyle. Giving up on your program entirely or to just a small degree is not a sin. However, since you have set your heart on being successful and you are trusting God to help you be successful, then if the devil can get you to fail your program in any way, he will use that to accuse you of having failed your God.

Do not let him do that. Even if you slightly get away from your healthy lifestyle or you go off in a big way, and you hear the accusations in your head, "See you can't do this. You are a failure. You may as well give up totally." Do not listen to those accusations. You are not a failure; you are a world overcomer. Even if you did go off your program, it is not a sin, and you are not causing your God to be displeased with you. The scripture says resist the devil and he will flee from you. This is true but look again at the very first part of the scripture. It says submit yourself to God. That is the first step, and you have already done that, so remember your commitment and be bold and courageous. Resist any temptation, no matter how many times a day you have to do it, and the devil will flee from you. You will be successful in the end because you are a child of God and can do all things through Christ who strengthens you.

Lord Jesus, You have already defeated the devil for me. He has no authority over me and cannot make me do something I do not want to do. He knows when and where I am weakest, but in my weaknesses, I become strong because of Your strength. You have given me authority over the devil and all his lies. Your Word says that if I rebuke him, he will leave. I choose to believe Your Word. I am a world overcomer, and I will be successful with my healthy lifestyle program with Your help. In Your name, Jesus, I pray. Amen.

Nutrition Thought for the Day.

The next subject to be discussed is antioxidants. If you pay any attention to news articles, TV commercials, magazine ads, etc., I am sure you have heard antioxidants mentioned. You probably have some idea from the things you heard that antioxidants are good. Antioxidants are helpful for the body but in excess could be harmful. The first thing to learn is what antioxidants are and what they do. Antioxidants can prevent oxidation. Great, you say, what is oxidation? Simply put, oxidation is an interaction between oxygen molecules and any other substance with which they may contact. There is not enough room or time here to teach a chemistry course, but an atom of oxygen has electrons circling the atom in an orbit similar to the way the planets revolve around the sun. In straightforward language, when an oxygen atom steals one of these electrons from another element, it is called oxidation.

Day 122
You Can Endure All

Then the Lord knows how to rescue the godly from temptation, and to keep the unrighteous under punishment for the day of judgment. (2 Peter 2:9)

This scripture promises us that the Lord will rescue the godly (this is you as a born-again Christian) from temptation. Refer back to day 63, read 1 Corinthians 10:13 again, and note that you can overcome any temptation that comes your way for it says that you will receive no temptation that is not uncommon to man. There is nothing new under the sun. It may not seem like it at the time you are tempted, but God is faithful and will not allow you to be tempted beyond what you can bear and will rescue you from the temptation if you listen to Him. He will provide a way out from the temptation, but you will have to call on Him and depend on Him for help during that time. If you give into the temptation, He will not stop you but will be there to help you out of it. He will not do that for the unrighteous.

This temptation that Peter was talking about, I'm sure, was concerned with something sinful. However, it can easily be applied to other things such as temptations for you to go off your diet or skip your exercise period. While giving in to such temptations is not a sin, it is still a temptation. You can have victory over those types of temptations also because your God wants you to be successful in everything you do and not just spiritual matters. Do not hesitate to call on Him even for worldly temptations that may seem to be very small and not very spiritual. Your God wants to help you in every way.

> Thank You, Jesus, that You will provide an escape route for me in any kind of temptation I may have. Whether it be something spiritual or something minor that is worldly, You have a way out of it for me. I know that every temptation or trial I go through is nothing new to man. Sometimes it feels like I am being persecuted more than anyone else around me, but I know that this is just another attack of the enemy and I refuse to give into it. I also know that any temptation will not be from You but the enemy, and therefore I have authority over it. I thank You for being my safety valve, escape hatch, and secret escape door. You are all those things for me. In Your name, Jesus, I pray. Amen.

Nutrition Thought for the Day.

There may be several orbits circling an atom, and there may be more than one electron in the outer orbit of that atom. Some chemical elements are much more stable than others and do not easily give up electrons. When an element reacts with oxygen by donating an electron (or you could say by having an electron stolen), the process is oxidation. So what is the big deal about oxidation? There are a few places where this could be a benefit, but for the most part, oxidation is harmful. An example of oxidation that you are familiar with is metal sitting out in the open air that begins to rust. The formation of rust is the oxygen in the air reacting with the iron in the metal, stealing electrons from the outer orbits encircling iron atoms. In this case, you know that rust is not pretty to look at and in time it will weaken the metal. The elements in our body do not rust, but they can be harmed due to oxidation reactions.

Day 123
Overcome Evil with Good

Do not be overcome by evil, but overcome evil with good. (Romans 12:21)

This is not saying that going off your healthy lifestyle program is evil, but it is saying overcome evil with good. Remember, when the Scriptures tell you something like this you need to understand that it is not a suggestion but a command. God would not tell you to do something that you are not capable of doing. If He tells you to overcome evil with good, it is because you have the power to do so. Thus, if you have power to overcome evil, then surely you have power to overcome the temptations that try to cause you to go off your diet plan. When temptation comes and tells you to eat more than is on your diet plan (or eat less if you are trying to gain weight), try to eat slightly less just to prove to yourself and the temptation (devil) that you will not give in. When the temptation comes trying to get you to stop exercising, exercise another ten minutes just to prove to yourself and the temptation (devil) that you can do it. No, this will not always be easy, and sometimes you may not win the battle, but it if you continue to hang in there and trust in your God, you will win the war. Be bold and courageous.

> Father God, I resolve that I want to prove to myself and to the devil that I am an overcomer and I will do that with Your help. I will refuse to give into temptations, be it temptations to sin or temptations to quit my healthy lifestyle program. I know that if the devil can get me into a sinful situation that has nothing to do with my healthy lifestyle program, he will have the leverage to try to show me that I am a failure. The spiritual and the physical are very much connected. If he can defeat me spiritually, he will try to bring that over into the physical and vice versa. I resolve to be victorious in all areas with Your help, and I thank You, Father, in Jesus's name. Amen.

Nutrition Thought for the Day.

Another example of oxidation that we have already looked at is the oxidation of polyunsaturated fatty acids. The double bonds between two carbons of the polyunsaturated fatty acid are oxidized by oxygen in the cell or the blood, wherever the oxidation is taking place. An electron in the outer shell (or orbit) is stolen from one of the carbon atoms by oxygen breaking the double bond. This creates a different fatty acid then we had at the start. If this occurs when it is in food before being eaten, it results in rancidity. If it occurs in cells of the body after the food has been eaten, digested, and absorbed, it could be the start of inflammation.

Day 124
Prayer Avoids Temptation

"Keep watching and praying that you may not enter into temptation; the spirit is willing, but the flesh is weak." (Matthew 26:41 and Mark 14:38)

When He arrived at the place, He said to them, "Pray that you may not enter into temptation." (Luke 22:40)

…and He said to them, "Why are you sleeping? Get up and pray that you may not enter into temptation." (Luke 22:46)

All four of these scriptures took place after the last supper on Mount Olive the night before Jesus's crucifixion. Jesus went off to pray and talk to His Father, came back, and found His apostles sleeping when He asked them to watch with Him and pray. What did He tell them to do to avoid temptation? Pray! The Bible says this four times so we know it must be important. If this was the formula for the apostles to use, in Jesus's presence no less, do you think it is not the formula for us to use today when temptation comes? If we resist the devil, he will flee (see James 4:7–8). Here is an important observation: if Jesus expected His apostles to be tempted in His presence, how can we think we will never be tempted? We will, but we have God's promise that we can resist it. We will not be tempted beyond what we can bear, and He will provide a way out and rescue us. Be comforted by this thought today and be an overcomer for anything the devil may present to you. He will not let us be tempted beyond what we can bear, and He will provide a way out and rescue you.

> Father God, I thank You that You are the all-powerful God that can always rescue me from any situation. I know that You speak to me regularly, but the cares and daily activities of the world prevent me from hearing You. Help me to be more attentive to Your Word and spend more time listening so that I can learn to hear Your voice in all situations. I thank You, Father, in Jesus's name. Amen.

Nutrition Thought for the Day

There is no way to prevent anything from eventually being oxidized permanently but antioxidants can help to some extent. Whenever we have metabolism taking place (and this occurs continuously in every cell in our bodies), we have the possibility of oxygen reacting with another substance causing the creation of a free radical. A simple way to explain this would be with water. Water has the formula H_2O, which means it is a compound consisting of two hydrogen atoms and one oxygen atom. Each hydrogen has one electron in its outer orbit. Oxygen has room for two electrons in its outer orbit. Therefore the two available hydrogen electrons are shared with the oxygen atom. This makes a complete substance that we call water. In reactions, water disassociates. That means one hydrogen atom separates from the water and results in $H+1$, or it has one available hydrogen electron. The remaining substance is called a hydroxyl group which is $OH-1$. The hydroxyl group needs one electron to fill its outer orbit, the electron it lost when the hydrogen atom separated from it. This hydroxyl group is now called a free radical. It travels through the cell looking for a hydrogen to steal from another compound to make its outer orbit complete. Hence, free radical damage takes place.

WAYNE E. BILLON, PH.D., RDN, LDN

Day 125
You Will Receive Your Crown

Blessed is a man who perseveres under trial; for once he has been approved, he will receive the crown of life which *the Lord* has promised to those who love Him. (James 1:12)

This scripture can also have a spiritual and a physical meaning. When James wrote this, I am sure he was referring to trials that Christians were undergoing because of persecution from their fellow man and the devil. While the persecution you may be going through today is not the same, it still results in you being tormented by the world and the devil. Physically, you may be going through trials and persecutions because of your healthy lifestyle. In either case, this scripture still pertains to you. It was written for all of us. Persevere, and you will be blessed no matter what your trial may be; in due time you will receive the crown of life that is promised by our Lord in the Scriptures. It is promised for those who love Him, and that includes you. Even though you may not seem like you are blessed when you have a victory, no matter how small it may be, you are indeed blessed. Today count your blessings and recall how many times the Lord has helped you. Encourage yourself with your past accomplishments that you have made by His strength. Do not be discouraged. Be bold and courageous!

Father God, You have made so many promises to me in the Scriptures that it is completely overwhelming. I know there will be trials and temptations throughout my life, but I also know that no matter what I go through You will always be there to help me. I am not in this life alone. You have already blessed me with so many wonderful blessings, and I am thankful to You for them. I look forward to continue receiving Your blessings and to see more and more victories down the road for Your praise and glory. I thank You, Father, in Jesus's name. Amen.

Nutrition Thought for the Day.

Yesterday I gave a straightforward explanation of the formation of a hydroxyl radical from water. There are numerous types of free radicals that come from many other reactions besides the splitting of water into hydrogen and oxygen. Normal metabolism produces free radicals. One very strong oxidizing substance is hydrogen peroxide. You probably have put hydrogen peroxide on a cut at some point to kill bacteria without realizing how it worked. The chemical formula for hydrogen peroxide is H_2O_2. From the previous example, you saw that the outer orbit of hydrogen has one electron available to give up. The outer orbit of oxygen requires two electrons to be complete.

In the case of hydrogen peroxide, the compound is unstable because it is looking for two electrons to complete the outer orbit of the extra oxygen. This makes it a stronger oxidizing agent then the hydroxyl radical (OH-1). Another term you may see in articles is a reactive oxygen species (ROS). This term is given to any oxygen-containing molecule that is capable of being highly reactive. Examples are the two mentioned above, and a compound called a superoxide anion radical, nitric oxide radical, singlet oxygen, hypochlorite radical, and several compounds known as lipid peroxides.

Bottom line: We need antioxidants in our diet.

Day 126
Everyone Is Tempted

When the devil had finished every temptation, he left Him until an opportune time. (Luke 4:13)

Is this an exciting scripture? Everyone that walks the face of this earth is tempted by the devil. The scripture above is referring to Satan tempting Jesus right after Jesus received His water baptism and the Holy Spirit baptism. The devil then took Him out into the desert and tempted Him. Jesus did not fall for any of his temptations. His victory over every temptation was a victory for you and me and defeats the power of sin in our lives. Also, note that the scripture says he (Satan) left Him (Jesus) until an opportune time. As far as the devil was concerned, he was not finished tempting Jesus but he left Him until he could find a more opportune time. And what time might that be? He looks to see what our weakest point is. In your case, since you are on a healthy lifestyle regimen, it may be when you are hungry, and it would be an opportune time to tempt you to overeat. Or it may be when you are exhausted it would be an opportune time to convince you not to exercise. Jesus was tempted so how can we expect not to be tempted. Jesus defeated the devil every time He was tempted. I know you cannot say that about yourself, none of us can for we have all fallen. But, the good news is, because of what Jesus did, you have the victory! Thank You, Jesus, for defeating the devil for us. Use this knowledge to give you strength when temptations come your way. You are not being picked on more than anyone else; you are being picked on because you are God's creation and God's child. Hold your head high and walk tall because of that honor.

> Lord Jesus, You set the standard for me as my role model by defeating the devil every time he tempted You. Every one of Your victories is a victory for me. Every time You defeated the devil I reap the benefits. Thank You, Lord Jesus for humbling Yourself and coming to this earth to walk out a lifespan in the limitations of a human body. You did that for me! I receive what You did and I glorify You for Your great sacrifices. I know that I will be tempted and I know that if I fail, I will always have You as my advocate before my Father God. I thank You, Jesus, for what You did for me. Amen.

Nutrition Thought for the Day.

You put hydrogen peroxide on a cut because it is a potent oxidizing agent. It breaks the cell walls of bacteria, causing them to die. It is so strong that today there is a recommendation it not be used on cuts because it could also damage living tissue. Here is a kicker, the next time you pick up a bottle of hydrogen peroxide, look on the label and note that it is 2% hydrogen peroxide. If only 2% of the hydrogen peroxide solution can do that much damage to tissue, how much damage could 100% hydrogen peroxide do? Every time metabolism takes place in your body, hydrogen peroxide is produced. Sounds terrible, doesn't it? Do not be alarmed, this is a standard procedure and the antioxidants in your body neutralize hydrogen peroxide. It happens continuously in your body and there is nothing you can do about it except to make sure that you get ample antioxidants in your diet. These antioxidants help to neutralize free radicals.

Day 127
Jesus Was Tempted

For since He Himself was tempted in that which He has suffered, He is able to come to the aid of those who are tempted. (Hebrews 2:18)

Yesterday was about Jesus being tempted in the desert by Satan, and the scripture stated Satan left Him to come back at a more opportune time. Today's scripture also mentions Jesus being tempted, and it makes another point. Because Jesus was tempted in the same way you are tempted (different time, different place, different emphasis, same results—temptation to cause you not to follow God's Word) He, as a man, fully understands exactly what you have to go through. You are not an island standing alone in the middle of a violent sea being overwhelmed by waves of the enemy. Sometimes it may feel like that but if you look around, you will see standing on that island with you is the one and only Jesus. If you could see into the spiritual world, you would also see legions of angels surrounding your island. The Holy Spirit is moving over the island sending down grace and wisdom to you, and your Father God is looking down from above, waiting for His opportunity to bless you for all eternity. So, close your eyes, envision the description I just gave you, and try to remember that vision every time you feel like things are closing in on you. You are not alone; you are one of God's chosen!

Lord Jesus, You set me in the place I am for a reason. You have a call on my life, something that You want me to do. There are people I can reach with Your Word that pastors and churches may never get an opportunity to reach. There are a lot of hurting people in the world that I come in contact with each day. They do not have the ability (yet) to see the vision that I can now see with You, the angels, the Holy Spirit, and God the Father surrounding me with grace, love, and forgiveness. Thank You, Jesus for giving me that vision and help me to bring others that I meet every day into that vision with me. In Your name, Jesus, I pray. Amen.

Nutrition Thought for the Day.

Free radicals are produced by metabolism in the mitochondria (this is where a lot of energy is created in the cell and is known as the power pack of the cell). Free radicals are produced when inflammation occurs. Free radicals are also produced during exercise. Yes, exercise is included in this list. Exercise increases metabolism and also causes muscle damage. Thus it is going to produce some free radicals. But if the exercise is appropriate for your body makeup, metabolism, and diet, it will not be harmful but helpful. Free radicals that are produced from environmental factors include cigarette smoke, environmental pollutants, radiation, toxins that you may get in the environment (such as pesticides, herbicides, cleaning solutions, etc.), and results of the ozone level being too high. Thus, counteracting free radicals is very important, and I am sure now you will now pay closer attention to antioxidants.

Day 128
Jesus Was Tempted II

For we do not have a high priest who cannot sympathize with our weaknesses, but One who has been tempted in all things as *we are, yet* without sin. (Hebrews 4:15)

This scripture also emphasizes that Jesus, your intercessor, is also your high priest. You do not have a high priest that cannot sympathize with your weaknesses because He was also tempted in all things and in all areas that you are tempted. To defeat sin, He took all the sins of the world on His body on the cross. To defeat all sins, He had to be tempted in every possible way so He could defeat all forms of sin. He became sin for you and took your sins, all your sins, on Himself on the cross. That may sound strange but, if Jesus defeated all sins, then He had to face all forms of sin so that He could defeat them. You cannot defeat something you do not encounter.

But here is the difference, the last part of the scripture says, "yet without sin." This means that He faced all these temptations but He did not succumb to any of them. He was tempted in all ways, but without sinning. Thus, since He was a human when He walked the earth, He knows what it is like to be tempted as a human and can sympathize with your weaknesses when you fall into temptation and sin. No matter what you have done or how many times you have done it, Jesus understands and will forgive you. No, He does not like it, and He wants to see you walk away from all temptations victoriously, but when you do not, He is still there with you and forgives you. Walk with confidence today that you are a forgiven child of God that is completely understood by Jesus!

Thank You, Jesus, for taking my place on the cross and taking all of the sins I have ever committed and ever will commit with You to the cross. Thank You for allowing Yourself to be tempted in all ways that I am tempted and for defeating each and every one of those temptations. Your life, death, and resurrection have set me free from the bondage of sin and placed me in heavenly places with You. I know that You understand me when no one else does. I also know that You sympathize with me for all that I have to go through and You still love me. I thank You, Jesus, for Your incredible love. Amen.

Nutrition Thought for the Day.

A simple definition of an antioxidant is a compound that inhibits oxidation thus preventing the deterioration of cells in our body, foods in a refrigerator, or foods on our cabinet shelves. An antioxidant technically is not a substance, but it is any compound that is capable of donating electrons to neutralize a free radical. So it is not one particular substance but any substance that will accomplish this. Antioxidants come in several different forms. Some are more effective in water-soluble situations, and some in fat- soluble situations. There are even a few that are effective in both. Some antioxidants are enzymes that the body makes. Some vitamins are antioxidants (vitamin C and vitamin E), some are minerals that act as cofactors with enzymes such as selenium, iron, copper, zinc, and manganese. However, before trying to take in large doses of these vitamins and minerals, wait until I discuss them one at a time because excessive doses can be harmful.

Day 129
You Are an Overcomer

"I have been crucified with Christ; and it is no longer I who live, but Christ lives in me; and the *life* which I now live in the flesh I live by faith in the Son of God, who loved me and gave Himself up for me." (Galatians 2:20)

When you became a born-again Christian, Christ took up residence in you. Since He took your place on the cross and took all of your sins upon Himself, past and future, He is always with you to guide you and be your Lord. You can deny His authority at times and do things your way, but it does not chase Him away from you. If you receive His help, ask and depend on His guidance, then the life you live in your flesh (that is in your body), you live by faith that He is indeed with you. As you realize and receive all of this as truth, you accept it on faith and you acknowledge that, because of His love for you, He gave His life for you. It may take some meditation on this scripture, but once you get it down in your spirit, you will realize how remarkable this fact is. You can walk through your day today knowing that your God is walking with you and in you and there is nothing that can come your way that can separate you from Him.

Lord Jesus, I am so glad that I asked You to be my Savior and my Lord. Thank You, Jesus, for accepting me and dying for my sins. I do not have to walk around wondering what is going to happen to me in the next life. Instead, I can walk in confidence that my future is bright, literally very bright in heaven. I do not need to worry or have any concern whatsoever about my future with You or my walk on this earth. Thank You, Lord Jesus, for what You have done for me. Amen.

Nutrition Thought for the Day.

You may have heard it said that too much of anything could be harmful. This is undoubtedly true in nutrition. Even though a nutrient may be extremely important and necessary, too much of that nutrient may be equally dangerous and toxic. You need a balance of carbohydrate, protein, and fat but an excess of either one will cause weight gain and sometimes complications beyond weight gain. In the area of antioxidants, a trace amount of selenium is necessary for a healthy body but much more than a trace amount can be very toxic to the human body. Do not read one little fact about a vitamin or mineral and then start taking them indiscriminately.

Important! We tend to believe that if one recommended serving of a vitamin or mineral will do some good, then twice as much will do twice as much good, and three times as much will do three times as good, and so forth. **That Is Not True!** That type of thinking can cause people a lot of trouble. It has been my observation over the last forty years of being a registered dietitian that this is a common practice among people. It is also a fact that frequently deficiency symptoms of a vitamin or mineral are very similar to the toxicity symptoms of the same vitamin or mineral. Please remember that.

Day 130
God's Grace Is Sufficient

And He has said to me, "My grace is sufficient for you, for power is perfected in weakness. Most gladly, therefore, I will rather boast about my weaknesses, so that the power of Christ may dwell in me." (2 Corinthians 12:9)

This is Paul speaking in his second letter to the Corinthians, telling them what God revealed to him, "My grace is sufficient for you for power is perfected in weakness." The "My" mentioned here is God the Father. He tells you that His grace is sufficient for you. Remember that no matter how down or discouraged you may feel, or how tempted you may feel, God's grace is sufficient. If you trust in Him, He will see you through any temptation. His power is perfected in weakness which means that when you are weak in your flesh in regards to sin, then you rely on Jesus's strength because He defeated sin and has power over it. So through His Word, you can develop power over sin in your life by receiving what Jesus did for you. Paul says that he would rather boast about his weaknesses so that the power of Christ would dwell in him. If he had an area where he was weak, and he bragged about that weakness but admitted that in his own strength he could not overcome that weakness, then he was boasting in the power of Jesus. Walk through your day today boasting about the power of Jesus that is in you and has overcome the weaknesses that you once had. If those weaknesses are still there, continue to defeat them through God's Word.

Lord Jesus, thank You for Your power that is at work in me. When I am weak, I am really strong in You because of what You have done for me. I thank You, Jesus, for the strength, You give me and how You help me to realize each day, by the power of Your Holy Spirit, the power that I have through Your Word. I know with confidence that I can overcome every obstacle that comes my way today and that I can continue to be successful in my healthy lifestyle because of Your power that is at work in me. I thank You, Jesus, for Your work in me. Amen.

Nutrition Thought for the Day.

Another big class of antioxidants, besides those mentioned as vitamins and minerals, are those found naturally in foods, and there are thousands of them. The antioxidants in plants are called phytochemicals (phyto- means plant), but some phytochemicals have properties besides antioxidants. Plant phytochemicals that are antioxidants are grouped into several different categories. Some phytochemicals are alkaloids, anthocyanins, carotenoids, flavonoids, isoflavones, organosulfides, phenolic acids, phyterosterols, stylbenes, and xanthrophylls. Under most of these categories, there are several examples of phytochemicals, and this is by no means a complete list. Some have antioxidant activity, some act like hormones, some are antibacterial, and some seem to be anticancer. They are not yet considered to be essential (required) for human health, but many are important for optimal health. They are found in an extensive variety of fruits and vegetables and add impetus to why we should eat a variety of fruits and vegetables every day.

Day 131
Do Not Let Yourself Be Carried Away

But each one is tempted when he is carried away and enticed by his own lust.
(James 1:14)

People sin because they want to, it is fun for the flesh but painful for the spirit. If you continue to think about a sinful act, you will eventually want to participate in that act. What you do not think about you will not do. That is true in the spiritual but also true in the physical. If you keep thinking about the big piece of chocolate cake you will eventually go and eat that piece of chocolate cake. That would not be a sin, but the devil will use it to make you think of yourself as being defeated. If he can make you feel defeated in the physical, he can carry that over to the spiritual. You have to learn to nip all temptation in the bud and not give it a place in your mind. You can do this. When temptation comes, turn your thoughts to something in God's Word and rebuke the temptation. Go and do something wholesome with your hands, exercise, call and talk to a friend, do anything to take your mind off your thoughts. Get an accountability partner to help you. Get up, do something positive, and remember that Jesus is always with you.

> Lord Jesus, thank You that You are always with me and always at work in me. By the power of Your Holy Spirit give me ideas of things I can do when temptation comes. I know I should pray and talk to You, but I need something to do in my idle time that is wholesome. I look to You for advice and guidance. I do not want to give in to my worldly desires, I resolve to replace them with godly ideas, and I look to You for guidance. In Your name, I pray. Amen.

Nutrition Thought for the Day.

Some examples of these phytochemicals that you may have heard of are as follows: 1) isoflavones are found in soy products and are *claimed* to help ease the symptoms of estrogen deficiency; additional claims are concerned with preventing some cancers and cardiovascular disease. *Not all the research agrees with the claims.* Having soy products in your diet is probably a good thing but taking in excessive isoflavone supplements is probably not a good idea.

Allicin is found in onions and *is claimed* to be antibacterial and to help with preventing atherosclerosis. It could also decrease blood clotting.

Anthocyanins are found in blueberries and other fruits that are blue, purple, or red. They are associated with reducing the risk of cancer, urinary tract infections, inflammation and could result in reducing heart disease, and promote healthy aging. Research still needs to confirm the full effects of anthocyanins in a healthy diet.

An example of stylbenes that you may have heard of is resveratrol. This is found in grape skins, red wine, peanuts, blueberries, and cranberries among others. It has been associated with preventing heart disease and may lower high blood pressure. The research is still out with this compound also. Some other antioxidants we will talk about associated with specific vitamins and minerals include the carotenoids. There are entirely too many to go into detail here, but you can find numerous websites that can give you more information.

Day 132
His Power Is within Us

Now to Him who is able to do far more abundantly beyond all that we ask or think, according to the power that works within us. (Ephesians 3:20)

Read this scripture, meditate on it for a few minutes, and let its meaning sink into your spirit. Paul says in this scripture, alluding to Him (Him being God the Father) as one who was able to do far more abundantly beyond what any of us can ask or even think according to the power that works within us. According to what? According to the power that works within us. All the power of Jesus Christ is at work within you and is available to you once you strengthen your faith and learn how to use it. This is an extremely powerful scripture and deserves serious meditation. This should be a tremendous encouragement to you and should strengthen you. I am sure that most of us are not at the point we can fully understand and put this scripture into practice but we need to study it, memorize it, believe it, and in time we can see the scripture at work within us. Do not leave room for fear or doubt to enter your mind. Remember that there is a power at work within you that is greater than any power in the world. I know this is awesome and amazing, but it is the power of our God!

Lord Jesus, Your Scriptures never cease to amaze me. Your power is at work within me; it is available to me to use for Your glory. Thank You for that power and revealing to me that it is beyond what I can imagine or even ask. There is nothing too hard for You. There is nothing that will test Your strength or ability. You have passed that on to me, and no, I do not deserve it. I am aware of that, but it is not given to me based on what I deserve, but based on what You have done for me. I thank You, Jesus, for Your power that You have given me. Amen.

Nutrition Thought for the Day.

Besides the antioxidants and phytochemicals, there is another large set of supplements that have many claims that are not yet founded by solid research. Ginseng and ginkgo are a couple of examples. I mentioned these two because they have one thing in common that I am going to give to you as an example of how you can get in trouble by just taking a bunch of supplements without thoroughly researching them. For instance, suppose heart disease runs in your family, and you want to prevent this from happening to you. Most doctors will recommend that you take a baby aspirin a day to prevent blood clots. Another popular supplement is omega-3 fish oil. Another is garlic with claims that it may help prevent cardiovascular disease. So to be proactive, you begin to take each of them without researching them. On most of the labels of these supplements, if not all, you will not find a statement that one of the side effects of each of these compounds is reducing blood clotting. Ginseng and ginkgo fall into this category also. If you take some of each of these, you could very well cause yourself a more severe problem of internal bleeding without any warning signs. Too many of these types of supplements, or doses too large of just a few of them, could cause spontaneous bleeding. Please research any supplements that you take and consult with a registered dietitian or physician before doing so.

Day 133
Put on the Full Armor of God

Put on the full armor of God, so that you will be able to stand firm against the schemes of the devil. (Ephesians 6:11)

In addition to a remarkable unmeasurable power that is within you, there are additional weapons in which to use in your fight against the devil. Ephesians 6:11 tells you to put on the full armor of God. You should go to Ephesians 6, read the entire chapter, and look at all the armor that is available for you. Much of the armor you already have on you but may not even realize it. With the armor God gives us we can not only just stand, but we can stand firm against the schemes of the devil. We can still be overcome but only if we put down our armor and we do not utilize the power that is within us and succumbs to temptation. But remember that nothing can make you succumb to temptation; you succumb because you want to. You have to be strong and show resolve and stand up against all the attacks of the enemy. You are fully equipped to do so. These attacks include any spiritual attacks that he may come at you with, but also any physical attacks to try to get you off track with your healthy lifestyle. Do not listen to the temptations. Instead, listen to the still small voice within you and be victorious!

Father God, You have given me so many weapons to use to overcome the attacks of the enemy that it is incredible. Only through the power of Your Holy Spirit will I be able to remember all the things I need to win the attacks when the enemy comes. Thank You for the armor that You have given me to clothe myself with at all times. And thank You for the immeasurable power that You have put into me. I know that I will be victorious with Your help in not only my new healthy lifestyle but also in my spiritual life and everything else that I try to accomplish. In the name of Jesus, I pray. Amen.

Nutrition Thought for the Day.

One critical reminder is the need for a balanced diet. No one food on the face of the earth is the perfect food and will provide us with all of the vitamins, minerals, protein, carbohydrate, fats, water, and phytochemicals that we need for a healthy existence. Any time you see a diet plan that eliminates one of the food groups, it should throw up a red flag and tell you not to even think about that diet plan. Some commercials that you see on TV and other places make it sound like the product they are advertising will do everything from causing you to lose weight, lower cholesterol, gain muscle, decrease aging—you get it, anything that claims to do all of that is not worth even considering. Balance is the key.

Day 134
We Can Overwhelmingly Conquer

But in all these things we overwhelmingly conquer through Him who loved us. (Romans 8:37)

Romans 8:35 asks, "Who will separate us from the love of Christ? Will tribulation, or persecution, or famine, or nakedness, or peril, or sword?" In the above scripture, Paul answers his own question. He says that all the things mentioned in verse thirty-five we can overwhelmingly conquer through Him who loved us. Three things to note here: 1) you can overwhelmingly conquer; 2) you conquer through what Jesus Christ did for you, and 3) He loves you. You do not have to fear any of the things listed in Romans 8:35 nor any other type of calamity not listed. You can overwhelmingly conquer whatever comes your way because of the love of Jesus. Walk in His love today with another scripture to add to your memory list concerning who you are in Christ. Be bold and courageous! You are an overwhelming conqueror!

Father God, You have given me another scripture that tells of Your power and love for me. I know that nothing can separate You from me and I choose to be the conqueror today that You called me to be. I know that nothing that comes up against me, whether it is a spiritual attack on my spiritual life or a physical attack on my healthy lifestyle, it cannot cause me to be distracted from my goal. I know this is true because of Your love and the power that You have given me. I thank You, Father, in the name of Jesus. Amen.

Nutrition Thought for the Day.

Vitamins are divided into two major groups and can be classified three different ways. There are organic vitamins, natural vitamins, and synthetic vitamins. Organic vitamins are grown with nothing but organic seeds in organic soil, organic fertilizers, and organic pesticides/herbicides. This means that everything was natural with no chemicals added. The vitamins extracted from these plants are called organic vitamins. The USDA definition of organic as quoted directly from their website is as follows: "Organic food is produced using sustainable agricultural production practices. Not permitted are most conventional pesticides; fertilizers made with synthetic ingredients, or sewage sludge; bioengineering; or ionizing radiation. Organic meat, poultry eggs, and dairy products come only from animals that are given absolutely no antibiotics or growth hormones."

Day 135
Greater Is He That Is in Us

You are from God, little children, and have overcome them; because greater is He who is in you than he who is in the world. (1 John 4:4)

1 John 4:1 says, "Beloved, do not believe every spirit, but test the spirits to see whether they are from God because many false prophets have gone out into the world." In 1 John 4:4 it says that we have overcome them. The "them" that is spoken of here is the false prophets that John was referring to in 1 John 4:1. And yes, you are a child of God since you have received Jesus Christ as your Savior and Lord. He is in you, and He is greater than the false prophets who are in the world. If you diligently seek God with all your heart, continue to meditate on His Word, and fellowship with like-minded believers, you will be able to hear the Holy Spirit when He speaks to you, and this will give you a much greater ability to test the spirits of the world. You are a child of God. Greater is He who is in you than he who is in the world! Walk with confidence again today knowing who you are in Christ.

Thank You, Lord Jesus, that You are greater than all the false prophets combined that are in the world. And the Scriptures tell me the power You have over false prophets is also in me. I ask for the Holy Spirit to daily provide me with wisdom and discernment that I will be able to test and uncover the false prophets that try to lead me astray spiritually and physically. I know that I have that power because of Your Word and I ask that Your Holy Spirit continue to reveal it to me as I learn more about who I am in Christ. Thank You, Jesus, for revealing this to me. Amen.

Nutrition Thought for the Day.
Natural vitamins are derived from plants that have been fertilized with natural fertilizers (man-made fertilizers) and pesticides. Synthetic vitamins are synthesized (man-made) in a lab. So which are best? If you are comparing them as to which are the most efficient, there is virtually no difference. If you are comparing them as to cost, synthetic is the cheapest, natural is next, and organic is the most expensive. As to which is the safest, organic may have a slight edge but maybe not. Here are the augments: since organic has safer pesticides reportedly, there should be less of a chance of contaminants. However, if synthetic vitamins are made according to the law, they are prepared in environments that prevent contaminants. In practice, synthetic is usually recommended because they are cheaper and are just as effective. I use synthetic.

Day 136
Enter His Courts with Praise

Enter His gates with thanksgiving *and* His courts with praise. Give thanks to Him, bless His name. (Psalm 100:4)

We should each have days that we put everything aside and do nothing but praise our God for all that He has done for us and will do for us. Today's devotion is dedicated to that. Psalm 100:4 says to enter His gates with thanksgiving and to enter His courts with praise. Give thanks to Him, and bless His name. Reflection is an excellent thing when we can reflect back on the good things that we have seen in our lives. Every good thing comes from above. Think back to all the things God has done for you in the past and just spend a few minutes, alone with Him if possible, and give Him praise and thanksgiving. He alone is worthy of praise, honor, and glory. Glorify His name today in everything that you do. Each day we spend on this earth should be expended for the glory of our God, but many times we go through the day without even thinking about praising Him. Let today be a day spent praising His name.

Father God, Lord Jesus, and Holy Spirit, I want this day to be a day for praising You. I dedicate everything I do this day to Your praise and glory. I glorify Your name. All praise, honor, and glory be to my God. I thank You for all the blessings that You have granted to me through the years. I thank You, Lord Jesus, most of all for dying on the cross for me and granting me eternal salvation. May every day I spend on this earth be for Your glory, but I particularly want to give praise, honor, and glory to You this day. I declare this in Your name Jesus. Amen.

Nutrition Thought for the Day.

The term natural was mentioned when I talked about labels. For your information the term natural is currently not defined by the FDA or the USDA. From a food science perspective, it is difficult to define a food product that is natural because the food has probably been processed and is no longer the product of the earth. That said, the FDA has not developed a definition for the use of the term natural or its derivatives. However, the agency has not objected to the use of the term if the food does not contain added color, artificial flavors, or synthetic substances."

WAYNE E. BILLON, PH.D., RDN, LDN

Day 137
Know God's Power in You

That the God of our Lord Jesus Christ, the Father of glory, may give to you a spirit of wisdom and of revelation in the knowledge of Him. *I pray that* the eyes your heart may be enlightened, so that you will know what the hope of His calling, what are the riches of the glory of His inheritance in the saints, and what is the surpassing greatness of His power toward us who believe. *These are* in accordance with the working of the strength of His might. (Ephesians 1:17–19)

This is a long scripture, but it is an excellent prayer that Paul wrote to the Ephesians. He told them that he prayed this for them without ceasing (Ephesians 1:16). Read it slowly and break down the parts of the prayer and pray it for yourself on a regular basis. Ask for the spirit of wisdom and of revelation in the knowledge of Him and that the eyes of your heart may be enlightened so that you will know the hope of His calling and that you may also see the riches of the glory of His inheritance. The next to last verse is particularly good—that you may know the surpassing greatness of His power toward you who believe in Him. There is so much in these verses to get down into your spirit. This is huge in helping you understand who you are in Christ. Be encouraged today knowing that you have an incredible inheritance and power greater than you can imagine available.

Lord Jesus, I pray Ephesians 1:17–19 as a prayer for myself and I thank You for the inheritance I have waiting for me and the surpassing greatness of Your power for me. I also look forward to the spirit of wisdom and revelation to help me know You better. I know that I am more than a conqueror and a world overcomer. I want to become stronger and stronger with each passing day against all temptations that come against me, whether they are spiritual temptations or physical temptations trying to get me to turn away from my healthy lifestyle program or You. I know I can do that because of Your great power that is available to me. In Jesus's name, I pray. Amen.

Nutrition Thought for the Day.

Vitamins are divided into two major groups, water-soluble and fat-soluble. The reasons for divisions are obvious, the water-soluble vitamins are soluble in water and not in fat. The fat-soluble vitamins are not soluble in water but are soluble in fat (oil). Many of the water-soluble vitamins have two names or two methods of nomenclature. Some can be called by a letter (i.e., vitamin C), a letter with a number (i.e. B1, also called thiamin), or by a name (i.e., niacin, also called vitamin B2). The water-soluble vitamins are B1 (thiamin), B2 (riboflavin), B3 (niacin), B6 (pyridoxine), B12 (cyanocobalamin), biotin, folic acid, and pantothenic acid. These are grouped together and commonly called the B vitamins. Another water-soluble vitamin outside of this group is vitamin C. The fat-soluble vitamins are A, D, E, and K.

Day 138
By Grace You Have Been Saved

But God, being rich in mercy, because of His great love with which He loved us, even when we were dead in our transgressions, made us alive together with Christ (by grace you have been saved), and raised us up with Him, and seated us with Him in the heavenly *places* in Christ Jesus. (Ephesians 2:4–6)

Paul once again speaks of God's mercy and great love for us and points out that even when we were lost and dead in sin, God made us alive again with the new birth. While we are still walking on this earth, we are raised up with our Savior and seated with Him in heavenly places. This planet God has created has a lot of beautiful sights but it is not our home, we are only passing through. God has something even more fabulous for us. Rejoice in this fact, but the sobering truth is that there are so many lost souls that still do not realize this. I am sure there are many around you in your workplace, your circle of friends, perhaps your family, and others that may be working with you on a healthy lifestyle regimen. Praise God for your inheritance this day but also ask Him for wisdom to be able to witness to the lost and see more people be able to share this inheritance with you.

Father God, I thank You for Your mercy and grace and for saving me. I also thank You for my inheritance that is waiting for me in Your Kingdom in heaven, but my heart is heavy for those that cannot share this inheritance with me since they do not know You. I pray for them now (you can mention names here) and ask for Your Holy Spirit to give me wisdom and direction to lead others into Your Kingdom. I pray in the name of Jesus. Amen.

Nutrition Thought for the Day.

There is a lot of controversies today about taking vitamins on a daily basis or not taking vitamins at all. Many myths about vitamins exist, and there still are many things we do not know. First, I will talk about some of the controversies and some of the things we do not know. One of the first questions that is frequently asked is, "should I take a multivitamin daily?" The answer is simple: if you need one, yes; if you do not need one, no. Sounds like a cop out and in a way it is. Preferably we should get all of our vitamins and minerals from the foods we eat. A vitamin supplement, whether it is a multivitamin or an individual vitamin, should never be a substitute for food. I have heard people say, "I did not get in all the fruits and vegetables today that I should be eating so I will just take a vitamin tablet in his place." It just does not work that way.

Day 139
We Can Control Our Thoughts

We are destroying speculations and every lofty thing raised up against the knowledge of God, and *we are* taking every thought captive to the obedience of Christ. (2 Corinthians 10:5)

Paul tells us that we can destroy speculations and every lofty thing that rises up against the knowledge of our God. He also says that we can take every thought captive to the obedience of Christ. Does this mean that this will be easy? No, of course not, it will not be easy, but it is certainly doable. Remember God will never call us to do something that He does not equip us to do. He will not ask us to do the impossible. If there is a command in God's Word that He gives us, then it is because it is possible for us to complete that command. If we try to do everything in our flesh we will fail, but He expects us to be victorious in His power by calling on Him in our times of trouble and every temptation. As long as we put Him first and seek His guidance in everything we do, He will provide us with the wisdom and direction to be successful in all our undertakings. It is when we get cocky and think that we can accomplish anything and everything on our own wisdom and strength that we end up in a setback or even failure.

Thank You, Father God, that I have the power, through Your Word, to take every thought captive and make it obedient to Christ. First of all, I know to do that I must know what Your Word says so that I can put it into practice. By knowing Your Word, when trials and temptations come, I will know what scriptures I can use to speak directly to the trials and temptations. Trials and temptations will have to bow to Your name when I speak to them in faith. You have given me the faith to accomplish that, and I ask You for the wisdom to remember what Your Word says about each situation that faces me. I thank You again for Your love and grace in Jesus's name. Amen.

Nutrition Thought for the Day.

There are those who advocate that everyone should take a multivitamin every day because we overeat processed foods and the processing destroys some vitamins. This is partially true in that processing food does destroy many of the vitamins. Processed grains have vitamins added back, and that should help to some degree with the losses but does not cover all of the vitamin/mineral losses in processing. If we all ate unprocessed foods, that is we obtained fruits and vegetables fresh and prepared meals from scratch, we would get a lot more vitamins and minerals than eating processed food.

While that sounds really good and would be the best thing, but in our fast-paced world today it is just not practical because too many people work and do not have the time to shop fresh and prepare fresh food each day. So, are vitamin/mineral tablets the answer? It still depends. If you are eating a well-balanced diet and getting in five servings of fruits and vegetables a day, having a source of dairy products, whole grains, and high- quality protein daily, your need for vitamin/mineral supplements would be at an absolute minimum if not zero.

Day 140
Our Battle Is Not against Flesh and Blood

For our struggle is not against flesh and blood, but against the rulers, against the powers, against the world forces of this darkness, against the spiritual *forces* of wickedness in the heavenly *places*. (Ephesians 6:12)

Sometimes your trials and tribulations come in the form of one of your peers or family members giving you a hard time about your unsuccessful lifestyle or inability to lose/gain weight. According to today's scripture, your battle is not against other people, that is, not against flesh and blood. If people are bullying you, whether knowingly or without realizing it, their actions are the result of demonic influence. This is not me talking; this is what today's scripture says. That does not mean that the people who are bullying you are evil but they are just not in tune with God's Word and are giving into a tormenting spirit. They would not even realize what is happening. Not to worry! These are the very spirits that you have authority over, and you can control your thought life against their temptations no matter what form they use to attack you. Just remember where your trials come from and remember where your strength comes from and you will be okay. Also, examine your own actions because you could become a bully without realizing it. None of us are immune to outside influence. Maintain your focus and consider how you are treating those around you today.

I am not afraid of any of the attacks of the enemy, and I know that he may use some of my loved ones to say harmful things to me or against me inadvertently. He may even try to get me to say harmful things against them. That is not a time for me to get angry with them (or myself) and to create an argument because that is exactly what the enemy wants me to do. It is a time for me to show them love and understanding and explain to them why I will be successful in everything that I do, and that is because of God's Word. I must remember not to do this in an obnoxious, argumentative way but to show love and compassion. I thank You, Father that You will give me the understanding and wisdom to be able to accomplish this. I pray in Jesus's name. Amen.

Nutrition Thought for the Day.

The makeup of your diet can affect vitamin/mineral absorption. While we advocate a high-fiber diet as being healthy (and it is), it does have some cautions in that the high-fiber tends to bind with several different minerals rendering them non-absorbable. If you were to review a list of vegetables that indicated how much of the various minerals they contain per serving, it does not mean you will absorb all of those minerals. Certain compounds in fiber affect mineral absorption, in some cases a significant effect. Fiber supplements, like Metamucil, have a warning on the label suggesting you not take a vitamin/mineral supplement within an hour of taking the Metamucil because of the effect of fiber on some nutrients. You should not take in less fiber but make sure you are taking in adequate minerals (from foods) to counteract what may be lost from the fiber.

Day 141
Principalities and Powers Have Been Destroyed

When He had disarmed the rulers and authorities, He made a public display of them, having triumphed over them through Him. (Colossians 2:15)

Good news!! Jesus has already defeated the powers and principalities of the air. When God defeated the powers and principalities in the air, the rulers of the darkness of this world, He then totally disarmed them and made a public display of them showing that He triumphed over them through Jesus's life, death, and resurrection. They have been defeated, and they have no power or authority over you unless you give them power and authority. The only authority they can claim is the authority that you give to them. When temptations or even just distractions come, know that you have authority over those distractions and that you can take every thought captive and make it obedient to Christ. This may not be easy, but if the Word says you have authority over the powers and authorities (demons) in the heavens, then you have that authority. This is part of who you are in Christ. Take your authority and do not be discouraged!

Thank You, Father God, for what You did through Your Son in conquering the powers and principalities that ruled over this world in darkness. I do not have to contend with them unless I choose to give them a place in my life. They have been defeated, and You have given the power and authority over them to me. I thank You again for that, and I look forward to the victories that lie ahead. In Jesus's name, I pray. Amen.

Nutrition Thought for the Day.
Other diet nutrient interactions take place in addition to those with fiber. An example would be drinking excessive amounts of tea daily because tea is high in a compound called tannin that can bind with iron and render some iron unavailable. Taking mineral supplements together could also be a problem. Too much iron could prevent the absorption of copper and vice versa. Too much calcium can prevent the absorption of phosphorus and vice versa. Too much calcium could prevent the absorption of magnesium and vice versa. This is not all of the possible diet-nutrient interactions that could take place; there are far too many to discuss on this platform. You really should consult a registered dietitian to make sure your diet is adequate in all nutrients, particularly if you are on a low-calorie diet and/or if you are taking supplements.

Day 142
Do Not Make Your Lifestyle Program Your Idol

Therefore concerning the eating of things sacrificed to idols, we know that there is no such thing as an idol in the world, and that there is no God but one. However not all men have this knowledge; but some, being accustomed to the idol until now, eat *food* as if it were sacrificed to an idol; and their conscience being weak is defiled. (1 Corinthians 8:4, 7)

It was intended by Paul for these scriptures to be used for those that thought it was evil to sacrifice food to idols and then eat that food. But this scripture also points out that there is no such thing as an idol in the world for there is only one God, and the only worship you should be giving is to your one and only God. Sometimes we can want something so bad, even something that is good for us like healthy weight loss, that we unconsciously begin to idolize our goal. We can do this in our work, we can do this in our, play as in sports, and we can idolize money. You can even idolize your healthy lifestyle as an idealistic goal and want it so bad that it becomes your idol. Worship the Lord your God only, and everything else will fall into place. Continue with your new lifestyle regimen as an important goal in your life for it is that, but do not idolize it.

I have only one item of worship, and that is my God. The Trinity, three distinct persons, but they make up one God, and that is all that I worship. If I ever begin to look at my lifestyle regimen as an idol, I ask for Your Holy Spirit to make me immediately aware that I am off course. I do not ever want to idolize anything other than my God. My healthy lifestyle is important, and I will succeed with it, but it is because I honor my God and not my goal. I confess this in the name of Jesus. Amen.

Nutrition Thought for the Day.

Other factors to consider that may interfere with vitamin/mineral absorption include any ongoing disease states. For example, if you have osteoporosis and need high doses of calcium each day, it may not be practical to take in as much dairy products as you would need to meet your calcium requirement. People with osteoporosis or osteopenia would benefit from a calcium supplement. Some people have lactose intolerance and cannot tolerate dairy products. They may also benefit from a calcium supplement but Ca found in food naturally is better than supplements. Also, both of these groups of people would benefit from vitamin D supplementation. Vitamin D is not found in many foods naturally. The primary source of vitamin D is found in dairy products and, if you cannot take in dairy products, you would probably need a vitamin D supplement. Vitamin D is also synthesized in the skin in the presence of sunlight. Not everyone can tolerate sunlight and during the winter, because of the earth's rotation, the sun is too far away to produce very much vitamin D in our skin. People not exposed to the sun may benefit from vitamin supplementation.

WAYNE E. BILLON, PH.D., RDN, LDN

Day 143
Stay on the Path of Life

He is *on* the path of life who heeds instruction, but he who ignores reproof goes astray. (Proverbs 10:17)

This proverb is another key to be successful in your healthy lifestyle program and provides direction to receive God's help continually. Well, this scripture may give you a bit of encouragement to do that. If you follow God's Word and keep His instructions close to your heart, then you will be on the path of life and on your way to success. If you ignore God's Word, you will not hear from God as you should, and you could end up going astray. This has been mentioned several times in several different ways so far, and this is just another way of encouraging you to stay in God's Word.

Do not be discouraged, you are on the path of life, and all you have to do is to decide to stay there. Unfortunately, all of us have to be reminded of this on a regular basis. As you very well know, in our routine daily walk, life happens, and sometimes we can be quickly derailed. Sometimes just looking at the six o'clock news can ruin my day and I have to get alone with my God and sort things out. Whenever you are derailed (led off or knocked off the path of life), do not allow the distraction to get a hold of you. As soon as possible you should have quiet time and read God's Word. As long as you stay in God's Word and heed His instruction, you will be okay.

Thank You, Father, for leading me to the path of life through Your Word. It is my intention and desire to stay on the path of life and to follow Your Word in everything that I do. I know that if I take heed to your instructions, I will be successful not only in completing a healthy lifestyle program, but with everything I do during my walk on the face of this earth. I thank You again for your mercy, grace, and love. I choose this day to glorify Your name. I confess this in the name of Jesus. Amen.

Nutrition Thought for the Day.

Some medications can change our vitamin/mineral requirement. If you have reflux disease and take one of the drugs that inhibit acid production in the stomach, you are also inhibiting calcium absorption, magnesium absorption, iron absorption, and vitamin B12 absorption. Someone that takes this type of medication probably needs to take supplements of each of these. Some people take diuretics that cause a loss of fluid through the kidneys to help lower blood pressure or to help keep the kidneys functioning properly. Diuretics also can cause loss of certain electrolytes like potassium and sodium. In some cases, potassium should be taken as a supplement with these diuretics. If you take a diuretic, do not start taking potassium but talk to your doctor first. Some diuretics cause you to retain potassium in which case you would be getting too much if you took a supplement. Also, part of the reason for taking the diuretic may be to lower potassium in the blood.

Day 144
Watch out for Pride

When pride comes, then comes dishonor, but with the humble is wisdom. (Proverbs 11:2)

You should always keep a watchful eye out for pride. If you start to do very well on your healthy lifestyle regimen, you could end up being prideful about your accomplishments. The Scriptures say pride comes before a fall (Proverbs 16:18). Pride can creep into your daily life without you even realizing it. The devil is very subtle with his tactics. He will not try to get you to take giant steps into darkness but will lead you to what seems to be harmless baby steps. Before you know it, you will be far from the path of righteousness. Some people see humility, the opposite of pride, as a sign of weakness. The truth is, humility is a sign of strength. It takes a strong person to admit that they were wrong or to keep from bragging about something that they accomplished that was very well done. Be alert and keep an eye out for pride. Do not let it have a foothold in your life. If every time you make an accomplishment you get in the habit of thanking Jesus immediately, that habit will grow on you and will help you to avoid pride.

Lord Jesus, I do not want to be a prideful person. Instead, I want to be known as a person with great humility but I know that all the good things I accomplish are not completed by my own strength but by the strength of You in me. Help me to remember that I owe all to You. I know that one day I will be very proud of the success I have made with the healthy lifestyle program I am following, and there will be great temptation to let everyone know how great I did. There is nothing wrong with me receiving accolades for my accomplishments but they must be received with the glory reflected to You. I want to give You all the glory for everything I accomplish. In Your name, Jesus, I pray. Amen.

Nutrition Thought for the Day.

Some people may not be taking prescribed diuretics but could be taking over the counter diuretics. Once overweight people find that diuretics cause water loss from your body, and that causes weight loss, some start taking over the counter diuretics. There are all sorts of teas that can be bought over the counter in health food stores that work as diuretics. There are also pills that you can buy, many of which are high in caffeine. Caffeine is a diuretic, but it does other things in your body too. An excessive caffeine intake can affect glucose levels, blood pressure, and heart rate and rhythm. If you take any such supplements over-the-counter to help you to lose weight, you need to thoroughly research them and talk to your doctor about them before you add them to your diet/exercise routine. Diuretics can cause electrolyte imbalances that can lead to heart problems. They can also cause dehydration. It would be good for you to talk to a registered dietitian about any supplements that you take.

Day 145
Watch out for a Crushed Spirit

The LORD is near to the brokenhearted and saves those who are crushed in spirit. (Psalm 34:18)

All of us will have days when we feel like we have nothing to be prideful about, nothing to brag about. Maybe you have a really bad day at work, with your friends, or with your family. Maybe instead of losing weight, you have gained a few pounds, or if you are trying to gain weight, you lost a pound. This may happen from time to time, but it is not the end of the world. It is a bump in the road maybe but not a sinkhole that you fall into and cannot get out. Just pick up where you left off and continue with your efforts, whether that is with work, friends, family, or your healthy lifestyle program. Today's scripture will help you to be encouraged. Psalm 34:18 says, "The Lord is near to the brokenhearted and saves those who are crushed in spirit." No matter how down you may get, your Lord is right there with you. I know, it may not feel like He is there with you, but remember that He suffered every type of persecution and temptation that you have or will ever experience, and He overcame all of them for you. Call on Him and do not get discouraged. Tomorrow is another day. Put today behind you and look for a victorious day tomorrow.

Thank You, Jesus that You are always with those that are crushed in spirit and thank You that the brokenhearted can always turn to You for consolation. You do not want to see me suffer or be in pain of any kind, and I know that You are reaching out to all those in need. Come Lord Jesus and bring me encouragement from Your Word by the power of Your Holy Spirit. In Your name, Jesus, I pray. Amen.

Nutrition Thought for the Day.
You probably have heard people say you should take B vitamins to give you energy. Most of the myths and controversies about vitamins/minerals have some truth, but not everything about them is true. The B vitamins are all needed to produce energy in your body—that is true. But, if you are getting the recommended amount of B vitamins, taking in additional B vitamins will not give you more energy. This is probably one of the places where we make the biggest mistake. We think that if a little bit helps with something if we double the amount we take, it will help twice as much. That is absolutely not true and may indeed cause harm and we are taking in a balanced diet, we should be getting adequate B vitamins to meet the needs of our bodies. I will discuss each vitamin and mineral and give you information about good sources of each.

Day 146
Joy Comes in the Morning

In this you greatly rejoice, even though now for a little while, if necessary, you have been distressed by various trials. (1 Peter 1:6)

If you have been stressed out for any reason, as it says in 1 Peter 1:16, it will be for just a little while. No matter what trials and tribulations or stresses you are going through, they are all only temporary. Your entire life on this earth is only temporary. One day you will be with Jesus where there will be no pain, no suffering, no trials, and no tribulation. I know that when you are going through a trial, it sometimes does not seem like it is temporary but seems like it is taking forever to get through it. Do not be discouraged! You will get through it. There is another side to the trial, and when you get there, you will be better off and stronger in your faith. Always turn to your God, seek His help, and do not give up. I went through Hades serving my country in Vietnam. I was not saved at that time, but even without being saved and knowing all that God had for me, I made it through by continually reminding myself that what I was going through was only temporary. There would be a day when I would be able to return to the real world. The real world you have to look forward to is much better than what I was looking forward to; yours is heaven with Jesus. Keep your eyes on Him and off your problem, and you will make it.

I know that trials and tribulations are temporary even though while I am going through them they seem very, very long. I know that my God will see me through every trial that I encounter and I know that He loves me and will never leave me. I choose to be content in everything that I do and I choose not to complain or be bitter but to look to my God for I know my help comes from Him and Him alone. I confess this in the name of Jesus. Amen.

Nutrition Thought for the Day.

Continuing with foods that can cause a diuretic effect, regular tea that you drink with your meals (as with sweet tea in the south) or green tea also contain caffeine unless they are decaffeinated. Coffee contains caffeine. Many of the diet sodas contain caffeine, particularly most of the dark sodas like Coke and Pepsi unless they are caffeine free. Some root beers do, and some do not contain caffeine; another reason for you to read the label. The clear colas like Sprite and 7-Up do not contain caffeine, but regular Mountain Dew is high in caffeine. Energy drinks usually contain caffeine, and some have very large doses.

Other caffeine-containing foods include chocolate and cocoa. If you drink a cup of coffee or two in the morning, have tea with meals, have a diet cola that is not caffeine free, eat a piece of chocolate, and have an energy drink to get you through the afternoon, you could be ingesting a very large dose of caffeine. Under these conditions you may be losing more fluid then you should because of the diuretic effect and anything that causes you to urinate more is also going to cause you to lose more of the water-soluble vitamins, some minerals, and electrolytes.

WAYNE E. BILLON, PH.D., RDN, LDN

Day 147
Joy Comes in the Morning II

Weeping may last for the night, but a shout of joy *comes* in the morning. (Psalm 30:5b)

For your continued encouragement, know that whatever you are going through today or whatever you went through yesterday, it is once again, yes, only temporary. Today's scripture tells us that while weeping may last for the night (the night in some cases may be longer than what we usually consider one night period of darkness), a shout of joy comes in the morning. After your period of distress, however long that may be, there will come a time of joy as long as you keep your eyes on Jesus. Know where your help comes from and do not ever give up on God's promises. Know that He is with you in your darkest times as well as in your brightest times. There is no room for discouragement if you keep your mind filled with His Word. He loves you the same on your darkest day as He does on your brightest day. I know this is easier said than done but you can do it. Do not give up do not be discouraged!

> Lord Jesus, I know that You have great plans for me in this life and the next. I know that trials, tribulations, and various forms of discouragement will come my way as long as I am on the face of this earth but I know they are only temporary. After my trials are over, there will be great joy and celebration, and it will all be because of Your love and grace. I know I can endure and I resolve this day to continue striving to glorify Your name and be Your faithful servant. In Your name, Jesus, I pray. Amen.

Nutrition Thought for the Day.

Another major diuretic that some people consume on a regular basis is alcohol. If you ever had just one beer, you know that it causes you to go to the bathroom more often. Someone that drinks alcohol on a regular basis could be at risk for a deficiency of several vitamins and minerals. Alcoholics are at great risk for some vitamin and mineral deficiencies. Alcohol is also a source of calories providing seven calories per gram of alcohol (100% alcohol which is 200 proof). If you are trying to lose weight and you are taking in alcohol on a regular basis, you probably will not be successful. Mixing alcohol with caffeine drinks and/or energy drinks is very dangerous and is an invitation for disaster.

Day 148
Treasure God's Word in Your Heart

Your word I have treasured in my heart, that I may not sin against You. (Psalm 119:11)

Do not ever take any of God's Word for granted but always treasure His Word in your heart. Every word written in the Bible is there for a reason. There is nothing that is insignificant, no matter how minor it may be to you. The more time you spend in God's Word, the more you will learn about Him. If you come in from work and just say hello to your spouse, roommate, parent or whomever you live with, and maybe only have a brief conversation over the evening meal, you would not get to know much about them. To develop a real relationship you need to spend time with a person in different circumstances, such as under pleasant conditions, adverse conditions, at different times of day, etc. The same is true for your relationship with your God. You can spend time with Him by reading His Word, fellowshipping at church, listening to lessons about His Word, or just talking to Him. Do not turn to God's Word only when you need something and you approach Him asking for something. Seek Him when all is going well just to thank Him and praise Him. He loves you and wants to fellowship with you all the time.

Lord Jesus, I desire to have a greater appreciation for Your Word and to treasure Your Word in my heart at all times. I know that I need to develop a closer relationship with You and that I must find a way to spend more time with You. I ask the Holy Spirit to give me wisdom as to how I can arrange my daily schedule to make more time to talk to You and to listen to You. In Jesus's name, I ask. Amen.

Nutrition Thought for the Day.

The environment also plays a role in vitamin/mineral needs. In very hot environments you naturally sweat and lose water that you need to replace, but sweat also contains sodium, potassium, some magnesium, a trace of chloride, a trace amount of iron, and other nutrients. So those in very hot environments need to watch their intake of water and the nutrients mentioned above. Humidity also plays a factor. The lower the humidity, the more water you lose without realizing it. It would be good to drink some of the fluid/electrolyte replacement drinks whenever sweating a lot. The vitamin replacement drinks do little good if any.

WAYNE E. BILLON, PH.D., RDN, LDN

Day 149
You Are under Grace

For sin shall not be master over you, for you are not under law but under grace.
(Romans 6:14)

For further encouragement, you should memorize this scripture that Paul gave to the Romans, "For sin shall not be master over you, for you are not under law but under grace." The law of the Old Testament covered more than just the Ten Commandments. The Pharisees made up over six hundred rules that the Jews had to follow. The law was so involved and detailed that no one was able to obey it to completion. Jesus came and obeyed all of it without sin, therefore He fulfilled the law and defeated sin. Then the New Testament comes with grace that was given to you when you accepted what Jesus did for you and you asked for His forgiveness. That breaks the effects of sin over you and sin is no longer your master. Do not come under condemnation when you sin. This is really talking about sinning spiritually, but you still may have some guilt when you do not follow your healthy lifestyle regimen to the letter, just as the people in the Old Testament had a hard time following all the laws they had imposed on them. Just as you can master sin, you can also master your healthy lifestyle regimen. Do not be discouraged! Be bold and courageous and stick with your program.

> I confess with my mouth that I shall not be mastered by sin because God's Word says that I am under His grace. Sin cannot condemn me. If I fail to follow my healthy lifestyle regimen to the letter, I am not under sin for missing it, nor am I under any kind of condemnation. I am more than a conqueror! I am a world overcomer! I can do all things through Christ who strengthens me! I thank You Father God for the grace You pour out on me. I know that I will be successful in all that I do in Your name. In Jesus's name, I pray. Amen.

Nutrition Thought for the Day.

Toxins in the environment can also be a problem. Drinking water that comes from wells or city water, or even bottled water, could contain compounds that interfere with the absorption of certain minerals. Contaminants in drinking water could also be a problem. At the time of this writing, Flint, Michigan was undergoing some severe issues with excessive lead in the drinking water. The lead by itself is toxic but, in addition, the lead could bind with some of the good minerals in the water and prevent them from being properly absorbed. Numerous toxins in the environment could present problems, too many to discuss here and they vary from region to region. A registered dietitian in your region should have some knowledge of potential problems in your area.

Day 150
Think on Things above

Finally, brethren, whatever is true, whatever is honorable, whatever is right, whatever is pure, whatever is lovely, whatever is of good repute, if there is any excellence and if anything worthy of praise, dwell on these things. (Philippians 4:8)

This is another excellent scripture to memorize so that when thoughts that come from the enemy, the world, or from your own flesh, you can take authority over them by recalling and acting on this scripture. Set your mind on "whatever is true, whatever is honorable, whatever is right, whatever is pure, whatever is lovely, whatever is of good repute, if there is anything of excellence, and if anything is worthy of praise, dwell on these things." When any distracting thoughts come into your mind, whether they are sinful thoughts, thoughts of going off your healthy lifestyle regimen, or just everyday distracting thoughts, they are not bringing glory to God. If you replace those thoughts with any of the subjects mentioned in the above scripture, then you are bringing glory to God, and you are living each day for His glory. We all know that this is not an easy task, but if it was easy, anyone could accomplish it. To achieve this, it takes resolve and consistency. As a child of God, you have access to everything you need to be successful. You can reach another level in your walk with the Lord by doing this. Do not be discouraged!

Father God, I want Your thoughts to be my thoughts. When sinful thoughts or just distracting thoughts come into my head, remind me of Philippians 4:8 so that I can replace them with thoughts of excellence, thoughts worthy of praise for You. I know that I have authority over my thought life and I know that with consistency I will have less and less of a problem controlling my thought life. I thank You for Your guidance through the Holy Spirit, and I know that I will overcome. In Jesus's name, I pray. Amen.

Nutrition Thought for the Day.

Another factor that will influence your vitamin/mineral needs is the amount, intensity, and length of time you exercise. Obviously, exercise can cause excessive perspiration so the loss of minerals and electrolytes should also be considered. Exercise works the muscles and causes them to get stronger and increases your protein requirement—maybe only slightly, but still it demands that you at least have adequate high-quality protein—not an excess of protein.

WAYNE E. BILLON, PH.D., RDN, LDN

Day 151
Encourage One Another

But encourage one another day after day, as long as it is *still* called "today," so that none of you will be hardened by the deceitfulness of sin. (Hebrews 3:13)

Everybody needs encouragement. You know how good it makes you feel when someone approaches you and says something like: "Have you been on a diet? You look great, really physically fit." That is a good feeling, isn't it? The Scriptures tells us to do that for each other every day. Granted the writer of Hebrews intended for this to be as it pertains to God's Word, and you should encourage each other in your walk with the Lord, but you should encourage those around you in everything, not just in healthy eating. If you see one of your peers on a diet/exercise program losing weight (or gaining weight if that is what they are trying to do), let them know it and encourage them. You can do this while giving praise to your God such as, "You are losing weight and looking so good, to God be the glory!"(Or it could be: "You are gaining weight and looking so good," depending on what their goal is) "I praise God for your success." There are many ways you can sneak in a witness for the Lord.

Father God, I do not want to miss any opportunity to witness for You. Encouraging those around me in my everyday activities is a great way to be a witness. I ask the Holy Spirit to remind me of every opportunity to witness for You. I want to be an encourager of Your Word. I also look forward to being encouraged by others through Your Word. In Jesus's name, I pray. Amen.

Nutrition Thought for the Day.

Gender differences in vitamin/mineral requirements also exist. Females before menopause have a higher iron requirement than do males. This will be discussed in greater detail when I get to iron, but the way we lose iron, for the most part, is by bleeding. Females' monthly menstrual cycle causes them to lose more iron until after menopause. The differences in the requirements between males and females for most vitamins and minerals are slightly higher for males in all cases except in the case of iron.

Day 152
Do Not Lose Courage

"But you, be strong and do not lose courage, for there is reward for your work."
(2 Chronicles 15:7)

It is good to stop now and then and make an evaluation of where you were, where you are, and where you are going. I will use this scripture to help you to look at where you are going. An encouraging note to know that if you overcome all the trials and tribulations and temptations to go off your lifestyle regimen, there is a reward for your work. The reward is a multilevel reward. First of all and most importantly, your success is giving glory to your God. Next, your heavenly reward is eternity with Jesus in your heavenly home. Earthly rewards include successful weight loss (or weight gain, whichever is your goal) which should also precipitate more stamina and improved mobility and exercise performance. You will also have the self-accomplishment that includes a long list of things such as an improvement in your appearance, your confidence, your well-being, and your overall improved health. This flows over to joy for those that are close to you as family, friends, and coworkers. There is a lot to look forward to and a lot to get excited about no matter how successful, or unsuccessful; your healthy lifestyle program has been so far. Whatever your progress, do not give up. Do not be discouraged; you can do this!

Father God, I know that no matter what I have been through, be it good, bad or indifferent, I have a bright future ahead of me. I know that as long as I follow Your Word, I will be giving You glory and will be able to look forward to an eternity in my heavenly home. I know that I will improve my health by continuing with my healthy lifestyle program and that will result in many benefits for me and those around me. I give all the credit for my success to You and give You all the praise and glory. I look forward to the accomplishments I will continue to have in the future with Your help. In Jesus's name, I pray. Amen.

Nutrition Thought for the Day.
Probably the hardest vitamin/mineral requirement to get a grip on is age. As we get older, we need more of certain vitamins/minerals and less of others. The problem here is, what is older? The recommended daily allowances (RDAs) for vitamins and minerals have this broken down for us by age brackets and gender, but not everyone ages the same. There is chronological age, and there is physiological age. You could probably go to any nursing home in this country and find someone in the mid-60s, maybe even early 60s, sitting on a porch in a rocking chair with nothing to do. You can find someone above 80 years old who is still holding down a forty hour a week job. If someone stays active as they age, the more active they are, the greater the need for vitamins and minerals. Some people just do not seem to age as fast as others do and it is difficult to determine what their real needs are. To determine all of these requirements, a complete nutritional assessment should be done by a registered dietitian.

Day 153
Stand in the Presence of His Glory

> Now to Him who is able to keep you from stumbling, and to make you stand in the presence of His glory blameless with great joy, to the only God our Savior, through Jesus Christ our Lord, *be* glory, majesty, dominion and authority, before all time and now and forever. Amen. (Jude 1:24–25)

This could be a sermon and a half. I will cover part of it today and part tomorrow. First of all, Jude is giving credit to Him (Jesus) who is able to keep you from stumbling. As you walk through your daily life, Jesus walks with you. I know it does not always feel like He is there with you, but He is with you and can keep you from stumbling. He is not going to guard every minute of your life if you are ignoring Him and doing your own thing. Even under poor conditions, however, the Holy Spirit will speak to you by your spirit, telling you where the stumbling blocks are. Yet, for you to hear Him you have to be listening, and that means you have to be in fellowship with Him at all times. Then, through the power of the Holy Spirit, Jesus—with a still small voice—can keep you from stumbling. If you do not stumble, He can cause you to stand in the presence of His glory. The "His," in this case, is referring to God the Father. Jesus causes you to stand in His glory blameless with great joy. Because of what Jesus did for you through His life, death, and resurrection, you are blameless. The only way you can stand in His presence is to be blameless. Because of Jesus you can walk without stumbling and stand blameless in His sight. As you walk through your day today, know that you are blameless in the sight of your God, not based on what you have done, but based on what Jesus did for you. Be thankful and be gracious. Be encouraged as you continue with your healthy lifestyle program.

> Lord Jesus, the only way I can stand in front of my Father God, is as an innocent child of God. That is something that I can only accomplish through Your blood. I thank You for shedding Your blood for me on Calvary and for helping me to walk without stumbling. It is because of You that I can. I thank You for the joy You are giving to me today. In Your name, Jesus, I pray. Amen.

Nutrition Thought for the Day.

I concede that some vitamins and minerals may be rendered unavailable due to processing or even cooking in our home and that most of us do not eat a perfectly well-balanced diet every day. Therefore, there may be times when we could use a vitamin and mineral supplement in our diet, so I do not have a problem with taking a simple multiple vitamin/mineral tablet once a day. What do I mean by simple? There are vitamin and mineral tablets available that provide several times the Recommended Daily Allowances That is not a simple multiple vitamin tablet, and I do not believe that is needed. There are the super expensive brands of vitamins and minerals that I think are too pricey. I do not think that organic or natural vitamins are worth the costs and I take a generic synthetic vitamin/mineral tablet daily, but I researched the company to make sure that it is reputable and has the USP (U.S. Pharmacopeia seal of approval) seal on it.

Day 154
Stand in the Presence of His Glory II

Now to Him who is able to keep you from stumbling, and to make you stand in the presence of His glory blameless with great joy, to the only God our Savior, through Jesus Christ our Lord, *be* glory, majesty, dominion and authority, before all time and now and forever. Amen. (Jude 1:24–25)

To continue with yesterday's scripture, you can stand in the presence of His glory blameless and with great joy for your God and Savior because of what Jesus did for you. Remember that the condition and appearance of your spirit before your salvation was not admissible in the presence of your God. If you stood before your God without salvation, then you would not be standing there blameless, and it would not be with great joy. Instead, it would be standing there in your sinful nature for the sake of being judged and condemned by your God. After salvation, because of what Jesus did for you, it is possible for you to stand blameless—that's right blameless—before your God with great joy because you know that you have entry into eternity in heaven. The last part of the scripture says to give glory, majesty, dominion, and authority, now and always to your God. Be encouraged today because of what Jesus did for you and give glory to God!

Lord Jesus, had it not been for what You did for me I would never be able to stand before my Father God blameless and in great joy. Because of Your great mercy and love, I can stand blameless before my Father God and give Him glory, honor, and praise. All authority is given to Him today and for as long as I live and then for all eternity in heaven. I choose to glorify my God and to praise Him. Thank You, Jesus, for Your mercy and love. Amen.

Nutrition Thought for the Day.

By way of review, remember that all processed grains in the United States are fortified with thiamin, riboflavin, niacin, folic acid, and iron. This would include any product that is made from processed grains such as processed flours, cornmeal, breads, cookies, crackers, snack cakes, processed rice, pasta made from processed flours, and processed cereals. These products are enriched because thiamin, riboflavin, and niacin are removed during the processing of the grains. Folic acid is added to prevent deficiencies in females because a folic acid deficiency can cause congenital disabilities. Iron is added because iron deficiency is usually a problem across the population. Whole-grain cereals or whole-grain flours do not have these added because they are not processed, and these nutrients are not removed. The 2010 Dietary Guidelines recommend that women capable of becoming pregnant consume 400 micrograms of synthetic folic acid per day from fortified foods or supplements.

WAYNE E. BILLON, PH.D., RDN, LDN

Day 155
We Can Draw Near to God's Throne with Confidence

Therefore let us draw near with confidence to the throne of grace, so that we may receive mercy and find grace to help in time of need. (Hebrews 4:16)

Because of Jesus, you can stand before your Father God blameless and with joy. Knowing that to be true, you can approach God's throne of grace with confidence because God's Word says that you can. And when you approach His throne you can receive mercy and find grace to help you in time of need. You do not have to approach your God with fear and trembling asking for something that you legitimately need while thinking in your heart "I hope He hears me. I hope He answers my prayer." You know that you can approach His throne in confidence without any condemnation whatsoever and you know that He hears your prayers. If He hears your prayers, then you know that they will be received with mercy and grace in your time of need. You should continue to give Him praise and glory ahead of time before you ask, when you ask, and after you ask with anticipation that He will answer your prayers.

Father God, I thank You that Your throne never closes. We can approach You any day, every day, any hour of the day or night and know that You are always there waiting for us with open arms. You are an amazing God! We do not have to second-guess if You will be responsive to our requests for we know that You are never too busy to hear us and that You are always available. Thank You, Father, for Your faithfulness even when I am not faithful. In Jesus's name, I pray. Amen.

Nutrition Thought for the Day.

I have one caution concerning water-soluble vitamins in general. Water-soluble means precisely what it says; the vitamins are soluble in water, which is what our blood and urine are. Some people are under the impression that if we take in more water-soluble vitamins than we need, the excess will come out in our urine and not cause a problem. For years we used to believe that and were not concerned about taking in excessive amounts of water-soluble vitamins. However, we have found that even though we excrete the excess, we can still ingest toxic levels of water-soluble vitamins. Examples will be given with some of the vitamins as we cover them. The point is, you do not want to take in megadoses of vitamins, even water-soluble ones.

Day 156
Love Your Neighbor as Yourself

Be devoted to one another in brotherly love; give preference to one another in honor; not lagging behind in diligence, fervent in spirit, serving the Lord; rejoicing in hope, persevering in tribulation, devoted to prayer, contributing to the needs of the saints, practicing hospitality. (Romans 12:10–13)

Today's scripture is three for the price of one, but they are three short verses that fit so well together they cannot be separated. The scriptures also lay out ideas for your daily plans. First, be devoted to one another in brotherly love. If you are to be a witness for your Lord and Savior you need to practice this on a daily basis. Second, give preference to one another in honor or treat one another fairly in business in your everyday activities. Thirdly, Paul says not to lag behind in diligence or be slothful in doing your Christian duties, and be on fire with the Spirit as you serve your Lord. Fourth, you should always be rejoicing in the hope that you have in your God and persevering in tribulation while you are devoting yourself to prayer. The last thing is to be generous and contribute to the needs of your fellow Christians and practice hospitality toward them.

This sums up the Lord's command to love the Lord your God with all your heart, mind, and soul and to love your neighbor as yourself. The things listed in the scripture are unfortunately a tall order for many people that call themselves Christians, but if you practice what the words say in Romans 12:10–13, you will indeed be a witness for your Lord and Savior Jesus Christ.

Father God, today's scripture is the essence of what it means to be a Christian and be a witness for You. To do each of the things mentioned in today's scripture on a daily basis would be a big task for many people. I do not want it to be a big task for me. I want to complete every step outlined in Romans 12:10–13 and be a walking witness for You. I ask for the Holy Spirit to guide me so that I may walk out this scripture in my everyday life and I pray in the name of Jesus. Amen.

Nutrition Thought for the Day.

The first water-soluble vitamin is vitamin B1, also known as thiamin. This vitamin can be destroyed by heat, so some would be lost in cooking, mainly if cooking at high temperatures over prolonged periods of time. Thus overcooking food will destroy some thiamin. It is also unstable in alkaline conditions which means when the pH is high. This should not be much of a concern in cooking unless for some reason you are cooking with large amounts of baking soda. Adding baking soda to green beans will give them a bright green color, and some people may add baking soda for that effect, but green beans are not a good source of thiamin to start with so that would not be losing much. Thiamin is stable when frozen so frozen foods should not affect thiamin very much.

Day 157
Be Patient

Therefore be patient, brethren, until the coming of the Lord. The farmer waits for the precious produce of the soil, being patient about it, until it gets the early and late rains. (James 5:7)

The Book of James was written to believers as a rebuke of the shameful way they were disregarding specific Christian duties. James wrote to them encouraging them to live based on the Gospel. In the scriptures before James 5:7, he reprimands them for they have been living a life of wanton pleasure with disregard for Christian principles. At the time this scripture was written many believed that Jesus was coming back for them in their lifetime. So in James 5:7 he encourages them to change their ways and be patient for the return of Jesus. He compares that to a farmer waiting for his crop to be fruitful. There are two keys in the scripture that can relate to you today. One, be patient not only in waiting for the next life of victory in heaven but be patient in everything you do now until that time comes. This includes being patient with your healthy lifestyle program. You did not gain your excess weight in a couple of weeks, and it is going to take you time to lose it. The best thing to do is to lose it slowly while developing new habits so that you can keep the excess weight off. The same is true if you are trying to gain weight. It takes time to gain weight appropriately by gaining muscle and not fat. The second key in the scripture is that while you are waiting, you give attention to the Gospel and follow God's Word. It would be great if all the excess weight on you just fell off in one day, but it does not happen that way. Be patient, be faithful, but be encouraged and you will be victorious.

Thank You, Father God, for the gift of patience. I know that patience is a virtue and I know that all of us need to practice it in our daily routine. I ask for You to increase my patience not only with my healthy lifestyle program but also in everything that I do. I also desire to make my walk with You closer and closer while I walk out my life on this earth in patience for Your coming. I ask for this in the name of Jesus. Amen.

Nutrition Thought for the Day.
Some tips to retain thiamin while cooking would be to use enriched whole-grain pasta or rice and, do not wash before cooking, or rinse after cooking. I know this is contrary to what many people are taught but is only a suggestion if you are concerned about losing thiamin. However, a deficiency in thiamin should not be a problem for most of us in the United States. Additional tips include cooking vegetables in a minimal amount of water. People in the south tend to cook vegetables to almost a mush while in the north people tend to like vegetables crunchy. I do not have research data to prove this, but the vegetables cooked in the south probably have a lower thiamin content if they are overcooked as described here. When cooking a roast, cook at a moderate temperature if possible and cook only until it is done; do not overcook.

Day 158
Walk in a Manner Worthy of the Lord

For this reason also, since the day we heard *of it,* we have not ceased to pray for you and to ask that you may be filled with the knowledge of His will in all spiritual wisdom and understanding, so that you will walk in a manner worthy of the Lord, to please *Him* in all respects, bearing fruit in every good work and increasing in the knowledge of God; strengthened with all power, according to His glorious might, for the attaining of all steadfastness and patience; joyously giving thanks to the Father, who has qualified us to share in the inheritance of the saints in Light. (Colossians 1:9–12)

This is a long scripture, but it contains several pearls of knowledge that summarizes much of what has been mentioned previously. I will break it down bit by bit over the next few days. First some background. Paul is writing to the Colossians, and in the first part of chapter 1:9, he tells them that he has heard good news about them serving the Lord and bearing fruit. Then in verse nine of chapter one, he tells them that since he heard the news, we (we—assuming his companions with him) have not stopped praying for them and asking that they be filled with the knowledge of God's will in all spiritual wisdom and understanding. This is the first step that you need to take after salvation, to be filled with the knowledge of God's will for your life and to be filled with understanding, so you know how to use that knowledge. It would be good to pray this prayer for yourself daily. Paul thought this to be the important next step for the new believers in Colossae. This is Paul's idea of walking out God's Word. It would be good to receive this as an example for you to follow.

Thank You, Father God, that we can know Your will and spiritual wisdom and understanding by seeking You and studying Your Word. In James 4:8 it says that if we draw near to You, You will draw near to us. The more I seek You each day by studying Your Word, praying to You, and staying in fellowship with like-minded believers, I know that I will be drawing closer to You. I also know that the fruit from these encounters will empower me with the wisdom and understanding that I need to be Your servant. That is my heart's desire, and I ask for Your wisdom and understanding in the name of Jesus. Amen.

Nutrition Thought for the Day.

There are compounds in some foods that could destroy thiamin, but this should not be of any major concern for most of us. Examples include tea, coffee, blueberries, Brussels sprouts, and red cabbage. Some fermented fish and shellfish also have a thiamin-degrading enzyme that could destroy thiamin or interfere with its absorption. Alcohol intake interferes with thiamin absorption also. Also, the metabolism of alcohol requires thiamin, and since alcohol is a diuretic and flushes fluids through the urine, people who drink a lot of alcohol lose water-soluble nutrients that include thiamin. So a person that takes in a lot of alcohol would be suspect for thiamin deficiency.

WAYNE E. BILLON, PH.D., RDN, LDN

Day 159
Walk in a Manner Worthy of the Lord II

For this reason also, since the day we heard *of it,* we have not ceased to pray for you and to ask that you may be filled with the knowledge of His will in all spiritual wisdom and understanding, so that you will walk in a manner worthy of the Lord, to please *Him* in all respects, bearing fruit in every good work and increasing in the knowledge of God; strengthened with all power, according to His glorious might, for the attaining of all steadfastness and patience; joyously giving thanks to the Father, who has qualified us to share in the inheritance of the saints in Light. (Colossians 1:9–12)

In the next part of the scripture Paul's prayer for the Colossians, after their salvation experience is that they walk in a manner worthy of the Lord to please Him in all respects, to bear fruit in every good work, and continue to increase in the knowledge of God. You should be witnesses for Jesus Christ in all that you do and, to accomplish that, you must walk in a manner worthy of the Lord. If you perform in this matter in your daily lives, you will bear good fruit for your Lord and Savior. Finally, in this sentence, Paul prays for an increase in the knowledge of God. Earlier in the same sentence, he prayed that they be filled with knowledge of His will in every spiritual wisdom. To mention that twice in the same sentence indicates he felt it was essential for you to know your God. Thus, he emphasizes the importance of staying in His Word and seeking Him through prayer, meditation, and fellowship.

Dear Father, my goal for the rest of my life on this earth is to walk in a manner that is worthy of You, not just with the healthy lifestyle program I am following, but for everything that I do. I know that I cannot do that on my own power and I know that I have to depend on Your guidance and the power of the Holy Spirit in me. Use me in this lifestyle program to be a witness for You and to walk in a manner that will bring You glory. I know that with Your strength I will be successful and I thank You in the name of Jesus. Amen.

Nutrition Thought for the Day.

Our thiamin requirement increases as we get older starting with a requirement of 0.2 milligrams per day for a baby up to six months old, to 1.2 milligrams per day for males nineteen years of age and older. The requirements for most vitamins vary between males and females but there is not much of a difference concerning thiamin. For a female that is nineteen years old and older, the recommended intakes are 1.1 milligrams per day. During pregnancy and lactation, the thiamin requirement goes up to 1.4 milligrams per day.

Day 160
Walk in a Manner Worthy of the Lord III

For this reason also, since the day we heard *of it,* we have not ceased to pray for you and to ask that you may be filled with the knowledge of His will in all spiritual wisdom and understanding, so that you will walk in a manner worthy of the Lord, to please *Him* in all respects, bearing fruit in every good work and increasing in the knowledge of God; strengthened with all power, according to His glorious might, for the attaining of all steadfastness and patience; joyously giving thanks to the Father, who has qualified us to share in the inheritance of the saints in Light. (Colossians 1:9–12)

In the last part of the scripture, Paul prays that the Colossians be strengthened with all power according to His glorious might. This is talking about the power that is given to you through the Holy Spirit. Then Paul says that the power according to His glorious might is necessary so that you can attain the steadfastness and patience needed to continue to bear fruit. This should be endurance and patience as you walk out your life on this earth but also endurance and patience as you complete your new program. As I pray for you to receive these godly qualities, as you should also pray and ask for these godly qualities, so Paul prayed and asked for the Colossians to receive the same godly qualities. You can receive, but you have to want to and be willing to walk them out. You can do this by the power of the Spirit in you. Do not ever question your ability to walk out God's gifts to you.

Thank You, Father God, for the gift of patience. As I prayed just a few days ago, I know that patience is a virtue and I know that all of us need to practice it in our daily routine. I know that if I increase my knowledge of You and my understanding of Your Word, I will increase my patience. During this healthy lifestyle program, there are many opportunities for me to lose patience and I especially need You to help me get through this program. I know that You will give me the wisdom and patience that I need and I thank You for it in the name of my Lord and Savior, Jesus Christ. Amen.

Nutrition Thought for the Day.

As we approach our elder years, our vitamin requirements usually decrease. Some exceptions will be discussed as we cover each vitamin. The question once again becomes, "What does age mean?" No matter what your age is, if you are very active and do not have disease states active in your body, your requirement for most vitamins would still be as for a person much younger than yourself. It is difficult to determine the vitamin requirements for older people because there are so many variations in the amount of exercise and mobility between people as they age. The change in the requirements is very small as we get older as evidenced with thiamin going from 0.2 milligrams per day to 1.2 milligrams per day over a range of seventy years. That is only 1 milligram per day difference. That should not be much of a concern, but since thiamin is so important in producing energy (as is all of the B vitamins), and since you should have to take in a very large amount to get an overdose, I do not have a problem with the elderly taking a general B vitamin supplement.

Day 161
Walk in a Manner Worthy of the Lord IV

For this reason also, since the day we heard *of it,* we have not ceased to pray for you and to ask that you may be filled with the knowledge of His will in all spiritual wisdom and understanding, so that you will walk in a manner worthy of the Lord, to please *Him* in all respects, Bearing fruit in every good work and increasing in the knowledge of God; strengthened with all power, according to His glorious might, for the attaining of all steadfastness and patience; joyously giving thanks to the Father, who has qualified us to share in the inheritance of the saints in Light. (Colossians 1:9–12)

In the last part of this scripture, Paul says we joyously give thanks to the Father. Giving thanks and praise to God your Father has been emphasized several times. It is something we all need to resolve to do each day. It is part of the walking in a manner worthy of the Lord and pleasing Him in all respects. As a result, it will help us to bear more fruit and to get closer to our Lord and Savior. And finally, Paul finishes up by saying, "Who has qualified us to share in the inheritance of the saints in Light." The "who" in this sentence is God the Father. As a result of you accepting Jesus Christ as your Savior and Lord, you get to share in the inheritance of the saints and he says you get to share in Light. The "Light" referred to here is Jesus, the Light of the world, and He will also be the Light of heaven in that there will not be a need for any other form of light. So, sharing in the Light is being in the light of Jesus in heaven.

Father God, I look forward to being in the light of Jesus in heaven, but I also want to be that light to the people around me on this earth. While on this healthy lifestyle program I have many opportunities to either show the light that is in me or let darkness come from me as the trials that I face sometimes get heavy. My body does not always respond in the way that I want it to concerning weight and fitness. This can be discouraging and can cause me to show a discouraging spirit. Help me, by the power of Your Holy Spirit, to let the light of Jesus shine through me instead of darkness shining through. I cannot do this on my own strength, but I know that I can accomplish it with Your help. In Jesus's name, I pray. Amen.

Nutrition Thought for the Day.

One important piece of advice that nutritionists tell their clients is to eat a variety of foods in moderation to prevent having any deficiencies and to prevent overeating. As we look at each of the vitamins and minerals, note that no one food is an excellent source of all the vitamins and all the minerals. Instead, you will find one vitamin to be concentrated very high in one food but low in another food, while a different vitamin might have a low concentration in both foods and very high in a different one, and so on. If you list all the B vitamins and the food source that has the highest concentration in each, they will all be different foods. Thus, if you ate a variety of foods, you lessen your chance of getting a nutritional deficiency.

Day 162
Be Strengthened in Your Heart

Now may our Lord Jesus Christ Himself and God our Father, who loved us and gave us eternal comfort and good hope by grace, comfort and strengthen your hearts in every good work and word. (2 Thessalonians 2:16–17)

Paul is praying to Jesus and God our Father for the Thessalonians, and he emphasizes explicitly that they are loved and have been given, by grace, eternal comfort and hope. Yes, this was written to the Thessalonians, but it is for all of us. Paul's letter also asks for us to be strengthened in our hearts in every good work and word. This is a scripture that we could easily read over and miss the impact it was intended to have. This is an active prayer being prayed for Christians today—there is no clock or time frame in heaven. God wants us to be strengthened in all that we do and say. This is an excellent scripture to memorize and recite every time you feel discouraged, having a hard time at work or any disappointment with your healthy lifestyle program. Ask your Father God to give you eternal comfort and to strengthen your heart (spirit) in every good work and deed. Be encouraged today by this scripture and keep it close to your heart.

Thank You, Father God, that Your Word was true yesterday, is true today, and is true tomorrow. This prayer is for me today, and I receive it. Whenever I feel discouraged, or I am having a hard time with anything, I know that by grace, Your will for me is that my heart be strengthened in my every word and deed. Remind me of this by the power of Your Holy Spirit whenever I may be down or in a trial of endurance. Give me the strength to overcome so that I can be a witness for You and point my peers to You as the reason for my success. I ask this in the name of Jesus. Amen.

Nutrition Thought for the Day.

Sources of the water-soluble vitamins are abundant. However, a significant note about water-soluble vitamins, in general, is that we do not store water-soluble vitamins in our body per se. Since they are water-soluble, any excess comes out in the urine. This is not true for fat-soluble vitamins since they are stored in fatty tissue. The liver is usually an excellent source of B vitamins, not because they are stored there, but because there are so many reactions taking place in the liver that require B vitamins as cofactors, there is always a concentration of B vitamins in the liver. You will typically see liver listed as a source of many of the vitamins and minerals.

Day 163
Why Seek Godly Wisdom?

But the wisdom from above is first pure, then peaceable, gentle, reasonable, full of mercy and good fruits, unwavering, without hypocrisy. (James 3:17)

Essentially there is no wisdom outside of God's wisdom. Man's wisdom cannot save us. God's wisdom helps to unite us through our spirit with the Holy Spirit. God's wisdom is pure, peaceable, gentle, reasonable full of mercy and good fruits, unwavering and without hypocrisy. Man's wisdom cannot function in this manner. It is only by God's wisdom that we can fully understand God's Word. Conventional wisdom will not save us but can lead to death. It would be a good practice when you get up in the morning to dedicate your day to the Lord and ask for His wisdom to guide you through the day in everything that you do. You need to be ever conscious that your dependence is on the wisdom of your God and not only your own wisdom. If you make this prayer at the beginning of every day, it will help you to become aware during the day who you depend upon—yourself or your God.

Thank You, Father God, for Your wisdom and the fact that Your wisdom is free for the asking. I know that I need Your wisdom to be able to follow Your Word and to be able to make wise choices in my everyday life for my work, home, and in all my activities. As it says in Your Word, I ask for wisdom this day so that I may be a better witness for You. In Jesus's name, I pray. Amen.

Nutrition Thought for the Day.

I do not recommend liver as an everyday food even though it is a good source of many of the vitamins, iron, and protein. The reason being is that all nutrients that come into the body from the digestive tract go directly to the liver (except for the chylomicrons discussed previously). All toxins that come into the body through the digestive tract also go through the bloodstream directly to the liver. If an animal grazing on a pasture ingests a pesticide or some toxin that got into its feed supply, when the toxin gets to the liver, the liver will pull it out to try to detoxify it, so it does not harm the rest of the body. This is the same way the liver detoxifies alcohol. If you then eat the liver, you are getting all the vitamins and minerals that are there plus all the toxins that are stored there.

Day 164
Do Not Lose Heart

Let us not lose heart in doing good, for in due time we will reap if we do not grow weary. (Galatians 6:9)

You are about six months into this healthy lifestyle program, and perhaps you have been doing well. Maybe not as good as you would like to be doing, but you are making accomplishments. Perhaps you are trying very hard to be successful. Meanwhile, spiritually you may be working very hard to follow God's Word, but you do not see the fruit you would like to see. I am going to interpret today's scripture from a physical and a spiritual point of view. You may be competent in your goals in a physical arena but not in the spiritual arena. Whatever your situation is, do not be discouraged and do not lose heart for trying to do well. Until the next life, you may never know how many seeds you have planted in people's hearts. You plant, somebody else waters, someone else fertilizes, and then someone comes and reaps a harvest. That harvest may be a spiritual harvest of saving souls or maybe a physical harvest of people getting inspired to engage in healthy lifestyles. Do not grow weary in trying to be successful in both arenas, physical and spiritual. Eventually, you will reap the rewards in both areas. Do not be discouraged!

Father God, I do not know how many people are watching me on my healthy lifestyle program I am undertaking. They may be watching me to see if my program works, and at the same time they will see me profess my faith. Perhaps many people around me are being touched by my resolve to be successful with my program and my spiritual walk. I desire to be successful with both and to be an inspiration for those that choose to watch me. Let them watch me and be encouraged by my outcome in both areas. Continue to give me wisdom so that I do not do anything to lead anyone astray. I thank You, Father, in the name of Jesus. Amen.

Nutrition Thought for the Day.

The liver is also a very rich source of cholesterol. Having said all of that, if someone is exceptionally anemic and needs to increase their number of red blood cells, liver is probably the best source of natural iron that they could consume. If it was a question of staying anemic and eating liver to save a life, I would have no problem giving someone liver. After their blood supply is stabilized, I would eliminate liver from the diet. There is a place for liver but it is not in my regular rotation of foods. If you know where the animal was raised, and you know that the farmer was trustworthy, then it would make a difference. However, one more fact to consider is that the liver is very high in cholesterol.

Day 165
Wait on the Lord

Yet those who wait for the LORD will gain new strength; they will mount up *with* wings like eagles, they will run and not get tired, they will walk and not become weary (Isaiah 40:31)

Those who wait for the Lord will gain new strength, and they will mount up with wings like eagles, they will run and not get tired, and they will walk and not become weary. This is undoubtedly a compelling promise. To accomplish this, you will have to practice patience because the *wait on the Lord* phrase is the big key to following this advice. Trust is very important here also. You must have trust in your Lord if you are willing to wait on Him. As you mature as a Christian, these attributes will become more evident in your walk with the Lord. As you practice patience in your spiritual walk, that same patience will spill over into your physical life, and you will be able to master your new healthy lifestyle changes. This kind of patience and trust will develop the closer your walk with your Lord becomes. The more you know Him, the more you will trust Him. This will require you to put into practice all the things mentioned thus far such as reading God's Word, meditating on it, staying in fellowship with like-minded believers, praying to your Father God, etc. I know that is a mouthful, but you have a choice. You can follow your new regimen, or you can decide not to follow your regimen. Follow it and be successful, do not follow it and be unsuccessful. The choice is yours, but the wise thing to do is to wait on the Lord and let Him guide you and give you new strength.

Father God, I want to wait for You and Your guidance. I expect to gain new strength as I run my race on this earth, both spiritually and physically. I expect not to get tired or become weary because of Your strength. I know that You are with me, but it does not always feel like it. At those times that I feel defeated, revive me with Your Word. Send Your Holy Spirit to remind me of who I am in Christ and of all the help I have available in You. In Jesus's name, I pray. Amen.

Nutrition Thought for the Day.

Thiamin is widely distributed throughout many foods. Looking at a chart listing the foods that are highest in thiamin, you see pork to be at the top of the list. Other foods that are good sources of thiamin include sunflower seeds, wheat germ, yeast, and liver. Yeast and liver are probably the richest sources of thiamin. All enriched cereal grains are sources of thiamin and are perhaps the most important sources in the United States because just about everybody eats some form of processed grain such as bread, crackers, cookies, pastries, etc.

Day 166
Do Not Carry Your Own Yoke

"Come to Me, all who are weary and heavy-laden, and I will give you rest. Take My yoke upon you and learn from Me, for I am gentle and humble in heart, and you will find rest for your souls. For My yoke is easy and My burden is light." (Matthew 11:28–30)

Jesus is speaking, and He says that His yoke is easy and His burden is light. While the things that we are expected to do as a Christian may seem like a long list that would be very difficult to keep, it is not so. When we start to follow Jesus in the manner suggested, He puts His yoke on us but, as the scripture says, His yoke is easy and is light. In my own life, it frequently does not seem to be easy to follow Jesus's Word, and it often does not seem to be light. When we feel overwhelmed, we need to stop and consider what Jesus had to go through for us. We also need to consider what His Word says. He loves us, will never leave us, and He gives us the strength to complete our task. If He says His burden is light, then His burden is light. He cannot lie, and He will not ask us to do something that is impossible for us to do. If our burden is heavy, then it is because we are trying to carry it with our own strength and we cannot do that. Give your burden to the Lord and take up His yoke in its place. You may be surprised how much easier your task will become.

Lord Jesus, I need help remembering that my burden is heavier than Your burden and that when I take Your yoke on me, my burden gets lighter. In the natural, this does not make sense, but in the spiritual, it makes all the sense in the world. I give my yoke to You, Lord Jesus, and I am willing to take up Your yoke in its place. I know that You will give me the strength to accomplish this and I thank You for it in advance. In the name of Jesus, I pray. Amen.

Nutrition Thought for the Day.

Thiamin has several important roles, a primary function being the formation of energy. Energy that our body uses for everything it does including breathing, heart beating, kidneys filtering, exercise, and so on is in the form of ATP (adenosine triphosphate). Energy is stored in the body in the form of ATP. Without thiamin, we cannot produce ATP. As mentioned previously, if you take twice as much thiamin, you are not going to make twice as much ATP if you are already at your maximum capacity. Thiamin is also necessary for other metabolic pathways including maintaining membranes around nerve endings and proper nerve conduction.

Day 167
God Has Plans for You

"For I know the plans that I have for you," declares the LORD, "plans for welfare and not for calamity to give you a future and a hope." (Jeremiah 29:11–13)"

Okay, so the scriptures have established that you should not be overwhelmed and that you should take on Jesus's yoke and give your yoke to Him. In this scripture, the Lord declares that He has plans for you, plans for your welfare and not for calamity. Another version says He has plans to prosper you and not to harm you. It also means that He has hope for you in the future. There is nothing for you to fear, there is no burden that the Lord cannot carry. No task is too hard for our God to handle. It is impossible for Him not to love you. He is your Creator and your Savior and your help in a time of need. Keep this information ever before you so that it gets down into your spirit to such a degree that you could never forget it. Type out these scriptures on notecards and stick them on your refrigerator or someplace where you will see them every day to constantly remind yourself of who you are and what power is available to you through Him.

Father God, I know that Your plans for me are all excellent and that You want to see me be successful in everything that I do. I know that You want to see me prosper and not be in any harm and to have hope in the future. I do have hope and my hope is in You and You alone. I also know that I will be successful in my everyday experiences including my healthy lifestyle and my spiritual walk. I will be successful and will accomplish a great deal because of Your love and grace. I give You praise and thanks for all that You have done and will do for me. I thank You in Jesus's name. Amen.

Nutrition Thought for the Day.

Thiamin deficiency in the United States is uncommon except in cases of alcoholism and starvation or intense dieting. Most every vitamin has a deficiency name, and a thiamin deficiency is called beriberi. For adults, it could be what is known as wet beriberi or dry beriberi. There is also an infantile form of beriberi. Little information exists about the toxicity of excessive amounts of thiamin but, as mentioned earlier, too much of anything could cause some harm. Some megavitamin doses have as much as ten times the recommended daily allowance (RDA). There is no advantage or reason for taking that much thiamin.

Day 168
Be Content

Not that I speak from want, for I have learned to be content in whatever circumstances I am. (Philippians 4:11)

One of the things that can cause us to be discouraged is a lack of contentment with the progress or lack of progress that is taking place in our workplace, our homes, or other activities such as your healthy lifestyle program. In this scripture, Paul is telling the Philippians to be content in whatever circumstances they find themselves. He says that he is content no matter what the circumstances. In the next verse (Philippians 4:12) he explains that he has known what it is like to get by with just humble means, and he has known what is like to live in prosperity. He says that he has learned the secret of being filled and being hungry, both of having abundance and suffering need. The secret he has learned is found in Philippians 4:13, "I can do all things through Him who strengthens me." This does not mean that you should be happy when you are being persecuted or when things are going badly for you, but knowing where your strength comes from you will know that God is going to take care of you. With that knowledge, you can find contentment. It does not mean that you have to stay in that place of tribulation because you know that God is going to see you through it and when you come out the other side you are going to be a stronger person because of it. Learning to be content does not mean you are willing to settle for status quo, but you will accept status quo until you can improve your situation with God's help.

> Thank You, Father God, for the strength that You give me because I know that no matter what circumstances I have to go through I will be able to be successful because I can do all things through Christ who strengthens me. You have a plan for me, a direction You want me to go, and You will give me the wisdom to fulfill that plan. You will not allow me to be tested beyond what I can bear, but You will provide a way out. I trust in Your guidance and direction, and I choose this day to believe that what Your Word says is true, "I can do all things through Christ who strengthens me." In Jesus's name, I pray. Amen.

Nutrition Thought for the Day.
The next B vitamin is vitamin B2 or riboflavin. Riboflavin is found in a variety of foods, but for the most part, the best sources are animal products. The best source of thiamin was pork. The best source of riboflavin is dairy products, mainly milk. The next best source is meat and then legumes (beans and peas). Green vegetables are fair sources of riboflavin and fruits, and cereal grains are minor sources. However, remember that riboflavin is one of the vitamins that is enriched in processed grains. Thus enriched grains are fairly good sources of riboflavin. Since most people in the United States eat some form of grains, cookies, crackers, bread, etc. every day, riboflavin deficiency is not common.

Day 169
Do Not Receive Condemnation

Little children, let us not love with word or with tongue, but in deed and truth. We will know by this that we are of the truth, and will assure our heart before Him in whatever our heart condemns us; for God is greater than our heart and knows all things. (1 John 3:18–20)

Maybe you are at a place in your walk with the Lord that you know His strength is sufficient for you, but something has happened to make you feel like you are not worthy of His strength and power working in you. Something you may have done that you have asked forgiveness for has been recalled over and over in your mind by the devil. As a result, you feel condemned, and you start condemning yourself. This scripture tells us that we should love the Lord our God not with just our words but with our deeds and with truth in the way we live our lives. Walking in truth will assure your heart before Him when your heart tries to condemn you. God's forgiveness is greater than your heart, and God knows all things. He knows your heart, and as long as you belong to Him, there is no place for condemnation in your heart. The devil will try to tell you differently but know what God's Word says, there is no condemnation for those who are in Christ Jesus (Romans 8:1).

Thank You, Father God, that You know my heart and You know that my heart is for You and You only. I rebuke any condemnation that the enemy tries to bring against me. I have been forgiven of all my trespasses, and I walk in the light of Jesus. I am Your child. I do not ever have to be concerned with condemnation for I know that condemnation comes from the devil and not from You. I choose this day to walk in the light of Your Word and be free of any condemnation that the devil tries to bring against me, even condemning me for going off my healthy lifestyle program ever so slightly. I thank You, Father, in the name of Jesus. Amen.

Nutrition Thought for the Day.

Most riboflavin ingested is absorbed into the small intestines, but some naturally occurring nutrients tend to bond with riboflavin and render it unavailable in the G.I. tract. These substances are what are known as divalent metals such as copper, zinc, iron, and manganese. This is probably good to know, but unless you are taking in large doses of these metals, the amounts naturally found in foods should not cause a problem. If someone has iron deficiency anemia, they may be taking iron supplements. During the winter and the cold/flu season, some people take in large amounts of zinc. These are two examples that could possibly cause a problem with riboflavin but deficiency symptoms are still uncommon.

Day 170
Fix Your Eyes on Jesus

Therefore, since we have so great a cloud of witnesses surrounding us, let us also lay aside every encumbrance and the sin which so easily entangles us, and let us run with endurance the race that is set before us, fixing our eyes on Jesus, the author and perfecter of faith, who for the joy set before Him endured the cross, despising the shame, and has sat down at the right hand of the throne of God. (Hebrews 12:1–2)

In yesterday's devotion, you were encouraged to rebuke condemnation when it comes into your mind. The scripture today will help you to the next step. It tells you to lay aside every encumbrance and any sin that can so easily entangle you—even as strong Christians we all still have problems with sin. Some people say that life is but a stage and we are actors. Some people say that life is but a race and we are running to win. Paul uses the analogy of a race, and he says to run it with endurance by setting our eyes on Jesus, the author, and perfecter of our faith. Note in the last part of the scripture Paul says that Jesus, for the joy set before Him, endured the cross. What joy could have been so great that it caused Him to willingly accept all of the humiliation, beating, crowning with thorns, scourging, and crucifixion? The joy was saving you from Hades! You are the apple of His eye. Run your race with endurance and keep your eyes on Jesus and you cannot lose. Let the joy before you be winning other souls to Christ and looking forward to your eternity with Him.

Thank You, Jesus, for what You went through for me. You set me as your trophy, and that is what kept You going through all of the terrible persecutions that You endured. I want to set a joy before me such as well on this earth and doing well in my healthy lifestyle program. I want that joy to be something that will bring an extreme amount of joy to You. I know the first thing I need to do to make You joyful is to obey Your Word. I can also make You joyful by being a witness for You and see people receive You as Lord and Savior. Lord Jesus, give me the strength and wisdom to be able to accomplish this joy. In Your name, Jesus, I pray. Amen.

Nutrition Thought for the Day.
Being a water-soluble vitamin like thiamin, riboflavin is not stored in the body per se, and an excessive amount would come out in the urine. Because of the significant amount of metabolism that takes place in the liver, much of which is riboflavin dependent, liver is an excellent source of riboflavin. If you take a multivitamin with 100% of your riboflavin requirement, you can expect to have a bright fluorescent yellow color to your urine for a couple of hours after you ingest the vitamin. The vitamin naturally gives this color to the urine, and this is perfectly normal.

WAYNE E. BILLON, PH.D., RDN, LDN

Day 171
Make No Provision for the Flesh

But put on the Lord Jesus Christ, and make no provision for the flesh in regard to *its* lusts. (Romans 13:14)

Earlier in chapter 13 of Romans, Paul tells us that we should lay aside the deeds of darkness and put on the armor of light. He was speaking to the Romans about the carousing that was taking place during the nighttime and says that they should behave properly as during the daytime, that is not in sexual promiscuity and sensuality, nor in strife and jealousy. When running your race with endurance, you cannot leave any provision for the flesh. The only way to be successful in your race to obtain your trophy (which remember from yesterday is obedience and being a witness for the Lord) is to have Jesus's Word ever before you.

The only provision you want to have is for His Word and nothing for your own lust. Know that lust does not have to mean sexual desires. Yes, it can be that, but it can also be an unhealthy desire (or lust) for fame, money, power, and yes, even food or laziness. You can add anything to that list of unhealthy desires. Let your provision be Jesus's Word and walk through your day looking to Him for your joy.

Father God, I know that You are my provider and that I need to look to You in everything that I do. I am well aware of that but it is not always easy for me. The everyday hustle and bustle of the busy schedule that I have can be very distracting for me. By the power of Your Holy Spirit give me guidance and wisdom so that each day I can look to Your Word for my provision. Trying to be successful in so many things in my home life, my work, my healthy lifestyle program and others areas cause me to look to my own strength to be successful. I know that is not the road for me to take and I trust in You to guide my steps through Your Word. In Jesus's name, I pray. Amen.

Nutrition Thought for the Day.

Riboflavin is important as a coenzyme in energy production. There is a compound in the body called flavin adenine dinucleotide (FAD) that is necessary for energy production. Like thiamin, if you take in excess of riboflavin above your needs you will not make additional energy. The excess riboflavin will be excreted in the urine. Riboflavin has other functions, but energy production is by far its primary function.

Day 172
Become a Slave for Christ

Do you not know that when you present yourselves to someone *as* slaves for obedience, you are slaves of the one whom you obey, either of sin resulting in death, or of obedience resulting in righteousness? (Romans 6:16)

I believe this scripture is important not only from a spiritual standpoint but also from a physical standpoint. Yesterday's devotion was concerned with not leaving provisions for the flesh. Continuing with that thought, let's look at what Paul said to the Romans in today's scripture. Paul says that if they (the Romans) continue in sin, then they become slaves to that sin; but if they continue in obedience, then they become slaves of the one to whom they obey. If you continuously seek to obey God's Word, you will eventually become a slave to God.

In Jesus's time, after a slave served his master for an expressed period, he could be set free, or he could choose to be a bondservant to his master forever. Paul referred to himself as a bondservant of his Lord Jesus (Romans 1:1, Galatians 1:10 and Titus 1:1). James declared himself to be a bondservant of Jesus Christ (James 1:1) as well as Peter (2 Peter 1:1) and Jude (Jude 1:1). Several others in the New Testament made this declaration, but I think the major one was that Jesus took on the form of a bondservant to His Father God (Philippians 2:7). A bondservant for a Christian today would mean to be obedient to God's Word and follow Jesus Christ forever. Choose this day to be a bondservant of Jesus.

Dear Father God, I understand that a bondservant in the times Jesus walked the earth meant that a slave, after serving the required amount of time for his master, had the choice of becoming a free man or of becoming a bondservant to his master. That meant that he agreed to be his slave for life. Lord Jesus, You agreed to be a bondservant to Your Father God. I choose to be a bondservant for You. I want to be Your servant, or be it a slave, for life. I know I will need Your strength to accomplish this and I know that You will give it to me. In Jesus's name, I pray. Amen.

Nutrition Thought for the Day.

The riboflavin requirement for adult men is 1.3 milligrams per day, and for adult women it is 1.1 milligrams per day. This is not a very large quantity. Considering that riboflavin is found in an abundance of foods, is enriched in all processed grains, and we have a low requirement explains why riboflavin deficiency is not widespread in our country. When we started processing grains without adding riboflavin back to the processed grains, deficiencies were more common.

WAYNE E. BILLON, PH.D., RDN, LDN

Day 173
Be Filled with the Fullness of God

That He would grant you, according to the riches of His glory, to be strengthened with power through His Spirit in the inner man, so that Christ may dwell in your hearts through faith; *and* that you, being rooted and grounded in love, may be able to comprehend with all the saints what is the breadth and length and height and depth, and to know the love of Christ which surpasses knowledge, that you may be filled up to all the fullness of God. (Ephesians 3:16–19)

Part of the fruit of being a bondservant to Jesus would be as this scripture describes. You would be strengthened with power through His Spirit in your inner man, and Christ would dwell in your heart through your faith. You would be rooted and grounded in love, and you would be able to comprehend with all the saints the breadth and length and height and depth of the love of Christ which surpasses all knowledge. I believe that there are very few Christians today that fully understand the love that our God has for us. Paul tries to explain it in these verses. Finally, you would be filled with the fullness of God. That sounds like a pretty good deal. This was Paul's prayer for the Ephesians, but it is all the result of being grounded in Christ as a bondservant. You can do this, it just takes commitment, resolve, and daily putting your commitment into practice.

Father, I receive the prayer that Paul prayed for the Ephesians in Ephesians 3:16–19 for myself. I know I am being strengthened through the power of the Holy Spirit in my inner man and I believe that Christ dwells in my heart. I am still trying to comprehend the tremendous love that Jesus has for me, but I know that His love is in my heart. It is my desire to be filled with the fullness of Your love. In Jesus's name, I pray. Amen.

Nutrition Thought for the Day.
Deficiency symptoms of riboflavin include cheilosis (cracks in the corner of the mouth) and glossitis (inflammation of the tongue—a swollen beefy red tongue without any papillae). It would take as much as four months of an inadequate intake of riboflavin in the diet per day to produce deficiency symptoms. Since riboflavin is water-soluble, an excessive fluid intake, causing excessive urination, could cause deficiency symptoms to show up sooner.

Day 174
Let the Lord Be Your Rock

The LORD is my rock and my fortress and my deliverer, my God, my rock, in whom I take refuge; my shield and the horn of my salvation, my stronghold. (Psalm 18:2)

David wrote this Psalm after the Lord delivered him from his enemies and the hand of Saul. Look at the number of different ways David describes his protection from the Lord. He calls Him his rock, fortress, deliverer, shield, horn of his salvation, and stronghold. That covers just about everything more than once. David was a mighty warrior and a conqueror, yet he depended on God for his strength in just about every way imaginable. The Bible says that David was a man after God's own heart, but do you realize that David messed up big time? He committed adultery with Bathsheba and had her husband killed to cover it up. How many of you have messed up that badly? David sought forgiveness from God and received it, and he moved on. This was during the period of law and not grace.

How much more would we be forgiven today since we are under grace? David is an excellent example for us to follow when we mess up. Not many of us are guilty of adultery and murder. In spite of this, God not only forgave David but also blessed him tremendously. No matter what you have done, or how many times you have done it, or how often you have failed with your healthy lifestyle program—God still loves you! Do not be discouraged if you are not meeting your expectations. Most of us are our most severe critics. Pick up where you left off and continue with your quest to be a godly example for Jesus.

> Thank You, Father God, for the examples and role models You give me in Your Word. No matter what I have done, I know that You are still with me and that You still love me. It is impossible for You not to love me. By an act of my will, I choose to declare along with David that You are my rock and my fortress. I take refuge in You, and I have received my salvation through You. You are my stronghold and my shield. Help me by reminding me constantly that I need to call on You whenever I encounter a problem in my life. I know You will be there to help me. In Jesus's name, I pray. Amen.

Nutrition Thought for the Day.

Vitamin B3 is also called niacin. The best source of niacin is animal products and, in the animal products category, the best source is fish. As mentioned previously, the best source of each vitamin is usually different in that no one food contains everything that we need. This is why it is important to have a variety of foods each day. The greater the variety of foods we have the less chance we have of developing a vitamin or mineral deficiency. As discussed with the previous two B vitamins, enriched cereals is a decent source of niacin as well as whole grains, seeds, and legumes.

Wayne E. Billon, Ph.D., RDN, LDN

Day 175
I Belong to Christ

But God demonstrates His own love toward us, in that while we were yet sinners, Christ died for us. (Romans 5:8)

I am sure that you are like most believers in that many times you believe that you do not deserve God's love or forgiveness. You are absolutely correct in that; you do not deserve it. None of us do! There is nothing you or any of us can do to deserve the love we get from our God. That's why it is called unconditional love—He loves us unconditionally. That means when you do not love back He still loves you. His love for you never fails. When you were still a sinner and did not even realize how far away from God you were, and/or you did not even want to get closer to God, He chose you. When Jesus walked the face of this earth as a man, He knew every sin you would ever commit and every abusive thing you would ever do. Yet He was willing to die for you so that you might spend an eternity in supreme happiness with Him. This was without you even asking. Your God loves you that much, and there is nothing you can do to separate His love from you. Walk out this day knowing that you are loved, but not just loved, you are loved with an unconditional love that no one on earth can match. Be at peace today and rest in His love.

There is no way I can ever thank You, Father, for the love You have shown me, particularly while I was still a sinner. Even after I asked Jesus to be my Lord and Savior, I continued to fall from time to time into some of my old ways. He is still there with me, and He still loves me. It is hard for me to imagine the kind of love that You have for me—absolutely unconditional love! I thank You for that love and I resolve to strive to do better with my daily walk for You Father. In Jesus's name, I pray. Amen.

Nutrition Thought for the Day.
One thing to note is that only about 10% of the niacin in some plants is thought to be absorbed, so animal products are the best bet for niacin. There is another source of niacin for our bodies, and that is our liver can synthesize some niacin from the amino acid tryptophan. However, only about 3% of tryptophan that is metabolized can be converted to niacin. This would not be enough to meet our needs, and an external source is necessary.

Day 176
Praise Be to God for His Comfort

Blessed *be* the God and Father of our Lord Jesus Christ, the Father of mercies and God of all comfort, who comforts us in all our affliction so that we will be able to comfort those who are in any affliction with the comfort with which we ourselves are comforted by God. (2 Corinthians 1:3–4)

God created us for His glory. He wants us to serve Him and glorify His name. He is the God of all mercies and all comfort, and He comforts us whenever we are afflicted. The next part of the scripture is a part that we frequently overlook or just do not realize how important it is. He comforts us so that we will be able to comfort those who are also in any affliction with the same comfort that we receive from Him and He gives us comfort so that we will be at peace and be full of joy. He not only gives us comfort for our own being but He also wants us to share our comfort with others. When we bless others in this way, we are in return blessing the Lord because He loves all mankind the same. He has given us gifts (spiritual gifts) such as the gift of mercy, the gift of exhortation, and the gift of serving. But He does not give us these gifts just for our own good. He gives us gifts so that we can use them for those around us and the building up of the body of Christ on earth, ultimately glorifying God our Father. As you go through your day today look around you and see who needs comfort or encouragement that you can lift up in the name of the Lord.

Heavenly Father, I know that You give me comfort in times of affliction and in times of peace as well. I know that You want me to be at peace, but You also want me to share the comfort and peace You give to me so that I can lift up the members of the body of Christ around me and glorify You. Every good gift comes from You, and You give us spiritual gifts to use for each other and ultimately for Your glory. Do not let me miss an opportunity today with my peers, family, and coworkers to give them comfort and joy in Your name. My fellow dieters are a good place to start comforting people, for I have so much in common with them. Continue to give me the wisdom I need for this purpose, and I pray in the mighty name of Jesus. Amen.

Nutrition Thought for the Day.

There is a compound in our bodies called nicotinamide adenine dinucleotide (NAD). This compound is absolutely necessary for the production of energy. The nicotinamide is niacin. Just like the other vitamins, taking an excess of niacin will not cause us to produce more energy. Any excess will be excreted in the urine. Like the other water-soluble B vitamins, we cannot store niacin in the body per se but also like the other B vitamins, a high concentration of niacin is found in the liver because of a large amount of metabolism that takes place in the liver involving energy.

Day 177
Praise Be to God for His Comfort II

"As one whom his mother comforts, so I will comfort you; and you will be comforted in Jerusalem." (Isaiah 66:13)

As children, we knew we could always depend on our mother to give us comfort whenever we ran into a problem, whether it was falling and scraping a knee or not getting something that we wanted. She always had the words to say to help us. Our God is like that, but above and beyond everything she could ever do. He always has the words to say, and they are found in the Bible; God indeed is our comforter. As a child, we knew to run to our mother when we needed comfort, even if it was for a very small, minute thing. Do you know to run to your God for comfort? Even for small and minute things? If you do not do that, you should. Your God wants to comfort you in everything and not just the big things, He cares about your every move and your every thought. When I was young, I used to wonder how in the world one God could hear everyone's prayers at once. That is still beyond my comprehension, but it is true. As a young Christian, you might not want to bother God with the small petty things because you think He is too busy. Your God is never too busy for even the smallest problem that you might encounter. Do not ever feel like you cannot go to your Father God for comfort, advice, or wisdom. He is always ready to hear you and to help you.

> Thank You, Father, that You are always available. You are never too busy with managing things in the universe or listening to the requests of your people. I do not understand how You do that, but I know it is true. Nothing is too hard or too big for You to handle and at the same time nothing is too small or too petty for You to consider. I know I can always call on You in a time of need—every need—great and small! Thank You Father God for Your great understanding and love for me. I thank You in the name of Jesus. Amen.

Nutrition Thought for the Day.
Besides being involved in energy production so heavily, there are approximately two hundred enzymes that require NAD as a coenzyme. That means that those enzymes would not be active without NAD. Thus whatever reaction those enzymes are necessary for would not take place. All the B vitamins are important in reactions other than energy production, but this makes niacin even more essential.

Day 178
He Is My Hiding Place

You are my hiding place; You preserve me from trouble; You surround me with songs of deliverance. (Psalm 32:7)

Besides being our comforter, our rock, our refuge, and all the other attributes attributed to our God, He is our hiding place. He preserves His children from trouble, and He surrounds them with songs of deliverance. The Book of Psalms is full of songs of deliverance and encouraging words about how much our God loves us and protects us. It will not be until we get to heaven that we will realize how many times we were preserved from trouble. I am willing to bet that almost daily something happens in the spiritual that we cannot see that He protected us from—that is if we are calling on God's help and His angels to surround us in times of need, even when we do not know we are in need. I begin each day by presenting my day to the Lord and asking for His protection around me, my family, my home, and everything that belongs to me. I ask for protective angels, warring angels, guardian angels, and angels of all kinds to be around me and to protect me. I ask for the Holy Spirit to fill me afresh and anew and give me wisdom, understanding, and direction for the day. If you are not already doing that, I highly recommend it. Do not be afraid or do not hesitate to speak God's blessing over yourself and all that is yours.

Heavenly Father, I wonder how many times each day You have directed my steps or ran interference for me that protected me from harm. If I could see into the spiritual realm, I believe I would see angels all around. I know that bad things still happen to good Christian people, but I also know that You are with us through everything that comes our way. I am sure that Your Holy Spirit is speaking to my spirit at all times, but I am not always able to hear Him because of the hectic daily routine that I have to face. Help me to be more in tune with Your Word so that I do not miss any words of wisdom that come from the Holy Spirit. I ask this in the name of Jesus. Amen.

Nutrition Thought for the Day.
The niacin requirement for adult males is 16 milligrams per day, and for adult females, it is 14 milligrams per day. This is a much larger requirement than the other two B vitamins discussed; however, niacin deficiency in this country is still not common. Deficiencies of niacin do exist, and it is sometimes called the four D vitamin because it can produce four deficiency symptoms, all of which start with the letter D; dermatitis, diarrhea, dementia, and death.

WAYNE E. BILLON, PH.D., RDN, LDN

Day 179
He Is My Shield

"As for God, His way is blameless; the word of the LORD is tested; He is a shield to all who take refuge in Him." (2 Samuel 22:31)

Five days ago, we had a scripture that said the Lord is our shield. This scripture repeats that and adds the way of the Lord is blameless and that His Word is tested. God's Word goes back about six thousand years. During that time there have been many prophecies that have been given and have been fulfilled. The only prophecies that have not been fulfilled are those predicting the end times, and gradually those are being fulfilled. This means that God gave us His Word and then fulfilled it. His Word has been tested and has been proven to be true; to question God's Word is foolishness.

So the scriptures that we have looked at over the past few months that proclaim your protection, your peace, your comfort, etc. have all been fulfilled not only in your life but also in the life of hundreds of thousands of Christians since the time of Christ. There is no need for you ever to doubt God's Word. God's Word is truth and God cannot lie—it is impossible for Him to lie. Every promise that you can find in God's Word, you can receive as a promise that is intended for you. As you walk through your day today, walk with such confidence that nothing will shake you because you know that God's Word is true and it is your shield.

Thank You, Father, that Your promises were true yesterday, they are true today, and they will be true tomorrow and until the end of time. Thank You, Father that You are a shield about me and I know this is true because You cannot lie. Your Word has been tested and retested and has been proven to be true. I resolve to walk through this day believing that Your Word is true for me in every situation that I might encounter. I also resolve that You are my shield and my protection. By an act of my will, I choose to rely on Your promises. I thank You, Father, in Jesus's name. Amen.

Nutrition Thought for the Day.

Since you may encounter this next bit of information about niacin in the media, I think it is worthwhile mentioning here. Sometimes niacin can be used as a drug and not just as a vitamin. Niacin taken in very large doses has been reported to increase HDL levels. There are not very many things that can increase HDL, and so some physicians suggested people take niacin in pharmacologic doses rather than dietary doses to raise their HDL levels. This has since been found to be ineffective and may even produce harm to the human body. Taking niacin in large doses is no longer recommended.

Day 180
He Is My Dwelling Place

"There is none like the God of Jeshurun, who rides the heavens to your help, and through the skies in His majesty. The eternal God is a dwelling place, and underneath are the everlasting arms." (Deuteronomy 33:26–27a)

There is none like our God, like the God of Jeshurun. What does that mean? *Jeshurun* is a Hebrew word (Strong's H3484) that means upright one and is a symbolic name for Israel that describes her ideal character. So this says there is none like the God of Israel, an ideal character, who rides the heavens to get to us for help. Our God is eternal and is a dwelling place that is everlasting. Our God always was and always will be—He is the everlasting God, the Alpha, and the Omega. He is our dwelling place, and His everlasting arms are always there to catch us and guide us. Walk through your day today in peace knowing that you serve an everlasting, eternal God in whom you can always find peace. Your God will never leave you nor forsake you. Continue in your healthy lifestyle regimen in peace knowing that you are a child of the everlasting God.

Father, I thank You for being my dwelling place where I can always go to find peace and solitude in Your everlasting powerful arms. I know that You will always be with me and will never leave me. That thought is comforting to me and gives me strength for the day. Any success that I have accomplished so far in my life has been done because of Your grace and guidance. I resolve to approach my day today without any fear or doubt of the power that works within me. I thank You, Father, in the name of Jesus. Amen.

Nutrition Thought for the Day.

Recent research has shown that while HDL does tend to go up with very large doses of niacin, it had no effects on reducing heart attacks or strokes. I do not believe very many physicians, if any, are recommending niacin any longer. The large doses of niacin also had side effects, some of which could be very dangerous such as liver failure. I do not recommend that you take niacin in these large doses. If you have a family history or personal history of heart disease and low levels of HDL, you should talk about what you can do to treat that with your physician.

Day 181
Nothing Can Separate Me from His Love

For I am convinced that neither death, nor life, nor angels, nor principalities, nor things present, nor things to come, nor powers, nor height, nor depth, nor any other created thing, will be able to separate us from the love of God, which is in Christ Jesus our Lord. (Romans 8:38–39)

This scripture does not leave any question about what could separate us from our God. Everything that is said here is probably something you already know, but it is very comforting to read it all together in one scripture. Paul tells the Romans that he is convinced nothing, not death, nor life, nor angels, nor principalities, nor things present, nor things to come, nor powers, nor height, nor depth, nor any created thing (which would include anything else that may have been missed in the above liturgy) will be able to separate us from the love of God. This also includes sin which cannot separate us because Jesus died for our sins and they have been forgiven and removed. It is impossible for God not to love us and not to forgive us. We are His loving children that He created. When the walls are closing in on you, and you feel like you are at the end of your rope, remember that nothing can separate you from the love of God. He is with you, He will help you, and He will never leave you. Be comforted this day by His love.

Nothing from the past, the present, or the future can separate me from the love of my God. No heavenly thing such as angels, no earthly thing that has ever been created, and no demon can separate me from the love of my God. My thoughts, my actions, or sinful ways cannot separate me from the love of my God because Jesus died for my sins and I can receive forgiveness for any mistakes that I make. The only thing that could separate me from my God is me. I would have to, by an act of my will, completely turn my back on my God and decide never to follow Him again. Of course, I will never do that so I can walk with confidence this day that I am not separated nor will I ever be separated from my God who loves me so much. Thank You, Father God, for Your love in the name of Jesus. Amen.

Nutrition Thought for the Day.

Vitamin B6 is the next water-soluble vitamin. Vitamin B6 is found in many forms including pyridoxine, pyridoxal phosphate, and pyridoxamine phosphate. Pyridoxine and its phosphorylated form are just about exclusively found in plant foods. Pyridoxal phosphate and pyridoxamine phosphate, for the most part, are found in animal products. Rich sources in the plant Kingdom include vegetables in general, grains, nuts, and some fruits such as bananas. The rich sources in animal products include sirloin steak, salmon, and the white meat of chicken.

Day 182
His Thoughts Are the Highest

"For My thoughts are not your thoughts, nor are your ways My ways," declares the LORD "for *as* the heavens are higher than the earth, so are My ways higher than your ways and My thoughts than your thoughts." (Isaiah 55:8–9)

Isaiah 55 is a short chapter in which God tells His people to come to Him and to listen to what He has to say. He tells the wicked to forsake their ways and the unrighteous man his thoughts and return to the Lord, and He would have compassion on them. Then comes verse 8 where He says that His thoughts are not our thoughts and His ways are not our ways. He tells us that His thoughts are much higher than ours. I do not think any of us will have a problem admitting that we cannot think as God can and that we are certainly not perfect in our actions. Sometimes we may even condemn ourselves because of our actions, but as you read the scripture, you should realize that our God knows that His thoughts and ways are higher than our thoughts and ways. He knows that we do not think or act as He does, nor will we ever be able to while on this earth. That is why He sent His Son to pay for our sins and our unrighteousness. So, if you realize that at times you are not reaching your potential, spiritually and physically, you need also to realize that your God still loves you and forgives you for any miscoming.

Father God, I know that I certainly do not think as You do and I certainly do not act as Jesus did when He walked the face of this earth. I know that Your thoughts are higher than my thoughts. No matter how much I try to reach perfection, I know I will never be able to get there, but I believe I can do better than I am doing now. Because Your ways and Your thoughts are so much higher than mine does not mean that I should not strive to do the absolute best I can. I resolve this day to try to do better, spiritually and physically, in everything that I do and I continue to ask for Your Holy Spirit to give me wisdom and understanding to accomplish that task. In Jesus's name, I pray. Amen.

Nutrition Thought for the Day.
Vitamin B6 is absorbed in the small intestines with the help of a zinc-containing enzyme. Rates of vitamin absorption vary greatly from individual to individual depending on many factors but the range of absorption for vitamin B6 is from 61 to 92%. Ultimately, larger doses result in larger amounts being absorbed but, as with most vitamins and minerals, the larger the dose, the less efficient is the absorption. This is good since it will help prevent us from getting a toxic dose but we can still take in so much that we could cause harm to ourselves.

WAYNE E. BILLON, PH.D., RDN, LDN

Day 183
He Is with Us Always, Even to the End of the Age

"Go therefore and make disciples of all nations, baptizing them in the name of the Father and the Son and the Holy Spirit, teaching them to observe all that I commanded you; and lo, I am with you always, even to the end of the age." (Matthew 28:19–20)

These are the last verses in the book of Matthew. Jesus gave this command to His disciples as He was ascending into heaven. They give us the everlasting hope that no matter what we do, He is always with us—even until the end of the age. This is Jesus's command to us to go and make disciples of all nations baptizing them in the name of the Father and the Son and the Holy Spirit. He tells us to teach everyone how to know and obey His Word. Even though you may have heard this verse and you know that He is always with you no matter where you go, how often have you obeyed this scripture?

Verse 19 starts out as, "Go therefore and make disciples…" this is a command, not a suggestion or something that would be nice to do. He did not say, "All you who have been ordained or have been through Bible College go, therefore." The command was to you and to me to go and make disciples. Man added the seminary and ordination part years later. Do not feel like you cannot do this, because you can. It does not mean that you have to stand on a street corner with a Bible and yell at people as they pass. You can use your everyday dealings with the people where you work to be a witness for your God. Ask Jesus to give you an opportunity to lead someone to Him and be ready at any moment to witness and watch to see what happens.

> Father God, I understand now that when Your Word says there is something we should do that is not a suggestion but a command from You. I realize that the command is for every other born-again Christian and for me. Each of us has the opportunity to witness to someone every day, but because of the cares and pressures around us, we often forget. Forgive me for not taking every opportunity to be a witness for You. Give me the wisdom and understanding to know the timing and person that I should talk to on Your behalf. All of us that are born-again Christians are ambassadors for Christ. Help me to remember that and to speak up on Your behalf as often as You present me with an opportunity. In Jesus's name, I pray. Amen.

Nutrition Thought for the Day.
Vitamin B6 is frequently abbreviated as PLP. It functions in the body in many different diverse areas, but it is associated with over one hundred different enzyme systems. Just about everything that happens to protein is a result of a PLP containing enzyme. When amino acids are broken down, and when amino acids are synthesized, PLP is required. Many other protein functions require PLP. It is an essential vitamin in protein metabolism.

Day 184
Keep God's Word in Your Heart

My son, give attention to my words; incline your ear to my sayings. Do not let them depart from your sight; keep them in the midst of your heart. For they are life to those who find them and health to all their body. (Proverbs 4:20–22)

If we are to listen to God's Words, keep them in our hearts, and not let them out of our sight, then reading and meditating on His Word cannot be overemphasized. We know that the closer we get to Him, the closer He is to us, and the better we can hear Him. We know that His Word gives us guidance and protection. The proverb for today is another aspect of keeping God's Word in the midst of our hearts for it is life and health to our body. His Word tells us that by Jesus's stripes we are healed (Isaiah 53:5, 1 Peter 2:24). As we read God's Word and pay close attention to all the promises, we should make a list of them and memorize each promise. Everything that God says He will do in His Word is not just a statement, but also a promise. We can read over these promises lightly and say something like, "Wow that is nice," but it is more than nice, it is a promise from our God Himself. Remember that He cannot change His mind and take His promises away. Any promise that is in God's Word is for all His children and is there forever. One problem non-believers have with is that see God's Word as too good to be true. We know that the Gospel means good news and refers to God's Word and God's Word is truth. The word "gospel" was hardly ever used in Jesus's times because it meant more than "good news," it meant too-good-to-be-true news. Isn't that amazing? God's Word is too good to be true! However, we know that God's Word is in itself truth. So, as you read His Word, look for His promises and claim them for yourself. This is not a name-it-and-claim-it mentality, but it is believing God's Word for its face value. Release your faith to receive God's promises for you.

Father God, I know that Your Word is truth and is indeed good news. To the unbeliever it seems like too good to be true news but, as believers, we understand that it is indeed good news and is truth. When I read Your Word, I need to make it a regular practice that I read it with the understanding that every promise I find in Your Word is a promise for me, and I should claim it for myself. I resolve to read Your Word with a new understanding and a new perspective to find every promise that is there and claim it for myself. I know that for Your Word to work in my life, I cannot just claim anything for the sake of having things but for the sake of my health, protection, and prosperity. I know that I also have to make these claims based on my faith in You. I pray for this in Jesus's name. Amen.

Nutrition Thought for the Day.

PLP also functions in glycogen degradation. Remember glycogen is stored glucose in our liver and our muscles. This is important in energy production for the body. PLP is also important in the metabolism of all macronutrients for converting them into energy as was the three vitamins previously discussed. PLP is necessary for red blood cell formation. Finally, PLP is also necessary for proper nerve function. Thus PLP is important in energy production, protein metabolism, carbohydrate metabolism, red blood cell formation, and maintaining nerve cells.

WAYNE E. BILLON, PH.D., RDN, LDN

Day 185
Fear the Lord and Shun Evil

Do not be wise in your own eyes; fear the LORD and turn away from evil. It will be healing to your body and refreshment to your bones. (Proverbs 3:7–8)

Sometimes as born-again Christians, even though we know the Lord and we know His Word, we can get cocky and think we can do things on our own—even simple things. While we do have the ability to accomplish some things on this earth, we cannot come near to our potential on our own power. We must depend upon the Lord. It is when we become wise in our own eyes that we start going down the road to failure. This verse in Proverbs tells us to turn away from evil and fear the Lord. While this is indeed something we should do, we can become wise in our own eyes with things that do not even relate to something that is necessarily evil, but something that is just distracting us. In this case, we may not think about turning away from it because we do not see the distraction as evil. However, the fear of the Lord mentioned in this verse means fear, but it also means to revere or to stand in awe. It is a kind of reverent fear with honor and respect.

Distractions can cause us to refrain from giving respect to our God. If we can them, we will find that we can also avoid going down the road to failure, whether a spiritual failure or physical failure. Revering God's Word can give healing to our body and refreshment to our bones. This is really an interesting verse because in the King James Version it says, "it shall be health to thy navel." The Hebrew word used here is *shor* (Strong's H8270) and means umbilical cord or naval. So this verse is saying that a reverent fear of our Lord is nourishment to us as a mother's umbilical cord is nourishment to her baby. How awesome is that? Have a reverent fear of your God today and seek Him with all your heart knowing that you are attached to Him like an unborn baby is attached to its mother.

Father God, I thank You so much for keeping me as close and attached to You as a newborn baby is still attached to its mother by the umbilical cord. I have a reverent fear of You and honor You with all my heart. I do not want to be wise in my own eyes, but I want to have Your wisdom and avoid evil. I even want to avoid distractions that are not necessarily evil but are preventing me from giving You respect. Continue to give me the wisdom and understanding so that I may accomplish this in my walk. I will approach today knowing that I am spiritually, and in a way physically, attached to You. In Jesus's name, I pray. Amen.

Nutrition Thought for the Day.

Since PLP is vital in muscle metabolism, particularly in the synthesis of amino acids, and results in the synthesis of muscle, do bodybuilders need additional vitamin B6? Since muscle metabolism is being increased, yes there would be an increased need for the vitamin, but the increased need would be so negligible that additional supplements are not necessary. Remember that vitamin B6 is found in a variety of foods and anybody eating a balanced diet should be getting more of the vitamin than they need. Muscle builders are usually very good eaters and eat a lot of meat, and the vitamin is abundant in meat. While there may be a slight increase in the requirement, there should be no need for additional supplementation.

Day 186
Acknowledge Him in All Your Ways

Trust in the LORD with all your heart and do not lean on your own understanding. In all your ways acknowledge Him, and He will make your paths straight. (Proverbs 3:5–6)

"Do not lean your own understanding"—a command, not a suggestion. This is another way of saying, "do not be wise in your own eyes," that was discussed yesterday. At the time we have to make a decision, we may quickly make a rash decision if we lean on our own understanding. This is true even if the decision is one that may not seem to be very important in our eyes at the time. Every decision we make is important because it will ultimately leave a memory in our minds. If we rashly rush into a decision without acknowledging our God or asking Him what we should do, we may end up going down the wrong path and making the wrong decision. As the scripture says, "if in all our ways we acknowledge Him, He will make our paths straight." Notice that it says, "in all our ways." This means even those decisions that we might not even think twice about because they seem to be such an obvious or unimportant decision. Keep this thought with you and rely on your God to help you in making all decisions. The choices that you have to make concerning your healthy lifestyle program may be second nature to you by now, but do not take them for granted either. If you make any changes or substitutions, carefully consider them and research them if necessary.

Dear Father, I know that I am here for a purpose and that everything I do is being watched by someone. If I take too many things for granted, then my family, my peers, or my coworkers may think that I am being compulsive and not trusting in You. I do not want to give anyone the impression that You do not come first in my life. I want to acknowledge You in all my ways and lean on Your understanding and not my own. I trust totally that when I do that, You will make my paths straight. I thank You, Father, in the name of Jesus. Amen.

Nutrition Thought for the Day.

Several days ago I mentioned that we used to teach excessive amounts of water-soluble vitamins would not be dangerous because the excess is excreted out through the kidneys. While this is true, I also said that you can always get too much of anything. Vitamin B6 is an excellent example of this. I heard of a report several years ago that some bodybuilders discovered vitamin B6 was necessary for muscle synthesis and therefore they concluded that if they took an excess, it would help them build muscle faster. This is not true, in fact, it can be very dangerous. Some of these bodybuilders took 2500 times the required amount, which resulted in dire consequences.

WAYNE E. BILLON, PH.D., RDN, LDN

Day 187
Be Careful of the Power of the Tongue

Death and life are in the power of the tongue, and those who love it will eat its fruit. (Proverbs 18:21)

One of the hardest things for us to get under control is our tongue. It is so easy to put your tongue in motion before you put your brain in-sync with what you really should be saying. The tongue can get you in more trouble than anything else. As the proverb for today says, "life and death are in the power of the tongue." It also says, "those who love it will eat its fruit." One thing about words that come out of your mouth that is very important to remember is this: they are like toothpaste. Once the toothpaste is out of the tube, there is no putting it back. You can say something hurtful very quickly without meaning it and without thinking. And yes, you can ask for forgiveness and the person may very well forgive you, but it leaves a scar in the person's mind, maybe even a small spiritual scar, but a scar just the same. In years to come, that thought may resurface and open up like a bad wound and still cause trouble. The best thing to do is to think before you put your tongue in motion and only say those things that will be edifying to the person you are talking to and to God.

Father God, I know that my tongue can be used for very hurtful comments or for edifying and praise. It is easy to speak quickly without first organizing my thoughts. Forgive me for times in the past when I have done this, and I do not ever want to do it again. I resolve to practice thinking things through before I put my tongue in motion. Before I say anything help me to remember to filter what I say through Your Word. If it lines up with Your Word, then I know it will be good to say. Let my words be fruitful to those that I speak them to and to You. Let them not cause grief now or in the future. In Jesus's name, I pray. Amen.

Nutrition Thought for the Day.
Frequently a toxic amount of a vitamin or mineral will produce the same symptoms as a deficient amount. That reportedly happened in the case with vitamin B6. Since B6 is also necessary for protection of the sheaths that cover the nerve endings, a deficiency will produce pain and possible paralysis in the feet and hands. The toxicity of this vitamin produced the same symptoms, and some of the bodybuilders were paralyzed to such a degree that they could not lift their arms and legs against gravity. With IV fluids the excess of the vitamin was washed out of their bodies, but some subjects had permanent damage. Never take that large of an excess of any vitamin or mineral.

Day 188
Keep from Having a Broken Spirit

The spirit of a man can endure his sickness, but *as for* a broken spirit who can bear it? (Proverbs 18:14)

If something happens to make us sick or ill, but our spirit is healthy—that is, if our spirit is in tune with God's Spirit—then we can endure the hardship. But if our spirit is broken and is not in tune with God's Spirit, then we will have a hard time dealing with adversity of any kind. When we get discouraged, depressed, or get down for any reason we want to examine our spirit first before anything else. If there is something that is not right between our spirit and God's Spirit, then that is the first thing we need to correct: that can be easily done by confessing whatever it is that is causing separation between our spirit and God's spirit. Whatever it may have been, we need to forgive ourselves, then we can move on and face the adversity. God is always there waiting for us to come to Him for help and for healing of our spirit. Do not ever wait or put off until tomorrow correcting something that is not right in your spirit today.

Dear Lord, there are times when adversity can slowly and quietly sneak into my spirit without me realizing it. Things may tend to seem off kilter a little bit and I do not know why. I need to learn that when that happens, I should sit down and examine my spirit to make sure that it is in tune with Your Spirit. I do not ever want to get out of sync with Your Spirit. I know that a healthy spirit leads to a healthy mind and a healthy body. Help me to always keep communication open between my spirit and Your Spirit. In Your name, Jesus, I pray. Amen.

Nutrition Thought for the Day.

A deficiency of vitamin B6, can cause a microcytic hypochromic anemia in addition to neurological damage. That means our red blood cells are smaller than normal and have a pale color. This will affect oxygen transportation through the body and will cause us to be short of breath and get tired easily. Many things can cause us to be short of breath and get tired, so if you have those symptoms, do not immediately blame it on a deficiency of vitamin B6. You should be evaluated by a physician to find out the cause.

Day 189
The Fear of the Lord Leads to Life

The fear of the LORD *leads* to life, so that one may sleep satisfied, untouched by evil. (Proverbs 19:23)

The reverent fear of God leads to life. When you honor your God and you show reverence to Him, it means that you are seeking His presence and staying in His Word. When that happens, besides uniting yourself to your God as a newborn is attached to his mother via the umbilical cord, you may also find that your sleep will be satisfied. You will not be in fear of evil or of any adversity that comes your way on this earth. Peace with your God is manifested when your heart does not condemn you. You can walk in peace, you can work in peace, and you can sleep in peace. The key is staying full of God and staying in His Word. This does not put you in a protective bubble where nothing can get to you because you still have to walk through this evil world, but nothing has to affect you and you do not have to succumb to anything. Practice walking in God's presence today and feel His peace as your spirit is united to His Spirit. 1 Corinthians 6:17 says, "But the one who joins himself to the Lord is one spirit with Him." This is true, or it is not true—let your faith decide.

> Father God, I choose this day to unite my spirit with Your Spirit by staying in Your Word. I expect to be at peace at home, in my workplace, and any place else I go. I expect to have a peaceful, restful sleep. I know that the devil will still try to tempt me and that natural adversities will come my way, but I also know that I do not have to succumb to any attack of the enemy or any adversity that I may face. I know that You are with me and will never leave me. I thank You for the honor and privilege that You have given to me by allowing my spirit to be at one with Your Spirit. In Jesus's name, I pray. Amen.

Nutrition Thought for the Day.
Some advocate taking larger doses of vitamin B6 for carpal tunnel syndrome, morning sickness, and PMS. No strong documented research says this is correct, even though some physicians prescribe extra vitamin B6 for these conditions. Taking a little extra will not be harmful since an excess would be excreted out through the kidneys but taking megadoses should be avoided as previously discussed.

Day 190
Listen to the Lord

"But he who listens to me shall live securely and will be at ease from the dread of evil." (Proverbs 1:33)

So far in Proverbs, we see that if we listen to the Lord our God, He will give us life, direct our paths, bring health to our bodies and nourishment to our bones, satisfy our sleep, and protect us from evil. Today's proverb adds that we will be at ease from even the dread of evil. We do not even have to think about what evil can do to us. The Hebrew word for evil in this case is *rà* (Strong's H7451) and means evil but also could mean bad, malignant, unpleasant, unhappy, and several other similar meanings. Thus, if we listen to the Lord our God, He will keep us from even the dread of all these wrongful/evil connotations, even conditions that we may not consider to be evil such as something that is unpleasant to us. This includes being unhappy. All of these conditions may be a subtle start of something bigger that the devil has planned for us down the road. Nip his plans in the bud and do not let such feelings get a hold onto your spirit.

> Father God, I thank You for the book of Proverbs and all the wisdom it contains. From just the verses that I have read so far, I can easily see that by staying in Your Word and listing to Your Holy Spirit I can avoid all sorts of evil and even the dread of evil. I resolve today to continue to study Your Word and seek You with all my heart. I expect to have the peace that surpasses all understanding (Philippians 4:7) and guards my heart and mind. In Jesus's name, I pray. Amen.

Nutrition Thought for the Day.
Vitamin B6 requirements are 1.3 milligrams per day for adult men between the ages of 19 and 50. For men 51 years of age and greater the requirement goes up to 1.7 milligrams per day. Adult women between 19 and 50 of age have a requirement of 1.13 milligrams per day. Women 51 years and above have a requirement of 1.5 milligrams per day.

WAYNE E. BILLON, PH.D., RDN, LDN

Day 191
Commit Your Works to the Lord

"Commit your works to the LORD and your plans will be established." (Proverbs 16:3)

You can comply with this scripture by dedicating your day to the Lord when you wake up in the morning. This does not have to be a formal prayer per se, but you can just tell Him that you want to dedicate everything you do that day to Him. This will include your work, your play, your communication with all those around you, and your healthy lifestyle program. If you do this every day and stop at times during the day to remind yourself of the dedication you completed in the morning, it will help you to remember who you are in Christ and your Christian goals. If you can develop a habit of doing this when things are closing in around you and the opportunity presents itself for you to get angry or discouraged, then you can remind yourself that your day is dedicated to your Lord. This will provide you with strength because you do not want to give something to the Lord that is filled with anger or discouragement.

I know it is not always easy to do this, nor is it easy to stay completely joyous all the time, but it is possible. God would not call you to do something that He does not give you the strength to do. In 1 Thessalonians 5:15 it says, "See that no one repays another with evil, but always seek after that which is good for one another and all people." So when people do you wrong, do not do wrong to them in return, but seek to do that which is good. This verse is followed up by 1 Thessalonians 5:16–18, "Rejoice always; pray without ceasing; in everything give thanks; for this is God's will for you in Christ Jesus." I think the statement in between the two verses just mentioned, "pray without ceasing," is the key to being able to be joyous on all occasions. If we submit everything we do to the Lord and pray about it first, we will constantly be reminded of who we are in Christ and what our role is on this earth. Commit everything you do this day to the Lord and rejoice in His grace for you.

Lord Jesus, I rejoice in You today for all You do for me. I submit everything I do today to You for Your praise and glory. Today I resolve that I want to do only those things that will be a good witness for You and will bring You glory. If I begin to do anything this day that will discredit my witness or will not bring glory to Your name, remind me, by the power of Your Holy Spirit, of the dedication that I made to You today and give me the strength to change my direction so that everything I do points to You. In Your name, Jesus, I pray. Amen.

Nutrition Thought for the Day.
Vitamin B12 is next and has several factors that make it different from the other water-soluble B vitamins. Vitamin B12 belongs to a group of compounds called cobalamins and has an atom of cobalt attached to it. Cobalt is not a required mineral per se because we do not make vitamin B12 in our bodies, but cobalt comes in our bodies already attached to vitamin B12. Animal products are the only natural sources of vitamin B12.

Day 192
Pursue Righteousness

The way of the wicked is an abomination to the LORD, but He loves one who pursues righteousness. (Proverbs 15:9)

This proverb should undoubtedly be no surprise to any Christian. The way of the wicked is an abomination to the Lord, but remember that Jesus died for the wicked. God does not like the way of the wicked, but He is ready to forgive the wicked and bring them into the Kingdom. There are times in the lives of each of us that we come across someone that is truly wicked. We need to be careful about saying this about someone so that we do not pass judgment, for this is not our place. However, if we come across a person whose actions and words are truly vile, and they even profess to be wicked, our reaction should be to avoid that person; this is probably a wise choice. I say probably because if the person is someone that is very close to you, it may not be possible. In either case, the correct approach is to pray for that person and look for an opportunity to be a witness to them for your Lord. If we use our daily actions and words to be a witness for someone that is acting wicked around us, then we are pursuing the second part of this proverb—seeking righteousness. The Lord loves one who pursues righteousness. Do you want to be someone who hates the wicked or do you want to be a person who seeks righteousness and prays for the wicked? As you go about your day today look for an opportunity to bless someone and be a witness to them. If you see someone who is being contrary or rebellious or just plain wicked, be ready to pray for that person.

Father God, I want to pursue righteousness in everything that I do. When I stand before You one day in the final judgment, I want to be able to hear, "Well done my good and faithful servant." To accomplish that, I realize that I have to walk through an evil world and will come in contact with evil people. I need to avoid the presence of evil, but at the same time, I need to be aware of which people need a witness and which need prayer. By the power of Your Holy Spirit, I ask that You continue to guide me so that I can be a righteous pursuing person that is a witness for You. In Jesus's name, I pray. Amen.

Nutrition Thought for the Day.
The best sources of vitamin B12 are meat, poultry, fish, shellfish, and egg yolks. As mentioned previously, the liver is an excellent source of vitamin B12 because so much activity takes place in the liver that requires vitamin B12. Vitamin B12 can be synthesized by microorganisms but not by our bodies. There are a few important things about the absorption of vitamin B12 and the preparation of the vitamin for absorption that takes place in the stomach that you should be aware of and will be covered next.

Day 193
Keep a Cheerful Heart

All the days of the afflicted are bad, but a cheerful heart *has* a continual feast. (Proverbs 15:15)

Have you ever noticed people around you that seem to want to do their own thing and never mention the Lord? Surely you have been in contact with people who rely on their own strength and help from the government or their family instead of looking to the Lord. I certainly have, and I often wondered why this type of person seems to be blessed more than I am. I think the devil loves for you to see this happening to other people and he likes to make you aware of it so that he can introduce jealousy into your heart. Guard your heart and do not let this happen. Such people may seem to be doing well now, but as today's proverb says, their days are bad—maybe not visibly bad to you or to them—but the time is coming when they will pay for their rebellious ways.

On the other hand, if you know who you are in Christ and you continue to seek Him, stay in His Word, and in fellowship, you will have a cheerful heart. It is as if a person with a cheerful heart is having a continual feast, even when things go wrong they can have the peace of the Lord with them at all times. This is the way you want to be in everything you do today—have a cheerful heart! How is your healthy lifestyle program coming? Is it causing you stress, or are you able to accept slow progress or a lack of progress? Trust in God to see yourself eventually be victorious. If you can do the latter, you will have a cheerful heart and will be encouraged to continue your program.

I am so thankful that my Father God loves me so much that I can walk through a storm and have the peace of Christ reign in my heart. Colossians 3:15 says to let the peace of Christ rule in my heart and to be thankful. I want the peace of Christ to rule in my heart today no matter what trials and tribulations I have to face. I know that You will keep me in perfect peace and I know that I will be victorious in the end. I thank You for Your peace in the name of Jesus. Amen.

Nutrition Thought for the Day.

Vitamin B12 comes into the body with food bound to polypeptides found in animal products. Hydrochloric acid, and an enzyme in the stomach called pepsin releases vitamin B12 from these polypeptides. A cobalamin binding protein attaches to the vitamin at this time. The same cells in the stomach that produce hydrochloric acid also produce a compound called the intrinsic factor. This intrinsic factor becomes very important later on in the small intestines as it concerns the absorption of vitamin B12.

Day 194
Walk in Wisdom

I have directed you in the way of wisdom; I have led you in upright paths. When you walk, your steps will not be impeded; and if you run, you will not stumble. (Proverbs 4:11–12)

Wisdom is a gift from God. James 1:5 says, "But if any of you lacks wisdom, let him ask God, who gives to all generously and without reproach, and it will be given to him." God wants you to walk in the way of wisdom and when you do He will lead you in upright paths. He promises that when you walk in wisdom, your steps will not be impeded, and if you have to run, you will not stumble. This does not mean that if you ask for wisdom you will all of a sudden be the wisest person on earth and will know everything there is to know. It does mean that when you are making decisions, and you need to make the right decision by using godly wisdom, it will be given to you if you ask for it and know how to hear from your Father God.

It also does not mean that you can live your life the way you want to without communicating with God on a regular basis and then when you need wisdom, you all of a sudden turn to God and expect to have the wisdom you need. When you walk with God on a daily basis and you stay in His Word, then you can ask for wisdom and receive it. In your healthy lifestyle program be sure to keep this in mind. If you hear about some food, supplement, or some new miracle diet that will cause you to lose weight or gain weight so much faster, do not jump at the thought of it. Ask for wisdom and research it before you make any rash changes. If you keep close to God's wisdom, He will lead you down a straight path.

Father God, I thank You for Your promise that if I need wisdom, all I have to do is ask of You. I know that I cannot use You like a grocery cart, going up and down the aisles and asking You for anything I want, and filling my basket up. I know I have to walk with You daily and stay in Your Word. When I do so, I know that You will direct my paths in everything that I do, including my healthy lifestyle program. I resolve this day to continue to seek You with all my heart and to use godly wisdom in all my decisions. I praise You and thank You for Your direction in my life, in Jesus's name. Amen.

Nutrition Thought for the Day.

Why is this information about vitamin B12 necessary at this point? It is very important because millions of people today are taking compounds that inhibit the production of hydrochloric acid in the stomach due to reflux disease or ulcers. People that are taking these medications also decrease the production of the intrinsic factor and the cobalamin binding protein. The reduction in hydrochloric acid, the cobalamin binding protein, and the intrinsic factor all decrease the absorption of vitamin B12. If you take medications to decrease acid secretions in your stomach, you probably need to supplement with vitamin B12. Large doses of vitamin B12 can cause more of B12 to be absorbed even without the intrinsic factor available.

Day 195
Walk in Wisdom II

He who walks with wise men will be wise, but the companion of fools will suffer harm. (Proverbs 13:20)

In 1 Corinthians 15:33, it says, "Do not be deceived: 'bad company corrupts good morals.'" If we fellowship with like-minded believers who walk in godly wisdom, then we will learn from them, and we will also be wise. Have you ever heard the old saying, "iron sharpens iron?" It is a true saying. If we walk with fools, even though they may be believers but do not walk with God on a regular basis and are used to going their own way, then we can be led astray by them and eventually turn to worldly wisdom. No matter how strong you may think you are this is possible. It can happen to anyone and must be taken into consideration when choosing friends. I know this is not always easy to do because you may have some long-term friends whose company you enjoy, but they just do not lead you in the way of God's Word. You must choose your friends wisely, and sometimes that may bring about a hard decision. As hard as it may be, the bottom line is that you may have to choose between your God and your old friend. It is tough, but God will give you the grace if you trust Him. Another possibility is to pray for your old friend to come to know the Lord.

> Thank You, Father God, for wisdom and direction for not only guiding me in my daily steps but also in directing me towards godly companions. If I am being misled by someone that is close to me, I ask that You give me direction so that I can make wise choices as tough as they may be. I resolve to choose Your companionship over that of any person on the face of this earth. I know that may not always be an easy thing to do when it comes to long-term friends, but I trust You to give me the grace and wisdom to accomplish that task. I also pray that You bring laborers across the paths of my close friends that do not know You so they can witness with me of Your salvation. In Jesus's name, I pray. Amen.

Nutrition Thought for the Day.

Once vitamin B12 reaches the small intestines, it is broken free from the cobalamin and binding protein and is attached to the intrinsic factor. It then moves through the small intestines to the end of the small intestines called the ilium and is absorbed at that point, particularly in the last third of the ilium. Only a small percentage of vitamin B12 that is not attached to the intrinsic factor is absorbed by diffusion. However, when large doses are taken it can be absorbed by diffusion all along the small intestines.

Day 196
Keep a Joyful Heart II

A joyful heart makes a cheerful face, but when the heart is sad, the spirit is broken. (Proverbs 15:13)

Contrary to popular belief, joy is not an emotion but is a state of being. I know that pleasant things can make us happy and under these conditions, we say that we are joyful. This is a form of joy, but we can be joyful under unpleasant conditions—it is our choice. I am not saying it is an easy choice, but it is still a choice just the same. Even when things are not going our way, we can choose to be joyful. The way we do that is by looking to our God for our joy and not to the circumstances we see on the face of this earth.

An excellent scripture to look at here, in addition to the one listed, is Hebrews 12:2 which says, "Fixing our eyes on Jesus, the author and perfecter of faith, who for the joy set before Him endured the cross, despising the shame, and has sat down at the right hand of the throne of God." Imagine all the suffering that Jesus had to go through. He knew exactly what was going to happen to Him, and He was not looking forward to it at all, but He endured it all because of the joy He knew He would receive by seeing all of us have the opportunity to have eternal life with Him in heaven. That is awesome! "But he who listens to me shall live securely and will be at ease from the dread of evil" (Proverbs 1:33). Another good scripture is Romans 14:17, "For the Kingdom of God is not eating and drinking, but righteousness and peace and joy in the Holy Spirit." I know you get much pleasure out of eating food, but our joy should come from the Lord. This is probably why Galatians 5:22 says that joy is a fruit of the Spirit.

> Father God, I thank You for the joy You have set before me. I know that when this life is over, I will spend eternity with You in heaven and that is indeed something to make me joyous. If Jesus knew that spending eternity in heaven with us humans was going to give Him such great joy that it gave Him the power to endure the tremendous suffering that He had to go through, how much more can I endure the rest of my life on this earth to spend eternity with Him! In Jesus's name, I thank You. Amen.

Nutrition Thought for the Day.

As people age, as in their elder years, some produce less intrinsic factor as a natural part of the aging process. This does not happen to everyone, but it does happen. Also, the elderly tend to eat less meat for several reasons. As people age their taste buds change and sometimes meat does not taste as good to the elderly. The elderly may also have difficulty chewing and not eat as much meat. Elderly that are on fixed incomes may not be able to afford much meat in their diet. Thus these factors set up the elderly for a possible vitamin B12 deficiency and supplements should be considered.

WAYNE E. BILLON, PH.D., RDN, LDN

Day 197
Avoid Laziness

The way of the lazy is as a hedge of thorns, but the path of the upright is a highway. (Proverbs 15:19)

The Lord does not like laziness. There are two other Proverbs, both of which say the same thing. Proverbs 6:10–11 says, "A little sleep, a little slumber, a little folding of the hands to rest"-your poverty will come in like a vagabond and your need like an armed man. Proverbs 24:33–34 is almost identical. "A little sleep, a little slumber, a little folding of the hands to rest," then your poverty will come as a robber, and you want like an armed man. The way of the lazy is as a hedge of thorns. Ever try to hike through the woods and find that between you and where you want to go is a hedge of thorns? Which is easier, to try to climb through the thorns or walk uninhibited down the highway?

I do not think that if you are lazy, the Lord will cause problems to come your way because He would not have to, your laziness would cause your own share of problems. If you are trying to lose weight and exercise is a part of your program, there is absolutely no place for laziness. If you allow laziness to overtake you and you do not exercise, you will likely gain your weight back or at least not lose weight. This would not be the Lord punishing you for not exercising, it would merely be you punishing yourself. Resolve this day to put laziness aside and complete your exercise program. You can always do some extra things to increase exercise like do not park right next to the door of the grocery store or next to the building where you work. Park a little further away and walk a little extra. All these little things will add up and pay dividends in the end.

> Father God, I know that laziness is not part of Your plan for my life. This includes not only laziness like "a little folding of the hands, a little rest" but spiritual laziness too. I know that I need to be physically active to help me be healthy and I also need to be spiritually active by studying Your Word and staying in fellowship with like-minded believers. As I need to take care of my physical condition, I also need to take care of my spiritual condition. I resolve this day to put laziness aside, whether it is physical or spiritual, and seek Your will for my life. I ask for Your help and guidance in Jesus's name. Amen.

Nutrition Thought for the Day.

Unlike the other B vitamins, vitamin B12 can be stored in the body and is stored in the liver. This is another reason why liver an excellent source of vitamin B12. Our requirement for vitamin B12 is 2.4 micrograms (a microgram is one-millionth of a gram which is a very, very small amount). The body is capable of storing from about 2 to 4 milligrams (a milligram or a thousandth of a gram). Considering the small requirement for vitamin B12, 2 to 4 milligrams is a very large amount. Thus it may take a while before a vitamin B12 deficiency manifests if someone goes to a diet that is devoid of B12.

Day 198
Avoid Pride

Pride *goes* before destruction, and a haughty spirit before stumbling. (Proverbs 16:18)

One of the greatest weapons the enemy has is pride. Satan's great fall from God's presence was a result of pride. He was in charge of all worship in heaven and he was a masterful worshiper, but he wanted to be the object of worship instead of the one giving worship. Whenever we set ourselves up as the source of greatness or the best at whatever, we are giving in to pride. We are doing this when we decide to do things our way instead of God's way. The opposite of pride is humility. Numbers 12:3 says, "Now the man Moses was very humble, more than any man who was on the face of the earth." If the Bible says that Moses was the most humble man on the face of the earth, then I believe it to be true. Do you know who wrote Numbers? Moses did. In the modern vernacular this would sound like "Hey man, I'm the most humble dude on the face of the earth." Does this sound like humility to you? Not by today's standards but the reason Moses could say that was because he knew from where his strength and ability came from and he gave credit (but not in this verse) to God for his abilities.

Look at Exodus 17; Moses was leading God's people through the wilderness when they could not find water. In verse 6, God told Moses to strike the rock at Horeb with his rod and water would come out. Moses did, and water came out. Later during their journey, they needed water again. In Numbers 20:8, God told Moses to speak to the rock in front of the congregation and water would come out. Instead, Moses struck the rock twice. Water came out, but because of his disobedience and pride, he could not enter the Promised Land. Moses decided to do it his way instead of God's way in front of God's people. God's way is always best.

Father, I know that pride comes before a fall and that the devil is good at deceiving us to think that our way is better than Your way. I do not ever want to give in to pride. I realize that all my strength and abilities come from You and I choose to give You all the glory for everything I accomplish on this earth. I ask for guidance in all that I do so that I can quickly recognize when pride raises its ugly head, and I can reject it. In Jesus's name, I pray. Amen.

Nutrition Thought for the Day.

Vitamin B12 has several vital functions among which includes the synthesis of red blood cells. When deficient in vitamin B12, the person will have a megaloblastic macrocytic anemia. That is a condition where the red blood cells are much larger than normal but have much less hemoglobin in them than normal. This decreases their ability to carry oxygen and results in the person being short-winded and tired. Vitamin B12 deficiency in the elderly is not uncommon. About 10–30% of older individuals have changes that occur in their gastrointestinal tract and either prevent or slow down the absorption of vitamin B12.

Day 199
Listen to the Lord

For the LORD gives wisdom; from His mouth *come* knowledge and understanding. (Proverbs 2:6)

Recently, we were talking about wisdom and that if we want wisdom, all we have to do is ask. Today's scripture further tells us that not only does wisdom come from the Lord, but also knowledge and understanding. Knowledge is knowing facts. Understanding is realizing what knowledge we have and the meaning of the knowledge. Wisdom is using the knowledge and understanding for the glory of God. The modern secular man does not see it that way. They see someone that is smart as being wise and full of knowledge and understanding. Being smart is not necessarily being wise. Trusting in God to show us how to use the knowledge and understanding we have is wisdom. When we see ourselves as smart, we are setting ourselves up for pride. Choose this day to be wise, that is to be full of godly wisdom and rely on Him to direct you in your daily tasks.

Father God, I thank You for wisdom, but I also thank You for the knowledge and understanding that You provide me. Give me a greater ability to be able to use the knowledge and understanding I have wisely for Your glory. It is my desire not to become puffed up with my knowledge and wisdom but to use it for Your glory only. In Jesus's name, I pray. Amen.

Nutrition Thought for the Day.

The sheaths that cover and protect the nerve endings are dependent on vitamin B12 as well as vitamin B6. A deficiency of B12 can cause tingling, numbness, and pain in the peripheral nerves. It is possible that a deficiency of vitamin B12 could also cause ataxia (shaking movements and unsteady gait), muscle weakness, spasticity, and other problems. Not everyone that has a deficiency in B12 will have these symptoms, but it is possible. These are also symptoms that are not uncommon in the elderly but just because someone may have some of the symptoms does not mean that they have a vitamin B12 deficiency. One rule of thumb we have about making a diagnosis is that you never make a diagnosis on just one symptom.

Day 200
Love Wins All

Better is a dish of vegetables where love is than a fattened ox *served* with hatred.
(Proverbs 15:17)

We know from the Gospel of John that God is love and we know that in the New Testament Jesus tells us that a summation of God's laws can be found in the statement, "love the Lord your God with all your heart mind and soul and love your neighbor as yourself." Thus, we know that love is more important than anything else in our lives. Today's scripture from the Old Testament points out this very thing. It says, "Better is a dish of vegetables where love is that a fat ox served with hatred." To understand this, you need to know that in biblical days the fattened ox was eaten on special occasions and major celebrations. A meal of all vegetables was not considered to be something desirable. So to have a meal with all vegetables and to also have love at that meal, was better than to have the choicest morsels with hatred. Let this be the theme not only for today but also for your life. Try to see your peers, neighbors, family, etc. through the same eyes as Jesus sees them. Jesus sees all of us as someone He died for, and He loves all of us, even when He does not receive love in return.

It is sometimes difficult to do this when the people around us are criticizing us or treating us wrongfully. You may encounter this as an overweight person or underweight person and receive criticism because of your weight; maybe not to your face but you know people are talking about you behind your back. They may even be saying that you trying to go to a healthy lifestyle is a waste of time. Jesus does not think so and you should not think so either. It may be difficult to love these people, but it is God's command for you to do so. Forgive them, think about things from above, and move on. Do not be discouraged! Do not give up!

> Father God, I thank You that You love me no matter what I look like and no matter what I do. Even when those close to me may be making fun of me and criticizing me, I know that You still love me. I am also aware that I should take Your love and return it to those around me, even when they do not show love for me. There are times when this is very difficult to do, but I know that it is what You want me to do. I ask for Your Holy Spirit to continue to guide me and bring to my remembrance that I should love others as You love me. I resolve this day to show love for those around me and not to return criticism for criticism or hatred for hatred, and I ask for Your strength to accomplish this. In Jesus's name, I pray. Amen.

Nutrition Thought for the Day.

Very little of vitamin B12 is excreted from the body and turnover is approximately only 0.1% per day, hence the low requirement of 2.4 micrograms/day for this vitamin. People at risk for vitamin B12 deficiency, besides the elderly, include people taking medications to reduce acid production in the stomach and strict vegetarians since vitamin B12 is only found in animal products. True vegans should have a supplement.

WAYNE E. BILLON, PH.D., RDN, LDN

Day 201
Do Not Be Gluttonous

Do not be with heavy drinkers of wine, *or* with gluttonous eaters of meat; for the heavy drinker and the glutton will come to poverty, and drowsiness will clothe *one* with rags. (Proverbs 23:20–21)

The wisdom of this proverb should be obvious. Someone who is not overweight or a heavy drinker should already know that this can be true. The consequences that may run through your mind first is serious weight gain with alcoholism and all the unhealthy results that accompany both of those issues. Those conditions will occur if this was a continuous lifestyle but this proverb adds some additional woes. It says that gluttons will come to poverty and that the drowsiness that results from heavy drinking will clothe one with rags. We know that both of these results can be obtained. I once counseled a young man that was over 800 pounds. He was a high school football player that did not go to college, but upon graduation from high school he continued to eat as he did during football season but without exercise. The bigger he got, the less he could move around, and the more he ate. He ended up not being able to hold a job and resulted in poverty. Granted, this is an extreme case, but it does happen. It should not be difficult to believe that a heavy drinker may have a hard time keeping the job also and would end up in poverty, being clothed with rags. Hopefully, you are not anywhere near these two extremes. In fact, you are exercising your free will to avoid these extremes by your healthy lifestyle program. You are on your way to a healthier, more vibrant you, and if you continue studying God's Word, you will also be on the way to a healthier more vibrant spirit. However your healthy lifestyle program is progressing (or maybe not progressing), you should never give up. Continue with your goal and God's Word, and you will be successful. Do not be discouraged! Do not give up!

Lord Jesus, I thank You for giving me the grace to help me avoid excessive eating and drinking. I credit You with directing me to a healthy lifestyle program so that I can avoid these traps in my future. I want to continue to lose to a healthy weight and continue to exercise even after I reach my weight loss goal. I know that a healthy body supports a healthy spirit and vice versa and I resolve to become healthy and to stay healthy in all three parts of my being: my body, my mind, and my spirit. I know that I will be successful and I will give You the praise and glory for every ounce of success I obtain. In Your name, Jesus, I pray. Amen.

Nutrition Thought for the Day.
An oral dose of 100 to 250 micrograms per day is usually adequate to maintain vitamin B12 levels. However, patients with absorption difficulties may need 1000 micrograms (or 1 milligram) of B12 per day. If you want to have a physician check for B12 blood levels, it is more accurate to have him check for methylmalonic acid. If you are deficient in vitamin B12, methylmalonic acid cannot be metabolized and accumulates in the blood. This is a more accurate test for B12 deficiency then measuring serum B12 levels.

Day 202
Do Not Be Spiritually Slack

If you are slack in the day of distress, your strength is limited. (Proverbs 24:10)

We never know what awaits us when we first get up. Oh, we may have a plan for what we are going to do that day, and we may have high expectations; but, as the expression says, life happens. All of us have awakened to what we anticipated to be a typical day that turned out to be on the side of extremely stressful. If spiritually we happen to be down on the day that this happens, then our strength is limited, and we have a harder time rebounding. We may stay in a distressed, depressed, or irritable mood for some time. But, if we are prayed up, we are much more apt to take the day in stride and not have that day last longer than a day. We need to always be ready in our spiritual man to encourage our physical man because we do not know what is going to happen on a daily basis. This is such a tremendous advantage to staying in God's Word and staying in good Christian fellowship so that when the attacks of the enemy come, we are ready in season and out of season.

Father God, I know that if I continue in Your Word and keep feeding my spirit man, I will be equipped to face any trial or tribulation that may come my way. I know that Your grace is sufficient for me but that I must walk in Your grace and not try to conquer the world or my own power. I resolve this day to submit to Your will and guidance for my life and to face each task as if You were standing next to me with a shield about me. I know that I can do all things through Christ who strengthens me (Philippians 4:13). I thank You, Father, in Jesus's name. Amen

Nutrition Thought for the Day.
Another treatment for vitamin B12 deficiency is very small tablets of vitamin B12 called "B12 dots." These are small pills that are put under the tongue to dissolve. To my knowledge, research has shown that vitamin B12 in larger doses can be absorbed sublingually (means can be absorbed under the tongue) but I have not seen evidence that taking the same large dose would be any of the less effective if swallowed. The big difference may be in the cost of the vitamin. You will probably find that the B12 dots are more expensive than standard vitamin B12 supplements.

WAYNE E. BILLON, PH.D., RDN, LDN

Day 203
The Lord Is Our Strength

The name of the LORD is a strong tower; the righteous runs into it and is safe. (Proverbs 18:10)

Suppose you wanted to build a strong tower to protect you in stormy weather. You would build a tower that has a broad base for strength and made of the strongest materials known to man, you then want to reinforce it to withstand excessive winds as in a tornado. You would insulate the tower and roof materials so that they would not be blown away and will be water repellent. Any windows would be covered over with steel shutters. The tower would have its own generator so that there would never be a loss of power and if you had such a tower, then when a storm came you could run into it and feel safe. Well, as born-again Christians you have such a tower. While you cannot see this tower or touch it as something tangible, it is there nonetheless. This tower is the name of Jesus. All authority is in the name of Jesus; authority that can protect you from any storm that may come your way. Under the wings of your Lord, you are safe. Know that, as you walk through your day today, you have a strong tower to protect you from anything that may come your way. Walk with confidence and trust in your Lord and Savior, Jesus Christ.

Lord Jesus, I thank You that You are a strong tower for me. I thank You that Your name is above every name and that You have given me the authority to use Your name in times of dismay. I know that I can run to You whenever storms of any type approach me and I will be completely safe physically and spiritually. I, by an act of my will, decide this day that I am going to walk in confidence that You are with me and will protect me from any harm. Lord Jesus, I thank You and pray this in Your Holy name. Amen.

Nutrition Thought for the Day.

Another water-soluble vitamin that has some similar functions to vitamin B12 is folic acid. You may see folic acid called folacin (an old outdated term) or folate. Folate is a general term for a large group of derivatives of folic acid that are found in plants and have similar chemical structures and properties. Not all folates are active forms of folic acid. Folic acid is the synthetic form of the vitamin and is the active form found in the body. Folic acid is the form of the vitamin that is found in grain products that were mentioned earlier. This is one vitamin where the synthetic form is better than the natural or organic form.

Day 204
Acquire a Wise Counsel

A wise man will hear and increase in learning, and a man of understanding will acquire wise counsel. (Proverbs 1:5)

Recently we talked about wisdom and trusting our God for wisdom. Today's scripture gives us a little different view on wisdom. It says, "A wise man will hear an increase in learning, and a man of understanding will acquire wise counsel." To be wise, we must be teachable. Always look for an opportunity to learn something new from someone that knows more than you do. Do not be so prideful as to think that you cannot learn from someone that you may otherwise consider to be lower than you in socioeconomic status, younger than you, or on a lower rung of the corporate ladder. If you want to be a leader, you must be teachable. If you allow yourself to do this, you will increase in learning. This is true if you are learning from a secular point of view or a spiritual point of view. Maybe you will come across a new Christian that has not been in God's Word as much as you have but he may give you some godly advice. Do not reject it because he is younger in the Lord than you are but receive it in humility. The other part of today's scripture is also important. Is there something in your workplace you do not know how to do or something in the scripture you do not understand? Do not hesitate to seek advice from someone that knows more than you do; this in itself is wisdom. Follow these rules, and you will increase in favor with your peers and your God, not to mention the knowledge and wisdom you will acquire.

Father God, I know that I do not have all the answers and that there are many things I can do well because of the gifts You gave me, but there are many things I still need to learn. With all humility, I want to seek knowledge from those around me, both in the secular world and the spiritual world that has the ability to teach me what I do not know. I resolve this day to be open to learning from those around me by seeking wise counsel whenever it is prudent. I expect Your Holy Spirit to guide me to wise counsel. In Jesus's name, I pray. Amen.

Nutrition Thought for the Day.
You may have heard of para-aminobenzoic acid (PABA). This compound is a part of folic acid. If you are wondering where you have seen PABA before, look on your ingredient label of sunscreen; it is usually a component of sunscreen solutions. At one time, folic acid had other names and was also called vitamin Bx or vitamin B9. Those terms are no longer used but you may still see some calling it vitamin B9.

WAYNE E. BILLON, PH.D., RDN, LDN

Day 205
The Lord Is Righteousness

The righteous has enough to satisfy his appetite, but the stomach of the wicked is in need. (Proverbs 13:25)

The righteous rely on their God for their needs to be met and the righteous know that the Lord will always be there for them. They walk out their lives on this earth in a satisfied manner. The righteous do not need to be continually seeking the next big thing, for they already have the biggest thing and are satisfied. The wicked lack confidence and do not have anyone to look to for constant truthful guidance. They never have enough and are always looking for more. They are greedy and live in a continuous greedy state. So the appetite mentioned in this scripture could be a food-type appetite where the righteous are satisfied when they have eaten enough, and the wicked are gluttonousness and never have enough. This scripture could also pertain to appetite as a desire for material possessions or even evil things or practices. In any case, you want to practice righteousness and be satisfied with what you have and with the Lord's provision. This does not mean you should not want to better yourself, but just do not go after things as an obsession. Walk out this day as a satisfied righteous believer while trusting in your God. Remember, you are righteous, not based on what you have done but based on what Jesus did for you.

Father God, I thank You that You satisfy my every need, lack, and want. You are all I need and You will never let me down. I ask that You give me the wisdom to see the needs of others and the provisions to help others when they are in need. I do not want to be prideful and look at the lost and say how glad I am not like them. Instead, I want to look at the lost that are continually seeking things and ask how I can help them to find satisfaction in You. I resolve to be attentive to do that today. In Jesus's name, I pray. Amen.

Nutrition Thought for the Day.

Good sources of folic acid include green vegetables (especially greens and the cabbage family), legumes (beans and peas), citrus fruits, and strawberries. Since folic acid is one of the vitamins that is used to fortify all processed grains, they are a decent source of folic acid. Animal products are not sources of folic acid. However, how much folic acid that is in a food source is not necessarily a good indication of how much you will absorb from that food. The plants do not contain folic acid but they contain folate, and that is converted to folic acid in the body. As a result of food preparation and other factors, the folate found in plants varies from as high as 96% in cooked lima beans to as low as 25% in romaine lettuce. The results of thermal processing on folate bioavailability depend on the form of the folate present in food.

Day 206
Preserve Kindness and Truth

Do not let kindness and truth leave you; bind them around your neck, write them on the tablet of your heart. So you will find favor and good repute in the sight of God and man. (Proverbs 3:3–4)

Note that this proverb is describing an act of wisdom. It tells us not to let kindness and truth leave us but to bind them around our necks and to write them on the tablets of our hearts. It tells us that if we do this, we will find favor and good repute in the sight of God and the sight of man. Kindness and truth are godly qualities that we should always want to profess in everything that we do, regardless of what we may receive in return. However, God's Word promises us that if we walk in truth and show kindness, we will find favor and good repute in the sight of God and man. Repute means standing, reputation, or character. So if we profess these qualities, we will stand before God with a good reputation and a moral character. We will also stand before our peers and our bosses with the same excellent reputation and an excellent moral character. So let kindness and truth be embedded in your heart; hold on to them and practice them in your daily activities at home, work, play, and church. You will find favor with all those around you but most importantly with your God.

Father God, it is my lifelong goal to please You and to find favor in Your sight. I know that if I do that my earthly walk will fall into place and I will find favor in the eyes of my peers and superiors. I know that unfortunately there are people in this world that hate You, thus they hate me too. While I may see them as some one Your Son died for, they may see me as their enemy. That is unfortunate, but it is unfortunate for them because if they are my enemy, they are Your enemy, and You will fight my battles for me. I resolve this day to walk in kindness and truth in everything that I do, and I ask for Your guidance and strength in that endeavor. I pray for this in the name of Jesus. Amen.

Nutrition Thought for the Day.
Some factors that can affect folate bioavailability include zinc deficiency and chronic alcohol ingestion. Both of these will decrease the availability of folic acid to the body. Large doses of folic acid will cause it to be absorbed by diffusion all along the small intestines. Overall, about 50% of folate in food is absorbed while the folic acid absorption from supplements and from the fortified grains is higher, especially if taken on an empty stomach.

Day 207
Watch Your Heart with Diligence

Watch over your heart with all diligence, for from it *flow* the springs of life. (Proverbs 4:23)

Guarding your heart is a critical step to staying full of God and walking closely with Him. Guarding your heart means filtering everything you hear through God's Word, this includes filtering your friends and all those that you let get close to you. If you allow someone to get close to you that does not know the Lord, even though they may be a good person, this may be a first of several dangerous steps in the wrong direction. Sometimes this is very difficult to do if the person really seems to be a good person and you want to maintain a close friendship. The devil would not put thoughts in our minds to go and shoot someone or to rob someone at gunpoint. His attacks are much more subtle than that. He would start with something that seems to be very harmless like making friends with someone that is not a believer. That could lead you into another circle of friends, all of whom are not believers. Then you could end up in a compromising situation where to keep their friendship you need to do something that is not in line with God's Word such as some lewd party. Their lifestyle may very gradually break you down and pull you away from your Christian walk ever so subtly, ever so slowly. The first thing you know you are well down the path to destruction and you are no longer hearing the Holy Spirit's guidance.

This may sound like something that is far-fetched, but this is the way the devil operates. It all starts with you not guarding your heart. It may not be with friendships; it may be with watching certain TV programs that seem to be harmless and then gradually get worse and worse, leading you to watch others that are similar. The first thing you know you are going down the wrong path again. Choose your words, your friends, and your idle time carefully. Guard your heart!

Father God, I realize how important it is for me to guard my heart. I know that the devil is clever and cunning and can put up smokescreens that will lead me away from You. I ask for Your Holy Spirit to alert me anytime I am tempted to seek friendship with the wrong company, look at the wrong TV show, attend the wrong movie, or anything else that will cause the door to my heart to have a slight crack, allowing the devil to enter. I resolve this day to guard my heart and to follow Your direction in all that I do. In Jesus's name, I pray. Amen.

Nutrition Thought for the Day.

As previously mentioned, folic acid is added to all processed grains in the United States. This decision was made in an attempt to decrease the number of neural tube birth defects. An example of a neural tube defect is spina bifida (a defect of the development of the spine). If folic acid is not available in sufficient quantities during the very early formation of the spinal column, the baby could be born with this defect. Surveys showed that pregnant aged women tend to be deficient in folic acid. Since everyone eats some grain (bread, cereals, cookies, crackers—anything made with processed flour or corn meal), it seemed to be good to fortify such grains with folic acid. The results have been successful with a significant drop in spina bifida.

Day 208
Righteousness Is Greater Than Sacrifice

To do righteousness and justice is desired by the LORD more than sacrifice.
(Proverbs 21:3)

You have to remember that when this proverb was written, the Jews were sacrificing live animals to the Lord for forgiveness of their sins. This proverb says, "to do righteousness and justice is desired by the Lord more than sacrifice." The sacrifice of animals for the forgiveness of sins was a prototype of things to come, specifically Jesus becoming the sacrificial lamb for all of the sins of the world. It was not the killing of the animals that pleased God. The purpose was to show man that he needed a savior, someone to permanently forgive all his sins. What God desired greater than sacrifice was righteousness and justice. Today we do not sacrifice animals to the Lord for our sins for our sins have already been removed by the sacrifice of Jesus, but some people think that they need to make sacrifices as a means of redemption for something they did. Their idea is that they will give up a certain something that they like to please God like they are giving God a gift of some sort for not being the person they should have been.

While the idea behind that seems to be good, there are no scriptural precedents for that in the New Testament. The Lord prefers us to walk in righteousness and justice. To walk in righteousness does not mean we will never sin again because all of us have sinned and fallen short of the glory of God (Romans 3:23) and will continue to sin. It means that we accept the righteousness that we have received from Jesus based on what He did for us and we immediately ask for forgiveness whenever we fall again. We should resolve with all our hearts to walk in His light and do our best not to give into any evil temptation.

Lord Jesus, You are pure righteousness and You have given Your righteousness to me when I accepted You as my Savior and Lord. It is now my desire to walk in righteousness and justice every day that I am on the face of this earth. I know that there is no substitute for obedience to Your Word and to walking in righteousness and justice. That pleases You more than any sacrifice I could make. You have made the ultimate sacrifice for all the sins of the entire world. I thank You, Lord Jesus, for what You did for me. I resolve this day to walk in righteousness and justice to the best of my ability by the power of Your Holy Spirit. In Your name, Jesus, I pray. Amen!

Nutrition Thought for the Day.

Folic acid is also essential in the metabolism of several amino acids and thus would be necessary for muscle metabolism as well as anything that involves these amino acids. There is one particular amino acid called homocysteine that is synthesized in the body naturally as a result of metabolism. This amino acid, during normal metabolism, is converted to an essential amino acid called methionine. Folic acid along with vitamins B6 and B12 are necessary for this metabolism to take place. A deficiency of either of these could cause homocysteine to build up in the blood, and while not proven, elevated homocysteine levels have a possible association with heart attacks and strokes as well as several other diseases.

Day 209
Watch Your Tongue

The tongue of the righteous is *as* choice silver, the heart of the wicked is *worth* little. (Proverbs 10:20)

The power of life and death is in the tongue (Proverbs 18:21). Even though the tongue is a small part of our total body, it is a powerful instrument that can be used to curse or to praise. We control the power of our tongues and if we walk in righteousness, then the fruit of our time is as valuable as choice silver. In the days that Proverbs 10:20 was written, choice silver (silver that has been purified several times) was precious to the Jews. Those that read this proverb in biblical days would see a greater value to the silver then we would see today. The proverb goes on to say that the heart of the wicked is not worth very much. This tells us that we must choose our words wisely and to be ever aware that the words that come out of our mouth will bring either glory or shame to us. They will bring sadness or joy. They will bring insults or praise. The choice is ours, choose wisely this day every word that comes out of your mouth.

Father God, I know that my words can bring healing or inflict harm to those that I speak. My words can be comforting, or they can bring depression. When I walk in righteousness and I speak in righteousness, I know that my words will bring life and praise to those who hear them. In turn, this will bring joy and praise to You. This is my desire, to bring joy and praise to Your name. I resolve this day to be attentive to the words that I say and make every effort to speak in righteousness and love and to avoid conversations that promote negativity. I ask for Your Holy Spirit to bring direction and guidance to me this day that I only say those things that will bring praise to You. In Jesus's name, I pray. Amen.

Nutrition Thought for the Day.

Folic acid is also required for two vital enzymes that, in normal metabolism, produces creatine and phosphatidylcholine, two compounds that are extremely important in exercise performance. Both of these compounds can also go on to increase plasma homocysteine levels in the absence of folic acid. Folic acid, therefore, plays an important role in exercise but, as mentioned several times earlier, an increase in folic acid in the diet will not improve exercise performance. A deficiency could harm exercise performance.

Day 210
The Wise Seek Counsel

The way of a fool is right in his own eyes, but a wise man is he who listens to counsel. (Proverbs 12:15)

Have you ever known anyone that always has the right answers? They are never wrong and know everything about everything? This type of a person does not take correction very well and makes it difficult to be around them; this is what Proverbs 12:15 calls a fool. They have tunnel vision and only can see their side of the story. We have all known or currently know someone like that. While it is difficult to get along with such a person, we still need to keep in mind that Jesus died for that person. You would probably never win that person over by beating him over the head with the Bible or continuously quoting scripture at him. Each person is different, and you may use a different approach with everyone that acts like a fool. Trust in the Holy Spirit to guide you and He will show you how to deal with such people as each case arises.

The second part of this proverb says that a wise man is one who listens to counsel. The fool may be well educated, and that may be why he thinks he knows it all. The wise man may also be well educated, but a real wise man will know the limits of his intelligence no matter how much education he has and will always be open to counsel. As a result of the counsel, he will only get wiser. Always be open to learning new things and accept correction and instruction with a humble heart. Do not be quick to criticize the fool or you will become like him.

Father God, I desire to be open to correction and instruction with all humility. I do not want to be like a fool and know more than everyone else. With wisdom comes wise counsel and with wise counsel the wise become wiser. I want to gain more knowledge and be a wise person so that I can use that knowledge for the advancement of Your Kingdom. Help me this day to be humble and to learn from others, to accept criticism and instruction, and not to be critical of those that try to put me down or brag on how much they know. In Jesus's name, I pray. Amen.

Nutrition Thought for the Day.
Our requirement for folic acid is very small and is only 320 micrograms of dietary folate a day. This is equal to 400 micrograms of dietary folate equivalents (DFE) which is the way you may see folic acid listed on labels in vitamin supplements. In the wide variety of foods that folate is found, and the supplementation of all processed grains, we should not have a folate deficiency problem in our country, but in poverty levels we still do. Remember that animal products are not a good source of folate or folic acid.

Day 211
Be a Righteous Neighbor

The righteous is a guide to his neighbor, but the way of the wicked leads them astray. (Proverbs 12:26)

We always want to walk in righteousness and justice, and we want to accept instruction and correction with humility. On the other hand, if we have more knowledge about a particular subject than our neighbor has, we want to be a guide for him but not by being an obnoxious person to let him know how much more information we have about the subject than he does. As we receive correction and instruction with humility, we want also to give correction and instruction with humility and not put the person down that we are instructing or correcting. This is walking in righteousness for them to see and follow our example. The wicked would not do this. The wicked would rise up as the fool and criticize them for not doing things the way they would do it. No one wants to follow someone like that, but your neighbor will be eager to follow you if you approach him with humility and righteousness and gently give him ideas of how he may be successful in whatever he is attempting to complete. You may get an opportunity to give examples of dieting, exercise, or cooking to any peer group that you may be working with on your healthy lifestyle program. Do not ever approach them as the diet guru that is doing so much better than they are but approach them in humility and with love. This is a win, win, win situation. You help them, you feel good about yourself, and you glorify God.

> Father God, besides wanting to walk in righteousness and in justice and be humble, I want to try to make sure that I treat my neighbors with righteousness, justice, and humility. I desire to be able to be a light in the darkness for those around me. To do that I have to walk in righteousness and humility so I can guide my neighbor down the path that will bring glory to Your name. I can only accomplish that with the guidance and help of the Holy Spirit, and I ask that He show me every time an opportunity arises that I can be a guide to my neighbor. I pray in the name of Jesus. Amen.

Nutrition Thought for the Day.

Clinical symptoms of folic acid deficiency include an inflamed tongue, diarrhea, weight loss, nervous instability, and dementia. There are any number of things that can cause these symptoms so if someone has some of the symptoms it does not necessarily mean that they have a folic acid deficiency. Another clinical symptom that is similar to vitamin B12 deficiency is megaloblastic macrocytic anemia. Like vitamin B12, this is a large red blood cell with less hemoglobin in it and will produce the same side effects as discussed with B12 deficiency, and that is a lack of oxygen carried through the body resulting in tiredness and shortness of breath.

Day 212
Be Gracious to the Needy

He who oppresses the poor taunts his Maker, but he who is gracious to the needy honors Him. (Proverbs 14:31)

I do not believe that God created us with the idea that He would make some of us poor and some of us rich. I think circumstances pertaining to our family, our environment, and the country we are in all play a role in our financial success. Of course, the decisions that we make in our lifetime are probably the biggest factors that determine our financial success. Those who have an abundance, or at least have all their needs met, should not look at those who are less fortunate than they are as being subservient to them. God created all of us, and those who are not currently basking in the same blessings that we may have are still His creation and are people for whom Jesus died. You are taunting Jesus when you criticize or make fun of people that He died for. It is the same as saying something like, "You died for them?" On the other hand, if you recognize that you are blessed, and you want to take some of your blessings and pass them on to those who perhaps have not had the same opportunities, then you are honoring God because the people you are helping are people that He created and died for. As you walk out this day look for those around you who are less fortunate and could use a helping hand. Help them in the name of Jesus and let them know that the help is not coming just from you but from Jesus.

Father God, I thank You for the blessings that I have because I know that all good things come from You. I know that not everyone in this world has the same financial status and I know that even though this is true, You still love all of mankind, no matter how rich or how poor they are. I also know that Jesus died for all mankind and not just for the wealthy or the blessed. It is the call that You have on all of us to help the needy, and that is something that I want to do. Give me greater means to give more to those around me that are in need and to do so without insulting them or looking down on them. By the power of Your Holy Spirit show me the people that You would have me help and how You would have me help them. In Jesus's name, I pray. Amen.

Nutrition Thought for the Day.
Folic acid deficiency will occur after a severe depletion of the vitamin on the tissue level. This could be increased by several conditions: 1) a folic acid deficient diet for two to four months; 2) chronic alcoholism; 3) pregnancy or lactation without increased folic acid intake; 4) hypermetabolic states (due to various diseases); 5) disorders of the intestines that cause a decrease in folic acid absorption; 6) medications such as oral contraceptives and some anticonvulsants; 7) folic acid antagonists which are drugs that are used to treat cancer.

WAYNE E. BILLON, PH.D., RDN, LDN

Day 213
Draw Near to God

Draw near to God and He will draw near to you. Cleanse your hands, you sinners; and purify your hearts, you double-minded. (James 4:8)

God promises us if we draw near to Him, He will draw near to us. We draw near to Him by fellowshipping with Him. We fellowship with Him when we worship Him in song, when we read His Word, when we pray to Him, and when we fellowship with like-minded believers. Prayer is a form of communication with God, and it does not necessarily mean that we are continually asking for something. We need to spend time talking to God as I am talking to you now. We also need to spend time listening for God to speak to us with that small voice in our hearts. We can also draw near to Him by listening to teachings about His Word in church, through videos, through CDs, etc. The more time we spend in the activities mentioned above, the more we will learn about our Savior and the closer we will get to Him. When we know we are seeking Him with all our heart, it will give us confidence that we are close to Him and that He hears us and will respond back to us. However, God will not love us more because we seek Him; He already loves all of us so much that He gave His one and only Son to die for us.

It is not as if God is far, far away from us when we do not seek Him because He is always near us, yet when we are doing our own thing we cannot hear Him speak to us. By seeking Him, we remove the static interference between us and can hear Him better. When we get up in the morning, we can dedicate each day to seeking our God in everything we do during that day. We can make the whole day an offering to our God in addition to spending time with Him by the ways previously mentioned. This will help us to be ever conscious that we are God's child and we are walking out His will in our lives.

Father God, I thank You that You are always near me and the more I seek You, the closer You seem to be to me and the better I can hear You speak to me with that still small voice that speaks to my spirit. I resolve this day and every day to seek You with all my heart in everything that I do. I know that the cares of the world can easily distract me from seeking You, but I also know that by the power of Your Holy Spirit I can be victorious for You have already overcome the world for me (John 16:33). I expect to see Your manifest presence in my life more and more as I learn to seek You in everything I do. In Jesus's name, I pray. Amen.

Nutrition Thought for the Day.
One thing I failed to mention about vitamins so far is a simple definition of what we call a vitamin. A vitamin is an organic compound (means that it contains carbon as one of its main constituents) that is needed by the body in minute amounts for growth, pregnancy, lactation, maintenance, and repair. The last note here is that vitamins cannot be synthesized in our body but have to come from the foods we eat. This makes all the vitamins essential. The definition of a hormone is similar in that it is an organic compound that is needed in minute amounts for all the same reasons a vitamin is needed, but a hormone is synthesized in the body.

Day 214
Be an Overcomer

"He who overcomes, I will grant to him to sit down with Me on My throne, as I also overcame and sat down with My Father on His throne." (Revelation 3:21)

Just what is it we are to overcome? I think we can best answer that question with a question. Jesus says in this verse, "as I also overcame." The question is, what did Jesus overcome? He overcame every sin while He walked the face of the earth. In your mind, you are probably asking, "So am I to overcome every temptation, sin, every vile thought that comes through my mind, every opportunity to be rebellious in any way?" Yes, that is exactly what it means, but Jesus knows that at times you will fall. That is when you immediately ask for forgiveness because Jesus already overcame the world for you (John 16:33). You do not do this on your own righteous acts but by His righteous act. The key to remember here is that He accomplished this incredible feat by the power of the Holy Spirit that was in Him. You also have the same Holy Spirit in you and you can accomplish the same thing Jesus accomplished. In fact, John 14:12 says, "Truly, truly, I say to you, he who believes in Me, the works that I do, he will also do; and greater works than these he will do; because I go to the Father." You are probably asking, how will I accomplish these feats? The same way that Jesus did, by the power of the Holy Spirit in you that was in Him. You cannot accomplish anything good on your own; you have to depend upon the power of the Holy Spirit in you just as Jesus did when He walked the face of this earth. He does not expect you to be that strong on your own and that is the very reason why He sent the Holy Spirit to us after He ascended into heaven. Every day I ask for the Holy Spirit to fill my family and me afresh and anew, so that we may be able to take on the trials that may come our way that day. I strongly suggest that you do the same. This does not mean that everything will be perfect, but it does mean that when you come across obstacles, the Holy Spirit will give you the wisdom and strength to overcome those obstacles.

Father God, I thank You that You have given the same Holy Spirit to me that You gave to Your Son when He walked the face of this earth. You know my strengths and my weaknesses. You know that on my own I cannot accomplish the goals that You have for me, but by Your goodness and grace You gave me the Holy Spirit and all of His power to me to overcome all the obstacles I may face. I thank You for such a blessing and I ask for the Holy Spirit to fill me afresh and anew this day and to guide me and direct me in every step that I take so that I may be the witness You called me to be. In Jesus's name, I pray. Amen.

Nutrition Thought for the Day.

The next vitamin to review is biotin. This vitamin is not designated by a letter and a number but just its name. Biotin is a little different in that the helpful bacteria that inhabit our large intestines synthesize it. We do not synthesize it, but the bacteria in our large intestines do and release it from into the space (called the lumen) of the large intestines. While most digestion and absorption takes place in the small intestines, biotin and electrolytes can be absorbed in the large intestines. Thus we have a natural source of biotin without taking in any food. The bacteria cannot make all the biotin we need so some must come in the diet also.

Day 215
God Always Hears Us

This is the confidence which we have before Him, that, if we ask anything according to His will, He hears us. (1 John 5:14)

In addition to promising us the Holy Spirit, God's Word also promises us that if we ask anything according to His will, He will hear us. This is what Jesus did when He walked the face of this earth. He knew beyond any shadow of a doubt that whatever He asked the Father to do would be done for Him. This does not mean that every single thing we ask for is immediately given to us. Our God is not like an automatic gift dispenser that deals out whatever we need as we go along saying, "give me one of those, give me one of these, etc." Sometimes we may ask for things that would do us more harm than good if we receive them, such as large sums of money if we are poor managers of our finances. God knows what is best for us and He will answer us in His timing, which is not always in agreement with our timing. No matter how much time it takes or how little time it takes for us to get our prayers answered, we need to resolve that our God is still on the throne and we will forever serve Him. Trusting Him does not mean that we only praise Him or trust Him when we get the things that we want. We need to praise and trust Him regardless of what we seem to get in return. Know that your God loves you and will never abandon you. Resolve to praise Him and to continue to obey Him regardless of what you receive in return.

Father, I know that You always hear my prayer even when it does not seem like You do. I also know that You care for me so much that You allowed Your Son Jesus Christ to die for me. You cannot break Your Word to me that You will never leave me. I have confidence this day and every day that when I pray, You hear my prayers and will answer them by what is best for me. I also realize that You will answer my prayers in Your timing. I resolve to continue to praise You in all circumstances, regardless of whether my prayers are answered in the same way I asked for them or not. I pray in the name of Jesus. Amen.

Nutrition Thought for the Day.

Biotin is widely distributed in nature, but the best sources are liver, soybeans, and egg yolks. Most people today are trying to avoid liver and egg yolks because of the cholesterol content and soybeans are not commonly eaten, so these significant sources are not in the diet of most people. Since biotin is widely distributed in nature, this is not a major problem. There is a glycoprotein in raw egg whites that can bind to biotin and render it unavailable, but this is only a problem if you eat a lot of raw egg whites, which you should not be doing because of the salmonella threat in raw eggs. Cooked eggs do not affect absorption.

Day 216
God Wants Us to Prosper

Beloved, I pray that in all respects you may prosper and be in good health, just as your soul prospers. (3 John 1:2)

All three epistles, 1 John, 2 John, and 3 John, were written by the apostle John, the same John that wrote the gospel. John was the apostle that is referred to in the Bible as the one that Jesus loved. Jesus loves us all the same, but since Jesus walked the earth as a man, He may have had a closer bond with John just as each of us has a friend that we feel is closer to us. However, the only place we see John referred to as the one Jesus loved is in John's writings. It may have been that John saw himself as being closer to Jesus. The point is, John knew Jesus very well, and he saw Jesus heal many people and raise people from the dead. In fact, John himself healed many people. He knew that it was God's will for us to be healthy and prosperous and that is precisely his prayer for the people he was writing to in this epistle. Remember that the Bible was written for all of us, and while John sent this epistle to a particular group of people, the fact is that the Bible is intended to be for all of us.

Thus, in this epistle, he is speaking to you when he prays for you to be in good health and to prosper as your soul prospers because he knows that is God's will for you. John was writing to born-again believers just like you and I. How does your soul prosper? If you are born again, your soul is sealed by the Holy Spirit with an indelible mark that will always be there (Ephesians 1:13). Your soul could not be in any better shape than to be sealed by the Holy Spirit. John's prayer for you is that you prosper and be in health just as your soul prospers. Understanding what this means makes this an awesome scripture, knowing that it is God's will for you. Walk through your day today knowing that Jesus loves you and that His will is for you to prosper and be in good health.

Dear Father God, I want to thank You for the desire You have for me to be in good health and to prosper just as my soul is prospering. Since I am a born- again believer and have received Jesus as my Savior and Lord, I know that the Holy Spirit has put a seal on my soul that will be there forever. I know that I am Your child and that You love me as You love Jesus. I realize how awesome a statement that is but it is true because the Bible says it is true (John 17:23). I look forward to walking through this day with Your guidance knowing that Your will for me is that I prosper and be in good health. I thank You, Father, in the name of Jesus. Amen.

Nutrition Thought for the Day.

One of the functions of biotin in the body is that it is covalently bound to enzymes and thus considered to be a coenzyme. That means for the enzyme it is bound with to be effective, biotin has to be there. One of the most important enzymes that require biotin takes place at the beginning of what is known as the Krebs cycle or the tricarboxylic acid cycle (TCA cycle). This cycle is the way we produce energy in our bodies. Thus, like the other B vitamins, biotin plays a role in energy production. Biotin also plays a role in the body in non-enzymatic processes including possible effects on DNA and gene expression.

WAYNE E. BILLON, PH.D., RDN, LDN

Day 217
Do Not Be Afraid to Ask

"Ask, and it will be given to you; seek, and you will find; knock, and it will be opened to you. For everyone who asks receives, and he who seeks finds, and to him who knocks it will be opened." (Matthew 7:7–8)

Many times people do not seek God when they have problems because they are under the impression that the problem is too small or that they ask God for so many things He will get tired of them asking and not listen to them. God cares about the small things as well as the large things, no matter how small they may be. Jesus wants us to approach Him and to ask Him for everything that we need. This scripture assures us of that. "Ask, and it will be given to you; seek and you will find; knock and it will be open for you." This is God's will for us that we ask, seek, and knock and He will hear our prayer. However, the scripture does not mean that we will receive everything we ask for in prayer. I know that this has been covered several times, but many of us still do not understand why some of our prayers seem to go unanswered.

We have to be reassured that God knows what is best for us and sometimes we may ask for things that may not be exactly what we need. We may be asking for things out of our lust and not out of our true need. We may be asking for things in a selfish matter, and God will not cater to our selfishness. If our prayers are within God's will, and we ask for things that will bring glory to His name, and finally if we ask in faith, chances are our prayers will be answered in the manner we asked. Once again though, they may not be answered immediately or in our timing but in God's timing, which is perfect timing. So whatever your needs are, examine them with your heart to make sure it is something that you need, and not just something that you want, and that you are asking for it for God's glory and not for your pride. Then speak to Him in your everyday language. Your prayers do not have to be glorious sounding with perfect language, but in your daily conversational voice seek God with all your heart.

> Father God it is very comforting to know that we can ask You for anything and everything that is a legitimate need in our lives and You will hear our prayers. I know that You hear me and I know that You want me to be happy and have all of my needs met. I also understand that the things I ask for may not be in my best interest even though I am not aware of it. I also understand that Your timing is perfect and does not always line up with my timing. I resolve not to get disappointed if I do not see my needs fulfilled the way I ask for them in my timing. I also resolve that I will continue to ask for my needs and be patient in receiving from You. I pray in the name of Jesus. Amen.

Nutrition Thought for the Day.

As much as we know about nutrition and as advanced as our knowledge is, the RDA for biotin cannot be determined because there is not sufficient information to tell us exactly what our needs are. In such a case, an estimate is suggested that is called the Adequate Intake (AI). The AI for biotin is 30 micrograms (a millionth of a gram) for adults over 19 years of age. Even though this is a very small amount, the biotin produced by the bacteria in our large intestines is not sufficient for meeting our requirements, so additional biotin is required by the diet.

Day 218
You Are More Than a Conqueror

I can do all things through Him who strengthens me. (Philippians 4:13)

I raised my daughter on this verse; this is our family motto. It does not mean that we can do the impossible, but we can do the reasonably possible. It does not mean that we can jump off a tall cliff and fly without wings. It does not mean we can run 10 miles at the rate of 100 miles an hour or something that is equal to or more than superhuman could do. It does mean that we can accomplish any task that is set before us with the help of our God and the guidance of the Holy Spirit. Our strength to do what seems to be impossible comes from our Lord and Savior Jesus Christ. Whenever it seems like we are at the end of our rope and we do not know what to do next, hang on and trust God! I know this is easy for me to say and for you to read, but putting into practice is difficult for both of us. I have had recent circumstances that cause me to find myself in a corner with no apparent way out. I have been in that situation many times, but every time God has found a way to rescue me. Isaiah 50:7 says, "For the Lord God helps me, therefore, I am not disgraced; therefore, I have set my face like flint, and I know that I will not be ashamed." This is a verse that I have memorized and is one that can help you when it feels like things are coming in on you from all sides. Know that your God loves you and cares about you. Know that He will never leave you nor abandon you. He wants you to call on Him in time of need, no matter how small the need may seem to be to you. Do not be discouraged but continue to put your trust in your God.

> Father, I know that I can trust You to always be with me and to guide me through everything that I may face. I know that sometimes it seems like I am alone with my back to the wall and I do not know which way to turn. When those times come, help me by the power of Your Holy Spirit. Remind me continuously who I am in Christ and the authority that I have within me from You. I know that You will never abandon me but will always be with me. I thank You, Father, in the name of Jesus Christ. Amen.

Nutrition Thought for the Day.
In case you are taking a supplement called alpha lipoic acid, you need to know that the biotin requirement is increased because of this supplement. Alpha lipoic acid is a strong antioxidant that is unique in that it is both water-soluble and fat-soluble. There are claims that it will help with peripheral neuropathy, a numbing or tingling sensation in the fingers or toes that is sometimes a complication of diabetes. Many people with diabetes experience this condition and may be taking alpha lipoic acid. If this is the case, a supplement of biotin may be recommended.

Day 219
Be Careful of Who You Associate with

Do not be deceived: "Bad company corrupts good morals." (1 Corinthians 15:33)

The company we keep is extremely important for our walk with the Lord. As today's scripture says, "bad company corrupts good morals." This does not mean that we avoid anyone that is not a Christian or anyone we feel is not on the same spiritual level we are; we should associate with non-Christians so that we can be a witness to them. However, we should not have close friends or spend a considerable amount of time with people that are into sinful habits such as illegal use of drugs, alcohol, pornography, etc. It is undoubtedly necessary that we witness to such people but not have them in our close circle of friends. If we do, the more time we spend with them, the more their lifestyle will tend to influence our lifestyle. We should always be on guard for such distractions, but this does not always necessarily refer to sinful things. There may be people that are on a diet and exercise program working with you in an attempt to lose or gain weight that uses incredibly unhealthy and undesirable practices. The more you associate with these people, the greater the temptation will be to try what they are doing. If their methods are harmful or unhealthy, this may lead you to try the same methods and result in an unhealthy lifestyle. Always be on the lookout for people that will lead you astray, not intentionally, but in everyday experiences. Trust God to direct you to the people that will be like-minded with you in their beliefs and help you in your walk with Jesus.

> Thank You, Father, for the friends and family that You have given me. Give me wisdom that I can be ever mindful of the people around me that may, intentionally or unintentionally, lead me down the wrong path. I do not want to do anything that will compromise my walk with You. I realize how easy it is to get off the right path with You. If ever I go astray, even with good intentions, lead me back to the path that You would have me follow. Instead of me being led by others down the wrong path, help me to be the leader to lead others to You. In Jesus's name, I pray. Amen.

Nutrition Thought for the Day.

Some also claim that biotin is necessary for strong fingernails and toenails. If you are young and you are getting ample biotin in your diet, plus what you are getting from the bacteria synthesizing it in your G.I. tract, and you have brittle nails, I do not think a biotin supplement will work. As we age, we tend to lose the ability to absorb some vitamins and minerals, and our fingernails may become more brittle. There is a claim that biotin may help strengthen the fingernails of the elderly. However, remember what has been previously mentioned when talking about vitamin B6, too much of anything can be harmful, and I do not recommend megadoses of biotin. Biotin is also needed for healthy normal skin, and a deficiency can cause a scaly red dermatitis. This does not mean that if you have dermatitis, you are deficient in biotin because many other conditions can cause dermatitis. If you have dermatitis and you have ample biotin in your diet, taking extra will not make dermatitis go away. It will only help if you have dermatitis caused by a biotin deficiency.

Day 220
Do Not Fear

You drew near when I called on You; You said, "Do not fear!" (Lamentations 3:57)

Fear is a crippling spirit. In 2 Timothy 1:7 it says, "For God has not given us a spirit of timidity [some versions say fear], but of power and love and discipline." We may have a fear of not ever being able to lose enough weight or gain enough weight to get to a healthy weight. The fear does not have to be concerning something big; it can be a small thing. Whatever we may fear, it did not come from God. Since He did not give us a spirit of fear, we know that whenever fear tries to close in on us, we can call on His name and He will draw near to us as today's scripture says. It is easy to say, "do not fear," but I know it is sometimes difficult to put into practice. It involves a faith walk and trusting in our God that He will provide us with the courage and strength to overcome any fear that we may encounter. Do not be fearful today, trust in your God and remember that you are a world overcomer.

I thank You, Father, that You have not given me a spirit of fear but a spirit of power, love, and discipline. I know that I have to practice discipline in my life to overcome the shadows of fear and I know that I can accomplish that, not on my power, but on Your power. I make an act of my will today to choose not to let fear have a foothold in my life. Instead, I choose to rely on Your Word to guide me through the day without fear. I know that Isaiah 26:3 says, that You will keep me in perfect peace because I trust in You. I choose to walk in peace today by the power of Your Holy Spirit. In Jesus's name, I pray. Amen.

Nutrition Thought for the Day.

The next water-soluble vitamin is pantothenic acid and is the last B vitamin. Like folic acid and biotin, it does not have a letter or a number designation. Pantothenic acid consists of the amino acid alanine joined by a peptide bond to a compound called pantoic. The word pantos means "everywhere" in Greek. I guess this name was given to the vitamin because it is so widely distributed in nature and is present in virtually all plant and animal foods. To our knowledge, having a deficiency of pantothenic acid would only happen if you are in severe starvation and you have a deficiency of everything.

Day 221
Trust in Your God

Thus says the LORD, your Redeemer, the Holy One of Israel, "I am the LORD your God, who teaches you to profit, Who leads you in the way you should go." (Isaiah 48:17)

In this scripture the word profit means just that, to profit or to benefit or avail. The scripture also points out that the Lord is our Redeemer and is the Holy One of Israel. This is important because it points out who is teaching us. It is not just some earthly, everyday teacher but the Lord, our Redeemer, the Holy God of Israel, and He will teach us how to profit or benefit in all that we do. He leads us in the way we should go. This is not going to happen coincidentally as a leaf falls off a tree in the fall of the year. It is going to happen because we trust in our God and we look to and expect Him to lead us in our daily walk. Once we establish this fact, then we take steps to walk it out and call on Him to give us the guidance we need to be successful in our daily walk. This, coupled with yesterday's scripture to refuse to give in to fear, empowers us to walk in victory and success. This can be true in every phase of our daily living including our work and our struggles with dieting and exercising. Our God cares about our diet, our exercise, and our health. Do not try to walk out your daily routine on your own strength but rely on your God and you will be successful as He leads you in the way you should go.

> Father God, the scripture today in conjunction with the scripture yesterday encourages me in that I know I can be successful with Your leadership and protection from fear. I also know that trusting in You and walking in faith is not something that comes immediately but has to be developed as I grow closer to You. I ask that You give me the grace to develop a greater knowledge, trust, and faith in Your Word so that I can walk out my daily life trusting totally in Your guidance and freedom from fear. In Jesus's name, I pray. Amen.

Nutrition Thought for the Day.
The abundant availability of pantothenic acid is a good thing because it has many important roles in the body. When discussing biotin, it was mentioned that biotin was needed in the Krebs cycle (the cycle that produces energy for our body). To enter the Krebs cycle there is a compound required called acetyl CoA. The CoA of this compound is pantothenic acid. Thus, without this compound, energy cannot be produced in our bodies. Since energy can be produced by the metabolism of carbohydrates, proteins, and fats, pantothenic acid is needed for the metabolism of each.

Day 222
God Does Not Play Favorites

For there is no partiality with God. (Romans 2:11)

This concise verse is extremely meaningful. God does not play favorites. All of us, whether Protestant, Catholic, Jew, Muslim, atheist or whatever, all have been created by our God. We are all His children whether we acknowledge Him as our Father or not. Does God love the fact that Muslims, atheists, agnostics, and even Jews do not acknowledge His Son, Jesus Christ, as one who died for our sins? No, of course not, that does not please God. But does He love the children He created? Yes, of course He does! He loves us so much that He gave us a free will to choose whether to follow Him or not. He does not show partiality to any of us, but He does answer the prayers of those that believe in Him and obey His Word. Suppose you are trying your best to do what is right in the eyes of God, but you mess up. Also, suppose that someone close to you is making the same efforts that you are but they do not mess up the way you did.

Does God love them more than He loves you? No, He does not. He loves the fact that they did not mess up, but when He looks at you, He sees the grace that you have received because of what Jesus did for you. He is ready and willing to forgive you and to help you get back on the right path if you trust in Him. Do not condemn yourself or think of yourself as looked down upon by God because you did something stupid. Know that God does not show partiality for any reason and that He loves you just as much as He loves Jesus. Maybe you question this statement. If so, look at John 17:22—23, "The glory which You have given Me I have given to them, that they may be one, just as We are one; I in them and You in Me, that they may be perfected in unity, so that the world may know that You sent Me, and love them, even as You have loved Me." This is one of my favorite verses and is extremely powerful. God loves us as much as He loves Jesus, this should give you great encouragement to walk through your day in love.

> Father God, I cannot thank You enough for Your love or do enough to deserve Your love. Your love for me is awesome. Your grace is more than what I need. I know that You love me as much as You love Jesus and as You love anyone else on the face of this earth. I choose today to meditate on this fact and to make this realization of Your love a part of my everyday life. I will walk out this day in Your love with the help of Your Holy Spirit. In Jesus's name, I pray. Amen.

Nutrition Thought for the Day.

Pantothenic acid is also necessary for the synthesis of cholesterol, bile salts, ketones, fatty acids, and steroid hormones. The RDA for pantothenic acid is 5 milligrams per day for the typical adult and 6 to 7 milligrams per day for pregnancy and lactation. For as many essential pathways that require pantothenic acid, you would guess that a larger requirement would be necessary. When pantothenic acid is used for a coenzyme, only a very minute amount is needed and that is why the daily requirement is not any larger than what it is. Since pantothenic acid is so abundant there is no one recommending supplements of pantothenic acid for any miracle cures or disease states. Toxicities of pantothenic acid have not been reported.

Day 223
What Is Not Seen Is Eternal

While we look not at the things which are seen, but at the things which are not seen; for the things which are seen are temporal, but the things which are not seen are eternal. (2 Corinthians 4:18)

We have a saying today that "seeing is believing." Without really thinking about it, this is pretty much how we live our lives. We have a hard time believing in something that we cannot see or touch; the natural is more real to us than the supernatural. Spiritually speaking, this is the opposite. The things that we see will one day no longer exist. Our bodies will return to dust and all plants and animals will return to dust at some point in time. The only things that last forever are those which we do not see, and those happen to be our spirit and the Spirit of our God. We will all live forever but, depending on how we lived our lives on this earth, forever may be in heaven or Hades. We are eternal beings, we just have not received our everlasting bodies yet. Do not live your life based on what you can see, feel, and touch but based on the Word of God which is eternal.

Matthew 24:35 says, "Heaven and earth will pass away, but My Words will not pass away." As you walk through today you can look around and be ever mindful that everything you see is only temporary and will one day pass away, but the Word of God will never pass away, and your spirit will always remain—forever. As a born-again believer, your spirit will remain forever in heaven with your Lord and Savior Jesus Christ. Let this thought bring comfort to you today and encouragement to you in everything that you do. Your healthy lifestyle program is good for the now, but it is just to help you be healthier so that you can be a better witness for Jesus. Do not make this your ultimate goal, but rather make Jesus your ultimate goal.

Father God, I thank You that I will live forever with You in heaven. All the trials and tribulations that I am going through now are only temporary. The only thing that is eternal is Your Word and Your desire for me to spend eternity with You in heaven. I resolve this day to realize that everything I have and every physical thing that I am working to accomplish on this earth is only temporary and I will look forward to eternity with You in heaven. I thank You for loving me so much that You gave Your Son to die for me so that I may spend eternity with You. I thank You, Father, in the name of Jesus. Amen.

Nutrition Thought for the Day.

While not a B vitamin, vitamin C (also known as ascorbic acid) is a water-soluble vitamin and is the last water-soluble vitamin to be discussed. Vitamin C has been the subject of controversy for decades. If you know anything about vitamin C, you probably have heard that it will help prevent or cure the common cold. Numerous studies show vitamin C helps prevent a cold and there are numerous studies that show vitamin C does not affect a cold. Which is true? There are a lot of variables that need to be looked at to determine the effectiveness of vitamin C in fighting the common cold. First, let's look at what vitamin C does in the body, what our requirements are, where it is found, and finally examine some of the hype about vitamin C.

Day 224
We Have Everything We Need

Seeing that His divine power has granted to us everything pertaining to life and godliness, through the true knowledge of Him who called us by His own glory and excellence. For by these He has granted to us His precious and magnificent promises, so that by them you may become partakers of *the* divine nature, having escaped the corruption that is in the world by lust. (2 Peter 1:3–4)

Things to realize from this scripture are that the divine power of God has granted us everything that we need that pertains to life and godliness. He did this through the knowledge of Himself. True knowledge of God is knowing Him through His Word and having an understanding of who Jesus is and what He did for us. For through the true knowledge of God we have been granted His precious and magnificent promises. This also comes through God's Word. Through the promises made to us by God, we can become partakers of the divine nature of God and look forward to our heavenly bodies when we spend eternity with Him in heaven, being saved from the corruption that is in the world today by lust. The mention of lust does not necessarily mean an extreme desire for sexual pleasures, but lust can be for money, power, and possessions, such as new cars or houses. Lust can also be an excessive desire for our looks, that is, for us to be the most beautiful or most handsome person around. Be careful that this kind of lust does not drive your desire to lose weight but that you keep focus and lose or gain weight for reasons of promoting your health for yourself and your family's sake.

Father God, I thank You that You have given me everything I need to be successful in this world. You have made knowledge of Yourself available through Your Word and have given me precious promises that I can hold onto until the end of this world as we know it. Thank You that I can enjoy Your presence and company now while I am still walking on this earth and do not have to wait until my final destination, which is my mansion in heaven. I thank You for Your Holy Spirit, and I look forward this day to when I can share my days with You in heaven. In Jesus's name, I pray. Amen.

Nutrition Thought for the Day.

First of all, vitamin C is found in a large number of fruits and vegetables. Citrus fruits are probably the most commonly known as good sources of vitamin C with an 8 ounce glass of orange juice providing most people with their requirement for the day. Most tropical fruits are good sources of vitamin C. The cabbage family, tomatoes, cantaloupe, strawberries, bell peppers, greens, and potatoes are also good sources of vitamin C. Vitamin C can be destroyed by heat, so when cooking vegetables, if you want to preserve vitamin C and many of the B vitamins in the vegetables, cooking with a low heat would be the preferable method. Since fruits are such a good source of vitamin C and they are usually eaten raw (many vegetables are eaten raw too), this makes vitamin C more available.

Day 225
We Have No Reason to Be Condemned

Beloved, if our heart does not condemn us, we have confidence before God; and whatever we ask we receive from Him, because we keep His commandments and do the things that are pleasing in His sight. (1 John 3:21–22)

God does not grade on a curve. If you walk a better walk today than you did yesterday, that does not mean that God will hear and answer your prayers faster today. God does not hear your prayers based on how well you did on any given day. He is not closer to you one day because you were a better Christian that day than in previous days. He loves you the same every day, and He hears your prayers the same every day. If you do not perform as the Bible tells you to on any given day, then what, if anything, affects your prayers on that day? If you mess up, the devil is quick to tell you what a failure you are and how you do not deserve to receive anything from God. Unfortunately, many are quick to receive and believe his lies. As people of God, we let our own hearts condemn us while God sees us as His children for whom Jesus Christ died. If you walk your talk and your heart does not condemn you, then you can approach God's throne with greater confidence and believe that what you asked for you will receive. This greater confidence increases your faith. Your increase in faith raises your boldness and the effectiveness of your prayers. This results in you seeing more of your prayers answered. The bottom line for this message is when you do not follow God's Word as you should, immediately turn to God, ask for forgiveness, and resolve to obey His Word more closely. This will remove any condemnation from your heart and enable you to approach God's throne with confidence.

> I see that the key to approaching my Father God's throne is faith. I also see that to increase my faith I must have confidence in myself and not condemn myself for my misgivings. Lord, I know that will happen when I see myself as You see me and not as the devil tries to get me to see myself as a condemned sinner. I used to be a condemned sinner but now I am a child of God, and all of my sins have been removed by the blood of Jesus. I thank You, Father, for my forgiveness and for the boldness that You have given me to approach Your throne with confidence and to present my prayers and petitions to You knowing that You hear me and love me no matter what I have done. I declare this in Jesus's name. Amen.

Nutrition Thought for the Day.

The RDA for vitamin C is 90 milligrams per day for males and 75 milligrams per day for females. That that smoke has a slightly higher requirement, somewhere in the neighborhood of 10 milligrams more per day. There is something in cigarette smoke that destroys vitamin C. While 90 milligrams of vitamin C per day has been shown to be the requirement for males, additional research has shown that about 100 milligrams of vitamin C per day taken in by men maximizes the body pool of vitamin C. Remember that water-soluble vitamins are not stored in the body. When we reach the excess that the body can hold, vitamin C starts to spill out through the kidneys in the urine. It has also been shown that about 250 milligrams of vitamin C per day will supersaturate tissue.

Day 226
We Are Not under the Law but We Are under Grace

For the law of the Spirit of life in Christ Jesus has set you free from the law of sin and of death. (Romans 8:2)

Remember that the Old Testament was governed by law. When we think of the Old Testament, we think of the Ten Commandments, and yes, those were laws given by God to Moses. In addition to those laws etched out on the tablets of stone, other laws governed what the Jews should eat, as well as laws for criminal justice, property rights, slavery, sexual relations and many more. The Old Testament Jews had a total of 613 rules or regulations that they had to follow. Man could not follow all those rules but sinned daily and needed a savior. That savior was Jesus Christ, and He introduced us to the New Testament, which is not based on law but grace. The grace comes from the forgiveness we receive through the sacrifice that Jesus made for us with His life, death, and resurrection. Our sins are not covered by blood as the sins of the Jews in the Old Testament were covered by the blood of animal sacrifices. Instead, our sins are removed entirely by the blood of Jesus Christ. I know we say that Jesus's blood covers our sins, but it does more than that, it removes them, never again to be remembered by God. The result of disobeying the law in the Old Testament was death. The result of turning to Jesus for forgiveness in the New Testament is life and peace for eternity. Choose this day who you are going to serve and choose wisely. Choose Jesus to be your Savior and Lord, and His grace covers you and removes your sins.

I thank You, Father God, for setting me free from the law of sin and death dictated by the Old Testament. I thank You for the New Covenant You have given us through the life, death, and resurrection of Your Son, Jesus Christ. I thank You, Father, for the forgiving grace that is available to us through Jesus. I know that You have removed my sins from me and have separated them from me as far as the east is to the west (Psalm 103:12). As amazing as that is, You have also chosen to forget my sins and never to remember them again (Isaiah 54:4, Jeremiah 31:34). You are an amazing God, and I give praise and honor and glory to You through the name of Jesus. Amen.

Nutrition Thought for the Day.
According to at least one research article, anything over 250 milligrams of vitamin C taken by mouth daily would probably come out in the urine. Not everyone has the same requirement, so this is difficult to predict precisely. Some people may have a slightly higher requirement, some a slightly lower requirement. However, it is unlikely that anyone would have a tissue saturation level of two to three times the requirement. In spite of this some people recommend that we should take in at least 1000 milligrams of vitamin C a day to prevent a cold. That is a much larger dose then research has shown to be the saturation limit and our requirement is even much lower than the saturation limit. All the saturation limit means is that after that point is reached, any additional intake would go right through our bodies and come out in the urine. This is not to say that we could not obtain a toxic dose if we continued to take too much.

Bottom line: Stay within the requirements.

Day 227
Our God Is Gives Us Strength and Power

Do you not know? Have you not heard? The Everlasting God, the LORD, the Creator of the ends of the earth does not become weary or tired. His understanding is inscrutable. He gives strength to the weary, and to *him who* lacks might He increases power. (Isaiah 40:28–29)

Our God, the creator of heaven and earth, never wears out, gets tired, or gets sleepy. This is sometimes difficult for us to understand because we do get tired, sleepy, and we wear down easily. This scripture also says that His understanding is inscrutable. That means He does not give any hints or emotions about how He knows everything about us and it is, therefore, difficult to understand His level of knowledge. When we get tired and worn down, He will give us strength. If we lack the power or the ability to accomplish our purpose on this earth, He, the God of infinite power, will increase our strength so that we can overcome. This should give you excellent encouragement today knowing that no matter what you do or how hard your task is, it is not too hard for your God. He is always aware of your situation and is always willing to help when you call on Him. Our God is an awesome God. Remind yourself daily of the power your God has to be ever present and be ever understanding of every situation that you may face on this earth. Do not hesitate ever to call on Him for help with whatever you are trying to accomplish, no matter how small or insignificant it may seem to you. You have a God that cares about every situation.

Father, thank You that You are always on duty and You are forever watching over me no matter where I am or what I am doing. Thank You that You care about everything I do and every trial or tribulation I have to face. I thank You that You give me the strength and the power I need to accomplish whatever task is before me. I know that You never get tired or weary and You never sleep. I cannot understand that with my finite mind because I do get tired and weary but I accept the fact that You do not and that You encourage me in everything that I do. I thank You, in the mighty name of Jesus. Amen.

Nutrition Thought for the Day.

So does this extra vitamin C help to prevent a cold? Some research shows yes and some research shows no. What could some of the variables be that may cause a research trial to determine yes or no to vitamin C preventing a cold? Vitamin C has been shown to improve the immune system and some extra may very well help if we are deficient in vitamin C. Other factors also affect the immune system such as a lack of sleep decreases our immune system; a poor diet decreases our immune system if we are deficient in calories, protein, and vitamins and minerals. Stress and tobacco increase our vitamin C requirement, and diuretics cause us to lose more than usual vitamin C in our urine. Any of these factors could complicate the effects of vitamin C.

Day 228
We Need to Listen for Jesus's Voice

'Behold, I stand at the door and knock; if anyone hears My voice and opens the door,
I will come in to him and will dine with him, and he with Me.' (Revelation 3:20)

This scripture is more prevalent for nonbelievers than believers since believers would have already heard His voice and opened the door to let Him into their hearts. However, it does make a point in that Jesus pursues us even when we do not pursue Him. If someone does not know Jesus, then in some manner, shape, or form He is standing at their door and knocking. If Jesus will do this for nonbelievers, how much more is He standing by us as believers to come in and dine with us.

To share a meal with someone during the days Jesus walked the face of the earth was a big deal and a sign of intimacy and friendship. Jesus desires to share Himself with us, but we have to open the door to let Him into our hearts. He will not knock the door down to get our attention, but He is always close by waiting for us to invite Him in. As believers, He is always with us and is in our hearts, but many times we still try to shut Him out of our lives. We should never want to do that, but instead we should welcome Him to accompany us in our daily walk through this life. This pleases Him. As you walk through your day today, keep in mind that Jesus is with you and wants to spend time with you. Just as parents raising their children need to spend time with them, and not just any kind of time, but quality time. Try to find a way to spend some quality time with your Lord and Savior today.

Thank You, Lord Jesus, that You are always looking after me and that You want to spend quality time with me. I know that I do not always spend time with You as I should, especially quality time. Life moves so fast and gets so complicated that I end up spending all my time trying to just get through the day. I know I use that as an excuse and tack on many other excuses to account for why I do not spend more time with You. All of the excuses I can make up are not good enough. My priority should be to spend time with You first. I resolve to try to spend more time with You, and I can do that by just sitting quietly for a while and talking to You instead of continually asking You to do something for me. By the power of Your Holy Spirit continue to remind me that I need to spend more quality time with You. Thank You, Jesus, for hearing my prayers. Amen.

Nutrition Thought for the Day.

Psychology affects our immune system. For example, have you noticed that people who are very much upbeat and positive have fewer colds than people that are very negative and easily depressed? Do you know someone that says, "its flu season, I'm going to get the flu. I know it, I always get the flu." What usually happens to people like that? They tend to get the flu more frequently. Positive thinking does improve our immune system. Positive thinking helps when we are fighting diseases, but positive thinking cannot by itself overcome a cold or the flu; however, it too can complicate the evaluation of the effectiveness of vitamin C in the diet.

Day 229
Work As unto the Lord

Whatever you do, do your work heartily, as for the Lord rather than for men, knowing that from the Lord you will receive the reward of the inheritance. It is the Lord Christ whom you serve. (Colossians 3:23–24)

This scripture reminds us that the reason we are on this earth is to serve our Lord and God. We so often forget that and get so wrapped up in trying to serve our own needs and the needs of those around us. This includes serving the needs of our employer, or if we are the boss, the needs of our employees and customers or clients. However, everything we do should be done in a manner to give glory to our God, even small menial tasks that may be very boring to us should be done in a manner as unto the Lord. On awards day that will take place at the end of time, it will not be some person or some company that will be congratulating you on a job well done; it will not be your friends or family that give you accolades for accomplishments. For completing your job on this earth in accordance with God's Word, it is Jesus who will be giving you your inheritance. And what is your inheritance? It is spending the rest of eternity with Him on the streets of gold in heaven. There will be no more pain, poverty, or dissension, but only peace and complete satisfaction. Concerning your healthy lifestyle program, you should want to be successful at that program to please your God and not just to look good. Yes, you should always be striving to be healthier and take better care of the body that God has entrusted you with, but you continuously need to remind yourself that you should be doing that for God's greater glory and not your own.

Father God, I do not ever want to be slack in anything that I do while on this earth. Every job that I undertake I want to do with the best of my ability as if You were the foreman that was overlooking my work. I may never know when someone is watching me to see if I walk the talk for being a Christian. I know that my purpose on this earth is to serve You and to be a witness for You in everything that I do. I resolve to accomplish that this day in Your name, Jesus. Amen.

Nutrition Thought for the Day.

If a person does not get proper sleep, diet, takes some form of diuretic (this could be excessive coffee, tea, or caffeinated soft drinks, or some medications), is a negative person, and is under very stressful conditions—how much higher is his vitamin C requirement? If he took an excess of vitamin C beyond the 250 milligrams per day, would it help prevent a cold? It is very difficult to conduct research with so many different variables that can alter the effectiveness of vitamin C. This vitamin has probably been researched more than any of the other vitamins, and still we do not have definitive answers for many of the questions about vitamin C.

Day 230
Delight in the Lord

How blessed is the man who does not walk in the counsel of the wicked, nor stand in the path of sinners, nor sit in the seat of scoffers! But his delight is in the law of the LORD, and in His law he meditates day and night. He will be like a tree *firmly* planted by streams of water, which yields its fruit in its season and its leaf does not wither; and in whatever he does, he prospers. (Psalm 1:1–3)

Recently we have been talking about doing everything as unto the Lord and allowing God to be in our hearts to guide us in everything we do. Today's scripture is the icing on the cake, so to speak. If you follow the instruction given the last couple of days, you will also be following the instructions given in today's scripture by not walking in the counsel of the wicked or standing in the path of sinners. If you seek the Lord with all your heart, you will be delighting in His law and meditating on Him day and night. As a result, you will be like trees planted by streams of water. You will never thirst or want for your daily needs. Your fruit will be abundant, and you will prosper in all that you do. This will give glory to the Lord as it is your reason for being on this earth. If you are following the ways of the Lord, be encouraged today that you have good things coming your way. Continue to be diligent with your healthy lifestyle program knowing that you will also be successful with it and thus glorify God physically as well as mentally and spiritually.

Father God, thank You that I am so blessed because of Your promises. I do not knowingly walk in the way of sinners or in the counsel of the ungodly. I delight in Your law, and I resolve to make a greater effort to meditate on Your Word day in and day out, wherever I am and whatever I am doing. I know that I will be blessed for my diligence and I know that I have a tremendous inheritance waiting for me as Your child. I thank You again for Your promises that You cannot break, in the name of Jesus. Amen.

Nutrition Thought for the Day.

What if a person took a gram (1000 milligrams) or even more of vitamin C per day? Would this amount be harmful? For some people, it would. Here again, there are many variables that would affect this. Vitamin C is an acid, and an excessive amount might tip the acid-base balance of the body, depending on the person's normal balance and what else they are consuming in their diet. When some people take around a gram of vitamin C, it causes them to have an upset stomach and diarrhea. An excessive vitamin C intake has also been associated with kidney stones. Vitamin C in excess could cause inflammation.

WAYNE E. BILLON, PH.D., RDN, LDN

Day 231
God Will Supply All Our Needs

And my God will supply all your needs according to His riches in glory in Christ Jesus. (Philippians 4:19)

And what are His riches? A never-ending supply of all good and valuable things, physical and spiritual, found in the universe. He has at His disposal everything you will ever need, all you have to do is ask and believe, as it says in Matthew 7:7–8. He will not just pour out everything you ask for as soon as you ask, but He will provide for your needs according to His wisdom and not your whims. Not all you ask for are really needs, but many are wants. There is a big difference. Sometimes you ask for things that you think you need but if they were granted they might not be beneficial at the time you ask. Even in your healthy lifestyle program, you may be overweight or underweight and want to lose fifty pounds or gain several immediately, but that would take a miracle. We have to lose weight gradually, and we have to gain weight gradually. You may be overweight and want to lose to your ideal body weight, or you may be underweight and want to gain to your ideal body weight. In either case, weight loss/gain takes a long time. Be patient in everything you ask for and in due time God will provide your every need. The timing will be perfect.

I thank You, Father God, for Your timing is perfect. You know my every need and You will provide me with my needs in Your perfect timing. Help me to understand the difference between my needs and my wants. My wants I selfishly consume for my own flesh, my needs are used for the advancement of Your Kingdom. I know that if I continue to trust and seek You, I will not have any serious needs. I thank You, Father, in Jesus's name. Amen.

Nutrition Thought for the Day.

So what is vitamin C good for in addition to promoting a healthy immune system? There is a long list of functions of vitamin C in the body as an antioxidant that reacts with a variety of free radicals and prevents tissue damage. On the other hand, if an excess of vitamin C is ingested, it could become a pro-oxidant and help to cause inflammation in the body. One way this could come about is by vitamin C causing excessive amounts of iron to be absorbed. This is another caution about taking too much of the vitamin. Vitamin C is necessary for the metabolism of some amino acids, neurotransmitter synthesis, and other functions that take place in the liver.

Day 232
The Lord Hears Our Call

But know that the LORD has set apart the godly man for Himself; the LORD hears when I call to Him. (Psalm 4:3)

Know that you have been set apart for God Himself and know that the Lord hears when you call to Him. This is a short verse but has two powerful promises in it. If you ever have had a bad day, as all of us have from time to time, and you wonder where the Lord is, then just repeat this verse to yourself over and over. I know many times you wonder where the Lord is when you call to Him, but He is always there, even though you are not aware of it. It may be that the Lord is answering your prayers, but because of the interference, you cannot hear Him. That interference could be the world, the flesh, or the devil. The world includes the busyness and all the schedules that you have to keep along with your daily tasks that can be overwhelming. The flesh could be the things you let distract you, the lack of time you spend fellowshipping with like-minded believers and with your God, your failure to engage in fervent prayer, or reading and studying God's Word. The devil is responsible for the temptations that he throws at you because he does not want you to hear from your God. Sometimes things happen that you have no control over but most of the things listed here you can control.

You need to be careful not to overload your schedule and learn how to say no to some requests. You need to become more organized and efficient in your time management and make time to read God's Word and talk to Him. If you stay in close relationship with your Lord, you will be able to more easily recognize the devil's temptations and take authority over them. Do not let your healthy lifestyle program be one of the overwhelming things that consume you to such a degree that you cannot hear from your God. Keep everything in its proper perspective and know that no matter what is going on in your space, you have been set apart by your God and He does hear you.

Father God, I thank You that I am blessed in that You have chosen to set me apart for Yourself. Thank You that You hear me when I call and You know what is best for me. You know when and how to answer my call when the timing is perfect. I know that the cares of this world can seem to be overwhelming for me sometimes, but I also know that nothing is overwhelming for You. I know that You do indeed hear my call and that You will give me the strength to complete my task until my call is answered. I thank You, Father, in the name of Jesus Christ. Amen.

Nutrition Thought for the Day.

Vitamin C may have a role in the prevention of some cancers. This does not mean megadoses of vitamin C will prevent cancer but having sufficient vitamin C as an antioxidant may prevent a cancer from starting. Once cancer is established in the body extra vitamin C may not help. Vitamin C has been associated with elevated cholesterol levels, reducing heart disease, reducing blood pressure, and increasing HDL but there is not sufficient evidence to recommend vitamin C for any of these disease states. As many reports say it helps, there are as many reports that say it does not help.

Day 233
The Lord Is Our Shield

For it is You who blesses the righteous man, O LORD, You surround him with favor as with a shield. (Psalm 5:12)

Besides setting us apart and hearing our call, God also blesses us as righteous people and He surrounds us with favor as with a shield about us. Even though you may be seeking God and trying hard to please Him, there may always be a tendency to fall back because you do not feel righteous so you think the scripture is not for you. That is not so. The righteousness you have is not based on any good or any bad thing you have done, but it is based on what Jesus did for you. As a born-again believer, when God your Father looks down on you, He sees you covered with the righteousness of Jesus Christ. Remember that when you confessed your sins to Him, He forgave ALL your sins and separated them from you as far as the east is from the west (Psalm 103:12) and He chooses not to remember your sins anymore (Hebrews 10:17). Also remember that the Holy Spirit has put an indelible seal on your spirit (Ephesians 1:13) that God sees when He looks down at you. That seal designates that you are a born-again believer and that you belong to the almighty God. That seal also covers you with the robe of righteousness. You need to learn to see yourself as God sees you, not as a sinner but as a child of God, coheir of Jesus Christ and the one who was mentioned in this scripture—a righteous person surrounded with favor, as with a shield about you. Concerning your healthy lifestyle program, remember that when you look in the mirror you may see yourself as being overweight or underweight, but when God looks at you, He sees you as His child for whom Jesus died.

Do not see yourself as any less or degrade yourself for any reason including your weight or your appearance.

Father God, I thank You for seeing me in a different light than I see myself but help me to see myself as You see me. I know that I am covered with the robe of righteousness, not because of any good thing I have done or because of the evil things I have not done, but because of what Jesus did for me. I am covered with His righteousness and I am coheir with Him. This is indeed an awesome statement and one that is true but one that I need to get down into my spirit to encourage myself every day. I am indeed a child of God! Thank You, Father, in the name of Jesus. Amen.

Nutrition Thought for the Day.

Vitamin C has also been related to possibly preventing macular degeneration (note that in all of these discussions I say *possibly* preventing). One thing we know is that a lack of vitamin C will cause collagen deficiency. Collagen is a protein in our body that performs many different functions. The gums in our mouth are largely composed of collagen. With vitamin C deficiency the gums breakdown and our gums will become sore, bleed, and in severe cases, the teeth may fall out. Our blood vessels have collagen in them that provides strength. With a vitamin C deficiency collagen will become weak, and blood vessels may break and cause bruising. There are a number of things that can cause a person to bruise so if someone bruises easily it does not necessarily mean a deficiency in vitamin C.

Day 234
The Lord Is Near

The LORD is near to all who call upon Him, to all who call upon Him in truth. (Psalm 145:18)

If God repeats something over and over in the Scriptures, He must really want to make a point. Every line of scripture in the Bible has a purpose and can be used for your spiritual strength and God's glory. For the last several days, His Word has told us several different ways that He is near to those who call upon Him. Your God obviously wants you to call upon Him in all circumstances, and He promises that He will be near to you. The scripture also says, "...to all who call upon Him in truth." "To call upon Him in truth" means that you really do love Him and you believe that when you call, He will answer. Psalm 145:19 carries this a little further for it says, "He will fulfill the desire of those who fear Him; He will also hear their cry and will save them." Our God's promises are true, but they are only true if you believe them and receive them. He really does want you to call upon Him and believe that He is near to you and will rescue you whenever you call on Him in truth. This is true for everything you attempt to do in this life, including losing weight or gaining weight and exercising. Nothing is too small or too insignificant for God not to be concerned about for every little detail to us is a big deal to Him.

Thank You, Father God, for Your desire that I am close to You in every aspect of my life. Thank You that You care about every little detail of my life and that You are always close to me and You are always listening to hear my call. How that can be is an awesome wonder for me, but since Your Word says it, I decide to believe and receive it. It gives me great comfort to know that You are always near to me and You are always listening for my call. Forgive me for the many times that I do not call on You when I am in need, especially those times when I believe that my need may be too insignificant or too small for You to be concerned. I know there is nothing too small for You just as there is nothing too large. I thank You for this Father, in the name of Jesus. Amen.

Nutrition Thought for the Day.
When a wound heals, it leaves a scar. That scar is made up of collagen. Vitamin C is necessary for the synthesis of collagen. The cells in our body do not last forever but cells are continually dying, and new cells are continually being produced to take their place. If the cells that make up a scar die, the new cells will need collagen to be synthesized and thus have a need for vitamin C. If we are deficient in vitamin C, that new collagen will not be synthesized, and the wound will not heal. In fact, if someone has scars from previous surgeries and they go severely deficient in vitamin C, the scars may open up again, even if it is years later. This is called dehiscence.

Day 235
Wait on the Lord

For from days of old they have not heard or perceived by ear, nor has the eye seen a God besides You, who acts in behalf of the one who waits for Him. (Isaiah 64:4)

Wait for the Lord. There is no God like our God, from the days of old until now, and that God of ours acts on behalf of those that wait on Him. One possible reason our God may not always act immediately when we call on Him is that He sees the need for teaching us patience. Galatians 5:22 tells us that patience is one of the fruits of the Spirit. Patience bears fruit. We have to learn to trust in God's Word, that He will fulfill it and do what He says if we wait on Him. Patience would certainly be a virtue for you to master for your healthy lifestyle program. As you well know, an excess of weight does not come off quickly, nor is it easy to gain weight or just get in shape. It takes a lot of hard work and sacrifice to be successful in such a program. If you lack patience, you lack a good thing and will have a discouraging time. Decide this day to become more patient in all that you do and especially with your healthy lifestyle program. Rest assured that the Lord will act on your behalf in His timing. Be willing to accept God's timing but be careful not to fall into a trap where you think that since God will eventually help you to lose weight, you do not have to continue to work so hard because eventually the weight will come off anyway. No, it will not, you still have to do your part.

> I thank You, Father, for acting on my behalf, even if it is in Your timing and not mine. I know that You are doing what is best for me. I understand that by teaching me to wait for You, I am learning to practice patience. I know that patience builds endurance, and endurance builds hope. I ask for You to help me develop more patience in everything I do and especially in my healthy lifestyle program. I know that I will continue to lose weight and become healthier so that I can be a better witness for You. I resolve this day to practice patience in all that I do, and I will be willing to wait for Your timing. In Jesus's name, I pray. Amen.

Nutrition Thought for the Day.

Vitamin C is necessary for wound healing. If you have a large number of wounds, as due to an automobile accident or wounds obtained in war, would your vitamin C requirement increase? I have no data to show how much it would increase but it would because of the need for additional collagen to be synthesized to heal the wounds and the stressful condition you would be in due to the injuries. So, if you had several wounds and you took very large doses of vitamin C, would the wounds heal faster? No, they would not. While the wounds may increase your need for vitamin C, once that amount is met, any excess could cause problems as previously mentioned.

Day 236
The Lord Will Teach and Counsel Us

I will instruct you and teach you in the way which you should go; I will counsel you with My eye upon you. (Psalm 32:8)

The Book of Psalms is very encouraging to read. God tells us He will instruct us and will teach us in the way that we should go. He says He will counsel us with His eye upon us. God can teach us in many different ways. When we first think of being taught, we think of being in a classroom or a Sunday school room with someone teaching us about God's Word. That is certainly a form of teaching, but God can teach us in many ways that we do not expect. We have been speaking of asking God for things and maybe not receiving the things we ask for in our timing. Sometimes it may be that our God answers us in a way we do not expect, but we are not in tune with Him to hear His answers.

For example, there may be a problem that we need a solution for, and we ask God for an answer, but we have not been able to hear from Him. Someone that we may be in conversation with, maybe even a person who does not know the Lord, will say something off-the-wall that will go in one ear and out the other, but later we may think about what they said and realize that, without knowing it, they gave us the answer to our problem. We may hear it announced on a TV news show; we may read it in the newspaper, we could receive an answer in any number of ways. This indeed happened to me several times in my life. We miss it because we expect the answer to come out of the Bible or some person of God that is teaching us. Do not put God in a box. God could speak to us through a rock if He wanted to. Always be listening for the Lord to speak to you, even in ways you may not ever expect.

Father, I realize that You can speak to me at any time and through any person or thing. I know I have to be more diligent in listening for creative ways that You speak to me. Your Word is indeed a way that You can speak to me and I expect to hear from You through Your Word, but I have to keep alert for You to speak to me in the most unexpected of places. If I am not in focus with You on any given day, please remind me to be looking for You to speak to me through any aspect of Your creation. I ask this in the name of my Savior and Lord, Jesus Christ. Amen.

Nutrition Thought for the Day.

I mentioned earlier that an excessive intake of vitamin C might be a pro-oxidant. To carry that discussion a little further it is necessary that you understand another function of vitamin C. It promotes the absorption of iron. For iron to be absorbed through our small intestines, it must be reduced to a form that is readily available for absorption. The acid in your stomach does that naturally but any other acid that you ingest, including vitamin C (ascorbic acid), would also aid in iron absorption. If you ingested an excess of iron along with excessive vitamin C, this could cause you to absorb more iron than you need and that iron could promote oxidation in the body.

Day 237
The Lord Is Our Rock

For You are my rock and my fortress; for Your name's sake You will lead me and guide me. (Psalm 31:3)

This Psalm reminds us that God is our rock and our fortress and it also reminds us that He will lead us and guide us for His own name's sake. We are God's children, and He is our Father. As a father watches over his children in the natural, how much more would our Heavenly Father watch over His children that He created? We belong to Him, and He has promised in His Word that He will never leave us nor forsake us. He cannot go back on His Word. Therefore it is logical that He has to watch over us because of His name's sake. If we do not believe that this is true, then we probably will not see God moving in our lives very much, but if we do believe this scripture is true, and we seek our God with all our hearts and keep in fellowship with Him, we will be able to see His protective hand in our lives. This is true in everything we do whether it is in our home life, work life, social life, or even in our diet and exercise. God has our back and He will lead us and guide us in all that we do. Be encouraged today that He is with you.

Father God, I thank You for being my rock and my fortress not only in a time of trouble but also in the good times. Thank You that You will lead and guide me in everything that I do. I declare that I believe this to be true and I accept Your guidance and Your leadership in my life. I look forward today and always for Your guidance in everything that I do including my healthy lifestyle program. I declare this in the mighty name of Jesus, my Savior and Lord. Amen.

Nutrition Thought for the Day.

A few other facts about vitamin C that may be of interest to you is that it can cause a false positive for occult blood in the feces. This means that if you have a stool test to look for blood, and you take an excess of vitamin C, the test may show that you have blood in the stools when you really do not. Similarly, the structure of vitamin C is very close to the structure of glucose. If you took an excess of vitamin C in your diet, as mentioned, the excess would come out in the urine. If you are testing your urine for concentrations of glucose, the vitamin C could give a false positive for glucose in the urine.

Day 238
The Lord Is the Light of Our Life

"For You are my lamp, O LORD; and the LORD illumines my darkness." (2 Samuel 22:29)

A similar verse is also found in the book of Psalms. Psalm 119:105 says, "Your Word is a lamp to my feet and a light to my path." Just as yesterday's verse declares that God will lead us and guide us, this scripture declares that He can do this by being a lamp to our feet, illuminating our darkness. While God is certainly capable of doing this in the physical, I believe this refers to God being a lamp to our feet and illuminating our darkness in the spiritual sense. When we are confused and do not know which way to go, the Holy Spirit guides and directs us through communication with our spirit. Of course, this will not happen if we are not in tune to God's Word. We have to be walking with Him so that we can hear His voice and see the spiritual enlightenment that He provides to us through His Holy Spirit. If we have not been doing this as we should, there is no time like the present to turn things around and seek God this day with all your heart. Resolve today that you will listen for His voice and look forward to His spiritual enlightenment.

I know that You are with me and that You are a lamp to light my path. You illuminate the darkest corners of my mind by the power of the Holy Spirit. I know that when I am trusting and believing in my God, He will speak to me by the power of the Holy Spirit and I will be able to hear His voice. I know that once I hear Him the choice is mine to follow His lead or to go my own way. If I follow His lead, I will walk in the light. If I go my own way, I will sink deeper into a dark pit. I resolve this day to follow Your lead Lord and to walk in Your light. I thank You for your guidance and direction, in the name of Jesus. Amen.

Nutrition Thought for the Day.

The next several discussions will be about fat-soluble vitamins which are vitamins A, D, E, and K. First, some general information about the fat-soluble vitamins. As the name implies, there are soluble in oils but not in water. Since they are fat-soluble, they are found where fats are found in the body and, unlike water-soluble vitamins, they can be stored in fat tissue and the liver. Thus they have the potential of being more toxic than water-soluble vitamins if we take in too much, particularly vitamin A. For fat to be absorbed through the small intestines bile is required to be present in the intestines. A very low-fat diet may not promote bile to be excreted into the small intestines and thus interfere with fat digestion and absorption. Anything that interferes with fat absorption will also interfere with fat-soluble vitamin absorption.

Day 239
The Lord Satisfies All Our Needs

"And the LORD will continually guide you, and satisfy your desire in scorched places, and give strength to your bones; and you will be like a watered garden, and like a spring of water whose waters do not fail." (Isaiah 58:11)

Isaiah tells us that the Lord will continually guide us. I believe every single word in every sentence that God has given us is meaningful, so note here that it says that God will continually guide us. There is no end to His love or His guidance. The scripture says that He will satisfy our desires in scorched places, so when it seems like everything is going wrong and you are not sure of which way to turn, then turn to the Lord and you will never go wrong. The Lord will give strength to your bones (or to your body), and you will be watered like a watered garden. Have you ever noticed how after you water a garden the plants perk up and reach to the sky? When the Lord waters you spiritually, that is what will happen to you in your spirit. His water is like a spring that never runs dry and never slows down. I know that if you are in a bad place this all sounds like a pie in the sky type of an idea, but this is God's Word, and it is real. If you believe it and receive it, then you can walk in God's Word with grace and power. He will give you strength as you go through your healthy lifestyle program but remember that you must be reasonable and still eat sufficient food to maintain your physical strength. The Lord will guide you and direct you, but He will not miraculously make weight fall off you if you starve yourself to the degree that is unhealthy. Trust in His guidance but be sound in your decisions to eat and exercise.

> Lord, I thank You that Your guidance is a continuous factor and is not something that You turn off and on from time to time. I know that I can always depend on You to guide and direct me no matter how scorched my journey may seem to be. I thank You for the strength you give to me and that You refresh me like a well-watered garden. I resolve this day to be attentive to Your guidance so that I can walk through the fiery darts the enemy sends at me and receive Your strength in all that I do. In Jesus's name, I pray. Amen.

Nutrition Thought for the Day.
Vitamin A is a group of compounds called retinoids. Two examples of retinoids are retinol and retinal. These retinoids are active forms of vitamin A in our body and will be referred to again later. The active form of vitamin A is not found in plants but is only found in animals and animal products. There is a precursor to vitamin A that is found in fruits and vegetables sometimes referred to as a pro-vitamin. This precursor is a group of compounds called carotenoids and includes alpha-carotene, beta-carotene, and gamma- carotene. There are over 600 carotenoids, but the most important one is beta-carotene.

Day 240
The Lord Shows Us the Way We Should Go

You will make known to me the path of life; in Your presence is fullness of joy; in Your right hand there are pleasures forever. (Psalm 16:11)

Our Lord will make the path of life known to us—the path He would have us walk down, the path He lights for our feet—which leads to our heavenly mansion in heaven. If you have ever realized you were in the right place at the right time and felt God's presence, then you have felt an extreme peace and confidence to carry on. I have a jail ministry on Thursday nights that has been very fruitful. When I get to lead someone to the Lord in jail, I drive myself home with joy and peace that surpasses any other peace. I know that I was where I was supposed to be at that time and place. It is so much better than watching Thursday night football. I know that He is present with me and it is a fullness of joy that will last forever. While there is nothing wrong or evil with being left-handed, this scripture tells us that in God's right hand there are pleasures forever. Forever is a long time. As you walk on your path through life today, rest assured that if you are saved, you are on the path to your eternal glorious home and expect God to guide you down that path.

Father, I thank You for making the path of life known to me and for guiding me down the path that leads to eternal glory. Before knowing You Lord Jesus, I was headed down the path to Hades, but You brought me out of the fiery pit and set my feet on the rock of salvation. I resolve to continue to follow Your path and I expect to continue to see You guiding me to Your path of glory. In Jesus's name, I pray. Amen.

Nutrition Thought for the Day.

We cannot synthesize vitamin A in our bodies but we can convert the carotenes to one of the active forms of vitamin A. Beta-carotene is two units of retinal hooked together. We can split beta-carotene into two active units of retinal. The other carotenes can also be converted to retinal, but they do not produce two retinals per one unit of carotene. In other words, gamma-carotene can be converted to retinal, but only one unit is created and not two units like with beta-carotene. Thus we can indirectly get vitamin A from fruits and vegetables but only by converting the carotenes into the active form of vitamin A in our body.

Day 241
The Lord Rejoices over Us

The LORD your God is in your midst, a victorious warrior. He will exult over you with joy, He will be quiet in His love, He will rejoice over you with shouts of joy. (Zephaniah 3:17)

I think that sometimes we do not realize how much heaven and earth are connected. Luke 15:10 says that there is joy in the presence of the angels of God over one sinner who repents. When one person comes to know Jesus Christ as Savior and Lord, the angels in heaven rejoice. The scripture for today says that the Lord our God, while His throne is in heaven, He is in our midst and will exult over us with shouts of joy. When we make accomplishments on this earth in the name of Christ, there is a party going on in heaven. God very much wants us to succeed. He and the angels never sleep, they are always active in watching us. That is something that our finite minds are not able to understand, but it is true, and one day we will have the same ability to rejoice with them in heaven. Be confident this day that your God rejoices over you with shouts of joy and is an ever-present force that is with you. Use this as encouragement as you deal with any stressful event in your workplace, with your family, in your personal life, or with your healthy lifestyle program. Your God cares about everything you do, and He is with you.

I thank You, Father, for the love that You have for me and for the way You express it with Your angels in heaven. It gives me great comfort to know that You are in my midst and, along with the heavenly host, rejoice over my accomplishments that are done in Your name. I know that I frequently do things that cannot be pleasing in Your sight and that I am not Your perfect child as I see perfection, but You love me just the same. I resolve this day to be joyous on this earth and to rejoice with You and the angels when I accomplish something in Your name. In Jesus's name, I declare this to be true. Amen.

Nutrition Thought for the Day.

Beta-carotene is a plant pigment that has a deep yellow or orange color and the plants that are high in beta-carotene are usually deep orange or yellow. Examples include carrots, sweet potatoes, peaches, and cantaloupe. Any plant that is yellow or orange is a good source of beta-carotene. Technically, it is not a good source of vitamin A because vitamin A is not found in the plant; however, we frequently say that it is but what we mean is that it is a good source of beta-carotene. If you ask a dietitian what is a good source of vitamin A, many of them will tell you yellow or orange vegetables.

Day 242
The Lord Has Great Compassion on Us

"For the mountains may be removed and the hills may shake, but My lovingkindness will not be removed from you, and My covenant of peace will not be shaken," says the LORD who has compassion on you. (Isaiah 54:10)

The book of Isaiah gives us many prophecies about God's love for us. This scripture tells us that even if the mountains are removed and if the hills shake, the lovingkindness of our God will not be removed from us. God has made a covenant with us and remember that a covenant that God makes cannot be broken by Him. We can break a covenant that we make with God due to our weaknesses, but He cannot break any covenant that He makes. Even if the world starts to come apart physically, our God will not be shaken and He will not take His love from us. He will have compassion for us no matter what is going on in the world around us, another comforting thought that we need in this day and age. The world does seem to be coming unglued around us at the time of this writing, but our God is still on the throne. He is not wrenching His hands and pacing the clouds and saying, "Oh no, what will I do now?" He is not moved by the problems that we create on this earth. Be reminded of the scripture in Isaiah 26:3 that says God will keep us in perfect peace because we trust in Him. As you walk through this day, resolve to do so in peace knowing that your God has a covenant of peace with you and He will not be shaken.

Father God, I thank You for the peace that I have because I know that as a compassionate God, You grant me peace and will not be shaken even though at times there seems to be no peace on the face of this earth. You want me to be at peace and to feel the compassion that You have for all of Your children. I resolve to walk in Your peace and not to be shaken by any of the calamities that take place around me. I know that through everything that happens on this earth, You will give me peace. I thank You for this peace in the name of Jesus. Amen.

Nutrition Thought for the Day.

Chlorophyll gives plants their green color. If the plant is high in chlorophyll and beta carotene, the plant will be green instead of yellow or orange. An example is broccoli. Broccoli is a dark green vegetable, but it is also a good source of beta-carotene. Too much vitamin A in our diet can be very toxic; vitamin A is the most toxic of the fat- soluble vitamins. If we eat very large amounts of fruits and vegetables that are high in beta-carotene, we will not get a toxic amount of vitamin A because our bodies will not convert more beta-carotene into vitamin A than is needed. However, since beta-carotene is an orange pigment, an excessive dietary intake can cause our skin to turn yellow, even dark orange if we ingest enough.

Day 243
Put Your Trust in the Lord

Put your trust in the LORD your God and you will be established. Put your trust in His prophets and succeed. (2 Chronicles 20:20b)

We could say that the bottom line in this month's devotions would be to put your trust in the Lord your God. As long as we continue to trust in our God, even when it seems like He does not hear us at all, we will be safe and will be established in righteousness. He will guide our paths, He will be with us, He will have compassion on us, and He will never leave us. All of us have times in our lives when we are not able to hear clearly from our God, and it seems like He does not hear us. Set your face like flint, knowing that your God is with you and will never leave you. Trust in Him in all circumstances and do not be discouraged. Be bold and courageous in all your activities and continue to strive to be a healthier you for the glory of your God. Do not give up on healthy eating and exercise. Do not give up on daily devotions and talking to your God as often as you can. Trust Him, and He will deliver you from all harm.

> Father, I choose to trust in You no matter what comes my way; even when I do not feel like trusting You. By an act of my will, I choose to trust You. In my heart, I know that You are in my midst and You will never leave me. You have compassion on me and You rejoice over me with joyous singing. You are a lamp to my feet. You are my mighty warrior and You go before me in everything I do. You make me more than a conqueror, a world overcomer; and You care about my every need, no matter how small. I thank You for this in the name of Jesus. Amen.

Nutrition Thought for the Day.

Usually, if we ingest such an excess of beta-carotene that it will turn our skin yellow, the whites of the eyes and underneath the fingernails are the first places to see a change in coloration. This can be scary to some people because this can also be a symptom of a more serious disease, such as cirrhosis which can also cause us to turn yellow. Beta-carotene taken in excess as a supplement could be harmful. There was one classic study that showed that people who smoked and took beta-carotene supplements developed a higher incidence of lung cancer than people who smoked but did not take in beta-carotene supplements; do not ingest anything to excess.

Day 244
Be Confident in Yourself

Therefore, do not throw away your confidence, which has a great reward. (Hebrews 10:35)

Your God lights your path, directs you in the way that you should go, is always with you, and rejoices over you. As a result of all these positive things in the extent to which your God loves you, you should be able to show extreme confidence that you are God's child in that you can do all things through Christ who strengthens you (Philippians 4:13). If you think that you fall too many times, remember that no matter how many times you fall your God is always there to pick you up. It does not matter if this is a spiritual fall due to sin in your life or a physical fall due to not following your healthy lifestyle routine—your God is always with you and will always rescue you. Be confident in this and be confident that no matter what you try to do on this earth your God is always with you. Think things through, use wisdom before attempting any new endeavor, and ask God for guidance before you attempt anything but know that right or wrong, your God is with you.

I thank You, Father, that You are always with me and will always be there to pick me up when I stumble. This gives me great confidence in that I know that in my success as well as my failures I will always have You there to see me through. I choose this day to walk with confidence that You are my God and that You will never leave me. I thank You that there is nothing I can do that can separate me from Your love. I thank You, Father, in the name of Jesus. Amen.

Nutrition Thought for the Day.

Beta-carotene is an antioxidant like vitamin C, but beta-carotene is fat-soluble while vitamin C is water-soluble. The active form of vitamin A is sometimes referred to as an antioxidant, but it is not. If you take multi-vitamins, look on the label and see what it says about vitamin A. It will usually tell you how many units of vitamin A are in the tablet and how many units of beta-carotene are in the tablet. Sometimes the units of vitamin A are listed as retinol equivalents (RE) or as international units (IU). Both of these are old units but are sometimes still used on labels today. The current units for vitamin A are expressed as retinol activity equivalents (RAE). No matter which one is used on the label of a vitamin tablet, it would be wise if you do not take the entire day's requirement as the active form of vitamin A.

Day 245
Trials Bring about Perseverance

And not only this, but we also exult in our tribulations, knowing that tribulation brings about perseverance. (Romans 5:3)

I do not believe this scripture is saying we should exult in our tribulations for the sake that we have tribulations but, when we have tribulations, we should not be discouraged because we know that every trial we go through, we can come out on the other side stronger. Trials bring about perseverance. Do not believe God causes bad things to happen to you because you probably do a very good job of causing bad things to happen on your own, but when you do go through some trial, He is there with you and will use the trial to teach you something. When things do not go the way you think they should, do not despair, but stand on your faith in God's Word. You know that He is with you and will never leave you. Ask Him for wisdom and direction in the midst of your trial. Ask Him for strength and for the trial to be a learning situation for you. Do not let trials make you bitter; instead, let them make you better. The choice is yours, depending on your attitude. We all know that we are going to have trials to walk through. The Word does not promise us that everything will be rosy and easy. John 16:33 says, "These things I have spoken to you, so that in Me you may have peace. In the world you have tribulation, but take courage; I have overcome the world." Let every trial be a step closer to a stronger faith and a stronger walk with your Lord.

Lord Jesus, I know that in this world I will have trials, but I also know that in the midst of all my trials You are there with me. I know that with Your strength I can walk through any trial and come out victorious on the other side. Trials will make me stronger because I trust in You. You are my deliverer, my defender, the one who directs my every step when I allow You to do so. Give me the wisdom and the understanding to know when to call on You in the midst of any trial. I thank You, Jesus, that You will always be with me. Amen.

Nutrition Thought for the Day.
Vitamin A in the diet is found bound to fatty acid esters and needs to be separated in the intestines to be absorbed. Once it is separated, it is carried by bile acids to the intestinal lining where it crosses the intestinal border, goes into chylomicrons, and travels through the blood attached to the chylomicron with the lipids that we digest and absorb as previously discussed. Thus fat and bile need to be in the diet for the fat-soluble vitamins to be properly absorbed. Anything that inhibits fat digestion or absorption will also inhibit fat-soluble vitamin digestion and absorption. An example is potato chips that are fried in olestra. These chips include a compound that prevents fat absorption; therefore, they are advertised as chips that you can eat more of but not get as many calories as regular chips. True, but you will not get as much of the fat-soluble vitamins either.

Day 246
Perseverance Results in Hope

And not only this, but we also exult in our tribulations, knowing that tribulation brings about perseverance; and perseverance, proven character; and proven character, hope. (Romans 5:3–4)

Trials bring about perseverance. When we complete the trials with the help of our Lord and Savior, we come out on the other side of the trial a better person. This shows our character. As long as we maintain our walk with our God through the trial, we show who we are in Christ. When we as Christians are persecuted, those around us will look to see how we handle adversity. If we come apart at the seams and say or do things that we may be sorry for later, those watching us will not see any advantage to being a Christian. If on the other hand, we walk through the trial with our head held high and continue to trust in our God, we will show our true character as Christians. Not only will this be a witness to those that are around us and perhaps open doors for us to minister to the lost, but it will also give us confidence in ourselves and our God. This will not only build our hope, but it will give hope to those who are watching us. They will see that even though we go through trials and tribulations when we make it through them, we are in a better place as a result of the trials. This gives hope to those that are observing how a Christian handles adversity. As you go through your healthy lifestyle program, there will be plenty of places for you to get discouraged. Those who know you are on such a program will also be watching to see how you handle adversity and setbacks in your program. In a sense, your program is also a trial. Come out the other side stronger with the help of your God and be a witness to all of those watching.

> I am now aware that once I declare Jesus to be my Lord and Savior, I put myself in a fishbowl that allows all the people around me to watch and see how I handle situations that life throws at me. There may be many people watching me that I am not aware of and, if I rant and rave as a heathen, I will lose my opportunity to be a witness and to minister to those around me. I need to walk through every trial with character and prove that as a Christian I am different. I cannot do this without the help and guidance of the Holy Spirit. I thank You for giving me the Holy Spirit and seeing me through all my trials. I choose this day to hold my head high and walk through all the adversities that come my way in the character of a true Christian. I thank You for helping me do this in the name of Jesus. Amen.

Nutrition Thought for the Day.

Olestra is the compound chips are fried in and it does prevent a lot of the fat from being digested and absorbed, so that fat passes on to the large intestines. The bacteria that live in the large intestines digest this fat and break it down into volatile fatty acids (that is, turn them into gases) and cause more total particles to be in the large intestines. This draws in water, causes bloating, and diarrhea. If you overeat a product that contains olestra or a compound like olestra, you will decrease your fat-soluble vitamin absorption and could cause gas, bloating, and diarrhea. Eating a small portion of these on occasion would probably be okay for most people but eating a significant amount may have the ill effects mentioned.

Day 247
We Have Hope

For whatever was written in earlier times was written for our instruction, so that through perseverance and the encouragement of the Scriptures we might have hope. (Romans 15:4)

Every scripture can be used for instruction and reproof. Paul is telling the Romans that everything that was written before their time was written for their instruction so that they would know how to get through the trials that they were facing. We have available everything that was written for the Romans, and everything written after the Romans. The Bible is the handbook on how to survive trials and tribulations. Jesus is the living Word. The Bible is the written Word. Jesus came to this earth as a man and walked out everything the Bible said we should do to please our Father God. Look at the trials and tribulations that Jesus had and see how He walked through them with love. "Father forgive them for they know not what they do." These were Jesus's words as He hung on the cross for those that tortured and crucified Him. An assignment for today is to look up 2 Corinthians 11:23–28 and observe the trials that Paul had to go through. He did not despair, he did not give up, but he conquered, just as Jesus did. He followed Jesus's example, walked through the trials, and came out the other side as a better man. Follow their example by following the Scriptures in your daily walk. You can only do this if you know the Scriptures and spend some time studying them on your own and in fellowship with other believers. The Scriptures will show you how to persevere and will give you encouragement so that you might have hope.

Hebrews 11:1 says, "Now faith is the assurance of things hoped for, the conviction of things not seen." I know that the promises given in the Bible are for me and I have faith that they will happen even though I have yet to see them be fulfilled. The more I persevere trials and tribulations the more encouraged I am that my God is with me.

Father God, I know Your Word is true and I choose to follow it. I choose to believe that the promises in Your Word are for me and I set my faith on receiving those promises in due time. I thank You, Father, for giving me the encouragement I need to accomplish every task that lies before me. In the name of Jesus, I pray. Amen.

Nutrition Thought for the Day.

I mentioned that heat (as in cooking) could destroy some of the water-soluble vitamins. In the case of vitamin A, heat denatures proteins in plants and causes some of the carotenoids in the plant to be released, thus making them more available. Functions of vitamin A include proper vision, particularly night vision. One of the earliest symptoms of vitamin A deficiency is night blindness. Vitamin A is also necessary for cell reproduction. This makes it very essential for cells that have a short lifespan and have to reproduce frequently. Examples are the lining of all the tracts in our body such as the gastrointestinal tract, the respiratory tract, the reproductive tract, and the urinary tract.

Day 248
Endurance Brings about Perfection

Knowing that the testing of your faith produces endurance. (James 1:3)

The Scriptures are full of advice concerning perseverance and endurance. James gives us an explanation about the testing of our faith. Trials and tribulations are a test sometimes not only on our physical stamina but also on our spiritual stamina. To get through the trials of this life, it takes a firm faith. As we endure through the trial, we develop character, and we also strengthen our faith. As James says, we need to fully understand the things that test our faith produces endurance and perseverance. Perseverance develops character and results in giving us hope. Many things may test your faith. These tests may come in the form of financial problems, marital problems, relationships at work, illnesses, and as you well know, weight problems. All these need to be dealt with and can be considered as trials that we can conquer through Christ who is in us. We are more than conquerors and we can do all things through Christ who strengthens us (Philippians 4:13). After we emerge victorious from these trials, we can look back and see that the trials enable us to practice endurance and strengthen our faith. Do not be discouraged! Do not be overwhelmed! You are a child of God and a world overcomer (1 John 5:4). See yourself as God sees you.

Father, I continue to pray as I did several days ago. I again make this declaration because it is important that I get this matter down into my spirit, and that is the matter of trusting in You through all my trials. I choose to trust in You no matter what comes my way; even when I do not feel like trusting You, by an act of my will I choose to trust You. In my heart of hearts, I know that You are in my midst even though I may not always see it and I know that You will never leave me. You always have compassion for me. You are a lamp to my feet. You are my mighty warrior and go before me in every trial that I have to face. You make me more than a conqueror, a world overcomer; You care about my every need, no matter how small. I thank You for this in the name of Jesus. Amen.

Nutrition Thought for the Day.

Vitamin A can interact with vitamin K and interfere with its absorption. Vitamin A deficiency could diminish the mobilization of iron from iron stores in our body. The important thing to remember is not to ingest anything in excess but keep supplements and intake of foods to moderate levels. Research any supplements or vitamins that you may think you need before you start taking them. The absolute best thing to do is to consult with a registered dietitian.

Wayne E. Billon, Ph.D., RDN, LDN

Day 249
Endurance Brings about Promises

For you have need of endurance, so that when you have done the will of God, you may receive what was promised. (Hebrews 10:36)

This scripture in Hebrews tells us that we need endurance so that when we walk out our lives according to God's Word, we know we will receive what has been promised to us. When we reach our final goal, we will lack nothing. That is part of the promise, but the promise is so much more than that. Yes, it includes our mansion in heaven on streets of gold, and it includes a carefree existence forever with no more suffering, pain, or any trials and tribulations of any kind; but it includes even more than that. Something that we cannot imagine because of our finite minds includes being in the presence of our Lord and Savior and worshipping at His feet. To be honest, bowing down and singing, "Holy Holy Holy is the Lord" at His feet all day does not seem to be something we may want to do for the rest of eternity, but that is because we are so used to enjoying physical things here on earth. When we get to heaven, we will finally fully understand everything that our God did for us, and we will understand spiritually and not just physically. To be in His presence will be awesome and I am sure we will be doing more things than singing to Him. Whatever we will be doing, it will be the most fun and more enjoyable that we can ever imagine.

> Lord Jesus, You have a place for us in heaven, and You have a call for us in heaven. Whatever it is and whatever we will be doing will be more glorious than we can ever imagine. I know that my finite mind cannot imagine the magnitude of the glory in heaven—the sights, the sounds, the smells, and just being in Your presence. I thank You that You know what my needs are so much better than I do and the endurance that You are preparing me for on this earth is for the sole purpose of perfecting me. I look forward to the day of final perfection with You in heaven. I declare this in Your name, Jesus. Amen.

Nutrition Thought for the Day.

Since vitamin A is necessary for cells that reproduce rapidly, vitamin A is undoubtedly important during reproduction and the development of a fetus. Note that an excess of vitamin A taken during pregnancy (not beta-carotene but the active form of vitamin A) can cause severe birth defects. Since skin cells have a fast turnover, vitamin A is also necessary for healthy skin, and for bone formation. Thus vitamin A deficiency can cause growth retardation. The carotenoids (beta-carotene) in our body are also important as antioxidants.

Day 250
Our Tests Produces Endurance

And let endurance have *its* perfect result, so that you may be perfect and complete, lacking in nothing. (James 1:4)

James tells us to let endurance have its perfect result. That is, the results of enduring our trials results in the perfection of our character. If we can see hardships as a means of developing our character then we may be able to see the light at the end of the tunnel. If we see life as a tunnel and we know that we are going through that tunnel, we can see the light at the end of the tunnel. When we get to that light it will be a glorious light, and we will lack nothing. Imagine lacking nothing! You can be joyous today knowing that everything that happens to you is a process of perfecting you and bringing you closer to your Creator. The closer you get to Him the better you can hear His voice. The closer your walk with Him then the likelihood of you wandering off the path diminishes. Every accomplishment you make in your healthy lifestyle program gives you more confidence to continue with the program. You can see your "light at the end of that tunnel" being the accomplishment of your goal, a healthy weight, and a healthier lifestyle. This is certainly doable, and you can accomplish it if you do not get discouraged and do not give up. Keep your eyes on the Master Trainer and you will be successful!

Lord, I choose to develop a new attitude towards the trials that I face in my life. I do not want trials and I am not asking You for trials or tribulations, but I am expecting that when they come, I will be prepared to handle them because of Your Word. I know that as I endure the tasks that face me in this world, my character is being developed; and as I keep my eyes on You, I know that our walk will be closer. The light at the end of the tunnel is Your light, and I look forward to being able to stand in the glorious light with You, lacking nothing! I look forward to this, Jesus, in Your name. Amen.

Nutrition Thought for the Day.
The next fat-soluble vitamin to be discussed is vitamin D. If you have been paying attention to nutritional news at all, you probably have seen a lot of talk about vitamin D. Our knowledge of vitamin D is increasing daily and, in the last few years, several new things have been discovered about vitamin D that were missed entirely in the past. We use to teach that vitamin D was the most toxic vitamin there is. We now know that this is not true at all and most people should be taking larger doses of vitamin D than we previously recommended. Too much of anything can be toxic, and too much vitamin D can produce extreme toxic effects but, we are finding that vitamin D is needed in greater amounts than previously believed.

Day 251
You Are Blessed for Your Endurance

We count those blessed who endured. You have heard of the endurance of Job and have seen the outcome of the Lord's dealings that the Lord is full of compassion and *is* merciful. (James 5:11)

Think about the things that Jesus and Paul had to endure; many others in the Bible had a tremendous amount to endure too. In this verse James mentions Job. If you have never read the book of Job, you may not be aware of his trials, but he was tested with every type of trial and endured until the end. After all, when he was finished, he was blessed beyond imagination with the compassion of our merciful God. You can also look at the story of David and see the immense number of trials he went through. David also endured and was declared by God Himself to be a man after His own heart. The Bible shows that endurance always produces fruit that is acceptable to our God. It may not always be easy to remember in the midst of a trial that our God is compassionate and full of mercy, but He is indeed. He knows every small thing that bothers you. Your concern about your weight and physical fitness is understood by Him. He has compassion for you for that and will help to see you complete your program if you do your part. Be strong and courageous! Do not be discouraged! You are the only one like you in the world. God had no one else like you, which is why He made you. You are His. Do not forget who you are in Christ!

> Thank You, Father, for creating me exactly the way I am for I know that I am unique in Your eyes. There is no one else exactly like me on the face of this earth. All of us are individual cells that make up the body of Christ, and I am honored to be one of those cells. I have endured everything I have faced so far, and I am blessed because of it. My trials and tribulations have made me who I am, and I am a child of God, coheir with Jesus Christ, and it does not get any better than that. I thank You, Father, in the name of Jesus. Amen.

Nutrition Thought for the Day.

One reason why it is difficult to get a toxic level of vitamin D is that vitamin D is not present in many of the foods that we eat. To get a toxic level of vitamin D, one would have to take in large doses of vitamin D by way of supplements. For example, the primary sources of vitamin D are liver, eggs, and some fatty saltwater fish. Dairy products, (including margarine), and some breads and cereals are fortified with vitamin D. Since we are finding that vitamin D is so much more beneficial than we previously thought, you will probably see other foods being fortified with vitamin D but most of the foods that are fortified with vitamin D now are not fortified with more than the daily requirement, if that much. Thus, to get a vitamin D toxicity, one would have to eat very large amounts of these foods. This is not likely, but if someone were to consume large amounts of the foods mentioned and/or took in vitamin D supplements for an extended period, then vitamin D toxicity becomes more possible.

Day 252
Be Immovable

Therefore, my beloved brethren, be steadfast, immovable, always abounding in the work of the Lord, knowing that your toil is not *in* vain in the Lord. (1 Corinthians 15:58)

Here are a few additional aspects of endurance that are important to understand. When you endure and hold your ground, you become steadfast, immovable, and you grow in the Lord. As you grow in the Lord and increase your faith and your understanding, you are bound to God's work. You do not have to be told this because you know that your toil is not in vain. You may not see the fruit right now, but if you continue to be steadfast in God's Word, you will bear fruit. You never know who and how many are watching you to see how you respond to adversity. As a result of your steadfastness you may receive rewards in this world such as a promotion at work or a raise, or maybe just favors someone will want to do for you because of who you are. Just be careful to let everyone know that who you are is not someone that was self-created, but you are a child of God, coheir with Jesus Christ. Be steadfast this day in all that you do. Be steadfast and immovable in your healthy lifestyle program and your endurance will prevail as a blessing.

Dear Father, I choose this day to be immovable and steadfast in Your Word in everything that I do, including my healthy lifestyle program. I thank You for the grace You have given me to be immovable. Even when I do not feel Your presence, I know You are there. I am encouraged by Your Word this day, and I resolve to follow You in all that I do, and I thank You in Jesus's name. Amen.

Nutrition Thought for the Day.

Vitamin D, like all fat-soluble vitamins, can be stored in the body. Liver is the main place in the body that stores vitamin D and is therefore high in vitamin D. Liver is not a food that many people eat, but huge amounts of liver, along with the other sources of vitamin D and a high intake of vitamin D supplements, could cause a toxic amount to be ingested. However, this is highly unlikely. The egg yolk is another good source of vitamin D, but because of the cholesterol content in egg yolks, most people do not eat a large number of eggs each day either. Fatty saltwater fish can be high in vitamin D but here again, unless you live near the ocean and love fish, you are probably not eating large amounts of fatty fish. Cod liver oil is taken by some folks as a supplement for various reasons, and it can be very high in vitamin D, and vitamin A. Be cautious if you take cod liver oil as a supplement.

Day 253
Be a Servant of God

But in everything commending ourselves as servants of God, in much endurance, in afflictions, in hardships, in distresses. (2 Corinthians 6:4)

Commending ourselves as servants of God may be an area we need to have endurance because as it says, in serving our God we certainly may have afflictions, hardships, and be in distress at times. When we declare who we are in Christ, we will be challenged, ridiculed, and shoved out of the way. This seems like it should be the other way around but God's Word promises us that we will have tribulations in the world because of Him. The Scriptures say there will be afflictions, hardships, and distresses. We may think that because we are Christians people will look up to us but unfortunately, the opposite is true. Oh, some people will, but most of the world is anti-Christian, and instead of looking up to us they will look down at us, and this is another type of hardship that we have not discussed. The trials mentioned previously were our daily trials that everyone faces with finances, sickness, and relationships, etc. There will be additional trials the closer we get to the end times, and those trials will come about as a result of our stand for Christianity. Do not be dismayed, do not be discouraged, God is still on the throne and always will be. Put your hope in Him and move on.

Dear Father, it is my desire to be Your servant and to serve You in all situations. I realize that as Christians we will be ridiculed and persecuted. That is quite evident in our own country today as we see laws changing in favor of those that are ungodly. Rules on abortion, marriage, and the lack of prayer in school, to name a few, are anti-Christian. People are being threatened for professing Christianity in our country. In foreign lands, Christians are being mutilated and beheaded because if their faith. I know these are signs of the end times and I know that You said they must happen. I will not be moved by the signs. I will be immovable in Your Word. I thank You for Your grace and strength in these times, and I resolve to be Your servant in whatever persecution I face. In the name of Jesus, I declare this. Amen.

Nutrition Thought for the Day.

Vitamin D is sometimes called the "sunshine vitamin." We do not synthesize vitamin D in our body per se, but vitamin D can be made in the body from cholesterol and the UV light from the sun. This is a multi-step process, but when sunlight strikes our skin, it begins a process of converting cholesterol to the active form of vitamin D in our body. How well this works depends on our complexion (dark skin versus light skin), how long we stay in the sun, how much of our body is exposed, the season of the year, and finally where we live. In the winter the angle of the earth is such that the sun is very weak and converts very little cholesterol to vitamin D. Roughly speaking, anyone living north of Atlanta converts less cholesterol to vitamin D because of the angle of the sun. During the summer with, our arms and face exposed, about ten minutes of sunlight will produce enough of vitamin D for that day and perhaps some extra depending on our complexion and our location when we are when we are exposed to the sun.

Day 254
Endurance Produces Life

"By your endurance you will gain your lives." (Luke 21:19)

Your endurance may save your life and the lives of others. This would particularly be true if things get so bad that being a Christian results in death. There may be those who would deny Christianity to save their life on this earth but lose eternal life with our Lord and Savior as a result. If by your example you remain true to Christianity and even if it causes you to lose your life on this earth, you will gain eternal life with our Lord and Savior with special rewards. We all certainly hope this never happens to us, but it is happening around the world to Christians at the time of this writing. This type of steadfastness would be an example to those around you and would be like Stephen when he was stoned in the book of Acts (Acts 7:59–60). Just before his death, he cried out with a loud voice, "Lord, do not hold the sin against them!" Be bold and courageous and do not lose your faith in any circumstance. You know that your reward will be great.

Father God, I truly hope that severe persecution does not come upon those in our country as it has upon those in other countries. I know that the Bible warns us of persecution in the last days but I choose to stand my ground in Your Word regardless of what happens. I pray not only for myself but also for my fellow countrymen and for those that lead my country that they will come to know the only truth is in Your Word. May Your grace be poured out in abundance on all those around me and the leaders of my country in Jesus's name. Amen.

Nutrition Thought for the Day.

The conversion of cholesterol to vitamin D involves the UV light of the sun, our skin, our liver, and our kidneys. Thus if we have a disease that affects our liver, this conversion will not take place. Likewise, if we have kidney failure, the conversion will not take place. If we have adequate skin exposed while in the sun for an adequate period, at a location where the angle of the sun to the earth is good, and our liver and kidneys are healthy, we can convert enough cholesterol to meet our daily need for vitamin D. However, this is not true for everyone. For example, babies and little children who do not get to go outside very much cannot depend on the sun for the source of vitamin D. The elderly who do not get enough sun exposure will not meet their needs for vitamin D. These people need to obtain vitamin D from food and/or supplements. If we are in the sun for long periods of time, we will not convert more cholesterol into vitamin D than we need and we will not get vitamin D toxicity. However, we may increase our chances of skin cancer by excessive sun exposure.

Wayne E. Billon, Ph.D., RDN, LDN

Day 255
Produce Fruit

But the fruit of the Spirit is love, joy, peace, patience, kindness, goodness, faithfulness, gentleness, self-control; against such things there is no law. (Galatians 5:22–23)

As we endure in this impatient, selfish, prone to evil world, we will not despair, but we will continue to be led by God's Spirit. As we follow the Spirit of the Lord, we will enjoy the fruit of the Spirit. There are many fruits of the Holy Spirit, and they should be self-evident in our lives so that those around us can see them as a witness to our Christianity. This is the best way we can witness to our family, friends, and coworkers without ever saying a word to them about Jesus. The fruit of the Spirit is love, joy, peace, patience, kindness, goodness, faithfulness, gentleness, and self-control. All of these are necessary for us to persevere and endure. While the laws of our country may change in so many ways that are not pleasing to us or conducive with Christianity, there is no law against showing love or joy or peace or any of the rest of the fruits of the Spirit. These fruits can be evident when you are in the grocery store, at your workplace, in a restaurant, or in the gym as you work on your healthy lifestyle program. In any case, they are not to be evident only in church or inside your home with just your family seeing them. Yes, they are important in those places too, but they need to be seen by the world. Let your light shine and do not be discouraged, do not be dismayed.

Holy Spirit, I know that You are in me and that You guide me in all truth as the Word promises. I want to bear Your fruit for all to see abundantly. No matter what people say about me or how they may chastise me, I want them to know that I am Yours and that Your fruit is abundant in my life even though they may not understand what that is. I thank You for Your abundant fruit that You have given to me in Jesus's name. Amen.

Nutrition Thought for the Day.

Conditions that can prevent the conversion of cholesterol in the skin to vitamin D include the wearing of sunscreen. We are being discouraged to spend too much time in the sun because of the chance of skin cancer, and we are encouraged to wear sunscreen. This is very important and we should follow these recommendations, but if we use sunscreen that is over eight SPF, the UV rays that convert cholesterol to vitamin D are blocked. If you are concerned about sunshine and skin cancer, but want to obtain some vitamin D from the sun, then stay in the sun for about ten minutes before applying sunscreen. That will provide you with a significant dose of vitamin D.

Day 256
Forgive As You Have Been Forgiven

So, as those who have been chosen of God, holy and beloved, put on a heart of compassion, kindness, humility, gentleness and patience; bearing with one another, and forgiving each other, whoever has a complaint against anyone; just as the Lord forgave you, so also should you. (Colossians 3:12–13)

We are reminded that as born-again believers we have been chosen by God and are holy and beloved. In case you are not feeling very holy right now, let me remind you that your holiness is not based on what you have done, but it is based on what Jesus did for you; so if you are a child of God then yes, you are holy. The scripture tells us to show some of the fruit of the Spirit previously studied and includes having a heart of compassion, kindness, humility, gentleness, and patience. It tells us to bear with one another and forgive each other just as the Lord has forgiven us. This is another fundamental characteristic that we must show if we are to be God's children—and that is forgiveness. Christians do not hold grudges or take revenge. Romans 12:19 says, "Never take your own revenge, beloved, but leave room for the wrath of God, for it is written, 'vengeance is mine, I will repay,' says the Lord." If God forgives us for anything, we have done who are we to hold something against someone else? Forgive and move on. By doing this, you will let your light shine in the darkest of places.

Lord Jesus, because of Your life, death, and resurrection I am forgiven of every sinful thing I have done. You forgive me freely without question because I trust in You. Who am I to hold a matter against someone that something against me? I know that to be forgiven I must also forgive in the same manner that You have forgiven all of us. There are times when I do not feel like forgiving someone that did something very hurtful to me. When those times come up, I ask that You give me the wisdom and the grace to forgive. I vow today to forgive those who have trespassed against me in Your name, Jesus. Amen.

Nutrition Thought for the Day.
Another condition that can decrease the concentration of vitamin D in our body is obesity. Individuals that are obese have a problem with obtaining vitamin D from the sun because the vitamin is absorbed into the fat tissue and tends to be stored there. It is not easily released into the bloodstream and thus is not doing the body any good. Aging also can affect the body's effective production of vitamin D whether we spend time in the sun or not. These two groups of people should rely on their diet and/or supplements to obtain their vitamin D requirements.

WAYNE E. BILLON, PH.D., RDN, LDN

Day 257
Be an Example of Christ's Patience

Yet for this reason I found mercy, so that in me as the foremost, Jesus Christ might demonstrate His perfect patience as an example for those who would believe in Him for eternal life. (1Timothy 1:16)

In 1 Timothy 1:15 Paul tells Timothy the statement that says Jesus Christ came into the world to save sinners, among whom Paul was the foremost of all, is trustworthy and deserves full acceptance Then Paul says that because he was such a sinner, he found mercy so that Jesus might demonstrate His perfect patience for those who believe in Him for eternal life. In other words, Paul was saying that since he was such a great sinner, if God can save him, it demonstrates God's patience for waiting on him. As a result, others might see the mercy of God to save Paul and would also come to know the Lord and receive eternal life. Have you sinned more than Paul has? Have you persecuted the church by dragging members out of the church and having them imprisoned and even killed? I think not, but, even if you did, you would still receive God's mercy and be forgiven once you came to Him with repentance. So if you ever doubt that you are saved, you can rest assured that God's mercy is greater than any sins you have ever committed.

Thank You, Lord Jesus, for the great mercy You have shown to me by Your love and for forgiving me. Let those that know me see the change in me since I have become a Christian and let them understand without a doubt that the change is due to Your mercy and Your grace. There is nothing I can do, or anyone can do for me to save me from my sins. Only You and Your sinless life, death, resurrection, and ascension can grant me forgiveness for my sins. I thank You again for my forgiveness and I ask that my Christian walk will be a witness to others that they too may be saved and receive eternal life. I pray in Your name, Jesus. Amen.

Nutrition Thought for the Day.
As mentioned earlier, the complexion or color of our skin affects the conversion of cholesterol to vitamin D in our bodies. The darker the skin pigmentation, the more the production of vitamin D is blocked by UV exposure, and thus this reduces the production of vitamin D. If people with darker complexions do not take in adequate sources of vitamin D in their diet, they are subject to vitamin D deficiency. Consider the fact that most people do not eat a lot of liver (if any), do not eat a large number of eggs, do not drink adequate milk or are lactose intolerant, and do not eat large quantities of any kind of fish much less fatty saltwater fish, and you can see why vitamin D deficiency could be common.

Day 258
The Lord Is My Rescuer

Now you followed my teaching, conduct, purpose, faith, patience, love, perseverance, persecutions, *and* sufferings, such as happened to me at Antioch, at Iconium *and* at Lystra; what persecutions I endured, and out of them all the Lord rescued me! (2 Timothy 3:10–11)

In this scripture Paul reminds Timothy that since he was one of his disciples involved in his teachings, he knows what Paul had to go through. Paul tells of some of the hardships he endured and how he conducted himself with purpose, faith, patience, love, and, perseverance, through all of his persecutions and sufferings. Paul reminds Timothy that his persecutions took place more than once in three different places at least. He also reminds Timothy that he endured them all and that it was the Lord who rescued him. This has been discussed several times and, if the Scriptures repeat the importance of God's people enduring persecutions with patience, love, and perseverance, then it must be something that the Lord really wants to get across to us, something to which we should pay closer attention. Let this be just one more scripture to remind you that the Lord will rescue you out of any trial and any tribulation. Be content this day that you are the apple of His eye and He will save you from any calamity.

Thank You, Jesus, that You are my rescuer and that You will be with me everywhere I go and through everything I do. No matter what I face or how difficult or how easy my trials may be, I do not have to face them alone ever again. You are always with me. Help me to feel Your closeness and be aware of Your presence. Help me to be able to receive Your wisdom and understanding in my time of need. I thank You again, Jesus, for rescuing me. Amen.

Nutrition Thought for the Day.

Since vitamin D is a fat-soluble vitamin, it is found associated with fat in the foods that contain vitamin D. It is also absorbed in our intestines in association with micelles, the small particles of bile that enhance fat absorption. Anything that decreases fat absorption will also decrease the absorption of fat-soluble vitamins. Problems with bile production will be detrimental to vitamin D absorption as well as with any of the fat-soluble vitamins. Foods that are specially prepared to reduce the fat content, such as potato chips that are fried in olestra to reduce fat absorption, will also reduce fat-soluble vitamin absorption. An extremely low-fat diet will not only be low in vitamin D but will not stimulate as much bile to be secreted and such a diet will be lower in vitamin D. Normally about 50% of vitamin D ingested is absorbed.

Day 259
Be Ready in Season and Out Of Season

Preach the word; be ready in season *and* out of season; reprove, rebuke, exhort, with great patience and instruction. (2 Timothy 4:2)

The scripture for today shows Paul's instructions to Timothy as to how he is to conduct himself and walk as a Christian. He tells him to preach the Word. In case you are not aware of it, Timothy was a very young man and was not that educated as far as God's Word is concerned. What he knew was taught to him by Paul. It is upon all of us to teach God's Word, and we do not have to be seminarians or ordained to spread God's Word. Paul also tells Timothy to be ready in season and out of season—that means in all circumstances to be prepared to teach God's Word. He tells him to reprove, rebuke, and exhort those around him with great patience. This is the same call we have on our lives, and we should be ready in season and out of season, or as it is spoken today to be ready at the drop of a hat to stand up for God's Word.

As you go through your day, look for opportunities to do precisely what it says in this scripture: to teach, to reprove, rebuke in love, and to exhort God's Word with great patience. This is the call that is on you and me and all who proclaim to be Christians. Anybody can say they are a Christian, but only those who understand who they are in Christ can truly walk out their Christianity in faith and in peace. We could say that the bottom line is simply to put your trust in the Lord your God. As long as we continue to trust in our God, even when it seems like He does not hear us at all, we will be safe and will be established in righteousness. He will guide our paths; He will always be with us.

Father, as it says in Romans 12:1–2, I want to be a living sacrifice and be Your servant in all that I do. I want my everyday actions and relationships to be a reflection of who I am in Christ. I cannot do this in my own power, but I trust in You to give me the wisdom, understanding, and courage to walk out Your Word in everything that I do. I know this is a tall order and I know that there are times when I will miss the mark, but I also know that You will be with me and will rescue me if I go astray. I have full confidence in You as my rescuer. It is in Jesus's name, I pray. Amen.

Nutrition Thought for the Day.

Most vitamin D that is stored in our bodies is stored in our liver. If we took in toxic levels of vitamin D, it would cause damage to the liver. On the other hand, if the liver is already damaged due to some disease such as cirrhosis, its ability to store vitamin D would be greatly reduced. Since the liver also plays a role in the synthesis of vitamin D by the UV rays of the sun reacting on cholesterol in our skin, a damaged liver would also lose the ability to help convert cholesterol to vitamin D. Under these conditions vitamin D supplementation would be necessary on a regular basis.

Day 260
Faith and Patience Inherits the Promise

And we desire that each one of you show the same diligence so as to realize the full assurance of hope until the end, so that you will not be sluggish, but imitators of those who through faith and patience inherit the promises. (Hebrews 6:11–12)

Before the two verses quoted here, the author of Hebrews tells believers that God will not forget the love and the work they have been doing in ministering to the saints. Then in verse 11 he, and those that are with him, tell the believers that they continue to show the same diligence to realize the full assurance of hope until the end. I am sure they are referring to the end of their trials on this earth. He also tells them not to be sluggish but to be imitators of those who, through faith and patience, inherit the promises. So here is another scripture that tells us to hold on to God's Word for the assurance of hope and not to be sluggish but to take every opportunity to minister to those around us. This is not specifically stated but is implied.

The writer of Hebrews also tells the believers that they will inherit the promises given in God's Word through faith and patience. Once again I remind you that if something is repeated so many times in the scripture, God must have considered it to be important and indeed is something that should demand our attention. Be diligent to minister to those around you and do not be sluggish about it. Use faith and patience to minister to your family, peers, social contacts, and those who you may be in your healthy lifestyle program. You know you will inherit the promises granted in God's Word for an eternity with Jesus. Do not be discouraged, be bold and courageous, and walk out this day as a witness to God's Word.

Father God, You have told me a number of different ways in Your Word what I should do to maintain hope and to inherit the promises that You have given me. I desire to do exactly that and to be Your witness to all that I can as I walk through my daily endeavors. I know that You are always with me, but I ask that You guide me through Your Holy Spirit and remind me whenever an opportunity is being presented to me to be a witness for You. I hope for life eternal with You in heaven and I thank You again for giving me that opportunity through Your Son, Jesus Christ. It is in His name that I pray. Amen.

Nutrition Thought for the Day.

An interesting fact about vitamin D is that sometimes it is considered to be a hormone. The definition of a vitamin is an organic substance that is needed by the body in a very minute amount for maintenance, growth, repair, and reproduction. A vitamin cannot be synthesized in the body but must come into the body with the diet. The definition of a hormone is an organic substance that is needed by the body in a very minute amount for maintenance, growth, repair, and reproduction. A hormone is synthesized in the body. So we have vitamin D that can be synthesized in the body if the individual is exposed to adequate sunlight and has a properly functioning liver and kidneys. If these conditions are met, some consider vitamin D to be a hormone. If the above conditions are not met, then vitamin D cannot be synthesized in the body and has to come in with the diet and thus is considered a vitamin.

Day 261
Patience Endures

The end of a matter is better than its beginning; patience of spirit is better than haughtiness of spirit. (Ecclesiastes 7:8)

The Oxford dictionary defines haughtiness as the appearance or quality of being arrogantly superior and disdainful. When walking through our daily events, we have a choice of being patient with those around us and being a witness to them as the Lord opens the doors; or we can be very impatient, arrogant, and disdainful, looking down at them as being inferior to us because we are saved and they are not. That is like the behavior of the Pharisees, a behavior that Jesus constantly criticized and rebuked when He walked the face of the earth. We do not want to be like that, but instead, we want to be patient. Sometimes we can minister to someone when their heart is just not ready, and instead of doing good we may drive them further away from the Lord. We need to learn to rely on the Holy Spirit to direct us when it is the proper time to approach someone about the Lord. If we can accomplish this, we will indeed be fruitful and be practicing the gifts of the Spirit. As you go through your day today look for an opportunity to witness to someone that seems to be ready to receive God's Word. As the Scriptures say, be ready in season and out of season to profess God's Word (2 Timothy 4:2).

Lord Jesus, I know that to be successful I have to be in Your timing. If I get ahead of You then I am walking out on my own, and that can be very dangerous. Instead, I need to learn to let the Holy Spirit go before me and for Your lamp to guide my feet. Give me the guidance that I need to be fruitful in ministering Your Word to the lost. If I get out ahead of You, not only may I drive people away from You, but I may also miss those that are ready to hear about Your Word. I choose this day to be patient and to trust in the Holy Spirit to lead me and guide me. In Your name Jesus, I pray. Amen.

Nutrition Thought for the Day.
There is a lot about the functions of vitamin D that we have been aware of for decades and those functions will be discussed next. There is a large amount of data about the functions of vitamin D that we have not been aware of until the past decade and those will be discussed later. For a long time it has been common knowledge that vitamin D works with the parathyroid hormone to promote bone mineralization by promoting the absorption of calcium and phosphorus. When our blood calcium level drops below a certain level, vitamin D, along with the parathyroid hormone, increases the ability of calcium to be absorbed in our intestines, decreases the calcium excretion through the kidneys, and draws calcium out of bones to raise the calcium level in the blood. This is good news, and it is bad news.

Day 262
God's Kindness Leads Us to Repentance

Or do you think lightly of the riches of His kindness and tolerance and patience, not knowing that the kindness of God leads you to repentance? (Romans 2:4)

In Romans 1, Paul talks about those who are not following God's Word. He gives a long list of things that they are doing which are not proper such as, wickedness, greed, murder, strife, slander, and several more evil characteristics. Then in the first three verses of chapter 2, he asks the Romans that when they passed judgment on those who practice such things, and they are doing the same things themselves, do they expect to escape the judgment of God. That brings us to verse four which tells us that we should not take the riches of His kindness and tolerance and patience lightly because it is that kindness of God that leads us to repentance. If we see those around us that are participating in evil practices from something as severe as murder to something less severe like general strife, we are sometimes quick to judge them. When the Bible speaks of judgment, it is really speaking of condemnation. If someone that you are working with is constantly and obviously doing something wrong and bragging about it, and you say that what they are doing is wrong, that is not judgment. They are admitting to their wrongdoing themselves. But if you say that they are going to Hades because of their lifestyle that is condemnation and the type of judgment of which the Bible speaks. You do not know that at some point in time they may turn to the Lord, repent, and receive forgiveness for their sins. It is your job as a believer to point them in the direction that they are more apt to receive salvation than condemnation. So speaking of that type of judgment, do not be fast to judge but be patient and look for your opportunity to minister to them. Remember that Jesus died for them just as He died for you. Try to see them through the eyes of Jesus and know that He sees someone for whom He died. Amen or oh me!

> Father God, help me not to be judgmental by reminding me that I once to was a sinner and did not know of the salvation that was waiting for me because of Your life, death, resurrection, and ascension. I do not want to be arrogant and seem superior to those around me that are not believers. I want to be a good listener and to listen to their problems and the things they consider to be profitable so that when the timing is right, I will know how to minister to them by the power of Your Holy Spirit. In Jesus's name, I pray. Amen.

Nutrition Thought for the Day.

Many functions are consistent with a normal healthy body that requires sufficient calcium in our blood. For example, normal blood clotting, nerve conductions, and muscle contractions are a few examples of our needs for calcium besides just bone and teeth production. If our blood calcium levels drop too low, the kidneys and the parathyroid will do everything they can to increase the calcium level in the blood. This will enable our body to function in a normal manner, but it does so by drawing calcium out of the bones. If this were to continue for long periods of time, then we would end up with very porous and weak bones. In the past, the primary association of vitamin D was with healthy strong bones and teeth.

Day 263
We Are Strengthened with All Power

Strengthened with all power, according to His glorious might, for the attaining of all steadfastness and patience; joyously giving thanks to the Father, who has qualified us to share in the inheritance of the saints in Light. (Colossians 1:11–12)

This scripture encourages us by informing us that we can accomplish steadfastness and patience because we are strengthened with all power that is according to His glorious might. He has given us the power to overcome and has qualified us to share in the inheritance of the saints. Think about this; it should be a great encouragement to you to know that you have the power in you, the power given to you by your God, to be patient and to be steadfast in all that you do. As an old saying goes, when you have only one nerve left, and someone is grating it, you feel like coming unglued. Well, you may have that feeling but know that you have the God-given power to overcome. Be steadfast and patient and walk through your day as an overcomer knowing that God has your back.

Thank You, Father, that You have given me the power to overcome, to be patient, and steadfast. I know there are times when I do not feel like being patient, but instead I want to be angry and upset. Those times are real, and You know they are. However, faith is not about feelings; it is about trust in You. It is a fact that You have given me the power to overcome whether I feel like it is true or not. I choose to believe Your Word and be patient and steadfast this day in all that I do by the power of your Holy Spirit. I thank You for this power in the name of Jesus. Amen.

Nutrition Thought for the Day.

For a long time our recommended dietary allowances (RDA) for adults for vitamin D was four hundred international units (IU) per day. There was a time not too many years ago that I taught in class that if we took 2 to 4 times the RDA for vitamin D, it could cause liver disease. Today we have people taking between 1000 IUs and 3000 IUs with no obvious complications. PLEASE NOTE that I am not recommending you do this, vitamin D can be toxic but it is not as toxic as we previously thought. If you are going to take larger doses of vitamin D for extended periods of time, you should talk to your physician and have routine blood tests to make sure you are not taking too much.

Day 264
Be Worthy of Your Calling

Therefore I, the prisoner of the Lord, implore you to walk in a manner worthy of the calling with which you have been called, with all humility and gentleness, with patience, showing tolerance for one another in love, being diligent to preserve the unity of the Spirit in the bond of peace. (Ephesians 4:1–3)

This scripture calls for us to walk in a manner worthy of the calling with which we have been called. And what is that call you may ask? As a believer in God's Word, you have been called to the great commission as listed in Matthew 28:18–20. This is where Jesus tells us to go and make disciples of all nations baptizing them in the name of the Father and the Son and the Holy Spirit, and teaching them to observe all that He commanded us. He finishes this command with the words, "I am with you always, even to the end of the age." Many people believe that this calling was given to preachers or pastors, but that is not so, it was given to all believers. You accomplish this by studying God's Word and, by the power of the Holy Spirit, boldly proclaiming the Gospel to those who you contact. This does not mean that you have to stand on a soapbox on the corner of some busy street and scream at people as they pass. Not all of us have the same calling but as the saying goes, grow where you are planted. Your witness will be your calling and today's Word tells you to carry this out with ability, gentleness, patience and showing tolerance for one another in love.

Finally, today's scripture says to preserve the unity of the Spirit in the bond of peace. If we are children of God, coheirs with Jesus Christ, then we are also coheirs with every other believer. The scripture calls us to be in unity with believers with a bond of peace. This is a tall order, and it is for all believers. Many believers do not realize that this call is as real for them as it is for any pastor, priest, or preacher that is called to teach or preach God's Word. As you go about your day today, know who you are in Christ and walk with humility and patience, but also with boldness and confidence.

Dear Father, I understand that I have a calling on my life that is a general calling to be a witness to all those that I come in contact with. I know that You also have a specific calling on me and I pray that You reveal my calling. It may be just to be the witness in my workplace as mentioned above or it may be a calling that I am not aware of yet. In either case, I accept the general calling in my life and that of all believers, and I choose to be a witness for You in everything that I do. Strengthen me by the power of Your Holy Spirit this day to be the person that You have called me to be. In Jesus's name, I pray. Amen.

Nutrition Thought for the Day.

Just a few years ago the vitamin D recommendation for adults was changed from 400 IUs to 800 IUs. You may see a different unit used on vitamin labels instead of IU for vitamin D. Sometimes you may see the units as micrograms which is indicated by the Greek letter mu (μ) and the g for grams (μg). The 800 IUs of vitamin D is equivalent to 20 μg. Many researchers still believe that 800 IUs is not enough for most people. It is important to have blood work to determine your level of vitamin D.

Day 265
Endure Reproach for His Sake

You who know, O LORD, remember me, take notice of me, and take vengeance for me on my persecutors. Do not, in view of Your patience, take me away; know that for Your sake I endure reproach. (Jeremiah 15:15)

Even if we know our calling and we walk out that calling with all of our ability and with every good intention to please our Lord and Savior, it does not mean that we will be able to do that without difficulty. We all know that we will have people who come against us because of what we believe. Some may approach us face-to-face, but most will probably talk about us behind our backs. Our God knows who our real friends are and who our enemies are. Vengeance belongs to Him, and He will judge those who unjustly judge us. Do not be discouraged if everyone does not see things the way you do or does not respond to what may be a perfectly good witness that you presented them. There will always be people like this that you will encounter every day. In the Gospels, Jesus told His disciples to shake the dust off their sandals and move on if they were not accepted. You should do the same and not look back. If you present your life to the world with patience, humility, faith, and love, you are doing all that you have been called to do. The rest is up to those who witness what you say and do. If they judge you because of your righteous actions, then they will have to face the Lord and be accountable to Him. It is not your place to judge them but move on with patience and do not be discouraged.

Father God, I know that there will always be mockers who will be against Your Word and thus will be against my witness and me. I know I do not have to hold them to account for their actions for I am not there judge. I also know that one day we will all be held accountable by You for every word that we say. If I am mistreated because of my witness to You, I will move on and continue to be the witness that You called me to be. I will not be discouraged, but I will be bold and courageous for Your sake because I know that You are with me. I pray this in the name of Jesus. Amen.

Nutrition Thought for the Day.
The normal range for vitamin D in our blood is from 25ng/ml (nanograms per milliliter) to 100ng/ml (some labs have the higher end at 80ng/ml). Blood levels that are greater than 100 ng/ml are considered to be of concern. Many researchers prefer that the level of vitamin D be somewhere over 30 ng/ml and stay in between 50 and 60 ng/ml. The reason checking blood levels is so important is that some individuals could take 50 IUs per day and reach their recommended blood level easily. Others may have to take between 1000 and 3000 IUs to reach their recommended blood level. Those who can maintain their blood level with taking a lower dose might end up with toxic levels in the blood if they took 1000 IUs per day for extended periods. There are apparently other factors affecting vitamin D absorption and homeostasis in the body that we have not discovered.

Day 266
Again I Say Endure

And we toil, working with our own hands; when we are reviled, we bless; when we are persecuted, we endure; when we are slandered, we try to conciliate; we have become as the scum of the world, the dregs of all things, *even* until now. (1 Corinthians 4:12–13)

This scripture is similar to yesterday's in that it talks about when we work for the sake of our Lord we may be reviled. In the verses before this one, Paul talks about some of the hardships he and his companions were enduring. Toil or work with our hands can mean working as a witness for the Lord. When we are reviled under such circumstances, we should bless those who are coming against us. The word revile means to be criticized or abused with anger in an insulting manner. A synonym of revile is to condemn. We should bless people under such circumstances, endure their slanderous insults, and try to conciliate them. That means to try to keep them from being angry and try to appease those who accuse us. Paul and his companions were traveling about doing good for people and performing miracles in the name of Jesus. Yet, they were seen as the scum of the world, the dregs of all things. If they were seen in this light even though they were probably doing many greater things than we are doing, how can we expect to be seen with respect because of our ministering on behalf of God's Word? It is not always easy to bless someone who is cursing you but it is what Jesus did, and it is what the Word calls us to do. This does not mean we should be a doormat to everyone, but we should attempt every day to follow this scripture and be a blessing to those around us regardless of the circumstances.

Father, You know that I am not always eager to bless someone when they curse me but You know my heart and that is my desire to be a blessing to all those who persecute me. My flesh does not always act in the same way my spirit wants it to, but I resolve to continue to try to be the witness and the servant that You called me to be. I choose not to be moved when I am reviled by those around me, and I will try to conciliate them by the power and direction of the Holy Spirit. I thank You that You will give me strength in that area. In Jesus's name, I pray. Amen.

Nutrition Thought for the Day.

There are deficiency symptoms of vitamin D that we have known about for decades. When children are growing, it is very important for them to have adequate amounts of calcium and vitamin D. Taking in large doses of calcium with insufficient vitamin D will not be adequate for normal health. The child's bones will be soft and their legs will bow out or bow in as a result of the weight of their body pushing down on their legs. This deficiency is called rickets. Vitamin D deficiency at this age produces other problems, but this is the most common one. If vitamin D with adequate calcium is added to the diet and braces are put on the child's legs, the problem can be corrected if caught early enough.

Day 267
Endure and Reign

If we endure, we will also reign with Him; If we deny Him, He also will deny us. (2 Timothy 2:12)

We have been talking about enduring trials and how important that is if we are to be God's witness on this earth. This scripture adds another aspect of the importance of enduring, and that is we will also reign with Him if we endure. Paul's second letter to Timothy points out an important element of enduring hardship for Jesus's sake. The opposite of enduring hardship for Him is giving up and denying Him. One day we will stand in judgment before Jesus Christ, and if we endured for Him, then we will reign with Him. If we deny Him, He will deny us. That should give a little bit more incentive to enduring persecution for the sake of our Lord and Savior as well as for our own good. Every time you successfully go through a trial you are stronger after the trial and you are increasing the glory that you will receive on judgment day. So this will give you another all-important reason for putting up with persecutions you may receive in this life. While these persecutions may seem very bad and overwhelming to you now, in the future when you look back, they will seem like small stepping stones to a victorious everlasting.

Lord Jesus, it is a comforting thought to know that one day, when I stand before You in judgment for my life on this earth, I will hear well done good and faithful servant. Then I will cross over into eternity with You and will actually reign with You forever. This is an awesome thought! The trials and tribulations that I face on this earth will seem like child's play when I get to heaven with You. I am encouraged this day by Your Scriptures that declare I will reign with You as coheir to all that You have. I declare this in Your name, Jesus. Amen.

Nutrition Thought for the Day.
If someone has adequate vitamin D and calcium during their younger years, but has a deficient intake of vitamin D during their early adult years, they can develop a disease known as osteomalacia. This is soft bones in adults but does not produce the same symptoms as with rickets. Adult females are particularly susceptible to this condition if they do not have ample calcium and vitamin D in their diets. Pregnancy increases the need for both calcium and vitamin D, and if proper calcium is not provided, the calcium will come out of their bones to maintain constant blood levels and could cause this condition to take place. Adults that are shut-ins and do not get enough sunshine are also subject to this problem as well as patients that have fat malabsorption. Individuals with renal disease that are on kidney dialysis are also at risk because the kidneys are not available to synthesize vitamin D from cholesterol with the help of sunlight, skin, and liver.

Day 268
Our Father Disciplines Us

Then Jesus was led up by the Spirit into the wilderness to be tempted by the devil. (Matthew 4:1)

The enduring previously discussed has been concerned with enduring physical trials or trials that we have been going through because of someone persecuting us. It is important to point out that trials may not come from someone else, but they may be coming from inside our head. We all face temptations and overcoming those temptations are also trials. Sometimes it may seem like the devil will not leave us alone, that every time we turn around there is another tempting thought going through our heads. Overcoming those trials is enduring also. Our greatest battles against sin are in our minds. There have been many books written on the battlefield of the mind. When you feel like you are being tempted a lot, do not be discouraged. Think of today's scripture that points out that even Jesus was tempted by the devil. This scripture is a direct indication of the temptations He endured. In Hebrews 4:15 the Bible also tells us He was tempted in every way we are tempted: "For we do not have a high priest who cannot sympathize with our weaknesses, but One who has been tempted in all things as we are, yet without sin." So every type of temptation we face, He also faced and He defeated for us. When we sin by giving into temptation, that sin has already been accounted for by the life of Jesus and His blood. In 1 Corinthians 10:13 the Bible tells us, "No temptation has overtaken you but as is common to man; and God is faithful and will not allow you to be tempted beyond what we are able, but with the temptation will provide a way of escape also, so that you will be able to **endure** it (emphasis mine)." So take heart because you are not being tempted in any way that Jesus was not tempted and the Bible promises you that you are equipped to be able to overcome any temptation.

Lord Jesus, it is indeed a comforting thought to know that every temptation I face has already been faced by You. Every place I set my foot You have already traveled there before me. And every temptation that I face You are aware of and You will not allow me to be tempted beyond what I can bear but will provide an escape hatch so that I can overcome and endure it. I believe in Your Word, and I trust that You will fulfill it to the letter. Therefore today I will walk with confidence knowing that I am equipped to overcome any temptation that can come my way if I just trust in You. In Your name, Jesus, I pray. Amen.

Nutrition Thought for the Day.

Some symptoms of excessive calcium intake include diarrhea, mental confusion, and calcium deposits in soft tissues. Calcium deposits in soft tissues would include calcium deposits in muscle, calcium deposits attached to joints, and kidney stones. The test for this is a blood test that shows increased blood calcium which is a condition known as hypercalcemia. The parathyroid, the kidneys, and vitamin D join together to do a good job helping regulate calcium levels in the body, but when vitamin D is deficient because the kidneys are not functioning correctly, the symptoms may occur.

Day 269
Perseverance Bears Fruit

"But the *seed* in the good soil, these are the ones who have heard the word in an honest and good heart, and hold it fast, and bear fruit with perseverance. (Luke 8:15)

In this passage of scripture, Jesus is finishing up with the story about the sowing of seed, some of which fell beside the road, some on rocky soil, some fell among the thorns, and some that fell on good soil. His point concerned the seed that fell on good soil and He explained to His disciples what it meant. By keeping your heart pure, receiving God's Word in your heart, and holding fast onto it, you will bear fruit by your perseverance. This is out of the mouth of Jesus Himself. If you know that you have received God's Word and you hold onto it fast within your heart, you should fully understand that it is to you He is speaking when He says you will bear fruit with your perseverance. You may not see the fruit now, and it may take a while before the fruit ripens, but if you continue to persevere, and keep God's Word in your heart with perseverance, you will bear fruit. This is also undoubtedly true with your healthy lifestyle program. If you persevere with that program and you continue to diet in a practical healthy matter, and complete reasonable healthy exercises, you will bear fruit. Just as in a spiritual matter you know that you do not see the fruit right away, you do not see the evidence of significant weight loss or gain right away. But if you continue to persevere and stick with your program you will bear fruit physically while spiritually you will also be growing and bearing fruit also. Be encouraged by this today and continue with your program with renewed endurance and determination.

Father God, I am determined to be persistent and to continue to cherish Your Word in my heart and to follow it as closely as I can. I know that by doing this, I will bear fruit. I also am determined to continue with my persistence to get healthier by carefully choosing what and how much I eat and by completing sensible exercise programs. I know that I can do this with the help of Your Holy Spirit and that I will bear fruit by losing weight and increasing my physical endurance while also increasing my spiritual understanding. I know that You are with me in all that I do and I thank You in the name of Jesus. Amen.

Nutrition Thought for the Day.

If you research vitamin D and disease, you will probably find almost every disease under the sun is claimed to be related to vitamin D deficiency. There is sufficient evidence to substantiate many of the claims, but there are still a lot of claims that need additional investigation. The consensus is that most people are deficient in vitamin D because of the limited number of foods that it is available in and because of the lack of sun exposure. In addition to this we now realize that vitamin D does so many more things in the body than previously thought and thus our requirement is higher. For this reason, many researchers believe that perhaps we need more than 800 international units per day but how much more is difficult to determine since there are so many variables and each has their own unique genetic makeup.

Day 270
Pursue Righteousness

But flee from these things, you man of God, and pursue righteousness, godliness, faith, love, perseverance *and* gentleness. (1 Timothy 6:11)

In the verses before the one listed, Paul is telling Timothy about watching out for certain evils. The evils he was concerned with the most was the desire for "possessions" and money—that is people whose main desire was to get rich. There is nothing wrong with being rich or having money. In fact the more money you have, the more money you can give away to God's church and people in need. That is the reason why we should want money and not for the sake of squandering it foolishly on lavish living for ourselves. Instead, Paul tells Timothy to pursue righteousness, godliness, faith, love, perseverance and, gentleness. So it is okay to have money, just do not let the money have you. "Seek first the Kingdom of God and His righteousness and all these things will be given unto you as well" is a statement that Jesus made in Matthew 6:33. Be content where you are and grow where you are planted. Trust God to meet your every need and do not get greedy. Stay focused and do not get discouraged.

Father, Your Word is so full of wisdom and advice for me that I cannot thank You enough. Wealth can be good, and it can be bad. I know that all my needs will be satisfied through Jesus Christ and that I should pursue Your righteousness and not wealth. As I seek You, I expect to have all of my needs provided for and if You so choose to allow me to be wealthy, I will use my wealth for Your glory and spend it in a manner that You direct me. I thank You for this, Father, in the name of Jesus. Amen.

Nutrition Thought for the Day.

In addition to the diseases previously mentioned, vitamin D has been associated with helping to reduce the incidence of cancer. Not enough research has been completed to be definitive with vitamin D and cancer, but some twenty different types of cancer have been related to vitamin D deficiency. Vitamin D has also been associated with lowering the risk of cardiovascular disease, but this association is weak. Vitamin D has been associated with reducing blood pressure, but this association is also weak. There are so many variables that are involved with cancer, heart disease, and blood pressure that it is difficult to determine precisely what vitamin D's role is, if any. This is also complicated by genetics that can increase or decrease the incidence of these diseases and the need for vitamin D.

Day 271
Of These the Greatest Is Love

Now for this very reason also, applying all diligence, in your faith supply moral excellence, and in *your* moral excellence, knowledge, and in *your* knowledge, self-control, and in *your* self-control, perseverance, and in *your* perseverance, godliness, and in *your* godliness, brotherly kindness, and in *your* brotherly kindness, love. (2 Peter 1:5–7)

To understand this scripture fully we need to look at the two verses before it. In 2 Peter 1:3–4 he says, "Seeing that His divine power has granted to us everything about life and godliness, through the true knowledge of Him who called us by His own glory and excellence. For by these He has granted to us His precious and magnificent promises, so that by them you may become partakers of the divine nature, having escaped the corruption that is in the world by lust." Following this is today's scripture. You see how important it is to understand that God has given us everything pertaining to life and Godliness through knowledge of Him. It is by the power mentioned in this scripture that He has granted to us, along with all the precious and magnificent promises mentioned in this devotion. By those promises we may become partakers of the divine nature having escaped the corruption that is in the world by lust. So, it is because of this that we can apply all diligence to increase our knowledge, self-control, perseverance, Godliness, brotherly kindness, and end with brotherly love. This is some of the fruit that we can bear here on earth when we live by God's precious promises. Have confidence as you go through today that you have been granted the power to walk out these precious promises here on earth.

I thank You, Father, that You have given me an incredible and awesome power to be able to walk out Your Word and take part in the promises You have given us and, at the end, be rewarded with eternal life with You in heaven. Thank You that I have everything I need that pertains to life and Godliness through Your Word and that I can partake of the divine nature and escape the lust of the world by following Your Word. I choose to walk with my head held high this day knowing who I am in Christ. I thank You, Father, in the name of Jesus. Amen.

Nutrition Thought for the Day.

There are research articles that associate vitamin D with diabetes, particularly type 2 diabetes. Researchers have attempted to associate obesity with diabetes and vitamin D, but more research is needed. Vitamin D has also been associated with insulin secretion and insulin sensitivity in type 2 diabetes. Anyone with any of the diseases mentioned here that are associated with vitamin D would do well to have blood levels checked to see what their current vitamin D level is. If they are deficient according to their blood levels, it would be prudent for them to increase their vitamin D level with the counsel of a physician and/or a registered dietitian.

Day 272
The Lord Increases Our Strength and Power

He gives strength to the weary, and to *him who* lacks might He increases power. (Isaiah 40:29)

I know that we all have days where we feel like we do not have God's divine power or any power to help us through the day, but His Word says we do. If we believe we have the power to overcome and we step out in faith to exercise that power, I think we will be surprised to see that we can accomplish more than we have ever imagined. This is not just a mind over matter thing. It takes faith to step out. Today's scripture tells us that when we are weary He gives us strength and when we lack might He increases our power. Does this mean that we can have the strength to do anything? To lift any massive weight? No, it is not talking about that kind of power but a spiritual power by which we were able to overcome any obstacle we face. It is sometimes a hard concept to wrap our mind around but we are children of God, and our God loves us very, very much. So whatever gets in your way today, take a deep breath and ask your heavenly Father, by the power of the Holy Spirit, to give you the guidance and spiritual power to overcome.

Dear Father, there are days when I do not feel very powerful in the physical or in the spiritual. I know Your Word says that I have all power pertaining to life and godliness, so I choose to believe that Your Word is true and I am the person that You say I am. I believe that with the Holy Spirit guiding me I can do all things through Christ who strengthens me, as it says in Philippians 4:13. I resolve to walk through this day trusting in Your Word and looking forward to Your guidance through every obstacle that I may face. In Jesus's name, I pray. Amen.

Nutrition Thought for the Day.

Vitamin D has also been associated with helping to decrease viral infections, such as colds and flu. It appears that there may be at least two mechanisms by which this happens. One, vitamin D may help with the production of white blood cells which ward off infections. This would help to overcome some viral infections but also bacterial infections. When we come in contact with a virus that produces a cold or the flu, a chemical signal is sent through the blood that this foreign object (virus) has been detected in the body. The body sends T cells to counteract the virus. Some research indicates that the T cell has an antenna-like structure that recognizes the virus and destroys it. It has also been suggested that without sufficient vitamin D, that antenna is not functional, thus preventing the T cell from being able to recognize the virus. If you frequently catch colds or the flu, it would be interesting to get a vitamin D blood level checked to see if you are deficient.

WAYNE E. BILLON, PH.D., RDN, LDN

Day 273
The Bottom Line, Give Thanks

In everything give thanks; for this is God's will for you in Christ Jesus. (1 Thessalonians 5:18)

We are at the end of another month of the devotions. Most of devotions this past month dealt with enduring and persevering. In several places the scriptures tell us that as we persevere and endure, we end up as better Christians with hope for an eternal glory and with love for our fellow brethren. The bottom line of persevering is to build our character so that we can show love to our brothers in Christ, agape love—which is unconditional love—the same kind of love that Jesus shows for us. Because of the guidance we can receive through God's Word, we can accomplish this goal. So as we become the person God has called us to be because of His faithfulness, our response needs to be one of thanksgiving. Without the guidance of the Holy Spirit, without the strength He gives us to make it through the trials and tribulations, whether they are physical or in our mind, we are nothing. We need to be thankful and we should show thanksgiving to our Father every day. When you first get up in the morning it would be a good practice to start your day off with thanking your Father God for another day to be able to be His witness and His servant; thank Him for the guidance of the Holy Spirit and the immeasurably awesome promises in His Word.

Father God, I realize that I have so much to thank You for, it is hard to remember all that I am grateful. First of all, the obvious is thanking You for sending Your Son to die for my sins. There is no greater gift than that, and I cannot thank You enough for His sacrifice. Then You have given me a guidebook on how to live that is filled with incredible promises ending with an eternity with You in heaven. I want to spend this day as a day of thanksgiving for Your many blessings. I thank You in the name of my Savior and Lord, Jesus Christ. Amen.

Nutrition Thought for the Day.
Vitamin D has also been associated with possibly giving some protection against cognitive impairment and dementia. They have tried also to associate vitamin D with Alzheimer's disease but the evidence is not conclusive. Here again, chances are vitamin D may help with some or all of these diseases but there may be a multitude of factors that contribute to cognitive impairment, dementia, and Alzheimer's disease. Thus, in some cases vitamin D may seem to help a lot, or it may seem to help a little or not at all. A lot more research is needed to verify the role of vitamin D in these diseases.

Day 274
God Is Our Refuge

God is our refuge and strength, a very present help in trouble. (Psalm 46:1b)

For the next month, the scripture quotations will be from the book of Psalms. Most of the Psalms were written by David and they were written to praise God and to acknowledge His greatness, protection, faithfulness, love, and several other positive attributes, but the bottom line is they are, for the most part, encouraging. It is not known for sure who wrote today's Psalm but as you can see it acknowledges that God is our refuge and our strength and that He is a very present help in trouble. This is in tune with the devotions we looked at the last month. Our God is a cover over us, a real refuge. He gives us the strength to complete the simplest to the most difficult tasks. Whatever our needs may be He will help us. Some people may say that they do not feel His presence at a time of trouble. As previously mentioned, faith is not based on feelings, but it is based on our hope for things that we cannot see (Hebrews 11:1). Whether we feel His presence or not, He is with us in every difficult situation. Be encouraged today knowing that your God is with you and will never leave you.

Father God, I thank You that You are my refuge and my strength and that You are always with me in every kind of trouble or situation. Even though I may not always feel like I have Your presence, I know that You are with me and will never leave me. I am blessed to know that I have Your covering over me everywhere that I go and that You will give me strength for every situation I have to face. I will walk through this day knowing that Your presence is with me whether I feel it or not. I thank You, Father, in the name of Jesus. Amen.

Nutrition Thought for the Day.

It has also been reported that vitamin D may have a protective role in reducing the risk of preeclampsia in pregnant women. Vitamin D deficiency during pregnancy has been related to the several unfavorable conditions in childbirth. The last disease discussed that might be related to vitamin D is multiple sclerosis. Higher levels of active vitamin D in the blood are associated with a low incidence of multiple sclerosis in women. There is not as much evidence to indicate that this is true in males. There is considerable research available indicating that vitamin D may help reduce the risk of multiple sclerosis.

Day 275
Commit Your Way to the Lord

Delight yourself in the LORD; and He will give you the desires of your heart. Commit your way to the LORD, trust also in Him, and He will do it. (Psalm 37:4–5)

This verse is frequently misunderstood. This does not mean that if you follow the Lord's commands as best you can, and you desire in your heart a new Cadillac, He will give it to you. Instead, it means that if you seek the Lord with all your heart and you commit your way to Him and trust in Him, He will put in your heart desires for good things that originate from His heart. When you seek the Lord with all your heart and you are united to Him in Christ, then the Holy Spirit will influence you to want good things—that is things that can be used to help you but also used for the glory of God, the ultimate end to your desires. It does not mean that any whim that crosses your mind is something that God will pour out on you because you are following His Word. Yes, you should, by all means, be obeying the Word of the Lord, but that is not a ticket for you to receive any material thing that you want. Many times the desires in our heart are desires that we have created, and they are things that really will not benefit us and may even cause us harm. When God puts a desire in your heart, you know that it is going to be something wholesome for you and those around you and for the advancement of His Kingdom. So, when you seek God with all your heart, expect to receive revelation from Him concerning your desires. When you receive that revelation, and you know for sure that it is from the Lord, go after it with all your might.

> Dear Father, help me to realize the difference between my desire for material possessions that may not be the best thing for me and the desire that You have for me. I know that the desires that You put on my heart will be everlasting desires for the advancement of Your Kingdom and Your glory. I thank You for wanting only good things for me and directing my heart to those things. I receive Your will for my heart and I choose to seek You with all my heart this day and expect to have the wisdom to understand what desires You have placed in my heart. In Jesus's name, I pray. Amen.

Nutrition Thought for the Day.

There is still a long list of possible associations of vitamin D with various other diseases. Granted, additional research is needed in all of these areas, but it seems to be clear that vitamin D plays a much greater role in our health than previously believed and it would behoove everyone to have their vitamin D level checked and take appropriate levels of vitamin D to correct any deficiencies that may be found. The blood test is expensive but most, if not all, insurance companies will pay for it. However, many may only agree to pay for it once a year. I suggest you check with your provider and your physician about having your vitamin D levels tested if you have not already done so.

Day 276
The Lord Is Your Rescuer

"Call upon Me in the day of trouble; I shall rescue you, and you will honor Me." (Psalm 50:15)

Our God is so gracious that He wants us to call on Him whenever we are in any troubling situation. As a father wants to protect his children and be there for them at all times, so our Father God wants the same thing for us since we are His children. He says that He will rescue us from any trouble that we may have, and as a result, we will honor Him. The reason we were created is to worship our God and to fellowship with Him. If you do something extraordinary for your children, you naturally expect them to give you thanks and praise for it. Our Father God is the same way. Our spiritual Father and our biological father have a lot in common in this regard. Whenever you receive something from your God, always be careful to give Him praise and glory for that which you receive. Remember that all good things come from God and they come because He is a loving Father and wants to help and protect His children. Walk through your day today giving glory to God for all the wonderful things He has done for you.

Father God, I do not ever want to take You for granted or overlook even the smallest blessing that I may receive from You. I know that all good things come from You. I thank You and praise You for all that You have done for me from the smallest to the most awesome gift that You have given me—which is my salvation through Your Son Jesus Christ. I thank You this day, Father, in the name of Jesus. Amen.

Nutrition Thought for the Day.

The next fat-soluble vitamin to be discussed is vitamin E. Vitamin E has undergone significant controversy in the last few years. Most researchers and nutritionists were under the impression that even though vitamin E was fat-soluble, larger doses of it were not toxic. Remember, anything can be toxic if enough of it is ingested. With vitamin E it seemed to be true that no immediate toxicity was detected, but it turns out that there may be detrimental effects that show up after prolonged intake of larger doses of vitamin E. Bad associations with vitamin E include cardiovascular problems, particularly heart attacks. The research is still controversial as to whether or not we should be taking a vitamin E supplement. It is believed that between 200 and 400 international units of vitamin E will not have detrimental effects. Note that I am not recommending you take vitamin E supplements. If you can get your vitamin E from food, you will be better off than from taking supplements.

Day 277
Wait Patiently on the Lord

I waited patiently for the LORD; and He inclined to me and heard my cry. (Psalm 40:1)

The old saying is that patience is a virtue. You can find numerous examples in the Scriptures of prophets, teachers, apostles, etc. that possessed extreme patience. Jesus also exhibited patience. We as a people have become a very impatient society. We want everything done quickly. We have fast food, one-hour photo development, drive-through stations for food, coffee, banks, and whatever. Everyone you talk to is too busy to slow down. With this type of society we tend to do away with patience, and this becomes our way of life. Unfortunately, this will overflow into our spiritual life. We know that we have a God that loves us, and we know that He hears us when we call and will answer our prayers—but when? We do not want to wait for the answer or to wait for His timing in anything that we do. It is very easy to fall into this trap and we should by now realize that God's timing is not our timing. He not only knows what is best for us but He knows when the timing is best. He will incline Himself to hear our cry, but it will be done in His timing. Practice patience and learn to wait on the Lord. There is a saying that can summarize the way many of us sometimes feel, including me, but we must practice patience. The saying is this: Lord give me patience and give it to me now.

Father, I have to admit that sometimes I am caught up in the everyday hustle and bustle and trying to get everything done in a hurry. Some things take time and have to be developed slowly. Help me to develop a patient attitude in all that I do, particularly being patient in waiting for You to respond to my request. I know that Your timing is best for me and I choose this day to be content with Your timing. I declare this in the name of Jesus. Amen.

Nutrition Thought for the Day.

As with the other fat-soluble vitamins, anything that affects the absorption of fat in the intestines will affect the absorption of vitamin E. There is a water-soluble preparation of vitamin E that can be taken if someone has fat malabsorption, but there is at least one report that says the water-soluble vitamin E is not very well absorbed. If you have fat malabsorption, then it may be necessary to take vitamin E supplements. Between 200 and 400 international units should be more than enough to meet most needs. This would be a good place to talk to a registered dietitian to discuss your fat malabsorption problem and the need for taking vitamin E supplements.

Day 278
Despair Not

Why are you in despair, O my soul? And *why* have you become disturbed within me? Hope in God, for I shall again praise Him *for* the help of His presence. (Psalm 42:5)

(Also in Psalm 42:11: Why are you in despair, O my soul? And why have you become disturbed within me? Hope in God, for I shall yet praise Him, the help of my countenance and my God.)

Sometimes, particularly when we are impatient, if things do not happen the way we want them to, and when we want them to, we may begin to despair. All of us have experienced a time in our life when we were in despair. Maybe the desperation came as a result of something that was rather minor at the time or maybe it was a major state of desperation. Nonetheless, we all know what it's like to be in despair, and it is not fun. Our spirit gets disturbed—that is, we lose our peace. When that happens we cannot be settled, and we are lead to despair. In such cases we need to remember who we are in Christ and that Isaiah 26:3 says, "You will keep him in perfect peace because he trusts in You." We need to remind ourselves of that and put our hope in our God and praise Him in all circumstances for we know His presence will come to us; even when we do not feel like praising Him, we need to lift our hearts and minds to His throne room and give Him praise and glory. I know that when we do this our despair will turn to hope and You will be glorified.

Dear Father God, as hectic as the world can be in these trying times, it is easy to lose sight of the reality of who we are in Christ and to give into the thoughts of despair that constantly bombard our minds. In such times I must remember that my hope lies in You and that there is no reason for me to be in despair. You are my hope, my refuge, and my strength. I choose this day to embrace the hope that You give me and refuse to give in to despair. I make this statement in the name of Jesus Christ. Amen.

Nutrition Thought for the Day.

Vitamin E is in a class of compounds called the tocopherols and the tocotrienols. There are various forms of vitamin E. The different forms include alpha (α) tocopherol, beta (β) tocopherol, gamma (Υ) tocopherol, and delta (δ) tocopherol. There are also four forms of the tocotrienols with the same Greek letter designations. All of the different forms have different potencies. Most of the vitamin D supplements you will see on sale in stores will be alpha-tocopherol. Another thing that affects the potency of the vitamin is its chemical rotation which is too difficult to explain in detail here, but there are two different designations for the rotations, d and l.

WAYNE E. BILLON, PH.D., RDN, LDN

Day 279
Let Your Heart Take Courage

Be strong and let your heart take courage, all you who hope in the LORD. (Psalm 31:24)

Today's scripture tells us that all who hope in the Lord should be strong and let their hearts take courage. Our hope is in His name and the name of no one else. We need to encourage ourselves and lift ourselves up by trusting in our God and putting all our hope in Him. Look back on your life and remember all the things that the Lord has done for you through the years, starting with granting you salvation by His death on the cross. Remember the times that He answered your prayers. Think of all the promises He has given you in His Word. Such promises as, you can do all things through Christ who strengthens you, you are a child of God, and you have not been given a spirit of fear but of power, love, and a sound mind, to mention just a very few. Think of all the good things you have and have accomplished because of His blessings and encourage yourself. All this should give you hope, and hope produces courage. Be encouraged this day by the promises in God's Word and put your hope in Him.

> Father God, I remember all the things You have done for me and all the promises in Your Word. I remind myself who I am in Christ and that Your promises are for real and they are for me. I am not worthy of the promises or worthy of the good things You have done for me but, Your life, death, and resurrection were completed on my behalf, and Your blood has totally removed all my sins and unrighteousness. I am now a child of God and I am righteous, not based on what I have done, but on what You have done for me. I receive Your righteousness and I choose to take courage in my heart and to put my hope in You. In Jesus's name, I pray. Amen.

Nutrition Thought for the Day.

The vitamin E supplements you will find in stores will be either dl-alpha tocopherol or d-alpha tocopherol. The d-alpha tocopherol is absorbed much better than the dl-alpha-tocopherol. A way to remember this is to let the dl stand for *don't like* and the d stand for *delicious* or *desirable* The d-alpha tocopherol will cost a little more than the dl form, but its absorption is about 50% better and is worth the money.

Day 280
The Lord Hears the Righteous

The eyes of the LORD are toward the righteous and His ears are *open* to their cry. (Psalm 34:15)

Some of you may still be bothered by the word "righteous". When sinners are saved, it is sometimes difficult for them to get a grip on the fact that they are righteous. The more they were into the ways of the world, the more difficult it is to understand that they are now righteous. However, if you are saved that is exactly what you are, righteous. Today's scripture says that the eyes of the Lord are toward the righteous and His ears are open to their cry. You may say, "But I am not righteous, I have done too many things wrong, the Lord will not hear my cry." You are right; you are not righteous—that is not on what you have done on your own power. However, you are righteous based on what Jesus did for you. The devil loves to come and remind you (and all of us) of past failures—and we all have plenty of them. No matter what your past failures are or how many times you failed in your attempt to follow God's Word, you are righteous because of what Jesus did for you. When you became a born-again Christian, your spirit was renewed and covered with the robe of righteousness. Your sins were not just covered but were totally cleansed from all unrighteousness (1 John 1:9), separated from you as far as the east is from the west (Psalm 103:11—12), and forgotten (Jeremiah 31:34). Do not ever let the devil tell you that you are not righteous because, if you are saved, the Bible says you are righteous, a child of God, and coheir with Jesus Christ. The Lord's eyes are on you, and His ears are open to your cry.

Father, I know what Your Word says about my righteousness, but sometimes I do not feel like I am righteous. I need to remember that Your Word is not based on feelings but based on truth and Your Word is truth. I know that Your eyes are on me and that Your ears are inclined to hear my cry. I am righteous based on what Jesus did for me, and that is all I have to remember. Lord Jesus, I thank You for the righteousness You have given me. Amen.

Nutrition Thought for the Day.

Each form of vitamin E has a different role in the body. If you are going to take a supplement, you will be better off taking a supplement of mixed tocopherols. This means there would be some of each of the four forms in each pill (α, β, Υ, and δ). The best supplement would not only be a mixture of tocopherols but a mixture that will also include all of the forms of the tocotrienols. These mixtures are supposed to be more effective and have less of a chance of detrimental effects. Of course the more variety of tocopherols and tocotrienols in the supplement, the more the supplement is going to cost. You will find that mixtures of all the forms of vitamin E are not readily available. Unless you have a fat malabsorption problem, you probably would not need a vitamin E supplementation with a well-balanced diet.

Day 281
Lovingkindness Surrounds
Those Who Trust in the Lord

Many are the sorrows of the wicked, but he who trusts in the LORD, lovingkindness shall surround him. (Psalm 32:10)

This does not mean that we will never have any sorrows, but when we do, we will still be surrounded by God's lovingkindness. What is lovingkindness anyway? The dictionary says that it is tender and benevolent affection. God surrounds us with tender and benevolent affection. Lovingkindness frequently appears in the Scriptures but in Psalm 136 *lovingkindness* appears in each of the twenty-six verses of the Psalm. This is another instance whereby if God tells us over and over again about His lovingkindness, He must want to make sure that we are aware of the kind of love He has for us. God is serious about His lovingkindness towards us. Be encouraged today to know that you are surrounded by God's tender and benevolent affection for you. Whether you feel it or not, believe it or not, He is with you, He loves you more than you realize, and He will never leave you.

I rejoice today because I know that my Father God surrounds me with His lovingkindness. There are times when I do not feel like I am surrounded by the tender benevolent affection of my God, but God's Word is not based on my feelings—it is based on His reality. His reality is that I am surrounded by His tender benevolent affection. I am blessed and my God loves me, how awesome is that? Thank You, Jesus for what You did for me and thank You, Father, for Your lovingkindness. In Jesus's name, I pray. Amen.

Nutrition Thought for the Day.

Since vitamin E is a fat-soluble vitamin, it would be found in foods that contain some type of oil with a few exceptions. All of the plant oils, especially the polyunsaturated oils, would be good sources of vitamin E. Wheat germ contains vitamin E as does liver, egg yolks, nuts, and seeds. The exception to the oily foods that contain vitamin E would include dark green leafy vegetables and asparagus. Again, as with all the fat-soluble vitamins, some fat ingested in the same meal is necessary for vitamin E in the foods to be properly absorbed.

Day 282
There Is No Want for Those Who Fear the Lord

O fear the LORD, you His saints; for to those who fear Him there is no want. (Psalm 34:9)

Once again there are a couple of words in this scripture that you need to understand fully. First of all, the word *fear* does not mean what we usually take it to mean, and that is to be afraid, as with fear and trembling. Our God does not want us to be afraid of Him. The word *fear* used in this scripture is the Hebrew word *yare,* and it means to fear as to revere, to stand in awe, reverence, honor, or respect. So we should have a reverent awe of our God and not be afraid of Him.

The next word that could cause some people confusion is the word *saints*. You may not consider yourself to be a saint, but just like the word righteousness, you are a saint because of what Jesus did for you. The word *saint* used here is the Hebrew word *qadowsh* and means holy or holy one or set apart. You are holy based on what Jesus did for you, and you are definitely set apart by your God since He sees you as one of His many children. He will provide for all of your needs, and in Him you will not want. The Catholic Church has a different definition of a saint, but you need to live by the biblical definition, which says that you are holy and set apart because of what Jesus did for you. Do not let anyone tell you that you are not set apart by your God if you are a born again believer.

Father God, I have an awesome reverence for You as You are my God Almighty and eternal. As one of Your children, I am set apart by You. In Your eyes, I am a saint because of the righteousness that Jesus has given to me. I do not see myself as a saint but since Your Word says I am a saint and set apart, I will then receive it and believe it. I will walk out this day knowing that I have the righteousness of Jesus Christ covering me as a child of God, I am set apart by You, and all my wants will be resolved. I thank You in the name of Jesus. Amen.

Nutrition Thought for the Day.

Some examples of how much vitamin E may be in foods: a tablespoon of safflower oil (very polyunsaturated) contains about 4.7 mg of vitamin E while a tablespoon of corn oil or canola oil (polyunsaturated but neither are as polyunsaturated as safflower oil) contains approximately 2.9 mg of vitamin E. Sunflower seeds contains about 9 mg of vitamin E per 2 tablespoons. Sweet potatoes contain approximately 4.5 mg per one-half cup. Boiled shrimp contains approximately 3.2 mg of vitamin E per every 3 ounces. Vitamin E is usually measured in international units (IU). To show you how much vitamin E is in the foods above, 1 IU is the biological equivalent of about 0.67 mg d-alpha-tocopherol; so 4.7 mg of vitamin E would be equivalent to 7 IUs of vitamin E.

Day 283
The Lord Consoles the Anxious

When my anxious thoughts multiply within me, Your consolations delight my soul. (Psalm 94:19)

From time to time all of us become anxious and have anxious thoughts. Sometimes these thoughts may be results of a crisis that is going on in the world or around us. It may be a crisis that we bring upon ourselves that gives us anxious thoughts. If we give in to the anxious thoughts and spend time thinking about them, which means meditating on them, they will multiply and turn into fearful thoughts. We can control those thoughts because we have been given power by our Lord and Savior Jesus Christ (2 Corinthians 10:5). We need to learn how to exercise that power by commanding the thoughts to be gone in the name of Jesus. Isaiah 26:3 tells us that God will keep us in perfect peace if our mind stays on Him and we trust in Him. Note it says, "perfect peace." This is an awesome statement that we should memorize and use to speak to our anxious thoughts. Our God wants us to be at peace and wants us to trust Him. Once we do that, we will overcome these anxious thoughts. His Scriptures (such as mentioned here, 2 Corinthians 10:5 and Isaiah 26:3) are consolations that will delight our souls. We can rest assured this day that we have authority over anxious thoughts and we can replace them with meditations on God's Word.

Yes, like everyone else on this planet, I sometimes have anxious thoughts, but like the other believers on this planet, I have power and authority over those thoughts. I have an arsenal of consoling scriptures that I can memorize and meditate on whenever anxious thoughts come my way. I know that my Father God promises me that I will have perfect peace when I stand steadfast on His Word and trust in Him. I also know that my God's promises are true and will never fail. I thank You, Father, for giving me authority over anxious thoughts, and I thank You in Jesus's name. Amen.

Nutrition Thought for the Day.

Fat in the diet is necessary for vitamin E to be absorbed appropriately. For any fat or fat-soluble vitamins to be absorbed, bile is also necessary. Thus anyone with gallbladder disease, liver disease, or a pancreatic disease may have difficulty absorbing the fat-soluble vitamins. Once absorbed vitamin E is transported through the body in the same manner as fats and other fat-soluble vitamins, however, vitamin E is not stored in the liver in the same extent that vitamins A and D are stored, hence the lessening of the chance of a liver toxicity from excessive intake of vitamin E.

Day 284
Do Not Fear the Terror by Night

You will not be afraid of the terror by night, or of the arrow that flies by day;
(Psalm 91:5)

You have protection and freedom from fear and terror. This verse also mentions that you will not be afraid of the arrow that flies by day. You do not have reason to fear arrows coming at you in this day and time—that may not be the type of arrows that was being referred to in this scripture—but you do have many things coming at you that could take the place of those arrows. The arrows of your present day could be replaced by bullets, but I'm sure it includes even more than that. The arrows could be the piercing darts of the enemy and could come in the form of words and deeds that are done to harm you, discourage you, or bring you down into the dark pits of fear. You do not have to be afraid of any such things because your God will protect you by day and by night if you trust in Him and meditate on His Word. You can walk through your day today knowing that your God is looking over you and protecting you. Choose some appropriate scriptures and memorize them as your weapons against anxious thoughts. Meditate on the Scriptures that you memorize so that you can be ready for anything that may come your way. Ephesians 6 is an excellent place to look.

> Father, I thank You for the arsenal that You have given me in Your Word. There are many scriptures that I have available to memorize so that I can meditate on them during my quiet times every day and that I can use them to overcome any anxious thoughts that come my way. I know that I am more than a conqueror and I can overcome the world (1 John 5:4). I can accomplish this by the power of the Holy Spirit and Jesus's blood, and can defeat any attack that the enemy will use against me. I resolve this day to meditate on Your Word and walk with confidence that You are with me. I declare this in the name of Jesus. Amen.

Nutrition Thought for the Day.
Vitamins A and D had several functions in the body that were specific, but vitamin E is different in that it takes part in several different processes in the body but in each process, the function is the same, and that is as an antioxidant. Remember, antioxidants help to prevent free radical damage that can cause all sorts of diseases to occur in our bodies including heart disease and cancer. Vitamin C covered earlier is an antioxidant, but vitamin C is a water-soluble vitamin and would not be found in fatty deposits in the body. Vitamin E is found in fatty deposits.

Day 285
Your Sins Are Covered

You forgave the iniquity of Your people; you covered all their sin. (Psalm 85:2)

You know that you are one of God's people since you have received Jesus Christ as your Savior and Lord. Because of receiving what Jesus did for you on the cross, all of your sins have been forgiven and His blood covers you. A very small but important word in this verse is the word "all." I looked up the word all in the original Hebrew, and it is *kol*. It means everything, all, or the whole. **ALL** your sins have been covered by the blood of Jesus; not just small sins or the sins committed before you were saved, but **ALL** your sins that you ever committed or will commit in the future. Do not let the devil condemn you with thoughts running through your head saying, "maybe you were forgiven for all the small sins but that big one—ooh no, you couldn't be forgiven for that one—it was too big." That is a lie from the father of lies (John 10:10) so do not listen to it for a second. If you received Jesus as your Savior and Lord, all of your sins were forgiven by His blood and you are a redeemed child of God and coheir with Jesus Christ waiting to receive your eternal inheritance. Be encouraged today as you look forward to your eternal inheritance in heaven.

> Father, I know that in Your eyes sin is sin and every evil that we call sin is the same. There are no small sins, no medium-size sins, and no large sins—sin is sin. James 2:10 says, "For whoever keeps the whole law and yet stumbles in one point, he has become guilty of all." No matter how man may classify sins, they are all the same in Your sight until they are eradicated entirely by the blood of Jesus, and then they are no more. I thank You that I am covered this day by Your mercy and grace and totally forgiven of all my sins. In Jesus's name. Amen.

Nutrition Thought for the Day.
Functions of vitamin E has to do with the maintenance of membrane integrity and the physical stability of cells. For example, red blood cells are very fragile cells and can easily be broken and destroyed by free radicals. Vitamin E can react with the free radicals and prevent them from damaging red blood cells. In this way vitamin E can help prevent hemolytic anemia, that is anemia (loss of red blood cells) caused by damage to the red blood cells. Vitamins B12 and folic acid prevent anemia but in a much different manner in that they are necessary for the synthesis of red blood cells.

Day 286
He Heals All Your Diseases

Who pardons all your iniquities, Who heals all your diseases; who redeems your life from the pit, who crowns you with lovingkindness and compassion. (Psalm 103:3–4)

This verse has four points in that it says God pardons all of your iniquities, heals all your diseases, redeems you from the pit, and crowns you with lovingkindness. An iniquity, according to Strong's Concordance as used in this verse, refers to punishment, fault, sin, or guilt. All such iniquities are pardoned by your God. This verse adds another aspect to God's pardoning, and that is He heals all your diseases. Yes, I know you will immediately think of when you or someone dear to you was sick, and you did not see a healing, but the Word says He heals all of our diseases. This is a complicated subject, too much so to discuss here, but your God is a healer. The Hebrew word used in this scripture for heals is *rapha* and means to heal, physician, cure, or repaired according to Strong's Concordance. One of the names of your God is Jehovah Rapha, your God who heals.

The scripture also says that He redeems your life from the pit. Before you were saved, you were in the pits whether you knew it or not and by your salvation you were redeemed. And then the last part of this verse tells you something you have heard before in the Book of Psalms; you have been crowned with lovingkindness and compassion. You should be getting it by now, you are the apple of God's eye, and He loves you immensely. This is a tremendous encouragement for you to take on this day knowing that you are loved more by your God than by anyone on the face of the earth.

Father God, I admit that sometimes I do not realize how much You love me. When I get to heaven, if I can recall all the things that happened on earth, I know that I will see that there were so many times Your love protected me and guided me in the right direction when I was not at all aware that You were even anywhere near me. Help me to realize today, while I am still on this earth, that You are guiding me and protecting me in every step that I take. I thank You, Father, for Your love in the name of Jesus. Amen.

Nutrition Thought for the Day.
Vitamin E may also help in preventing precancerous changes in DNA by stopping chain reactions that occur from free radical damage. Vitamin E may also prevent the oxidation of cholesterol. Some research indicates that vitamin E may help in the prevention of Alzheimer's disease, but other research shows that vitamin E does not affect Alzheimer's at all. Even though we know a lot about vitamin E and many of the diseases that it is supposed to have an affect on, much more research is needed, and this is why we are hesitant to tell people to take vitamin E supplements. If vitamin E supplements do not help and all you lose is the money you paid for the supplements, that is bad enough; but if the supplements cause harm, that is another story.

Day 287
Wait on the Lord

Wait for the LORD; be strong and let your heart take courage; yes, wait for the LORD. (Psalm 27:14)

Sometimes waiting can be the hardest thing you have to learn how to conquer. The timing of your God is perfect but seldom does it precisely coincide with your timing. Remember, practicing patience strengthens your endurance and your endurance gives you hope. Your God knows precisely what He is doing when it comes to hearing your prayers and providing for your needs. If it seems like your God is not answering your prayers in your timing, do not get discouraged but stand fast, hold your ground, and endure. Ephesians 6:13 tells us to put on the full armor of God so that we will be able to resist the devil on the day of evil, and having done everything, to stand firm. So when you think you have done everything that you can do, stand firm. There is an old cliché that says when you reach the end of your rope, tie a knot and hang on. God knows your needs and He is with you and will not leave you. Do not be discouraged! This would be a good thing to remember for your program for a healthy lifestyle also. You may be at a point where you are plateauing in your weight loss (or weight gain—whatever your goal) but do not get discouraged and do not give up. Continue doing what is right with your program and see yourself being successful.

Father, I know that Your timing is the only thing that matters. You know what is best for me and You know the best timing for all of my needs. I trust in You and Your judgment. When I have done everything that I know to do according to Your Word, I resolve that I will stand firm and wait for You to move on my behalf. I choose not to be discouraged, and I choose not to give up. I am more than a conqueror, and I will be victorious with the guidance of Your Holy Spirit. I make this declaration in the name of Jesus. Amen.

Nutrition Thought for the Day.

I have mentioned the importance of having a balance of nutrients in our bodies, including a balance of vitamins and minerals. I can use vitamin E as an example of how that may work. Vitamin C is a water-soluble antioxidant, but one of its roles is to help regenerate vitamin E. After vitamin E reacts with a free radical, it is damaged and is no longer able to be effective as an antioxidant. If there is a balance in the body between vitamin C and vitamin E, the vitamin C can help to regenerate vitamin E.

Day 288
Seek the Strength of the Lord

Seek the LORD and His strength; seek His face continually. Remember His wonders which He has done, His marvels in the judgments uttered by His mouth. (Psalm 105:4–5)

A key to patience and enduring is to stay steady in seeking God's help. As the scripture says, we should seek His strength continually. That means to dedicate each day to the Lord and make your day a regular worship experience for the Lord. To accomplish that you have to practice ever being aware of who you are in Christ and that your purpose on this earth is to give worship to your God. As you walk through your day, use the second part of the scripture as a means of encouragement by remembering everything He has done for you. Remember that all good things come from the Lord. I do not believe in chance or coincidence, but I believe that whenever something good happens to us, it has been worked out by the Lord to our advantage. Have you made any accomplishments with your program for a healthier lifestyle? Maybe you have not made the achievements that you wanted to by this time, but you have made some achievements. If you seek His face and His strength continually, then you will continue to make additional achievements, not only in this program but also in everything you do, including spiritual achievements. Do not be discouraged, seek the Lord in everything you do, even the small things that may seem insignificant to you.

> Father God, if I start to get discouraged in my daily activities, including my new program, by the power of Your Holy Spirit remind me of the accomplishments I have already made because of Your guidance and Your love. Every good thing that I have has come from You. I give You credit for all that I have and all that I am for I am righteous in Your sight because of Jesus's finished work on the cross. I resolve to continually seek Your face and Your strength in all that I do. I dedicate my day to be a living sacrifice for Your glory, and I look forward to seeing the accomplishments I will make because of Your love. In Jesus's name, I pray. Amen.

Nutrition Thought for the Day.

Another example of interaction is between the mineral selenium and vitamin E. Selenium, even though it is a metal, is also a powerful antioxidant. Selenium and vitamin E complement each other as antioxidants, and each one makes the other one more effective. When sufficient selenium is present, less vitamin E is needed and vice versa. The problem with selenium is that selenium taken in a slight excess above the standard requirements can be very toxic, so you do not want to take in more selenium to make up for lack of vitamin E. Also, even if you have a good intake of selenium, you still need vitamin E to complement it.

WAYNE E. BILLON, PH.D., RDN, LDN

Day 289
God Is Ready to Hear Our Prayer

For You, LORD, are good, and ready to forgive, and abundant in lovingkindness to all who call upon you. Give ear, O LORD, to my prayer; and give heed to the voice of my supplications! (Psalm 86:5–6)

I think it is important to stop and ponder on this phrase *ready to forgive*. Many times when we experience a period of weakness and we fall, we tend to get down on ourselves. That's when the devil loves to come in and say things like "See, you can't be successful, you are constantly falling and messing up. Your God can't keep forgiving you!" Well, that's another lie from the devil. Your God is ready to forgive and wants to forgive you for all of your shortcomings at all times. Jesus died for all those mistakes you and the rest of us continually make. He took your place and walked the face of this earth as a man for some thirty-three years without ever sinning. He did that because you and I are not capable of living a lifetime without sin, so He did it for us and passed His victory on to us. The scripture tells us one more time that our God is abundant in lovingkindness to all of us who call upon Him. He gives heed to our prayer and the voice of our supplications without ever tiring or becoming weary with our mistakes. As this is true in the spiritual, carry it over in the physical in your program for a healthier lifestyle. No matter how many times you may get off the schedule for your program, forgive yourself as God forgives you and pick up where you left off and continue to push on. Do not be discouraged, do not be dismayed!

Father, I am continually astounded at Your resilience for forgiving me for my many shortcomings. I know that You are ready to forgive me no matter how many times I fall. In my finite mind, it is difficult for me to understand how You can be that forgiving because I would have such a hard time forgiving someone that offended me that many times. You never grow weary with my shortcomings and You continue to hear my voice as I call out to You. I am in awe of Your lovingkindness and I resolve to continue to seek You and to try to be like You in forgiving myself when I fail and when others fail me, no matter how many times that may be. In Jesus's name, I pray. Amen.

Nutrition Thought for the Day.
During the discussion about supplements other than vitamins and minerals, omega-3 fatty acids will also be a topic. Omega-3 fatty acids are obviously oils, and they are also subject to free radical damage, particularly oxidation. Note, products that contain fat- like omega-3 fatty acids, may have vitamin E added so that it can help prevent oxidation of the fat. This prevents rancidity and allows a greater effect of the omega-3 fatty acid.

Day 290
The Lord Is the Rock of My Refuge

But the LORD has been my stronghold, and my God the rock of my refuge. (Psalm 94:22)

Remembering all the things the Lord has done for you in the past should help you to see that He has been your stronghold as this scripture states. You know this is true. He is your rock and your refuge. This is certainly true in the spiritual as well as in the natural. Also, consider this with your healthy lifestyle changes. Even if your weight change and conditioning has been minuscule, the fact that you started a program shows that you are concerned about your health and well-being. Every good thing you have or that you do is accomplished because of the Lord since all good things come from Him. The desire on your heart to improve your health and well-being was certainly placed there by the Lord. His help and His guidance are with you when you are not even aware of it. When you believe His promises are for you and you stand on His Word, you are standing on the Rock of salvation. He is your refuge and your strength. Encourage yourself throughout this day knowing that your God is your rock and your refuge, your stronghold and is always with you.

Father God, I know that You are my refuge, my rock, and my stronghold. I also know that You have always been my stronghold even before I asked Jesus to be my Savior and Lord. All the good things that have happened to me in my life are the result of Your love for me. I encourage myself this day to know that I am standing on the Rock of salvation and I will never be shaken as long as I keep my eyes on You. Thank You for always being there for me and for Your lovingkindness that surrounds me. I thank You in the name of Jesus. Amen.

Nutrition Thought for the Day.

Still using vitamin E as another example of taking in a balance of nutrients, let's consider vitamin E's relationship with beta-carotene. Remember that beta-carotene is the precursor for vitamin A. Beta-carotene is converted to the active form of vitamin A in the body (called retinol). High levels of vitamin E may prevent beta-carotene from being converted to retinol. If this continued for an extended period the person taking the high levels of vitamin E could develop a deficiency of vitamin A. Thus one has to be very careful with taking supplements and should research every supplement that they intend to take before ingesting it and preferably discussing their diet and supplements with a registered dietitian.

Day 291
The Lord Will Sustain Our Falls

The LORD opens *the eyes of* the blind; the LORD raises up those who are bowed down; the LORD loves the righteous. (Psalm 146:8)

The Lord opens the eyes of the blind, we know that our God does miracles so opening the eyes of the blind is not a big deal. This is true from a physical standpoint as well as from a spiritual standpoint in that the Lord will open the spiritual eyes of those who are spiritually blind. The Lord also raises up those who are bowed down and loves the righteous. Are there times when you feel like you are bowed down? Like you are bending over under the pressure of the world? Of course, there are times you feel like that. We all have times like that. On such occasions call out to your Lord, and He will lift you up. He is always close to you, waiting for your call. He loves the righteous. Remember that as a born-again Christian you are the righteousness of Jesus Christ because of the ransom He paid for you on the cross. There is nothing you or I can do to declare our own righteousness; we do not have to, Christ has already done it for us. Be encouraged today to know that you are the righteousness of Christ and that your Lord loves you; He will lift you up if you get bowed down and will open your spiritual eyes if you lose sight of your calling.

Father God, I thank You that, as a believer, I am included in the righteousness mentioned in today's scripture. Every one of Your promises refers to me no matter what my past was like or how many times I fail. If I get bowed down, You will lift me up. If I lose my sight, you can restore me, physically or spiritually. I have confidence in Your Word, and I know that it is intended for me and all believers. I resolve this day to accept who I am in Christ and to walk the walk for which You called me. I can only do this with the strength of Your Holy Spirit, and I thank You for that strength. In the name of Jesus, I pray. Amen.

Nutrition Thought for the Day.
The RDA (recommended dietary allowances) for vitamin E is relatively small. In milligrams the recommendation is 15 mg. You will usually see it expressed as IUs and this comes out to be 22 IUs. If you look at the label on bottles of vitamins that contain vitamin E, you will probably see that the RDAs are 30 IUs. These recommendations are now only for the d-alpha tocopherol form of vitamin E. Recent research has indicated that intake above 400 IUs (267 mg) may be a problem with some heart patients. The problem may be more severe in that many of the patients may not know they have a heart problem. The best thing to do is not to take supplements in excess, research them first, and discuss them with a registered dietitian.

Day 292
Teach Me Your Statutes

You are good and do good; teach me Your statutes. (Psalm 119:68)

In this Psalm the writer is talking to God when he says, "You are good and do good." You may recall from reading the Gospels that in Mark 10:17 a man ran up to Jesus, knelt before Him and asked, "good teacher, what shall I do to inherit eternal life?" In verse 18, Jesus asked him why he called Him good. Jesus told the man that no one was good except God alone. Was Jesus not God? Yes, Jesus was and is God but He walked the face of the earth as a man and not as God. The Spirit of Jesus was God and was certainly good, but I believe the point here is that man is not good, only God is good. The psalmist in today's verse is acknowledging that and is asking God to teach him His statutes. The word *statute* in our current dictionary means a written law that is passed by a legislative body. The Hebrew word for statue in this scripture means the same, an ordinance or a decree. If God is the only good creature in the universe, and He is, then His statutes are also good. God cannot sin, and He can do no wrong. Therefore, any laws He makes are good. We cannot be good in the same sense as God is good, but we should always strive to be as good as we can using Jesus as our model. Just remember that anything you achieve that is holy or right is not due to your goodness but to the goodness of God and the power of Jesus in you.

> Father, I know that all good things come from You and anything I do on this earth that may have some merit is due to Your goodness in me. On my own, I am nothing. By the completed work of Jesus and the power of the Holy Spirit, I am righteous in the eyes of my God. Jesus walked the face of the earth without committing a single sin and laid out a plan for me to follow. I resolve this day to try with all my strength to follow the example that Jesus set for me, but I acknowledge that all good things come from my God and not for me. I make this acknowledgment in the name of my Savior and Lord, Jesus Christ. Amen.

Nutrition Thought for the Day.

The last fat-soluble vitamin is vitamin K. Vitamin K belongs to a group of compounds called the menaquinones. Like all the other fat-soluble vitamins, vitamin K requires fat in the diet and bile salts from the gallbladder to be absorbed into the body. Once absorbed, it is similarly transported through the blood to fats and the other fat-soluble vitamins. Vitamin K is a little different from the other fat-soluble vitamins in that it is not stored in the body and it breaks down rapidly with a turnover of about every two and half hours.

WAYNE E. BILLON, PH.D., RDN, LDN

Day 293
The Lord Hears the Righteous

The righteous cry, and the LORD hears and delivers them out of all their troubles. (Psalm 34:17)

We are the righteousness of God based on what Jesus did for us. When we cry out, He hears our cries and delivers us out of all our troubles. As talked about in previous devotions, His timing may not be what we would hope for, but His timing is perfect. Continue to develop patience in trusting on Him and be willing to accept His timing for your life. He does hear your cry even when you do not believe you are being heard because you are not receiving the answers in the timeframe you desire. Lauren Daigle, a popular Christian singer, has an excellent song out called "Trust in You." Some lines from this song include, "When You don't move the mountains I'm needing You to move/when You don't part the waters I wish I could walk through/when You don't give the answers as I cry out to You/I will trust, I will trust, I will trust in You." The words of the song are so good because they are so true and it sets the tone for us when we read a scripture such as today's Psalm 34:17. We know that our God will deliver us out of our troubles, but we do not know the timing. In the meantime, we should just continue to trust in Him.

Father, I know that You hear my cries I and I know that You will deliver me out of all of my troubles. I also know that You will see me through this healthy lifestyle program if I keep trusting in You. You are my hope and my deliverer. I resolve this day to trust in You no matter what comes my way, no matter what the timing may be, no matter how minor or how major my request may be. I will trust in You. I release this prayer in the name of Jesus. Amen.

Nutrition Thought for the Day.

Vitamin K is found in a variety of plants and leafy greens are a particularly good source. It is also found in a variety of animal products. Another factor that makes vitamin K different from the other fat-soluble vitamins is that it can be synthesized in the large intestines by the bacteria that live there. If you remember, the water-soluble vitamin that is also synthesized by bacteria in the large intestines is biotin. The body does not synthesize vitamin K, but the bacteria that live in our colon synthesize it. At one time it was believed that we could meet all of our vitamin K requirements by the synthesis from the bacteria in our colon, but it is now realized that we may have additional requirements for the vitamin to be taken into the body with food.

Day 294
The Lord Wants Your Burden

Cast your burden upon the LORD and He will sustain you; He will never allow the righteous to be shaken. (Psalm 55:22)

This is a great scripture with a powerful promise, one that in my early days as a Christian I relied on very heavily. The scripture promises that if we cast our burden upon the Lord, He will sustain us. There were so many times when it seemed like I could not go on because there were too many things going against me. Someone gave me this scripture and encouraged me to follow it and cast my burdens on the Lord—lay them at the foot of the cross and give them totally to Him. I did that, but I wanted to take them back. This is a common occurrence with all of us. You have to come to a place where you give your burdens to the Lord and refuse to take them back. This, to some, may seem like arrogance, but He wants you to cast your burdens on Him. That is why He died for you. Get rid of all of your baggage and turn it over to the Lord. He will take it from you, and He will sustain you. You are the righteousness of Jesus Christ, and He will never allow the righteous to be shaken if you trust in Him. Take the goal that you set for your new healthy lifestyle and give the burden of meeting that goal to the Lord. Let Him worry about what has to happen for you to reach that goal and do not try to take it into your own hands. Leave it at the foot of the cross and walk through your day today with confidence that your Lord will sustain you and meet your needs.

Father God, I understand that You want me to turn my burdens over to You no matter how heavy or how light they may seem to me. I know that sometimes, if the burden is not that heavy, I think I can carry it on my own. But as I keep adding more and more light burdens to my load, before long I am burdened down under a much heavier load. I resolve to lay all the burdens that I have at the foot of the cross and leave them there. By the power of Your Holy Spirit give me the guidance and strength to totally accomplish this and not take the burdens back. They are Yours! In Jesus's name, I declare this. Amen.

Nutrition Thought for the Day.
Anything that affects the movement of ingested material through our colon also affects the synthesis and absorption of vitamin K. Diarrhea, particularly from an origin in the colon, can affect vitamin K absorption. Also, the production of vitamin K in our large intestines varies a great deal from human to human, but if our G.I. tract is functioning properly and we are taking in a balanced diet that includes a variety of foods, including vegetables, we should not have a problem meeting our vitamin K requirement.

Day 295
The Lord Is Gracious and Merciful

The LORD is gracious and merciful; slow to anger and great in lovingkindness. (Psalm 145:8)

Do you know what the differences are between mercy and justice? Justice is receiving what you deserve for a particular act. Mercy is not receiving what you deserve but receiving forgiveness for the same act. God's mercy includes restoration and compassion. When we stand before our Lord and Savior for our final judgment we certainly do not want to receive justice but mercy. Justice is fair and is what we deserve, but all of us have sinned and fallen short of the glory of God (Romans 3:23). We can be thankful each day that our God is gracious and merciful. He is also slow to anger because He is so patient with us. Think of how many times you did something that was offensive to the Lord. If someone was that offensive to you for the same number of times, how would you respond? Would you become impatient and rebuke them or yell at them? Would you turn your back on them and not want to speak to them any longer? I think all of us would be aroused in anger, but our God will never do that to us no matter how many times we fall. Compared to our sense of timing, He is certainly slow to anger. The last word in this verse is one that we should be getting quite familiar with, and that is God's lovingkindness. Here it is again in another Psalm. This emphasizes one more time that if we keep seeing the word over and over again, it must be because it is something that God wants to get across to us. He is full of lovingkindness for us. Be encouraged this day that you have a God that is gracious and merciful, slow to anger, and is great in lovingkindness toward you.

> Father God, I understand that Your mercy toward me is not deserved by me. By all rights, I deserve justice at best, but because of Your graciousness and Your mercy, I will not receive the judgment that I deserve. Your patience with me is more than I deserve too. You are slow to anger, even when I continually offend You. Your lovingkindness surrounds me in all that I do, and yes, I do not deserve that either. I resolve to receive Your mercy and, although I will never be able to earn or deserve Your mercy, I will work harder to please You. In Jesus's name, I pray. Amen.

Nutrition Thought for the Day.

The principal function of vitamin K in our body is in the formation of blood clots. Prothrombin is a protein that our body synthesizes and is necessary for proper blood clotting. If prothrombin is low, our blood will not clot as it should, and anything that causes us to bleed could be a serious problem. Vitamin K is necessary for the synthesis of prothrombin. Some people have a problem with the blood clotting too fast and can form blood clots that could be fatal. These people may have to go on blood thinners such as Coumadin or heparin. Vitamin K can nullify the effects of Coumadin, but it does not interfere with the effects of heparin. Thus someone on blood thinner therapy needs to be sure and check with their doctor to see if their intake of vitamin K needs to be restricted.

Day 296
The Lord Is a Stronghold for the Oppressed

And He will judge the world in righteousness; He will execute judgment for the peoples with equity. The LORD also will be a stronghold for the oppressed, a stronghold in times of trouble; and those who know Your name will put their trust in You, for You, O Lord, have not forsaken those who seek You. (Psalm 9:8– 10)

I included three verses for today's scripture because they fit so well together and are a continuation of yesterday's devotion. As a born-again believer, you will be judged with righteousness and mercy and you will not receive the justice that you deserve. The equity that your Lord will use will not be based on the good works you did or what bad works you did not do, but will be based on who you are in Christ. Your acceptance of what Jesus did for you on the cross will guarantee God's mercy for you. The Lord is and always will be your stronghold and you can always run to Him in times of trouble. Because you are diligent in reading God's Word and fellowshipping with like-minded believers, you know your God and you put your trust in Him. You know that your Lord has not forsaken you nor will He ever forsake you. Be comforted this day that the God you serve is a righteous judge that looks at your life through a filter and that filter is the blood of Jesus Christ and enables you to be judged with mercy and never be forsaken. Praise be to the Lord our God for His righteous judgment and for His stronghold in a time of trouble.

This day I give praise and honor and glory to You Lord, for your righteous judgment and Your mercy towards me. You are my stronghold, the tower that I run into in times of trouble and You have never forsaken me nor will You ever forsake me as long as I seek You. I resolve this day to seek You in everything that I do, and I expect to receive strength and mercy, not based on my goodness, but based on what Jesus Christ did for me. It is in His name that I pray. Amen.

Nutrition Thought for the Day.

Our vitamin K requirement is very low being only 120 µg for adult males and 90 µg for adult females. Remember that a microgram is a millionth of a gram and by comparison, a teaspoon of most compounds (such as sugar) is 5 g. So you can see that the requirement for vitamin K is very small. It should be adequately met with a normal diet and a normal functioning G.I. tract.

Day 297
Trust in the Lord and Abide in Him Forever

Those who trust in the LORD are as Mount Zion, which cannot be moved but abides forever. (Psalm 125:1)

Mount Zion was another name for Jerusalem, this is one of the oldest cities in the world and is also known as the city of David. Jerusalem was destroyed twice according to the Bible and was besieged 23 times, attacked over 50 times, and captured and recaptured over 40 times. Jerusalem is still standing and is still in controversy between the Jews and Palestinians. Jerusalem will remain until Jesus comes back for us. The psalmist probably did not realize what he was saying when he said that it would abide forever. When we trust in the Lord, we are like Jerusalem—a fortress that will abide forever. We will not be overcome by any enemy as long as we continue to trust in the Lord. This is His promise in His Word. Just as Jerusalem has been besieged and attacked many times, so we are besieged and attacked many times by the devil. Jerusalem has been overrun on occasion but has always come back to being the Holy City. In like manner, we sometimes may lose a battle to the devil, but as long as we trust in the Lord we will never lose the war. Walk through your day today with encouragement in your heart that your God is with you and you will never be overrun as long as you trust in Him.

Father, thank You that You have made me like a fortress that cannot be overrun by the enemy as long as I trust in You. I know that the devil will never stop coming at me with temptations and besiege me with lies about who I am. I know who I am. I am a child of God and coheir with Jesus Christ (Romans 8:17, Galatians 4:7). I can do all things through Christ who strengthens me (Philippians 4:13). The devil is a liar and is the father of lies (John 8:44). His attacks cannot overcome me as long as I trust in You. You are the only true God and I declare that I will continue to trust in You in all that I do. I thank You for who You are, in the name of Jesus. Amen.

Nutrition Thought for the Day.
Vitamin K has other functions in the body that are important besides helping the blood to clot, including the formation of bone. Many vitamins and minerals are necessary for proper bone formation and mineralization. Vitamin K is one of those, and recent research indicates that it may be more important than previously thought. This would be one reason why our requirement for vitamin K may be more than the bacteria in our G.I. tract can synthesize but, still, vitamin K supplementation in a normal balanced diet with a normal functioning G.I. tract is probably not necessary.

Day 298
The Lord Is with Us When We Fall

The steps of a man are established by the LORD, and He delights in his way. When he falls, he will not be hurled headlong, because the LORD is the One who holds his hand. (Psalm 37:23–24)

When you were born again and dedicated your life to Jesus, He began in the spirit to establish your steps, even though you probably were not aware of it. When you follow in the steps that He establishes, He delights in you. If you fall He does not give up on you, but He allows you to go down the dark path you have traveled in the past. No matter how many times we fall, we need to turn back to Jesus and ask for forgiveness immediately. As the scripture says, He will always be there and will hold our hand and continue to establish our paths. If we go off that path it is not His fault but it is because we choose to go off the established path. Choose this day to listen for the Lord's leading in everything that you do and decide in your heart of hearts that you are going to do everything you can to follow the established path He has set for you. If you know you go off that path, do not get discouraged and do not give up but return to it and ask for His forgiveness. This is true in the spiritual, the physical, and in your healthy lifestyle regimen. If you go off your program, do not give up, do not get discouraged but turn back to the path that you were on and forgive yourself and move on.

Lord, I know that You have a call on my life and that You have a path that You want me to follow. I know that the Holy Spirit is leading me every day down the path that You have chosen. It is not You that is failing me. Instead it is me that is wandering off Your established path. I know that when I fall You are there to help me get back up and get back on the path. I declare this day that I will pay more attention to following the Holy Spirit's guidance and do all that I can to stay on the path that You have established for me. I declare this in the name of Jesus. Amen.

Nutrition Thought for the Day.

Our next discussion will be concerning minerals. Some background information about minerals is necessary before any discussion can begin. Minerals are necessary for countless functions in the body among which include electrolytes, cofactors for enzymes, cofactors with some hormones, actual components of tissue such as bone and teeth, direct action such as iron carries oxygen through the blood to all tissues of the body, pH balance, and fluid balance. Each of these will be discussed as we progress.

Day 299
Our God Is Merciful

He has not dealt with us according to our sins, nor rewarded us according to our iniquities. For as high as the heavens are above the earth, so great is His lovingkindness toward those who fear Him. (Psalm 103:10–11)

Our God is merciful and gracious, and He does not deal with you with the justice you deserve but with mercy that you do not deserve. He does not reward you or does not judge you according to your iniquities, but He judges you according to your righteousness which is the same righteousness as Jesus Christ—as awesome as that sounds it became true when you received Jesus as your Savior and Lord. The scripture says that as high as the heavens are above the earth—which is infinite—is how great His lovingkindness is towards those who fear Him. There is a lot in this scripture, and we find that wonderful word again—lovingkindness—a fact that He wants to really get down into our spirits so that we can understand the immense love He has for us. The scripture then says that this lovingkindness is towards those who fear Him. Fear in this scripture is the same as has been previously discussed, and that is not the shaking in your boots fear, although we should have that kind of fear for our God, but the awesome reverence that we should have for our God. Today be encouraged that you are not judged based on the righteous life that you lived because none of us have lived the life righteous enough to deserve heaven, but you are judged based on the righteousness of Jesus Christ that covers you.

Father, I thank You once again for Your lovingkindness and Your mercy and grace towards me. I know that I am not being treated with the justice that I deserve for my evil ways and thoughts, but I am being judged based on the righteousness of Jesus Christ, and that makes me coheir with Jesus. This is so awesome that I frequently have a hard time realizing that it is true but I receive it because Your Word says it and Your Word is truth. I thank You that Your lovingkindness is so great it is not even measurable. You are an awesome God, and I give You praise and thanks this day, in the name of my Lord and Savior, Jesus Christ. Amen.

Nutrition Thought for the Day.
Electrolytes are mineral elements that have either a positive charge or a negative charge. Our bodies maintain a neutral charge. The heart actually functions as an electric motor. The heart muscle, as well as all the muscles in the body, are stimulated by electrical impulses as different electrolytes (positive and negative) cross the membranes of the muscle cells. When the electrolytes are in proper concentrations they create an electrical charge that stimulates the muscles to contract. If some electrolytes get too high, it causes electrical impulses to be disturbed and can cause the heart to race or to fail. Balance in our electrolytes is essential for maintaining life. Electrolytes come into our bodies through our diet. Too many or too little can be fatal. We must pay close attention to obtaining a balanced diet so that we can maintain an electrolyte balance.

Day 300
Goodness and Lovingkindness Are Mine

Surely goodness and lovingkindness will follow me all the days of my life, and I will dwell in the house of the LORD forever. (Psalms 23:6)

If we were to explain what has been said over the last several days in this devotional, this scripture would be a good summary. Once again, it mentions God's lovingkindness for us and His goodness and these characteristics will follow each of us all the days of our life. When we finish the call that He has on our life on this earth, we will dwell in the house of the Lord forever. How encouraging is that? The scripture just before this (chapter 23, verse 5) says that He has prepared a table for us in the presence of our enemies and He has anointed our heads with oil. It finishes up by saying our cup overflows. All this is true of your God and of you because you have chosen to receive what Jesus did for you, not because you are so good, but because of what He did for you. Do not ever forget the word "lovingkindness" and that God has such an abundant love for you that it is not measurable. Be encouraged this day that as a born again believer you will spend an eternity in the house of the Lord with Him.

Father, I know and receive the fact that Your goodness and lovingkindness will follow me all the days of my life. I received the promise that You have given to me in Your Word that I will dwell in the house of the Lord forever. These are awesome promises, and I choose to believe Your Word and that these promises will come true for me in the future. I choose to worship and praise Your holy name this day by making my entire day a sacrifice for Your glory. I declare this in the name of Jesus. Amen.

Nutrition Thought for the Day.

There are tens of thousands of enzymes in our body, and virtually nothing happens by way of reactions in our body without the aid of enzymes. Enzymes require cofactors and if those cofactors are not present the enzyme is useless. Whatever function that enzyme was to be necessary for can no longer be performed. Vitamins and minerals are cofactors for enzymes. If we are deficient in a mineral that is required for a specific enzyme, that enzyme cannot perform its function, and various disease states or malfunctions of our body will exist. It is essential that we have the proper balance of minerals in our body so that our enzymes perform to the maximum of their potential.

WAYNE E. BILLON, PH.D., RDN, LDN

Day 301
God Leads Us and Teaches Us

He leads the humble in justice, and He teaches the humble His way. All the paths of the LORD are lovingkindness and truth to those who keep His covenant and His testimonies. (Psalm 25:9–10)

The Lord leads the humble in justice and teaches the humble His way. The Hebrew word for humble in this scripture is *'anav* and means humble but in the sense of being poor and either needy, or weak, or afflicted, or lowly and meek. Thus, it seems to be speaking of humble in the sense of being beaten down rather than the way we use humble today. The Lord leads those that experience such injustice and teaches them His ways. Have you ever felt lowly and meek or beaten down? I certainly have. In such times just remember that the Lord is with you and He will lead you in a way of justice. As the Lord leads you down His paths, all His paths lead to, guess what, lovingkindness and truth. Once again we see the lovingkindness of the Lord. This promise is for those who keep His covenant and His testimonies. His covenant is a pledge that He has made with us through His Word. The word for testimonies in the Hebrew used in this scripture is interesting. It means a testimony or a witness, but in the Old Testament it is always plural and always concerns laws as divine testimonies. As you follow God's Word and you put forth every effort to keep His covenant you have this promise. As you walk through your day, keep this in mind and be encouraged to know that your God will teach you His way and guide you in lovingkindness.

Thank You Father, God, for always guiding me down the paths I should be traveling. I know that many times I have wandered off the path but You did not abandon me. You are always with me and guiding me, even when I am off the path that You want me to follow. I declare this day to make every attempt to keep Your covenant and Your testimonies to the best of my abilities and I ask for Your Holy Spirit to speak to my spirit when I intend to wander off the path that You have chosen for me. I asked this in the name of Jesus. Amen.

Nutrition Thought for the Day.

Similar to the enzymes requiring minerals to be cofactors, some hormones cannot function properly without certain minerals as cofactors. An example of this is the thyroid hormone. The thyroid hormone controls our basal metabolic rate (BMR), which controls how fast or how slow we burn calories. The thyroid is responsible for many other functions. The thyroid produces thyroxine which is the hormone that regulates our BMR, and the production of thyroxin requires iodine as a cofactor. A deficiency of iodine will cause an underactive thyroid gland and can produce dire consequences, including obesity.

Day 302
Our God Is with Us to the End

For such is God, Our God forever and ever; He will guide us until death. (Psalm 48:14)

This scripture reminds us that our God will be here forever and ever and that He will guide us until death. That means, of course, until our death since Jesus died once and will never die again. After death we will be with Him, if we are born again, and will not need guidance. This verse is the last verse of Psalm 48, and the psalmist is finishing his psalm with a reminder that our God lasts forever and will guide us until our death. As mentioned so many times in this devotional, to hear your God when He speaks to you or guides you, you have to be listening for Him. You can hear Him in your spirit when you read His Word, but you can also hear Him when you are walking around doing your everyday duties if you decide to keep in tune with what the Spirit is telling you. Sounds like something that would be too hard to do? Think again because 1 Corinthians 6:17 says, "But the one who joins himself to the Lord is one with Him." If you choose to join yourself with the Lord, then you become one with Him in spirit. If you are one with Him in spirit then you can hear His voice if you learn how to listen with your spirit. This takes constant devotion to your Lord and not just an hour meeting on a Sunday morning. You have to be dedicated to reading His Word and fellowshipping with Him. In any case, make an act of your will to listen for His voice and be encouraged to know that you can hear His voice and that He will continue to guide you until your time on this earth is complete.

Father God, Your Word says that I can unite my spirit with Your Spirit and be at one with You. I do not always feel like I am one with You, but since Your Word says it, I receive it and I believe it. I thank You that this is possible. I also thank You that You will be my guide until the day I die. I resolve this day to listen for that still small voice in my spirit in everything that I do and everywhere that I am. I ask for Your Holy Spirit to give me guidance and direction to help me to hear You when You speak to me. In Jesus's name, I pray. Amen.

Nutrition Thought for the Day.

Some minerals are actual constituents of tissue such as calcium, phosphorus, magnesium, fluoride, and others are necessary for the formation of bones and teeth. Other minerals have a direct action as iron carries oxygen through the body and is obviously necessary to supply oxygen to all the cells of our body, without which the cells would die. The electrolytes that are important in electrolyte balance are also crucial in fluid balance and maintaining the proper fluids in our bloodstream. Another critical factor is maintaining the proper pH of our bodies; we have a very narrow pH range that is needed for survival. Minerals are vital in maintaining that pH balance.

WAYNE E. BILLON, PH.D., RDN, LDN

Day 303
I Will Receive Counsel unto Glory

With Your counsel You will guide me, and afterward receive me to glory. (Psalm 73:24)

As mentioned in yesterday's and today's scripture, after He has finished guiding you, which would be the end of your time on this earth, He will receive you to glory. His counsel in the scriptures simply means advice or purpose. How many times in the scriptures, particularly in the book of Psalms, has your God reminded you of His lovingkindness and promised you over and over again that He will lead you and guide you until the end of your time until you are with Him in glory forever and ever? The Psalms are very encouraging, and it would be good if you read one each day as part of your daily devotions. Be encouraged this day that you will be guided throughout your walk on this earth and when it is over you will meet your Creator and be with Him forever in glory.

> Father God, I am encouraged by Your constant promises and reminders in Your Word. I thank You for continuously giving me encouraging words and thoughts. There are still times when I get discouraged and I feel like You are far away from me. I know that is not true, but sometimes it feels like it. I ask for Your Holy Spirit to lift me up when those times come and to remind me of the promises in Your Word. I resolve today to make an act of my will to be encouraged by Your Word in every step that I take and everything that I do. I thank You, Father, for Your love in Jesus's name. Amen.

Nutrition Thought for the Day.

The first mineral to be discussed is sodium (the chemical abbreviation is Na). Sodium is one of the most important minerals in our bodies. It is a positively charged electrolyte that is important for many functions. Sodium is found in all tissues, but it is concentrated in the fluid part of the blood. Potassium (the chemical abbreviation is K) is also a positively charged electrolyte that is found in all tissues but is concentrated inside the cells rather than in the fluids of the body. Our bodies and all cells are neutral in charge. When a sodium ion (the smallest element of sodium in our bodies) goes inside of a cell, it carries a positive charge with it. To maintain a neutral charge either a negatively charged ion needs to go into the cell with a sodium or another positively charged ion needs to come out of the cell. Usually when sodium goes in potassium comes out. This is known as the sodium/potassium pump. You do not need to understand this now, but the bottom line is this is extremely important in helping other nutrients get into and out of cells and helps to maintain electrolyte balance in the blood. This function is extremely important, so our balance of sodium and potassium is critical for us to be healthy.

Day 304
My God Will Be with Me Twenty-Four Hours a Day

The LORD will command His lovingkindness in the daytime; and His song will be with me in the night, a prayer to the God of my life. (Psalm 42:8)

It is fitting that the last scripture for this month and the last scripture from the Book of Psalms be one that summarizes what we have been discussing. Once again, we see the word lovingkindness in this Psalm. This is a final reminder of God's lovingkindness, but note that this scripture says the Lord will command His lovingkindness. That is a strong statement. The word for command in the Hebrew means just that, to command, charge, and order. Note that the scripture also says He will do this in the daytime and His song will be with you in the night. The Hebrew word for "song" used here means a lyric song, a religious song, or a song of Levitical choirs. A song of God will be with you in the night and will be as a prayer to your God. His lovingkindness will be with you twenty-four hours a day, as the saying goes, 24/7. Be confident today that your God's lovingkindness is with you wherever you go, whether you can feel it or not. Know that you are loved and you are being watched over.

Father, I thank You for Your lovingkindness that will always be with me, twenty-four hours a day, seven days a week. You have told me so many times in the Book of Psalms about Your lovingkindness. I know that You want to make a strong point for me to understand how much You love me. I do not always feel Your lovingkindness but, since Your Word says that You give me lovingkindness continuously, I choose to believe it and to receive it, whether I feel it or not. I will walk through this day knowing that Your lovingkindness surrounds me with every step that I take. I thank You, Father, in the name of Your Son, Jesus Christ. Amen.

Nutrition Thought for the Day.

Our heart is really an electric motor. The beating of the heart is stimulated by electrical impulses, and these impulses are generated from sodium/potassium going across cell membranes. If either one gets too far out of balance, it can affect the rhythm and rate of the heart and possibly cause a heart attack. Maintaining a proper sodium/potassium balance in the body is absolutely essential. This balance is obtained by the kidneys excreting an excess of either one of the elements and/or re-absorbing either one of the elements that are low in the body.

Wayne E. Billon, Ph.D., RDN, LDN

Day 305
You Are Guarded By God's Peace

Be anxious for nothing, but in everything by prayer and supplication with thanksgiving let your requests be known to God. And the peace of God, which surpasses all comprehension, will guard your hearts and your minds in Christ Jesus. (Philippians 4:6–7)

Do not be anxious about anything but in every circumstance that you find yourself in you should present your prayers and supplications (needs, wants, asking: all possible translations of the Greek word for this according to Strong's Concordance) with thanksgiving be known to God. If you know who you are in Christ, and you realize how much God loves you, then will you make these petitions to your Father God and you should have peace knowing that He hears your prayers and will answer them in accordance with His timing. The peace that can come over us in such a situation will surpass all comprehension and will help us to guard our hearts and our minds against the lies and temptations of the devil. This is accomplished by the blood of Jesus Christ that we are covered with as born-again believers. This should be extremely comforting and encouraging to you. You should pick up your Bible and look at verse 8 of Philippians 4:8 tells us what we should be thinking about after we make such supplications to our Father God. It tells us that we should think on whatever is true, honorable, right, pure, lovely, of good repute, and if there is any excellence and anything is worthy of praise, then we should dwell on such things. Set your mind today to dwell on the things mentioned in Philippians 4:8 and be at peace knowing that your God is with you and hears your prayers and allow the peace that surpasses all understandings to envelop you.

> Father, I cannot thank You enough for Your peace that You give to me when I seek You and petition for the things I need to walk in Your lovingkindness. I understand the things that I should be thinking about that are listed in Your Word in Philippians 4:8 instead of paying attention to the anxious thoughts that the devil and the world bring into my mind. I have control over those thoughts by the power of the Holy Spirit and having been redeemed by the blood of Jesus. I thank You for Your peace, and I decide by an act of my will to walk through this day with Your peace in my heart. I thank You, Father, in the name of Jesus Christ. Amen.

Nutrition Thought for the Day.

We lose sodium by excretion through the kidneys and by perspiration. If we lose too much sodium, we upset the electrolyte balance and upset the fluid balance of our bodies. Sodium helps to maintain fluid balance by holding fluid in blood and tissues. If sodium gets too high in the blood, besides upsetting the electrolyte balance, it can cause too much fluid to remain in the body instead of being excreted through the kidneys. This causes weight gain due to excessive fluid accumulation but more important than that it can cause our blood pressure to rise.

Day 306
Jesus Wants Us to Be at Peace

"These things I have spoken to you, so that in Me you may have peace. In the world you have tribulation, but take courage; I have overcome the world." (John 16:33)

In chapter 13 of the Gospel of John the apostles shared the Last Supper with Jesus. Throughout chapters 13, 14, 15, and 16 Jesus is trying to prepare them for His passion and death that would soon be taking place. They did not understand the things He was trying to tell them. He knew that once they saw how He would be beaten and crucified they would be extremely distraught and have the opportunity to be very fearful. At this point no greater calamity could befall them, yet He is telling them that throughout His agony they are to be at peace. In these four chapters Jesus mentions that they should be at peace three times (John 14:1, John 14:27, and John 16:33). If it were not possible for them to have peace under such horrible conditions, He would not told them to be at peace. Granted it would be very difficult to be at peace in such a situation, but that is what He told them.

Today we have the entire Bible to look at to help us see what Jesus was talking about and we know what happens in the last chapter of the book. We know that as born-again believers we will be with our Lord and Savior. If it was possible for the apostles to have peace under the conditions they experienced on the last night before Jesus's crucifixion, even when they did not understand what was coming after the crucifixion, how much more would it be possible for us to have peace today when we know and understand what is going to happen to us after our walk on this earth? Be encouraged today that the command not to be anxious is for you. Resolve to walk through this day resting in Him and laying all anxious thoughts at the foot of the cross.

Father, I understand that I am not to be anxious about anything. I know that Your Word is true and that it tells me to be at peace. It is not always easy for me to be at peace in everything that I do when the world is closing in on me, yet I know I can have Your peace. I can also experience the peace that surpasses all understanding as I continue to go through with my healthy lifestyle regimen. When things are not going my way with my program or with anything else that I do, I know that Your peace is available to. I resolve this day not to be anxious about anything. I thank You in the name of Jesus. Amen.

Nutrition Thought for the Day.

Sodium comes into the body, for the most part, in the form of sodium chloride (NaCl) or what is known as table salt. Sodium chloride is 40% sodium. Foods are naturally low in sodium. Most of our sodium intake comes into our bodies as a result of added salt. There is a strong movement today by all professional medical associations (i.e., American Heart Association, Academy of Nutrition and Dietetics, FDA) to encourage the public to lower their sodium intake. Excessive sodium leads to high blood pressure which can result in heart attacks, strokes, and renal failure. Other forms of sodium in our diet could be as sodium nitrates and sodium nitrites. These are additives in processed meat. Baking soda and baking powder that are added to baked goods are another source of sodium.

Day 307
God Promises to Keep You in Perfect Peace

"The steadfast of mind You will keep in perfect peace, because he trusts in You." (Isaiah 26:3)

The steadfast of mind will be kept in perfect peace by our Lord because we trust in Him. "Steadfast in mind" means those that have their mind set on the Lord, the ways of the Lord, His Word, etc. If you are following God's Word and staying in fellowship with like-minded believers, and if you believe in and trust God's Word, then the scripture promises that God will keep you in perfect peace. The way this has worked in my life is that, when I am in tune with God's Word and a stumbling block, a disappointment, or anything that is unexpected or undesirable, comes my way, I think of this scripture. I then call on God's peace, and even though the things that have caused me a problem may not change, God's peace is there if I will accept it. This is also true for you and for all who are born-again believers if you can believe God's Word and accept it. So whatever may come your way today that is an undesirable outcome, be it in your home, your workplace, or your lifestyle program, rest assured that God will keep you in perfect peace if you trust in Him.

Father, I believe that You will keep me in perfect peace if I trust in You. I know that this does not guarantee that nothing bad or any grave disappointment will come my way, but if they do, I know that I can always rely on You to keep me in perfect peace. This is the peace that surpasses all understanding because even though things may look very bleak for me at times, I can still be at peace because of Your Word. As I complete my daily chores today, I know that as I meditate on what Your Word says, I will remain in a state of peace. I thank You for Your peace in Jesus's name. Amen.

Nutrition Thought for the Day.
Salt substitutes may or may not have added sodium to them. You need to read the label to see what is in the salt substitute. Many salt substitutes are potassium chloride (KCl) instead of sodium chloride. This is okay as long as you have normal kidney function. If there is a problem with your kidneys, you may retain potassium and cause extreme cardiovascular issues. Other salt substitutes, like Mrs. Dash, should be okay but to be safe read the labels.

Day 308
You Can Control Your Peace

Let the peace of Christ rule in your hearts, to which indeed you were called in one body; and be thankful. (Colossians 3:15)

You were called by our God to be part of His Body, and as a part of that Body, it is certainly His desire that you have all of the gifts and blessings that He intended for you to have. Among those blessings is His peace. You certainly know that God intends that the Body of Christ be in peace and you were called to be a part of that Body. It, therefore, makes perfect sense that you are called into peace. A key to the scripture is that you also need to be thankful. Receive God's calling for you as a member of His Body and with that receive His peace, let it rule in your heart no matter what may come your way. Rest in His love today knowing that to be at peace is a calling on your life, and not just any calling, but a high calling. There is nothing greater than knowing that you are God's child and that His lovingkindness is on you wherever you go.

Father, I know that I am not just another person but that I am called to be a part of Your Body and that as such I am also called to be at peace. I choose this day to let the peace of Christ reign in every shadow of my heart no matter where I go or what I do today. I am a part of Your Body, and I thank You for Your lovingkindness that will always be with me no matter how much the devil, the world, or my flesh will try to upset my peace. I thank You for the peace that surpasses all understanding (Philippians 4:7), in the name of Jesus. Amen.

Nutrition Thought for the Day.

It is very important to read labels concerning sodium. Foods that are usually high in sodium include any instant foods, like instant grits and instant gravy but there may be low-sodium versions of these products on the market. You need to read the label. All tomato products, unless otherwise designated as low-sodium, usually contain high sodium such as tomato juice, tomato soup, tomato paste, etc. All processed meats, unless designated as low-sodium, are typically high in salt and other additives like sodium nitrate and/or sodium nitrite. This includes all luncheon meats, hot dogs, bacon, and all smoked or cured meats. Smoked pork chops are high in sodium, but fresh pork chops are not. Cheese is high sodium unless otherwise indicated on the label. Thus, pizza would be very high sodium because of the salt and baking powder/soda in the dough, the cheese, the tomato sauce, and other toppings such as sausage and anchovies (very high in sodium).

Day 309
May You Abound in Hope

Now may the God of hope fill you with all joy and peace in believing, so that you will abound in hope by the power of the Holy Spirit. (Romans 15:13)

Remember that hope lifts you up and strengthens you. As you become filled with hope, your faith is strengthened. You serve a God that is the God of all hope, and it is His great pleasure to give you all joy and peace as you believe in Him. This is an upward spiral type of momentum. The more you get to know your God, the more you trust in Him, and the greater your hope becomes. As your hope increases, your God becomes pleased with your progress and fills you with joy and peace. This increases your hope even more and enables you to communicate better with your God, and you can abound even more in hope by the power of the Holy Spirit who resides in you. As long as you keep your eyes on Jesus, your hope is strengthened by the power of the Holy Spirit who becomes more and more evident in your daily walk. As you complete your daily chores today, including your healthy lifestyle regimen, do not lose hope for one second. Your hope is in your Lord and on the promises in His Word.

Father, I have hope in You and Your Word. I ask You to fill me with Your joy and peace this day so that my hope can be strengthened that much more. I know that the power of the Holy Spirit is in me and that power helps me to abound in hope. You are the God of hope, and I praise You for it. I know that the more I trust in You, the greater my hope will be and I resolve this day to put all my trust in You and expect to see my hope strengthened by the power of the Holy Spirit. I thank You for this in the mighty name of Jesus. Amen.

Nutrition Thought for the Day.

Most soups and broths, unless the label indicates low-sodium, are high in sodium. All fast foods are high in sodium such as hamburgers, French fries, hot dogs, etc. Snack foods are high in sodium such as potato chips, corn chips, pretzels, salted nuts, etc. Anything that has been pickled is high in sodium since they are pickled in a salt solution (for example, pickles, olives, sauerkraut, and pickled eggs). For all other canned vegetables or frozen vegetables, please read the labels. Some foods will surprise you as to how much sodium they contain. Be careful of so-called diet foods that are low in sugar. When sugar is taken out of foods, frequently either sodium or fat is added to make it taste good. Fresh fruit and vegetables are just about devoid of sodium while being good sources of potassium and other nutrients. Read the labels.

Day 310
Do Not Let Your Heart Be Troubled

"Peace I leave with you; My peace I give to you; not as the world gives do I give to you. Do not let your heart be troubled, nor let it be fearful." (John 14:27)

Chapter 14 of the Gospel of John took place the night of the last supper. Jesus was trying to prepare His disciples for what was about to happen to Him, but they did not understand. Jesus knew what was going to happen to Him and He knew that it would be terribly unsettling to His disciples. Even though the worst was about to happen, He told them that He was giving them His peace, but this was not the worldly kind of peace. Instead, it was a godly kind of peace, the kind that surpasses all understanding (Philippians 4:7). Have you ever wondered what that means, "peace that surpasses all understanding?" The only kind of peace that could settle the apostles on that dark night was the peace that surpasses their understanding, a kind of peace that was not possible without the help of the Holy Spirit. With that peace He told them not to let their hearts be troubled and not to be fearful. Knowing what was about to happen, it does not seem possible to us, but that is the nature of God's kind of peace. This peace is available to you. Accept it and believe it. Go about your day today knowing that you have the peace that surpasses all understanding available to you and your God wants to give it to you freely.

Father, the peace that You give us is not the same peace as we understand in a worldly sense, but it is a heavenly peace that we need help to understand. It surpasses all understanding which means it is above our understanding and seems too good to be true. Yet your peace is true and it is that great. Help me this day to understand how great Your peace is. I resolve to walk in Your peace and I thank You for it in the name of Jesus. Amen.

Nutrition Thought for the Day,

Some are under the erroneous belief that sea salt or kosher salt is lower in sodium than table salt. This is not true. Sea salt and kosher salt are very coarse and would fill up a teaspoon faster than table salt. This may end up having slightly less sodium in a measured teaspoon of salt, but it would not be a significant difference. Some think that the sea salt is better for you because it has more nutrients than regular salt. Sea salt does contain a few more minerals than table salt does but they are in such small quantities that there is no advantage to taking sea salt over table salt. Table salt has iodine added, and for many people, this is the only source of iodine and is another important mineral to be discussed later. Sea salt has less iodine in it then does table salt.

Day 311
Do Not Worry

"And who of you by being worried can add a *single* hour to his life?" (Matthew 6:27)

If you do not have peace, then you are filled with fear and anxiety and/or worry. That is a terrible threesome. Peace replaces all of these and certainly is what you should be seeking. In this scripture Jesus is talking, and He is asking us that if we worry about anything, can we add a single hour to our life? This question is for you just as sure as if you were sitting in front of Him some 2000 years ago listening to His message. Do you realize that to worry is a sin? When the Word tells us to do something or not to do something it is not making a suggestion; it is giving us a command. When the Word tells us not to worry (Matthew 6:25, 31, and 34), it is not saying it would be nice if we did not worry, but it is giving us a command. God does not want us to worry. When you are worrying you are showing a lack of faith in God, that He is not able to take care of you. I know that this is easy for me to say but difficult to do. I agree it is easy, but it is what God wants us to do. Resolve this day to trust in your God and not give into worrying.

> Father, I know that You do not want me to worry, but You want me to trust You so much that nothing that comes my way will produce anxiety, fear, or worry in my heart. This is difficult for me to achieve but I know I can do it with Your help and the power of the Holy Spirit. I resolve not to be worried or fearful of anything that comes my way today, and I ask for Your Holy Spirit to give me the power and wisdom to be successful. In Jesus's name, I pray. Amen.

Nutrition Thought for the Day.

So how much sodium do we need? The actual amount of sodium required by the human body is not known. We do not have a requirement but a recommendation. Numerous studies have indicated that when we take over about 2.3g (2300 mg) of sodium a day, we can be putting ourselves in harm's way. Some people are called salt retainers and they tend to keep sodium in their body for longer periods of time before it is excreted. This causes them to retain fluid and can cause the problems mentioned earlier such as high blood pressure. If not corrected, high blood pressure can lead to a heart attack, stroke, and kidney failure. For those people it is recommended that 1.5 g (1500 mg) of sodium a day be their maximum intake. A teaspoon of sodium is approximately 5 g of salt. Since salt is 40% sodium, 5×40% equals 2 g of sodium, so, slightly over one teaspoon of salt per day is the recommendation.

Day 312
Always Rejoice in the Lord

Rejoice in the Lord always; again I will say, rejoice! (Philippians 4:4)

If you are always in a state of fear or anxiety and you do not have peace, it would be very difficult for you to rejoice in the Lord. However, the converse of that is also true. If you trust your God so much that you are always in a state of rejoicing, then it would be difficult for you to be in anxiety and fear. Remember that when you see a statement in the Word, it is not there as a suggestion, but it is there as a command. Philippians 4:4 says, "rejoice in the Lord always" and in the same verse Paul repeats his statement and says, "again I will say, rejoice!" God wants you to rejoice, and He gives you the tools in His Word to be at peace and thus be in a position where you can rejoice.

How many times in the last week have you just sat down in quiet time or as you moved about your day and just gave praise and glory to your God? Most of us would be embarrassed at the small number of times we do that. Our God is so good to us that we should be praising Him and rejoicing in Him all the time. I know it is not that we do not want to, we just do not think about it because of our busy lifestyles. We need to make an extreme effort to give praise and glory to our God and just rejoice in Him. an excellent way to do this is when you get up in the morning, the first thing you do is praise your God and give Him glory for another day, another opportunity to be a witness for Him. Once you get in the habit of doing this, it will happen automatically, and you will be giving praise to your God at least once a day. It will also make you conscious of the fact that you should praise and rejoice in your God and make it more likely that you would think of it again during the day. Rejoice in Him today!

Father God, I rejoice in You this day, not for any particular reason or for any miraculous thing You just did for me, but I rejoice in You because of who You are and what Jesus did for me. I give You praise and honor and glory because You are my God, the Alpha and the Omega, the King of kings and You are worthy of all praise and all honor. Your lovingkindness surrounds me every day without me even asking for it. You are with me everywhere I go, and every step I take is ordered by You when I trust in You and follow Your precepts. I ask for Your Holy Spirit to remind me throughout the day to continuously be giving You praise and honor and glory. I thank You, Father, in Jesus's name. Amen.

Nutrition Thought for the Day.

Most people take in more than the recommendation for sodium. The recommendation is really a small amount of salt per day. There are many other ways of seasoning your foods besides salt. There are a large number of herbs and spices that can be used in place of sodium. Some of the salt substitutes that are acceptable should be considered too. Using other flavorings such as lemon juice is also helpful. Be creative and try different things instead of adding so much salt to your diet. If your salt intake is over 2.3 g per day, start your sodium restriction by gradually reducing the amount of salt until you get used to less salt and then reduce some more; get used to that reduction and reduce some more, etc.

Day 313
We Are Blessed with Peace

The LORD will give strength to His people; the LORD will bless His people with peace. (Psalm 29:11)

Another remarkable promise is that the Lord our God will bless us with His peace. Remember that the peace we are used to as citizens of this earth is not the same peace this scripture is referencing. When we think of peace, normally we think of it in earthly terms. That is, if we would say that we are at peace if we are sitting in a comfortable chair in our living room in front of a warm fire, all of our bills are paid, we have food in the house, and all of our family is healthy. That is a physical, worldly peace. Another type of peace we may declare is peace with our enemies, and we are not fighting or arguing with anyone. That is another type of peace that we can experience on this earth. I do not think our God is talking about either of those kinds of peace, but instead, He is talking about a genuine peace in our spirits that is supernatural. This type of peace is that which we experience when our bills are not paid, we do not have all the food we want, and people are aggravating us for one thing or another. When we have peace in spite of all of those problems, that is the peace that surpasses all understanding and is a peace that God gives us. Receive His peace today and know that since you are one of His people you can rest assured that you are blessed with His peace.

I understand, Father, that there is a difference between the worldly peace that we have on earth when everything is going our way and the supernatural peace that surpasses all understanding when things are not going our way. I thank You for Your supernatural peace that You bless me with on a daily basis. I do not always understand Your peace but I choose, by an act of my will, to receive it this day. I resolve to walk through this day knowing that I am blessed with Your supernatural peace, in Jesus's name. Amen.

Nutrition Thought for the Day.

Potassium is the next mineral and has already been discussed to a degree with sodium. Potassium participates in the sodium/potassium pump and is important for muscle contractions and proper heart function. Potassium also contributes to the acid-base balance. Excessive potassium in the diet can be a problem if the kidneys are not properly functioning. With normal kidney function, potassium should not be a problem. Fruits and vegetables are rich sources of potassium. For packaged foods read a label to see how much potassium is in the container. Remember that many salt substitutes are potassium chloride instead of sodium chloride. Potassium losses are through kidney excretions. Some may be lost with perspiration but not near as much as sodium because remember potassium is found inside the cells and not as much in the fluid around cells like sodium.

Day 314
Our Joy Should Be Full

"If you keep My commandments, you will abide in My love; just as I have kept My Father's commandments and abide in His love. These things I have spoken to you so that My joy may be in you, and *that* your joy may be made full." (John 15:10–11)

The joy of the Lord is our strength, and Jesus wants us to be filled with His joy. This is another account of what happened on the night of the Last Supper when Jesus was talking to His apostles and trying to prepare them for what was about to happen to Him. He had taught them the way of the New Testament, that is the way of grace versus law, and He explained to them how they were to keep the commandments through grace. In this scripture He tells them to abide in His love and by abiding by His commandments, just as He kept the Father's commands and abided in His love. He gave them the model of how this was to be accomplished, and He now tells them that He has told them these things so that His joy may be in them. In not so many words He told them that if His joy was in them, then their joy would be made full. There is no other joy greater than the joy of being in God's Word. Do you have the joy of the Lord today? Are you abiding by His Word? Are you trusting in Him? If the answer to these last two questions is yes, then you should be full of the joy of the Lord. If not, then you are letting the cares of the world, the lust of the flesh, and/or the wiles of the devil distract you. You have control over these things if you will take the control that Jesus gave you. Complete your day knowing that the joy of the Lord is in you and allow the joy to come out for everyone around you to see and to enjoy themselves.

Father, I thank You for Your joy that You have given me and that You desire for me to have so that my joy may be full. I know that there is no joy greater than the joy of knowing who I am in Christ and knowing what waits for me after life on earth. I resolve to follow Jesus's commandments and to receive the joy that He wants me to. I thank You, Father, in Jesus's name. Amen.

Nutrition Thought for the Day.

Another mineral that is important to our electrolyte balance is chloride (chemical symbol is Cl). Sodium and potassium both have a +1 charge but chloride has a -1 charge so it is considered a negatively charged electrolyte and is important in electrolyte balance. Chloride is not found in very many foods naturally. Our main source of chloride is salt. Some salt in our diet is required for healthy functioning; we just do not want to ingest too much. Our stomach secretes hydrochloric acid (HCl) which is necessary for digesting our food. One of the functions of chloride is obviously in the production of HCl. We lose chloride through kidney excretions and perspiration. If you are taking adequate salt in your diet, you should not have a problem with meeting your needs for chloride. Some additional factors that affect sodium, potassium, and chloride requirements are air temperature and humidity, whether someone is a salt retainer or non-retainer, the condition of the kidneys, heart functioning, hypertension, and medications. Many medications cause the loss of sodium or potassium through the kidneys, and sometimes replacements are required. If you are on such medications your physician should notify you of such.

Day 315
It Is by Faith We Stand in God's Grace

Therefore, having been justified by faith, we have peace with God through our Lord Jesus Christ, through whom also we have obtained our introduction by faith into this grace in which we stand; and we exalt in hope of the glory of God. (Romans 5:1–2)

There is an old cliché you have probably heard that says, "when you see a 'therefore' you need to look to see what it is 'there for.'" The last verse of the previous chapter, Romans 4:25, says, "He who was delivered over because of our transgressions, and was raised because of our justification." The "He," of course, refers to Jesus. In Romans 5:1, Paul says, "Therefore, having been justified by faith,…." First, let's look at this initial part of the scripture. You, as a born-again believer, are the one that Paul is referring to as being justified by faith. Your faith in your God and His Word is what enables you to have all of the promises given to you. In this scripture, the promise is peace with your God through your Lord Jesus Christ. This is because He was delivered over to the Romans for persecution because of your sins and all the sins of the world. He was raised from the dead by your Father God for your justification—that is to say, so that you may be justified. And what does that mean? This word justified has also been broken down to mean *just as if ied* never sinned. It means that you were made righteous in the eyes of your God by accepting what Jesus did for you. Faith in what Jesus did is the means by which you have peace with your God. The next verse, Romans 5:2, adds the icing to the cake. It is through Jesus Christ that you have been introduced, by your faith, into grace. Remember grace can be defined as not receiving what we earned or deserved, but receiving unmerited favor from our God. It is by this grace that you are exalted in the hope of the glory of God. This should make you feel special. Breaking this down section-by-section shows the peace and the glory of hope in which you now stand. Be encouraged by this today and walk in peace, hope, and God's grace in all that you do.

> Lord Jesus, I thank You for all that You have done for me through Your life, death, and resurrection. Yes, that has given me salvation and an eternal life with You, but in my walk through this world before the eternity with You begins, Your sacrifice gives me hope and peace through grace that covers me head to foot every day in every step that I take. This is an awesome realization of Your love and I thank You for it today. Amen.

Nutrition Thought for the Day.

The next mineral is calcium (chemical symbol is Ca) which plays a huge part in numerous functions in the body. Probably the most well-known function is calcium's major role in bone and teeth development. Ninety-nine percent of the calcium in our body is found in bones and teeth. The remaining 1% the body cannot live without for the remaining 1% is important in muscle contractions, nerve conductions, blood clotting, and numerous other reactions within cells. Probably the most common disease associated with calcium deficiency is osteoporosis.

Day 316
Jesus Himself Is Our Peace

But now in Christ Jesus you who formerly were far off have been brought near by the blood of Christ. For He Himself is our peace, who made both *groups into* one and broke down the barrier of the dividing wall, by abolishing in His flesh the enmity, *which is* the Law of commandments *contained* in ordinances, so that in Himself He might make the two into one new man, *thus* establishing peace. (Ephesians 2:13–15)

Today's scripture is a mouthful. Jesus' life, death, and resurrection have brought us into salvation by breaking down the dividing wall between us (Gentiles) and the Old Testament Jews. Before Jesus's life on earth, Gentiles were excluded from citizenship of Israel. Gentiles had no hope to participate in God's covenant promises. The Jews were bound by the Old Testament laws. Jesus broke down the dividing wall between Jews and Gentiles, allowing the Gentiles to participate in and receive God's covenant promises. He gave us the new commandments of the New Testament which are based on grace and not law. This also freed the Jews from the penalty of the law. This is good news for both the Jew and the Gentile who can now be one under God's grace. With this grace we can thus be established in peace with the peace that comes from Him, since He is peace. It almost sounds like double talk, but if you break down each section and think about it you will understand that through the life, death, and resurrection of our Lord and Savior Jesus Christ we have been delivered from law (that was impossible for man to keep) into grace that is freely given to all of us even though we do not deserve it. Once again today you can walk in peace and joy knowing what Jesus did for you. Remember that this peace is not an earthly peace but a godly peace that surpasses all understanding.

Lord Jesus, You are the only person that was able to walk on this earth for a lifetime and not commit any sins. You obeyed the law to the letter and was the only person that was able to do that. It is impossible for man to obey every ordinance and law that was in place in the Old Testament times even though the law was good and was put there by our Father God. As a result of Your obedience, the law has been kept for me, and in its place, I have been given grace when I received You as my Savior and Lord. It is by that grace that I can stand in righteousness before You and my Father God and the Holy Spirit. For this righteousness I thank You, Jesus, and I resolve to walk through this day in Your grace. Amen.

Nutrition Thought for the Day.
Osteoporosis means porous bones and results in bones that can fracture or break very easily. Adequate calcium in the diet is essential to prevent this, but other minerals and some vitamins are also essential in preventing osteoporosis also. The amount of calcium in the diet is, of course, important but there are a lot of different factors that are involved since some nutrients can prevent calcium absorption and some disease states can prevent calcium absorption. The type of calcium ingested is also important because some can be absorbed very easily and some forms are very difficult to be absorbed.

Day 317
My Lord Allows Me to Dwell in Safety

In peace I will both lie down and sleep, for You alone, O LORD, make me to dwell in safety. (Psalm 4:8)

We are promised to be able to lie down in peace and be able to sleep. This is because our Lord enables us to dwell in safety. When this psalm was written, men were not always able to lie down at night and sleep in peace because of the troubled times and the enemies that were around them. Amazingly we are in similarly troubled times today. It seems like every day there is a new world crisis and a new local crisis. Financial problems loom over us and our country as well as the world. Our enemies are all around us. We need to understand that this scripture was written for the people who trust in God as their deliverer. Jesus had not been born yet, so there was no accepting Jesus as Savior and Lord at that time and thus no equivalent to being saved. The psalm was written for God's people that trusted Him and believed in His Word as it was written up until that time. The psalm is still intended for us today, but it is a promise for those of us that have received Jesus as our Savior and Lord and trust in Him. Thus, if we are saved and are walking In God's Word, then we are assured of God's peace if we accept it and, in spite of what is going on in the world and around our dwelling, we can lie down and sleep in peace knowing that our God is the one that we trust and not the economy, our military, or our government. Be at rest this day knowing that your God will keep you in perfect peace if you trust in Him.

Father God, many things are going on in my world today that can keep me in unrest and steal my peace. Sometimes when I lay down at night to sleep I have to question if I am safe or not because of the turmoil that surrounds me. My government, military, and locked doors can bring me some degree of security and peace, but it does not change the chaos that is in the world. The only thing that gives me true safety and the lasting peace that surpasses all understanding is You Lord. I trust in You Lord Jesus, and I know that because of Your protection I can sleep in peace. I thank You, Father, in the name of Jesus. Amen.

Nutrition Thought for the Day.

Factors that improve calcium absorption include vitamin D, a proper ratio of calcium to phosphorus in the diet, some sugars such as lactose that help calcium absorption, and ample acid in the stomach. From this we can see obvious things that would decrease calcium absorption such as a lack of vitamin D in the diet, excessive phosphorus in the diet, a lack of some sugars in the diet, and a decrease in stomach acid. Those that have acid reflux and take any one of the various medications that reduce stomach acid or take a lot of antacids to neutralize stomach acid can inadvertently affect calcium absorption.

Day 318
Make Peace and Receive Peace

And the seed whose fruit is righteousness is sown in peace by those who make peace. (James 3:18)

In chapter 3 of James, the apostle is talking about controlling the tongue. He mentions that the way to be able to control the tongue is by depending on the wisdom that comes down from above instead of depending on man's wisdom. In verse seventeen he says, "But the wisdom from above is first pure, then peaceable, gentle, reasonable, full of mercy and good fruits, unwavering, without hypocrisy." That type of godly wisdom is awesome. It is pure wisdom, is peaceable and will bring about peace. It is gentle and will not cause us trouble. It is reasonable and full of mercy and produces good fruit. It is unwavering—never changes—and is without hypocrisy. Hypocrisy was a problem in the days that James wrote this letter. Then, in verse 18, he says that the seed will produce the fruit of righteousness when sown in peace by those who belong to God and work hard to be peaceful and to make peace. Are you a peaceful person? Are you impatient and lose your temper easily? Do you want to raise your voice to members of your family, friends, and coworkers? If so, resolve this day to sow a seed of peace in righteousness based on godly wisdom. It would do all of us good to stop and think before we put our tongue in motion. What will be the cost of the comments we are getting ready to make? Will they sow peace or will they sow discord? If you can control your tongue and think of these simple little questions before putting it into motion, you can sow peace and righteousness in everything you do. As you walk through this day resolve to look for opportunities to sow peace in everything you do.

I know that there are many times in a day that I have the opportunity to either sow peace, sow discord, or not sow anything at all. Sometimes I do not say anything for fear of saying the wrong thing. If I can control my tongue and say godly things, things that I receive from You Lord through Your wisdom, I know that I will be able to sow peace in righteousness and bring about a calmness to whatever situation I may find myself. I resolve this day, by an act of my will, to look for opportunities to be a blessing and to sow peace and not discord. I ask for godly wisdom to be able to do this for Your glory Lord, and I ask in the name of Jesus. Amen.

Nutrition Thought for the Day.

Other factors that affect calcium absorption are excessive fiber in the diet and certain compounds that are found in high-fiber foods such as phytates and oxalate. An excess of other minerals can interfere with calcium absorption such as magnesium. Does this mean we should quit taking the anti-reflux or anti-acid meds? Should we go on a low fiber diet? The answer to both of those is no. Instead, we should make sure that we are taking in ample calcium in the presence of a high-fiber diet and anti-reflux or anti-acid meds. This is why a balanced diet is so important.

Day 319
Avoid Those Who Devise Evil

Deceit is in the heart of those who devise evil, but counselors of peace have joy. (Proverbs 12:20)

This verse from Proverbs, a book of wisdom, in an indirect way tells us that we can destroy our peace by having deceit in our heart. Those who are deceitful are those who devise evil plans. This does not mean that everything you do has to be an evil plan for causing harm or destruction to someone or their reputation. However, if on a regular basis you make room in your thought life for evil plans, even though you may not intend to put them into action, you are allowing deceit to enter into your heart. This will put you in a place where eventually more and more evil plans will take place. This will destroy your peace. However, the second part of this verse says that counselors of peace, those who promote peace and counsel people about peace, will have joy. So you have a choice today to choose deceitfulness or to choose joy. The choice is yours. Decide this day that you are going to remove any deceitful thoughts from your mind. You will then be able to experience peace and joy in all that you do freely.

Lord Jesus, I want to be a person that spreads love abroad and promotes peace wherever I go. It is easy to allow some evil desire to answer my heart over some silly insignificant occurrence that can cause me to become angry and revengeful. If I give into such distractive thoughts, they can turn into hate and produce revengeful desires in my mind. I realize that this can steal my peace and I do not want to let that happen. I resolve this day to rebuke any demonic or deceitful thought that enters my mind. I will guard my heart and trust in You to give me wisdom and protection against such diverse thoughts. I ask for strength in this area in Your name, Jesus. Amen.

Nutrition Thought for the Day.

Calcium requirements vary from males to females and for different age groups, but most adults require about 1300 mg of calcium per day. Older adults require a little less, about 1200 mg a day. Taking in much larger doses probably will not be of additional benefit for most people. The tolerable upper limit, which is the most calcium that could be tolerated by most people, is 2500 mg per day. The calcium level in our blood is controlled by vitamin D and the parathyroid hormone. If someone has a problem with the parathyroid hormone, they may also have a problem controlling their blood calcium level. Proper functioning kidneys and liver are also necessary to maintain an optimum blood calcium level.

Day 320
Depart from Evil and Seek Peace

Depart from evil and do good; seek peace and pursue it. (Psalm 34:14)

Yesterday's proverb told us that deceitful people are those who have evil plans in their hearts but counselors of peace walk in peace. Today's Psalm tells us to depart from evil and do good, seek peace, and pursue it. This implies that if we are in a situation that leans to the dark side of life, then we will not find peace in that area. The Hebrew word for evil in this verse is *rá* which means evil but could also mean wicked, bad, unpleasant, displeasing, and several other similar words. If there is anything that pertains to any aspect of evil, bad, unpleasant, or displeasing, then you want to depart from it and avoid it at all costs. It does not necessarily mean hateful or bad actions; it could be any of those other adjectives that lead up to evil. If you want to have peace, the peace that surpasses all understanding, you need to rid your life of anything that would block peace. Any Habits that are evil or remotely evil should be eliminated. Then seek peace and pursue it—that is to follow after it or chase it. Seek peace at all costs. It would be good if you analyzed your life patterns and your thought patterns for anything that may pertain to something that is evil, displeasing, or distracting in any ungodly way and resolve to remove those patterns from your life.

Lord Jesus, I understand that if I want to have peace in my life that I need to separate myself from all those things that can block peace. That includes anything that is evil, but other distractions that may be related to evil, displeasing, or undesirable could also prevent me from being at peace. I ask You to help me identify those things in my life that would be in any way, shape, or form an evil distraction for me and prevents me from having peace. I now resolve to remove any such distraction from my life and walk in the peace that You intended for me to have. I ask for this, Jesus, in Your name. Amen.

Nutrition Thought for the Day.

When blood calcium levels drop slightly below the normal levels, vitamin D and the parathyroid hormone cause calcium to come out of the bone. If this were to continue over an extended period in our life, this could lead to osteoporosis. Other factors that contribute to calcium coming out of the bones include people that smoke, have a high alcohol intake, high protein intake, women past menopause, multiple pregnancies, and probably genetics. Most people are still adding calcium to their bones by about age 35. There is nothing magic about 35 years of age, and it varies from individual to individual, but most people begin to lose calcium from the bones around age 35.

Day 321
Love God's Word and Have Great Peace

Those who love Your law have great peace, and nothing causes them to stumble. (Psalm 119:165)

Psalms were, of course, written in the Old Testament, so the law that is being referred to here is the law of the Old Testament. Your first thought may be that we are no longer under that law but we are under grace, and that is certainly true. However Jesus's life on earth fulfilled the law, and even though man was not able to fill the law, the law was still good. If you love God's law, then you love God's Word with emphasis on the commandments Jesus gave us in the New Testament, which is found in John 13:34, "A new commandment I give to you, that you love one another, even as I have loved you, that you also love one another." This commandment summarizes the entire law of the Old Testament as is declared in 2 John 1:5, "Now I ask you, lady, not as though I were writing to you a new commandment, but the one which we have had from the beginning, that we love one another." John was writing this to a particular lady, but everything written in the Scriptures is intended for us also. If you love God's law, you will try with all your heart to keep the commandments of loving one another as Jesus loves us. If you can accomplish that, you will have great peace and even though trials and tribulations may come your way, they will not cause you to stumble. Keep your eyes on Jesus today and watch for stumbling blocks that will steal your peace.

Dear Father, Your commandments are so simple, yet so difficult to walk out in perfection. I know that I should keep Your law as written in Your Word but there are so many things to remember that it is difficult. However, the simplicity comes in if I remember this summation of Your law and that is: to love one another as You love us. If I can accomplish that, then all the other aspects of Your law will fall into place. To do that effectively, I have to see people in the same way that You see them, that is as someone for whom Jesus Christ died. As I interact with people today in my family, my workplace, my peers in my healthy lifestyle regimen, help me to see all of them as You see them and to love them as You love us. I ask in the name of Jesus. Amen.

Nutrition Thought for the Day.

Proper calcium intake along with the other nutrients mentioned above, while avoiding the bad health practices that cause calcium to come out of the bones, will help to maintain strong healthy bones in the latter years of life. Exercise also drives calcium into the bones and helps to maintain strong dense bones. Weight-bearing exercises are good for this also. If you cannot take in the proper amount of calcium because of some intolerance, calcium supplements may be in order, but not all calcium supplements are created equal. Calcium carbonate is best absorbed followed by calcium acetate and calcium lactate. Calcium citrate and calcium gluconate bring up the rear. Calcium carbonate is good but needs to be taken with food because it requires acid for proper absorption. Food will stimulate acid production. However, if you are taking calcium on an empty stomach, calcium citrate is best because it does not require as much acid for absorption. When taking supplements, read the labels to see the form of calcium contained in that supplement.

Day 322
All Our Provisions Come from Our God

The eyes of all look to You, and You give them their food in due time. You open Your hand and satisfy the desire of every living thing. (Psalm 145:15–16)

If you are following God's Word, then you are looking to Him to lead you and guide you in everything you do. You are also looking to Him for all of your provisions whether they are material, financial, health, food, etc. As you look to your God, you trust Him for all of your needs to be met. It would be good to pick up your Bible and read chapter 6 of Matthew, particularly verses 25 and 33. Jesus is speaking, and His teaching in this chapter is summed up with verses 33 and 34: "But seek first His Kingdom and His righteousness, and all these things will be added to you." He also talks about the Father providing for the birds of the air that do not sow, nor reap, nor gather into barns (Matthew 6:26). Every good thing comes from above, and God opens His hand and provides you with everything that you need. If there are still things that you want and do not have, it may be that you really do not need them but you just want them. If you had everything you wanted you may be so distracted that you would not be following God's Word and would not be dependent on Him. Resolve this day to seek first His righteousness and look for everything else that you need to come your way.

Thank You, Father, that You know my every need and You provide for all my needs. Sometimes I am too carried away with the things that I want and desires of my heart that I really do not need. I know Your scripture is true and correct when it says that if I seek first the Kingdom of God and His righteousness that everything I truly need will be provided for me. This involves faith on my part and trust in You. Help me to realize each day that my eyes need to be centered on Your Word and Your righteousness and not on my wants, needs, and desires. I resolve this day to concentrate more on seeking first Your Kingdom and Your righteousness. In Jesus's name, I pray. Amen.

Nutrition Thought for the Day.

Sources of calcium include dairy products, tofu, sardines with bones, shellfish, greens, broccoli, and legumes. Just because a table or chart may say a certain plant source is high in calcium, it does not mean that you are going to get a lot of the calcium from that source. If the plant is high in fiber, it could be high in phytates and oxalates also, and these can bind with the calcium and render it unavailable in the G.I. tract. Other foods typically do not contain calcium that producers are now adding calcium to make them more desirable. For example, you can find orange juice that has added calcium. Soymilk, which technically is not dairy, advertises that it has more calcium than cow's milk because of the added calcium. If you read labels, you will be able to find other foods that have calcium added.

WAYNE E. BILLON, PH.D., RDN, LDN

Day 323
Provision Brings Praise

"You will have plenty to eat and be satisfied and praise the name of the LORD your God, who has dealt wondrously with you." (Joel 2:26a)

In the verses before this one, God is telling Joel that in the last days man should not fear because God will hear and answer His people. Granted that this was the Jews Joel was talking to, but remember that we are grafted in by the blood of Jesus, and we are now part of God's people; that wall between us has been broken down by Jesus. Whatever is promised to the Jews is also promised to us as born-again believers. In this chapter, God tells them not to fear beasts of the field or any army that will come against them. He tells them that their threshing floors will be full of grain and their vats will overflow with new wine and oil. In verse 26 He tells them that they will have plenty to eat and be satisfied and they will praise the name of the Lord their God. Provision should bring praise. We all need to be aware that every good thing we have comes from our God and we should constantly be thanking Him for all He provides for us. We know that we should be thanking our God for our salvation and all that Jesus did for us by His life, death, and resurrection, but sometimes we forget or fail to realize that our family, our home, our job, our health, and every possession that we have is provision from our God. Sometimes it may seem that we do not have everything we want, but we should be thankful for that which we do have and constantly be giving praise to our God for His provision.

> Father God, I want to thank You today, not for just the big things in my life like salvation, but also the small things that often get overlooked. Everything that I have that is good comes from You. You know what my needs are before I even ask and Your timing to provide me with my needs is perfect. Even the small things in life You are concerned about and provide for me without me even realizing it or asking. Many times I take You for granted and do not thank You enough for all that You do. I now thank You for every good thing that I have and for all the small things that I take for granted. I do not ever want to take You for granted but want to give You praise in everything that I do. I thank You in the name of Jesus. Amen.

Nutrition Thought for the Day.

Phosphorus is the second most abundant mineral in the body (chemical symbol is P). Phosphorus is also necessary for the formation of strong bones. Many of the same elements that block calcium absorption also block phosphorus absorption in the intestines. These include phytates and oxalates and interference from other minerals that are in high concentration; an example is high concentrations of calcium will also block phosphorus absorption. The ideal ratio between calcium and phosphorus is a one-to-one ratio in the diet. Phosphorus is very important for the creation of a compound called ATP (adenosine triphosphate) which is the way energy is stored in the body.

Day 324
Be Satisfied and Praise the Lord

The afflicted will eat and be satisfied; those who seek Him will praise the LORD. Let your heart live forever! (Psalm 22:26)

This psalm says that even the afflicted will eat and be satisfied but afflicted may not be the best translation here since the Hebrew word that is used in this case can mean afflicted, but has several other meanings. The first choice, according to Strong's Concordance, is poor, then humble, then afflicted, then meek. The King James Version of the Bible says meek for this scripture. In actuality, the scripture probably means all of the possible meanings that include the poor, the humble, the afflicted, the meek and anyone that is low in spirit. The Lord's blessings do not stop there however because everyone, whether they are poor or afflicted, is blessed by the Lord. Just as today's scripture says, we are blessed. The blessing should result in praise to our God. Those who seek Him will also praise Him. The Scripture also says, "Let your heart live forever." All of us will live forever; it is just a question of where that forever will be—heaven or Hades. What the scripture would be implying is that by seeking our God, following His Word and praising Him would result in our heart living forever in His presence rather than separated from Him. Resolve today to be satisfied with what provisions you have been given by your God and to praise Him for everything that you have knowing that you will live forever in His presence.

Father God, I thank You for the provisions You have given me. I receive them from Your bounty and I choose to be satisfied with what I have. I know this does not mean that I should not ever ask for additional provisions, but I should be satisfied with what I have and look forward to what else You have for me. I also choose to thank You for the provisions I have and I will continue to seek Your face and praise You for who You are and what You are, not just for the things I have. I thank You in the name of Jesus. Amen.

Nutrition Thought for the Day.
Animal tissues are the best sources of phosphorus and include milk, eggs, fish, and poultry. In plants, legumes (beans and peas), nuts and seeds, cereal grains, and chocolate are fair to good sources. Another source of phosphorus that is a bad source is soft drinks. Soft drinks are high in phosphoric acid and this depletes calcium by causing it to come out of the bones. This can lead to osteoporosis and is strongly linked to this disease. This is one of the many reasons dietitians are against soft drinks. Our phosphorus requirement is around 700 mg for adult males and females, but more research is needed.

Day 325
Do not Despair but Put Your Hope in God

Why are you in despair, O my soul? And why have you become disturbed within me? Hope in God, for I shall yet praise Him, the help of my countenance and my God. (Psalm 42:11)

There are times when each of us goes through a dry place that leaves us discouraged. Understand that we do not have to go through a dry place if we can get to the point that we totally trust our God, but most of us have not yet reached that place of total dependence on our God. We hear people say they are on a mountaintop one day and in a valley the next. I understand what they are saying but we should not have mountaintop and valley days. Instead we should always be on the mountaintop or, worst-case scenario, we should be on a level plane and it should be an elevated plane. If you are not there do not come under condemnation but you can work on climbing the mountain and staying there. In the meantime if you find yourself in a valley, do not despair or get disturbed in your spirit. Put your hope in God and praise Him and He will lift your countenance. He will water your dry places with living water that will alleviate your thirst. Think on all the times your God has blessed you and think of all of the valleys He has lead you through. Encourage yourself with the remembrance of the good things in your past. Praise Him today for what you have and do not despair over what you do not have. God's timing is perfect and He will see you through any valley you encounter if you trust in Him.

Lord Jesus, I know You do not want me to be in a valley and despair, that is not in Your plans for me. You want me to be soaring like an eagle on the mountain tops at all times. My hope is in You Lord, and I trust You, but sometimes I get overwhelmed by the cares of the world and forget who I am in Christ and forget my place on the mountaintop. I know I can overcome the valleys and despair by praising You in every situation I find myself. The devil hates to see me praise You. If I resist him and stand firm in my faith, he has to flee as the Bible demands (James 4:7, "Submit therefore to God. Resist the devil, and he will flee from you"). I ask for Your Holy Spirit to remind me when I should be praising Your name and thus resist the devil. In Jesus's name, I pray. Amen.

Nutrition Thought for the Day.

Magnesium is another important mineral that is probably greatly overlooked in our diets (chemical symbol is Mg). Magnesium is also important for the mineralization of bones and teeth and is necessary as a cofactor for numerous enzymes. Magnesium is important in nerve transmissions and impulses and is important for a healthy immune system. Muscle contractions and proper muscle function depend on optimal levels of magnesium. A normal sinus rhythm, which is a normal heartbeat, is dependent on magnesium.

Day 326
Imitate What Is Good

Beloved, do not imitate what is evil, but what is good. The one who does good is of God; the one who does evil has not seen God. (3 John 1:11)

John wrote the letter 3 John to Gaius, a dear friend of his. He is encouraging his friend to be an imitator of what is good, for the one who is of God does good. One who imitates evil is evil and does not know God. Why this scripture for today? It is not that you are an imitator of evil, but with all of the worldly distractions and peer pressures we all face daily, you could easily end up trying to please someone because of peer pressure. It may not involve doing something seriously wrong but maybe just a small compromise. The next time it may be a larger compromise, and then a larger, and a larger until finally, you may realize that you have wandered off the path and are headed for a deep pit; and you may have damaged your witness. We all know this can happen subtlety and very slowly. The devil knows better than to come at us out of the blue and try to get us to commit some huge sin. No, he comes at us with small gradual shifts in our behavior until he can get us totally off course. Guard your heart and be aware of the slight compromises with which he may tempt you. Stay in Christian fellowship and be an imitator of God's Word.

Lord Jesus, I know that when I compromise Your Word, I am doing wrong, but the wiles of the devil may trick me into a compromise due to peer pressure without me ever realizing it until I am well off the path You would have me follow. I want to avoid such tricks at all cost. I never want to imitate evil, consciously or unconsciously. Instead, I want to be an imitator of You. If ever I wander off the straight and narrow path You have me on, by the power of Your Holy Spirit, guide me back to Your path. In Your name, Jesus, I pray. Amen.

Nutrition Thought for the Day.
Sources of magnesium include nuts and legumes, whole grains, leafy green vegetables, chocolate, cocoa, and seafood. Note that whole grains have been mentioned several times already and these are nutrients that dietitians encourage people to eat more abundantly. Another source of magnesium would be from hard water. Research has shown that people with good sources of magnesium in their diet are less prone to cardiovascular disease and sudden death than those with lower levels of magnesium in their diet.

Day 327
I Have the Robe of Righteousness

I will rejoice greatly in the LORD, my soul will exult in my God; for He has clothed me with garments of salvation, He has wrapped me with a robe of righteousness, as a bridegroom decks himself with a garland, and as a bride adorns herself with her jewels. (Isaiah 61:10)

Isaiah tells us that he rejoices greatly in the Lord and his soul will exult in his God. The reason being, God has clothed him with garments of salvation and has wrapped him with a robe of righteousness similar to a bridegroom and a bride that decks themselves out for their wedding. When you consider the salvation that you have as a result of Jesus's life, death, and resurrection and the robe of righteousness that you are covered with, all the physical needs previously mentioned pale by comparison. You have eternal life with Jesus Christ in a mansion in heaven where there will be no more pain, suffering, hunger, or financial needs. This is something to greatly rejoice about and to give praise and exalt your God. You are blessed to be able to practice your faith and praise your God freely while you look forward to spending eternity with Him in heaven. Give thanks and praise this day to your God for your salvation and for your robe of righteousness that you are covered with and be content as you walk through your day with the things that you have.

Father God, I thank You for sending Your Son to die for me an unworthy sinner. By accepting what Jesus did for me I am covered with a robe of righteousness, and when You look down you do not see me, but You see the robe of righteousness covering me. I have a mansion reserved for me in heaven after I leave this world because of what Jesus did for me. I exalt and praise You this day for all that I have through Jesus. Many times I get so hung up with my wants and my needs that I overlook who I am in Jesus and all that I have as a result of Him. Help me to be ever conscious of who I am in Christ and to be content with my salvation and my righteousness. I thank You in Jesus's name. Amen.

Nutrition Thought for the Day.

People who are on diuretics (pills that make you urinate more frequently) may need more magnesium in their diet because diuretics flush magnesium out of the body through the kidneys. People with high blood pressure and/or cardiovascular disease are frequently on diuretics and could be losing magnesium through their urine. Magnesium is necessary for both normal blood pressure and a normally functioning heart. Alcoholics tend to be deficient in magnesium because alcohol is a strong diuretic and flushes magnesium out of the body. People who take large doses of calcium as a supplement to prevent osteoporosis may also need more magnesium in the diet since the high calcium intake may prevent some magnesium from being absorbed.

Day 328
God Will Perfect the Work He Started in You

For I am confident of this very thing, that He who began a good work in you will perfect it until the day of Christ Jesus. (Philippians 1:6)

Paul is talking to the Philippians, and he is declaring that where they are in Christ is no accident, but it is due to a divine plan of the Father when he said, "He who began a good work in you." That work that He began in them when He granted them salvation is the same work He began in you when you were saved. The promise was for the Philippians but also for you. He started the work and He promises to perfect it but that does not mean that you can go and do whatever you want and not seek your Lord. It does mean that as long as you do seek your Lord, stay in His Word and fellowship, He will be there with you to guide you and see that His investment is completed when Jesus returns. Be encouraged today that your God has determined to perfect the good work that He started in you and had intended for you since the beginning of time. That is quite an awesome fact to meditate on when you may feel down.

Heavenly Father, You are worthy of all praise and honor and glory. I choose to rejoice in You this day and to give You praise and glory for all that You have done for me, including the good work that You started in me and that You intend to perfect in me. I know that I can do nothing without You and that You are my provider, my comforter, and my protector. I ask for Your Holy Spirit to remind me when I get off center and start looking away from the path that You have prepared for me. I choose to thank You and praise You this day and every day for not giving up on me. In Jesus's name, I pray. Amen.

Nutrition Thought for the Day.

The next mineral is iron (chemical symbol is Fe). Iron is considered a trace mineral or a micromineral, not because it is any less important but because there is just a trace of it in the body. All the minerals covered so far are needed in much larger quantities than iron. You have probably heard of iron deficiency anemia and know that iron is necessary for healthy red blood cells. The primary function of iron in the body is carrying oxygen to every cell and carrying carbon dioxide (CO_2), a waste product, from cells to the lungs for excretion.

WAYNE E. BILLON, PH.D., RDN, LDN

Day 329
Be at Peace and Avoid Envy

A tranquil heart is life to the body, but passion is rottenness to the bones. (Proverbs 14:30)

This scripture is really a story of the spiritual versus the physical. Let's break it down word for word. The New American Standard Bible (NASB) is the version quoted above, and it says, "a tranquil heart." The King James Version (KJV) says, "a sound heart." The actual Hebrew word according to Strong's Concordance means health or healing. The Hebrew word for heart does not refer to the physical blood pumping heart in our bodies, but it refers to the inner man, mind, will, and understanding. The NASB says, "passion is rottenness to the bones." The KJV says, "envy is rottenness to the bones." Strong's Concordance says that the Hebrew word really means jealousy passion, zeal, or sexual passion. So what this scripture is saying is that the healthy spirit of man is life to the body. If your spirit is in contact with God's spirit and is in unity with the Lord, then this will bring life to your body. However, if you are filled with envy and sexual passion then this is rottenness to the bones and will bring disease to the body. The bottom line is to worship God with spirit and with truth and believe what the scripture says so that your body will flourish as a result. Another good reason for going through your day with an attitude of worship and rejoicing in your spirit as you talk to your God.

Father God, I know that when I am in unity with You and Your Holy Spirit that I not only am able to hear from You, but I am also empowering myself to have a healthier body. I know that when I am not in unity with You and Your Holy Spirit, not only am I not able to hear You as I should, but I am also opening the door to the devil to distract me and I am decreasing my ability to walk in the healthy state that You have for me. I desire to be in unity with Your Holy Spirit and for my spirit to rejoice with You this day. I look forward to having a good day being blessed and being in unity with You. In Jesus's name, I pray. Amen.

Nutrition Thought for the Day.
Iron is different from the other minerals studied so far in that it has what is known as two different valence states. It is too complicated to explain in this short space, but it means that iron is available in two different forms. One is called the oxidized form and has a +3 valence, and the other is the reduced form and has a +2 valence. The reason why this is important to know is because iron is absorbed in the intestines in the +2 valence. Most of the iron ingested is in the +3 valence and thus needs to be reduced to the +2 valence to be made available to the body. How does that happen? That is tomorrow's discussion.

Day 330
Trust in the Lord and Be Fruitful

Blessed is the man who trusts in the LORD and whose trust is the LORD. For he will be like a tree planted by the water, that extends its roots by a stream and will not fear when the heat comes; but its leaves will be green, and it will not be anxious in a year of drought nor cease to yield fruit. (Jeremiah 17:7–8)

If the Lord is where our trust is, then we are blessed. We would be like a tree that is planted close to the water so that its roots can extend to the stream and receive constant moisture. If your roots are in God's Word, then they are receiving constant spiritual nourishment and biblical knowledge necessary for you to be watered with God's Spirit. You will not fear when heat comes, and that heat could be any kind of trial or temptation that comes your way, because you will be able to stay nourished through the heat by God's Word. As a tree's leaves under such circumstances would stay green, you would also stay healthy. If a tree had feelings it would not be anxious in a year of drought nor cease to yield fruit because of its connection with the water. If you have such a connection with God's Word, then you will not be anxious in a time of drought, and you will not cease to yield fruit. Drought for you would be anything that tries to cut off your nourishment but it will not be effective nor will it prevent you from bearing fruit for your God. As you go through today's life experiences, know that you are connected to your God, and you are receiving life through God's Word and His Holy Spirit.

Father God, thank You that You want me to stay connected with You and Your Holy Spirit and, by so doing, I will never find myself in a place of drought. I will never be anxious about the worldly cares and pressures that come against me constantly because I know I am connected to You and Your Word. It is my desire to always be able to bear fruit for You. Remind me by the power of Your Holy Spirit that I am connected to You, that I am a child of God, and I will walk in Your love this day in Jesus's name. Amen.

Nutrition Thought for the Day.

Acid reduces iron from the +3 valence to the +2 valence. Thus, the acid in your stomach helps to reduce iron so that it is available for absorption. An important factor to note here is that if something interferes with the acid production in your stomach, such as high intake of antacids or the medications available for reflux disease, then your acid production is reduced and, while this helps with reflux, it could contribute to iron deficiency. If you take an iron supplement, it is good to take it with something that is acidic such as orange juice or tomato juice. This will help to reduce the iron to the +2 valence and improve your iron absorption.

Day 331
Dwell in the Shadow of the Almighty

He who dwells in the shelter of the Most High will abide in the shadow of the Almighty. (Psalm 91:1)

If you dwell in the shelter of the Most High you will abide in the shadow of the Almighty. You dwell in the shelter of your God by staying in His Word and seeking Him continuously with all of your heart. There is fruit that is produced when you can accomplish that and the fruit includes you abiding or staying in the shadow of the Almighty. God's shadow covers you when you stand on His Word. Strong's Concordance says that the Hebrew meaning for shadow is shade. It is cooler in the shade and you are protected from the harmful rays of the sun. Similarly, God's shadow protects you from harm as well as giving you a hiding place. How can this be? You may ask because you know that you are seeking God, but sometimes you do not feel like you are protected or being hidden from harm. Yes, life happens to all of us and there are times when you have to face trials and difficulties. However, if you abide in God's Word, then He will cover you and, even though you go through the trials, you will come out on the other side a better person and closer to your God. Whatever happens today, trust in Him and He will be there for you.

Thank You, Father, that Your shadow covers me wherever I go when I trust in You. Your shadow will provide a place of refuge for me and will provide peace for me. I desire to be in Your shelter at all times. The second verse of Psalm 91 says, "You are my refuge and my fortress, my God in whom I trust!" I receive this scripture for my own life and declare that today, I will abide in Your Word and declare that You are my refuge and my fortress and I trust in nothing other than You. I declare this in the name of Jesus. Amen.

Nutrition Thought for the Day.

Too much iron in the diet can be harmful. Sometimes people with good intentions who try to eat healthily will take an extra dose of vitamin C because they think that is good and they may also take an iron supplement. If too much of both are ingested, it could cause more iron to be absorbed than you need. If you add to that a diet that has adequate or high levels of iron, you could be putting yourself at risk for iron toxicity. Excessive iron in the body could act as a pro-oxidant. That means it can cause free radical damage like the free radicals previously discussed and could possibly contribute to atherosclerosis. More research is needed in this area. Just do not overdo it but take in the requirements.

Day 332
Our God's Promises Are Yes and Amen

The Lord will rescue me from every evil deed, and will bring me safely to His heavenly kingdom; to Him *be* the glory forever and ever. Amen. (2 Timothy 4:18)

"Amen" at the end of a statement, according to Strong's Concordance, means so it is, so be it, may it be fulfilled. There was a practice followed in the synagogues during Jesus's times that carried over into the Christian assemblies after Jesus's resurrection, and that practice was that when someone read from the Scriptures, gave a discourse, or offered a prayer up to God, the others present would respond with Amen. This meant that they agreed with what was read, said, or prayed about as if they said it. So when someone praises Him, or makes a statement and the response is "Amen," that means, "Yes I agree with the statement you just made and I make the same statement with you," or it can mean "let it be so."

In today's scripture, Paul says that the Lord will rescue him from every evil deed and will bring him safely to His heavenly Kingdom. Where Paul says *me* in the scripture, you can put in your name for the Lord will rescue you also. For this Paul praises God and gives Him glory forever. He ends his declaration with Amen and is thus saying let it be so. After reading this scripture, it would be good if you also said Amen, declaring that you agree with it. As many as the promises of God—that is all the promises that you can find in God's Word—they all are in Him yes and Amen. It is saying that God's promises are real, that as born-again Christians we believe in His promises, and if we say Amen we are declaring that those promises are something we receive for ourselves. There are many promises in God's Word and they are all for you so today say Amen to everything that you read in God's Word and rest assured that they are real for you.

Father, I know that there are numerous promises in Your Word and I understand that they are all intended to be for me. I receive Your promises as if they had my name on them spelled out in Your Word. I declare that I say yes and Amen to every promise in Your Word and I receive them today for myself. Your Word is true and is for all believers, and that includes me. I make this declaration in the name of Jesus. Amen.

Nutrition Thought for the Day.

Remember that iron is fortified in all processed grains. This includes all breads, cereals, pasta, flour and, of course, anything that is made with these products. This even includes corn chips, cookies, pastries, etc. Iron is also found in both plants and animals, but the +3 valence (as found in plants) is not absorbed as well as the +2 valence (found in animal tissue). Thus all meat is a good source of iron from the standpoint of its content and valence state. Dairy products are not a source of iron. In poultry the dark meat is a better source than the white meat (the dark meat is darker because of the higher blood content which is rich in iron).

DAY 333
Not by Power or Might

Then he said to me, "This is the word of the LORD to Zerubbabel saying, 'Not by might nor by power, but by My Spirit,' says the LORD of hosts." (Zechariah 4:6)

You may have heard this read many times and may have quoted it yourself. So many times we try to do things by our own power and with our own strength, and it frequently gets us into trouble. Philippians 4:13 says that I can do all things through Christ who strengthens me, and I believe that scripture but if I try to do it in my own power, I am not able to. I have to accomplish it by God's power working through me. Even the miracles that Jesus did were done by the power of the Holy Spirit working through Him (Acts 10:38). That being true, who are we to think that we can do the works of Jesus by our own power? Everything that we accomplish, no matter how small or how big, we need to ask our God to give us the strength and ability to complete each task. Without Him, we can do nothing! We need to rely on His strength and power in everything we do every day, even your healthy lifestyle regimen.

Lord Jesus, it is really good news for me to know that I do not have to rely on my own power to get things done. I know that on my own I am weak, but when I am weak I am strong in You. It is not by my power that I can accomplish anything but by Your Spirit. I acknowledge my reliance on You today, and I declare that I ask for the Holy Spirit to give me the power and strength to accomplish everything that I set out to do this day. I also ask for the Holy Spirit to give me the wisdom to know what tasks He would have me take on and what tasks He would have me avoid. I ask for this in Jesus's name. Amen.

Nutrition Thought for the Day.

There are a number of things that will inhibit iron absorption besides the wrong valence and having an insufficient amount of stomach acid. An imbalance of minerals in the diet will affect iron absorption. An example would be if copper or zinc intake was very high, iron absorption would be affected. Excessive calcium, phosphorus, and manganese can also decrease iron absorption. Polyphenols (such as tannin in tea and coffee) decrease iron absorption. Sometimes you can find food additives listed on the label that includes EDTA. This is known as a chelating agent and chelating agents will also decrease iron absorption.

Day 334
We Are Blameless before Him

Blessed *be* the God and Father of our Lord Jesus Christ, who has blessed us with every spiritual blessing in the heavenly *places* in Christ, just as He chose us in Him before the foundation of the world, that we would be holy and blameless before Him. In love He predestined us to adoption as sons through Jesus Christ to Himself, according to the kind intention of His will. (Ephesians 1:3–5)

This says that we have already been blessed with every spiritual blessing in the heavenly places in Christ. We could talk a long time on just that—most of us have to come to the full realization of who we are in Christ and that we have every spiritual blessing that we need. It also says that He chose us before the foundation of the world. Our Father God knew that He would send His only Son into the world to die for us so that by His death we may be made holy and blameless before Him. This is another awesome part of this scripture that we could spend a lot of time discussing. We have been made holy and blameless before God our Father. How awesome is that! I know that we (me too) do not always feel like we are blameless and holy. That is because on our own power or by our own merit we are not. It is only through what Jesus did for us that we can make this claim, and it is not even us who make the claim, but it is the Holy Spirit Himself since He inspired the writing of the scripture. To get this fact into your spirit, you need to read this scripture over and over several times and look at it as often as you can. Profess each day who you are in Christ, not based on your merit, but on what Jesus did for you. The more you can get this realization into your spirit, the more you will be able to bear fruit in His name and be successful in your lifestyle changes.

Father God, there is no way I can thank You enough for what You have declared for me in today's scripture. I have every spiritual blessing that I need, and I am holy and blameless in Your sight. I do not always feel that way, but I believe it, and I receive it because Your Word says it. As discussed a couple of days ago, I say yes and amen to this promise that is in Your Word. I make an act of my will today to remind myself as often as I can of who I am in Christ—that is someone who has every spiritual blessing and is holy and blameless in the sight of my God because of what Jesus did for me. I make this declaration in the name of Jesus. Amen.

Nutrition Thought for the Day.
Just as plants will interfere with the absorption of some of the other minerals, the fiber in plants (oxalates and phytates) also interfere with iron absorption. Oxalic acid is high in spinach, berries, tea, and chocolate. Phytates are high in corn and whole grains. Oddly enough, many of these are foods that we say are good for us and we should eat more of them but yet they can hinder iron absorption. That does not mean we eat less of these foods, but we make sure that we are getting more of the foods that contain iron. This is another good reason for fortifying processed grains with iron.

Day 335
Cast All Your Care on Him

Therefore humble yourselves under the mighty hand of God, that He may exalt you at the proper time, casting all your anxiety on Him, because He cares for you. (1 Peter 5:6–7)

Many years ago in my early days as a Christian, someone gave me this scripture to live by, and it really helped me through years of anxiety. Humble yourself before your God by giving Him the praise and honor that is due Him in return for what He did for you through His Son, Jesus Christ. Acknowledge who you are in relationship to your God, that is He is your Creator, your Redeemer, your Savior, your Protector, and I could go on and on. If you do this, in due time it is true that He will exalt you but do not honor your God so that you will be exalted. I honor Him because of who He is, and I would be glad to honor Him if I received nothing in return. One way you can humble yourself before your God is to cast all your anxiety on Him as the scripture says because He cares for you. How does this cause you to humble yourself before Him? By placing all your anxieties at the foot of the cross you are saying, "I cannot overcome all the anxieties that come against me, but You can and have already done so by Your life, death, and resurrection. Therefore I give all my anxieties to You knowing that You will bear this burden for me." After you make such a statement you must be sure that you leave your anxieties at the foot of the cross—do not take them back. Leave them there and walk away in peace, the peace that surpasses all understanding. Any anxiety that you have about losing weight, gaining weight, or just getting healthier is certainly something you want to lay at the foot of the cross. God wants you to be healthy, and He wants to take that anxiety from you. Give it to Him and do not take it back.

I thank You, Father, and my Lord Jesus that I can give You all my anxieties and You will gladly take them from me. I thank You that You love me that much and I know that as I humble myself before You that You will exalt me in due time. However, even if You never exalt me, I still want to humble myself before You. I acknowledge that the weight of the world is too much for me to carry but You Lord Jesus have already overcome the world and I give the burdens of the world to You. I make this declaration in Your name, Jesus. Amen.

Nutrition Thought for the Day.

True vegans need to be concerned about iron deficiency anemia. The most available and best iron is that which is found in the flesh of animals. The high fiber content that a vegan would be eating is healthy on the one hand but can hinder the absorption of iron that is found in those foods. This sets up the vegan for iron deficiency anemia, and an iron supplement would be in order. Most of the iron in our bodies is recycled. When a red blood cell dies, the iron is removed and recycled to other cells. We do lose a minimal amount of iron in feces and a very trace amount in perspiration. When we bleed we are losing red blood cells so obviously we lose iron also. This is why females, prior to menopause, have a higher iron requirement than males because of the monthly bleeding. Red blood cells live about 120 days and die.

Day 336
God Will Not Forsake You

"The LORD is the one who goes ahead of you; He will be with you. He will not fail you or forsake you. Do not fear or be dismayed." (Deuteronomy 31:8)

Wherever you go, the Lord has already been there before you preparing the way. This is true whether you see it or not or you believe it or not because God's Word says it. He will always be with you and will never fail you nor forsake you. You may not always feel His presence, but rest assured that He will not leave you. From a worldly standpoint there may be all kinds of reasons why you should be fearful, but from an godly perspective you have no reason to be in fear or to be dismayed. When anxious thoughts or fear of any kind starts to come at you, do not give them a chance to get a foothold in your mind. Do not entertain them but instead immediately lay them at the foot of the cross. Remember that fear is not of God but is of the devil, and if you experience a fearful or anxious thought, you know that it did not come from your God but from the evil one. Knowing that it is from the devil, you should also know that if you resist, it cannot affect you or stay in your mind. This of course includes any fearful thoughts about not being successful with your healthy lifestyle program.

Father God, Lord Jesus, I know that thoughts of fear and anxiety are not from You. I know they are from the evil one and I refuse to listen to them or to be affected by them. I lay them at the foot of Your cross, Jesus and I give them to You as Your Word commands me to do. They are Yours now and I do not have to deal with them any longer. You have already conquered them, and I do not have to do what has already been done by You. I know that You will never fail me and will always be with me. I do not have anything to fear or that can cause me to be dismayed. I believe Your Scripture and I receive it. In Jesus's name, I make this resolution. Amen.

Nutrition Thought for the Day.

Another function of iron is in the production of energy in the mitochondria (sometimes called the power pack of the cell because it is where energy is produced) of cells. Our iron requirement is 10 mg per day for males and 15 mg per day for females prior to menopause. Post menopause, the female's requirement goes down to 10 mg per day. A final note about iron, cooking in iron skillets can provide a small amount of iron in the diet, particularly if you are cooking something that is acidic in the skillet such as tomato sauce.

Day 337
You Do Not Have a Spirit of Fear

For God has not given us a spirit of timidity, but of power and love and discipline. (2 Timothy 1:7)

To live your life in tune with the theme of the last two days, you should memorize this scripture. It is an excellent scripture to repeat to yourself several times a day. The NASB says that God has not given us a spirit of timidity. Some versions say that God has not given us a spirit of fear. If you look up the Greek word used here for timidity in Strong's Concordance, you will find that it means *timidity, fearfulness, or cowardice*. Any version that uses one of these three words is correct, and the bottom line is that everything that has to do with fear or intimidation, or causing you to be a coward would not have been given to you by your God. It comes from the devil and is trying to get you to believe that you cannot accomplish those things God has called you to accomplish.

Instead of such a spirit, you have been given a spirit of power, love, and discipline. Some versions say power, love, and a sound mind. Both are correct, a disciplined mind is a sound mind, or a sound mind is a disciplined mind. This is God's gift to you, that of power, love, and the ability to be able to discipline yourself and control your mind. When thoughts come that causes fear or any kind of temptation, stand your ground and do not give in. Thoughts do not have authority over you but you have authority over them. One area that the devil may see as a weakness for you at this time is the fact that you are trying to develop a healthy lifestyle. You may receive thoughts of discouragement that say you will never be able to reach your goal, that you will stay overweight/underweight for the rest of your life. Do not give into such thoughts. You are a world overcomer and a conqueror. Even if you have only lost a fraction of what you wanted to lose, or only gained slightly, you have still made a positive change, and if you continue with your program, you will accomplish even more. Stand firm in your thought life and do not give into anxious thoughts.

Thank You, Father, that You have not given me a spirit of fear or cowardice but You have given me a spirit of love, power, and a sound and disciplined mind. Thank You that I do not have to listen to the devil's lies and I do not have to be intimidated by him. I know that I am a world overcomer and more than a conqueror because the Word says I am. By the power of the Holy Spirit in my life, I choose to exercise the right and the power that You have given me, and I take authority over any demonic thought that comes my way. I declare this in the name of Jesus. Amen.

Nutrition Thought for the Day.

The next mineral is zinc (chemical symbol is Zn). Zinc is found in meats, shellfish (particularly oysters), liver, grains, cereals, and legumes. The same substances that inhibit iron absorption also inhibit zinc absorption such as high-fiber, phytates, and oxalates. An imbalance of other minerals in the diet will also affect zinc absorption; examples include excessive iron and copper in the diet. Zinc is necessary as a cofactor for at least seventy and perhaps over two hundred enzymes, most of which are not related.

Day 338
Do Not Let Your Heart Be Troubled

"Do not let your heart be troubled; believe in God, believe also in Me." (John 14:1)

Here is an additional promise that deals with being anxious. Remember that John 14, of the Gospel of John, took place on the night of the Last Supper. Jesus was trying to prepare His apostles for what was about to happen later that night and the next day. Even though He told them several times that He was to suffer and be crucified, it did not sink in. They knew He was the Messiah and they were expecting Him to lead an uprising and take over the world. They did not realize that the Kingdom the Messiah was going to lead them to was in another world, in another life. The point here is that Jesus knew how fearful the events of the night would be for them, yet He told them not to let their hearts be troubled. He told them to believe in God (He was talking about His Father) and to also believe in Him. Jesus will never tell us to do something that is impossible for us to do. If He gives us a command, it is because He knows we can carry out that command by the power of the Holy Spirit in our lives. The command He gave to them that night is still prevalent for us today. Thus, no matter what you are going through now, or what you will go through in the future, do not let your heart be troubled; believe in God your Father and also believe in Jesus. His Word never changes and is always appropriate.

It seems like every day there is some new crisis in my life that I have to overcome. I have numerous opportunities to be anxious. I know Your Word tells me not let my heart be troubled and instead trust in You, Father, and in You, Jesus. I do trust in each of You, but sometimes it seems like my anxieties managed to get a hold of me. By the power of Your Holy Spirit, I ask that You remind me of this scripture whenever anxieties come my way. I resolve today not to let my heart be troubled but instead to trust in You. I make this resolution in Jesus's name. Amen.

Nutrition Thought for the Day.
Some examples of concentrations of zinc in foods are as follows: 1 cup of yogurt has about 2.2 mg; ½ cup of peas has about 1.0 mg; ½ cup of cooked black beans has about 1.0 mg; crabmeat has about 3.6 mg per 3 ounces; sirloin steak has about 5.5 mg per 3 ounces, and finally oysters have about 154 mg per 3 ounces. So you can see that in plants the concentration is low, slightly higher in some dairy, higher in meat, still higher in seafood—especially oysters.

WAYNE E. BILLON, PH.D., RDN, LDN

Day 339
Count Your Blessings

"Only fear the LORD and serve Him in truth with all your heart; for consider what great things He has done for you." (1 Samuel 12:24)

When the going gets tough because of fear, anxiety, doubt or whatever else tries to fill your mind, remember the things that God has done for you in the past. All of us have made accomplishments that would not have been possible without the power of the Holy Spirit in our lives. We have received financial help, healings, material rewards, or all of the above and numerous other things. Every good gift comes from above, and everything that we have received that is good comes from our God. Nothing is too big or too small for our God to accomplish. Do not ever put your God in a box and think that the task you are facing today is much too great for your God to deal with. Some great things to remember that He has done is the creation of the world, your very existence, and perhaps the most important your salvation through the merits of His Son, Jesus Christ. Do not ever think anything is too much for your God or too small to ask of your God. Your healthy lifestyle program is an opportunity for the devil to come against you and try to discourage you. Do not give in to his lies but think of the truths that your God has told you instead. Always serve Him with truth in your heart and remember the things He has done for you.

Father, there are times when it looks like I will not be able to succeed in many of the things that I am trying to accomplish, including my new healthy lifestyle plan. However, as I think of past accomplishments that I have completed, not on my own power but on the power of the Holy Spirit working through me, I have to be amazed I give You the praise, honor, and glory for all accomplishments that I have. All good things that I have come from You. Help me to remember the blessings that I have already received and to know that nothing is too big or too small for You. I thank You for all I have in Jesus's name. Amen.

Nutrition Thought for the Day.
Some of the symptoms of zinc deficiency include growth retardation, inhibited sexual maturation in males, decreased taste and digestive function, and impaired immune response. None of these are directly related other than the fact that enzymes that are responsible for proper metabolism of all of these functions and to prevent these deficiency symptoms, while vastly different from each other, all require zinc as a cofactor. Additional deficiency symptoms include delayed wound healing, disruption of the thyroid function and metabolic rate, ill effects of vitamin A function, and others. When a mineral is part of so many different enzyme systems, many different deficiency symptoms will result.

Day 340
Avoid Selfishness

Do nothing from selfishness or empty conceit, but with humility of mind regard one another as more important than yourselves; do not *merely* look out for your own personal interests, but also for the interests of others. (Philippians 2:3–4)

In chapter 2 of Paul's letter to the Philippians he is encouraging them to be Christ-like and is giving them some characteristics to follow. Here he tells them to do nothing from selfishness or empty conceit but with humility regard one another as more important than yourself. That may be difficult to do at times. He tells them not to just look out for their own personal interest but to also look out for the interest of others. Why is he telling them this? This is the commandment Jesus gave to us in the New Testament when He said to love your neighbor as yourself (Matthew 22:39). If you are to follow God's Word as you follow Him, then you need to work on following this scripture. The closer we get to the Lord, the closer He will get to us. We can get close to Him by obeying His Word. This pleases Him. The closer we get to Him and the more we please Him, the better we can hear the Holy Spirit leading us. Examine your world and see who is in your circle of influence (family, friends, co-workers, church members) that you may not have been treating with love. Have you shown yourself to be selfish to any of them? If so, make an attempt today to regard them more highly. Remember that Jesus died for them just as He did for you and He loves them just as He loves you.

Lord Jesus, You have compassion for me and for everyone around me. I do not always see those who I have contact with through the same eyes that You see them. I do not always treat others as being more important than myself. Help me to humble myself more and be compassionate to those that I have to live with and work with every day. If I start to be selfish with anyone, I ask for the Holy Spirit to point out what I am doing wrong and guide me on the right path. I ask in Your name, Jesus. Amen.

Nutrition Thought for the Day.

One of the deficiency symptoms mentioned was an impairment of the immune response. Zinc is necessary for a healthy immune system, but if you have all the zinc in your body that you need, additional zinc will not make your immune system any better. In fact, too much zinc can be toxic. If you ever took some of the lozenges on the market that claim to reduce the length and severity of a cold, the claim is due to the zinc that is added to the lozenges. Zinc can help in this respect but be careful in that the lozenges usually contain around 15 mg of zinc. The zinc requirement for males is 15 mg per day and for females is 12 mg per day. You can see how you could build up an excess rather rapidly, especially if you are taking in a diet that is adequate to high in zinc and perhaps a multivitamin/mineral mix that contains your daily requirement for zinc.

WAYNE E. BILLON, PH.D., RDN, LDN

Day 341
Fear of the Lord Is the Beginning of Wisdom

The fear of the LORD is the beginning of wisdom; a good understanding have all those who do *His commandments;* His praise endures forever. (Psalm 111:10)

In James 1:5, it says that if we want wisdom we can ask for it and our God, who gives to all generously and without reproach, will give it to us. The reason why we want to ask for wisdom is not so that we will know how to win a lottery or accomplish something that would be for our good only, but we ask for wisdom so that we can use it for the advancement of God's Kingdom. This scripture tells us that another way to obtain wisdom is to have a fear of the Lord, that is an awesome respect and reverence for our God. As a result of that respect for our God, we will want to keep His commandments and do what pleases Him. Yes, we will fail from time to time, but we must continue with endurance to fight the good fight and do all that we can to keep His commandments. That will result in the beginning of wisdom and will give us a good understanding. Wisdom is a blessing, and we certainly need wisdom and should ask for it, but we also need to have an understanding as to how to use that wisdom for the glory of God and advancement of His Kingdom. Seek God with all your heart today, ask for wisdom as it says in the book of James, and then look forward to that general guidance that you will receive as a fruit of your efforts.

Father, I ask You for wisdom so that I may be able to be a wise person for Your glory and not just for my ego. I also ask for the understanding that goes with wisdom to be able to know how to use my knowledge of Your Word for Your glory and the advancement of Your Kingdom. I know that if I have reverence for Your name that will also bring about the beginning of wisdom in my life. Father, I revere Your name and ask for the Holy Spirit to guide me if I ever move in the direction that brings discredit to Your name instead of praise. I ask this in the name of Jesus. Amen.

Nutrition Thought for the Day.

Copper (chemical symbol is Cu) is another important trace mineral, but there is not as much to talk about copper as with some of the other trace minerals. Sources of copper are somewhat similar to that of zinc. Liver has one of the highest concentrations (about 4.48 mg per 100 g of liver) with oysters being next (approximately 4.40 mg per 100 g). It goes down from there with vegetables and beef being much lower; beef is in about the same range as vegetables. White bread has about 0.13 mg per 100 g. The variations in the concentrations of minerals in food illustrate another reason why we should have a variety of foods in our diet. The greater the variety of foods, the less chance we have of obtaining a deficiency of anything.

Day 342
Fear of the Lord Is the Beginning of Wisdom II

He will bless those who fear the LORD, the small together with the great.
(Psalm 115:13)

The Lord will bless those who fear His name – who give honor and glory to His name. The name of our Lord is elevated above all the earth. There is no name greater than His name, and we should constantly be revering and elevating the name of the Lord. No matter how lowly we may be on earth or how kingly or wealthy we may be, our call as created beings by our mighty God is to give Him praise, honor, and glory and revere His name. There is no name on heaven and earth above His name. I resolve this day to honor my God in everything that I do no matter how small or how great and I further resolve to give Him praise from my lips, from my thought life, and from every action that I do. I am participating in my healthy lifestyle regimen so that I can be healthy for the praise of my God. I give my God praise for any progress made in my program, and I want to improve my health and stamina so that I will have a greater ability to be a blessing to my God.

Father, it is obvious that I want to lose weight and get in shape so that I can be healthy for my own good and the good of my family, but also for a greater good. And that greater good is so that I will have more stamina and endurance to be able to do more for the advancement of Your Kingdom here on earth. I know that the progress I have made so far is because of Your guidance and wisdom that You have given me. I give honor, praise, and glory back to You for my progress and I revere Your name for all that You have done for me. I thank You in the name of Jesus. Amen.

Nutrition Thought for the Day.

Factors affecting absorption are similar to those of the metals just mentioned. Phytates and fiber, in general, will interfere with copper absorption. High intakes of other minerals will also interfere with copper absorption such as zinc, iron, calcium, and phosphorus. Things that help copper absorption include acid type foods and vitamin C (vitamin C is ascorbic acid). Also, various specific amino acids in the diet help copper absorption which points to the importance of high-quality protein in the diet (meat).

Day 343
You Have the Lord's Favor

The LORD favors those who fear Him, those who wait for His lovingkindness. (Psalm 147:11)

The Lord loves us all, but this scripture says that He favors those who fear Him. The KJV says, "The Lord taketh pleasure in them that fear him, in those that hope in his mercy." According to Strong's Concordance, the word used here for *favors* or *taketh pleasure* means *to be pleased with, be favorable to,* or *to accept.* You can see that each of the versions is correct to a point. For the second half of the scripture the NASB says, "those who wait for His lovingkindness" while the KJV says, "hope in his mercy." Strong's Concordance says that the word for hope means *to wait, to hope,* or *to expect.* The word for mercy is *goodness, kindness,* or *faithfulness.* It is interesting how the different versions vary in their interpretations but still have basically the same meaning. Yes, God loves us all but God does have emotions and He is pleased with us when we revere His name and obey His precepts. We wait with expectations (hope) for His mercy or lovingkindness. If you want to be in the greatest place to receive His mercy or lovingkindness (whichever you choose to call it), then show Him homage and praise. Spend this day praising and revering your God in all you do today.

Father, I know that You love all of us, even those that have not yet received Jesus as their Savior and Lord, but You are obviously pleased when we do accept Your Son for what He did for us. You are also pleased when we revere Your name. I want to please You this day, and I choose, by an act of my will, to revere Your name and praise You for what You have done for me but also just for who You are. In Jesus's name, I pray. Amen.

Nutrition Thought for the Day.

Another source of copper that is similar to that of iron is cooking in copper pots. Probably more people cook in pots that have copper bottoms then iron bottoms. Cooking acid foods in these containers can release some copper into the diet. Another strange source is copper pipes that we use for transporting water through our homes. If the water running through your pipes is acidic, then this would release more copper into the water with which you drink or cook. Normally this is not a problem, but it could be if you take in excess of copper through your diet and supplements. Copper is not claimed to be any miracle mineral that will cure a long list of diseases, so most people do not take in copper supplements.

Day 344
Your Father God Loves You As He Does Jesus

"I do not ask on behalf of these alone, but for those also who believe in Me through their word; that they may all be one; even as You, Father, *are* in Me and I in You, that they also may be in Us, so that the world may believe that You sent Me. The glory which You have given Me I have given to them, that they may be one, just as We are one; I in them and You in Me, that they may be perfected in unity, so that the world may know that You sent Me, and loved them, even as You have loved Me." (John 17:20–23)

This is a long quote, but it is one of the most awesome scriptures in the Bible. In chapter 17 of the Gospel of John, Jesus is preparing for His passion and is praying to His Father. He prays for Himself, His disciples, and us. In verse 19 He finishes praying for His disciples, and in verse 20 He starts praying for us, "all those who believe in Me through their word. The word *their* in this scripture is the disciples and *all those who believe in Him* are all born-again believers. All the glory that the Father gave to Jesus has been given to us so that we can be one with Jesus and the Father. If that is not awesome enough, there is more! Jesus prays that we be perfected in unity so that the world will know that our Father God loves us as much as He loves Jesus. This is so incredible that God the Father loves you as much as He loves Jesus. That ought to build you up to new heights today. Walk through your day with your head held high knowing that you are loved by your God as much as He loves Jesus!

Father, Your Word is so awesome it is sometimes hard to fathom. I know Your Word says that I am a joint heir with Jesus (Romans 8:16–17, Galatians 4:7) but saying it in the manner that it is stated in today's scripture—that You love me as much as You love Jesus—is incredibly awesome. I cannot do anything to deserve Your love, but it is given unconditionally by Your grace. I thank You, Father, in Jesus's name. Amen.

Nutrition Thought for the Day.

The function of copper in the body is also as a cofactor for many important enzyme systems. Copper itself is not an antioxidant, but it is necessary as a cofactor for an enzyme that is an extremely important antioxidant. Copper is important in the metabolism of iron too. A deficiency of copper can produce an anemia similar to the anemia produced from iron deficiency, but this is relatively rare. Copper, even though it is needed in small amounts, is also necessary for a healthy immune function, normal bone formation, and normal cardiovascular and pulmonary functions.

Day 345
Fools Do Not Fear God

But it will not be well for the evil man and he will not lengthen his days like a shadow, because he does not fear God. (Ecclesiastes 8:13)

Most of the devotions have been concerned with you as one that is righteous because you accepted Jesus as your Savior and Lord. This scripture points out the other side of the coin, those who have not received Jesus Christ as their Savior and Lord are unrighteous. The righteous will receive favor from God, but the unrighteous will not receive such favor. They will not have their days lengthened or have the Lord walking before them in whatever they do. God still loves them, and when He looks down upon them from heaven, He sees someone that Jesus died for but He does not see them covered with the robe of righteousness. That is reserved only for believers, children of God, and that is what you are. You were saved because you heeded to the call of the Holy Spirit on your life and you are therefore the righteousness of Christ. Be thankful for the Holy Spirit for calling you. Now avoid evil and walk in that righteousness. Be blessed this day knowing your inheritance that is yet to come.

Father, I thank You that I am covered with the robe of righteousness because of what Jesus did for me. You will never leave me nor forsake me, and when You look down from Your throne in heaven, You do not see me, but You see the robe that covers me because I have received what Jesus did for me on the cross. Help me to see nonbelievers as You see them and that is as someone for whom Jesus died. By the power of Your Holy Spirit help me to be a witness to them so that they may also be covered with the robe of righteousness. In Jesus's name, I pray. Amen.

Nutrition Thought for the Day.

The next trace mineral is selenium (chemical symbol is Se). Selenium is different from most other minerals in that it is an antioxidant, and a strong one at that. It was mentioned when we talked about vitamin E because selenium and vitamin E work synergistically together to be more potent antioxidants than either one by themselves. Selenium plays a number of roles in the body as an antioxidant and is important in many enzyme systems. Like copper, one of the enzymes selenium is necessary for is an extremely potent antioxidant.

Day 346
The Lord Will Uphold You

'Do not fear, for I am with you; do not anxiously look about you, for I am your God. I will strengthen you, surely I will help you, surely I will uphold you with My righteous right hand.' (Isaiah 41:10)

This reiterates the fact that you should not be fearful or anxious. When God says something in His Word over and over again it is not because He has a poor memory. It is another promise that He wants to get it into your head and your heart—do not be fearful or anxious. In this scripture, He tells you not to fear because He is with you. He even says that you should not anxiously look about. He does not want you to be in fear or to be anxious about anything that is going on around you. At the time of this writing many things are going on in the world that could cause fear and anxiety. If ever there was a need for assurance from God that we should not be fearful or anxious, it is today. In this scripture He reminds you that He is your God and you should have no other gods before Him. Then He tells you that He will strengthen you, will help you, and will uphold you. Three things in one sentence that He promises to do for you that all refer to your safety and freedom from anxiety. This should be a very comforting scripture for you as you go through your day today. Keep in mind that fear and anxiety are not from your God but are from the evil one, the world, or even your own imagination. Do not succumb to fear or anxiety but trust in your God who is with you. You may be fearful that you will not be able to reach the healthy goals you set for yourself but do not give into that fear. Continue to work hard and look to your God, and you will be okay.

Fear and anxiety are ever present in the world around me. Wars and rumors of wars are abundant. Critical elections for one thing or another are always taking place, and the future safety of our country may be uncertain. Gun violence is overwhelming worldwide. Radicalized terrorist are causing havoc worldwide. Economic unrest is increasing. Can all these events produce fear and anxiety in my life? Yes, they can, but I know that You, Father, do not want me to be fearful or anxious. I know that you will strengthen me, help me, and uphold me through any crisis and I ask for Your help this day, Father, in the name of Jesus. Amen.

Nutrition Thought for the Day.

Selenium is found in a variety of foods but the concentration of selenium in food and water strongly depends on the concentration of selenium in the soil. Also, some plants are selenium accumulators in that the plant will concentrate large amounts of selenium from the soil while other plants may not absorb very much selenium from the same soil. Eating a variety of foods from a variety of places is another important factor for this mineral.

WAYNE E. BILLON, PH.D., RDN, LDN

Day 347
The Lord Will Uphold You II

He saved us, not on the basis of deeds which we have done in righteousness, but according to His mercy, by the washing of regeneration and renewing by the Holy Spirit. (Titus 3:5)

The fear and anxiety should have already been taken care of because you have already been saved by the blood of Jesus. He saved you not based on your righteousness, but He saved you according to His mercy by the washing of regeneration which is the new birth you experienced when you became born again. The washing was done by the blood of Jesus shed on the cross for you. You were then renewed by the power of the Holy Spirit who remains with you to guide you and lead you. Titus is telling these facts to a group of folks that lived much closer to the time of Jesus than you did but they still needed to be encouraged. Titus' words are still being used to encourage people today as they remind you that you are saved by the mercy of Jesus and the renewing of the Holy Spirit. You do not have to keep asking Jesus to forgive you for your sins after you have confessed them once and received salvation, but it would be good to ask the Holy Spirit to continue to renew you and fill you each day afresh and anew. Ask for the Holy Spirit's guidance this day and ask Him to constantly be renewing your mind as to who you are in Christ.

Thank You, Jesus, that by Your mercy I have my salvation. Thank You that I have been washed by Your blood and no sin can be found in me because of Your righteousness, and I do not have to depend on my righteousness to save me because I could never be that righteous. Thank You that I have been renewed by the power of the Holy Spirit and I ask for the Holy Spirit to fill me afresh and anew this day and to guide and direct me in everything that I say and do today. In Jesus's name, I ask. Amen.

Nutrition Thought for the Day.

Selenium is acclaimed to prevent many different types of diseases, such as some cancers and prostate inflammation, but the research is not conclusive, and selenium should not be ingested without the guidance of a physician. At least one report claims that selenium may cause or aggravate prostate cancer. There is another grave concern I have about selenium. Our selenium requirement is very small (55 µg per day for adult men and women) with a small window between our requirement and the toxicity level. If you take in too much selenium, it can indeed be toxic. Moderation, as with all the other vitamins and minerals, is the key.

Day 348
You Have Received the Spirit of Adoption

For you have not received a spirit of slavery leading to fear again, but you have received a spirit of adoption as sons by which we cry out, "Abba! Father!" (Romans 8:15)

Before Jesus came to the earth, the Jews lived in fear. Paul is telling the saved Romans that they had not received a spirit of slavery that leads to fear again—that is the old fear they used to have. He is telling them that instead, they received a spirit of adoption as sons by which they cry out, "Abba, Father." When you received Jesus as your Savior and Lord, you became a child of God (Romans 8:16, Galatians 4:7). You are coheir with Christ. As strange as that may sound, it is true. Fear makes you a slave to whatever it is you are fearful of but you do not have to give in to the spirit of fear. As someone that is born again you are no longer a slave to anything or to anyone. Do not allow fear or any other emotion to take you captive. John 8:36 says, "so if the Son sets you free, you will be free indeed." The Son, Jesus Christ, has indeed set you free. Walk in freedom today knowing that you are not a slave to anything and you do not have to allow any fear, emotion, or lie take you captive. You are not a slave to your new healthy lifestyle program either. Do not let it control you but you should control it at your pace, even if that is a pace slower than you intended.

Father, I know that I am no longer a slave to fear or to anything or anyone else because I have been set free by my Savior and Lord and I have been delivered from all fear. Fear is a spirit that tries to take over my mind and control me, but it has no more control over me. I have been given a spirit of adoption by You, and I am coheir with Jesus. That is an awesome statement I know, but it is true because Your Word says it is and I choose to believe Your Word. I know that Your Son has set me free and I am free indeed. I thank You, Father, in the name of Jesus. Amen.

Nutrition Thought for the Day.

Chromium (chemical symbol is Cr) is an interesting mineral. We are talking about chromium—the same chromium that makes up chrome wheels on automobiles—this is a required mineral. The RDA requirement for chromium has not been established but the estimated safe and adequate intake is very low at 35 µg for males and 25 µg for females. As we get older, it drops to 30 and 20 µg respectively for males and females after fifty years of age. It is amazing how important this small amount of chromium is in our diet for us to be healthy. We could easily get a toxic amount of chromium by ingesting large amounts of chromium supplements which are readily available and encouraged by some people to be consumed.

Day 349
We Are the Righteousness of God

He made Him who knew no sin *to be* sin on our behalf, so that we might become the righteousness of God in Him. (2 Corinthians 5:21

This is how we obtained our righteousness. Jesus walked the face of the earth without ever committing a single sin of any kind. The Bible tells us that He was tempted in every way that we are tempted, yet without sin (Hebrews 4:15). Remember that Jesus walked the face of the earth as a man and can sympathize with our weaknesses as is described in Hebrews 4:15, "Yet, He did not commit any sin whatsoever." The wages of sin is death (Romans 6:23). So, if someone lived their entire life on earth without ever sinning as Jesus did, then, according to the Scriptures, He should never die. But we know that Jesus did die without committing any sin and in so doing, as today's scripture says, He took on all of our sins and sacrificed Himself for them so that they no longer have any effect or hold on us. Since He did not sin He is true righteousness, and He passes that righteousness on to us since He died on our behalf. That is a truly awesome event. We can never be worthy enough to thank Him for what He did for all of mankind. As you go through your day today, keep in mind what Jesus did for you and who you are in Christ as a result. This scripture should give you strength in all that you do. As you continue with your healthy lifestyle regimen, increase your endurance with the hope given to you in this scripture.

Father, I have hope in You and Your Word, and I see the awesome thing that Jesus did for me. It is beyond my comprehension how He could be tempted with everything that I am tempted with and yet never sin, not even once. He totally conquered and overcame sin of every type; then He took on Himself all the sins that have ever been committed since the beginning of time and ever will be committed to the end of time. He did this out of love for us. That is a kind of love that is difficult for me to grasp but I receive it, and I thank You, Jesus, for Your love. Amen.

Nutrition Thought for the Day.
Functions of chromium include its role in the production of what is known as the glucose tolerance factor (GTF). This factor is not completely understood, but when we are deficient in the GTF, insulin is not taken up as well by cells. When GTF is adequate, insulin is more effective. Therefore chromium is listed as an important mineral for preventing diabetes, and indeed it is. However, if the chromium level in a body is adequate to meet all requirements, taking an extra amount of chromium will not help and will not stop diabetes. Chromium is also given credit for increasing muscle gain and is used by many weightlifters. This may be of interest to some of you but do not put a lot of stock in those claims. Most of the research that has been completed with chromium and muscle gain does not warrant an increase intake for bodybuilders, and I cannot recommend it.

Day 350
Be Careful about What You Put in Your Heart

"You brood of vipers, how can you, being evil, speak what is good? For the mouth speaks out of that which fills the heart." (Matthew 12:34)

The Pharisees were not Jesus's favorite people because they were hypocrites and He frequently called them on their hypocrisy. In this verse He calls them a brood of vipers and asks them how they say anything that is good if they are evil. He tells them that they speak out of their mouths that which fills their hearts. Another version says, "out of the abundance of the heart the mouth speaks." He was saying that since they were evil and their hearts were full of evil, how could they say anything that would be considered good. It is important to remember that what fills your heart is also what is on your mind and this is what you are going to speak out of your mouth.

Saying this another way, what you put into your heart is what comes out of your mouth. If you fill your heart with God's Word, then when the going gets rough, it is God's Word that will well up in your heart and comes up out of your mouth. If you spend your time reading trash or looking at trashy things on TV, that is what will build up in your heart. If you watch a lot of violence on TV, then it will be easier for you to become violent if you were to get into similar situations as you saw on TV. Even if what you are watching is not really sinful but very worldly, then worldly ideas will come out of your mouth. You need to guard your heart and be careful of what you take in because that will determine what you say. This is also true of negative thoughts. If you continuously think on negative things, then negativity builds up in your heart and that is what comes out of your mouth. This is very true with your healthy lifestyle regimen. If you are constantly looking at the negative and saying, "Oh I'll never lose that much weight (or gain enough weight). I always fail at the diets that I try." This sets you up for failure from the beginning. Being positive does not make things happen the way you want them to, but being positive sets the stage for hope. Hope builds faith. Faith moves mountains. Are you ready to move a mountain today?

> Father, I want to guard my heart. I know that if I put in negative thoughts, negative words will come out of my mouth. If I put in evil or lustful thoughts, evil and lustful words will come out of my mouth. If I continue to do this, then the thoughts will turn into actions. To avoid this, I know that I must put in Your Word so when I need encouragement, Your Word will come out of my mouth. Help me to be thought conscious so I can allow only positive and wholesome thoughts in my mind today. I ask for this in the name of Jesus. Amen.

Nutrition Thought for the Day.

Chromium has also been related to reducing cholesterol, and some research articles indicate that it may be somewhat effective while other research indicates that it does not affect cholesterol whatsoever. There are medications available as well as other supplements that can help reduce cholesterol that would not be bordering on a level of toxicity as would be the case in taking large doses of chromium. Chromium has also been related to weight loss—a subject that would certainly be important to you—however, the research does not consistently verify that chromium is effective for weight loss and I cannot recommend it to you.

Day 351
Seek First His Kingdom

"Do not worry then, saying, 'What will we eat?' or 'What will we drink?' or 'What will we wear for clothing?' For the Gentiles eagerly seek all these things; for your heavenly Father knows that you need all these things. But seek first His Kingdom and His righteousness, and all these things will be added to you. So do not worry about tomorrow; for tomorrow will care for itself. Each day has enough trouble of its own." (Matthew 6:31–34)

In Matthew 6 Jesus is giving us several different guidelines for the way we should live our lives. Before verse 31, He tells us about concerns about food and clothes. In verse 31 he tells us not to worry about what we will have to eat or drink or what we will have for clothing. He separates the Jews from the Gentiles in this verse by insinuating that the Gentiles are worldly and they seek worldly things. He reminds us that our Father God knows what our needs are. The key to this verse and to every aspect of our lives is to seek first the Kingdom of God, and His righteousness and all these things will be added to us as well. Your primary goal should be to get closer to your God by following His Word and being a witness for Him daily. If you put God first, and seek His Kingdom, everything else will fall into place. This is a walk of faith, but it is what you, and all of us, need to do. The last thing He tells us in verse 34 is not to worry about tomorrow for each day has a new concern or new problem that we should be willing to take in stride knowing that our God will see us through. Put your faith in God and trust Him. A source of worry for you is your new healthy lifestyle program but do not let it be worrisome. Put everything you do in God's hands and trust Him.

> Father, Your Word is full of so much good advice and has the answers to all of my problems. I should not worry about material things that are even basics for life like food, clothing, and shelter. Each day has a worldly problem of its own, but You have already overcome the world (John 16:33). The key to a successful life on this earth is the same as the key to pleasing You and the very same key to have peace that surpasses all understanding, and that key is to seek first Your Kingdom, and Your righteousness and everything else will fall into place for me. I desire to do that today and to put all the cares of the world aside and not to worry but to trust in You. I thank You, Father, in Jesus's name. Amen.

Nutrition Thought for the Day.

Sources of chromium include liver as the best source and brewer's yeast is also an excellent source. Other sources include nuts, cheeses, whole grains, mushrooms, and some spices. There is not enough room in this book to talk about spices as much as I would like, but the fact that spices are a good source of some of the trace minerals and can be used to make food much tastier is certainly something for you to consider. By using spices you can also add many antioxidants to your diet besides the addition of nutrient content, and you can reduce salt to flavor foods. That in itself may be a tremendous aid in preventing cardiovascular disease and high blood pressure.

Day 352
Do Not Worry about Worldly Things

But the Lord answered and said to her, "Martha, Martha, you are worried and bothered about so many things; but *only* one thing is necessary, for Mary has chosen the good part, which shall not be taken away from her." (Luke 10:41–42)

Do not be concerned with worry and do not become obsessed with daily routines. It is an example given to us by Jesus when He addressed Martha's concern to detail. While Jesus was traveling, He was invited to enter into the home of a woman named Martha. Martha had a sister named Mary who was intent on listening to God's Word while Martha was intent on making preparations to get everything just perfect for Jesus's visit. While Martha was distracted from what Jesus was saying with all the preparations, her sister Mary was sitting at Jesus's feet listening to what He had to say. This irritated Martha, and she came to Jesus and said, "Lord, do You not care that my sister has left me to do all the serving alone? Then tell her to help me" (Luke 10:40). Jesus's response was verse 41 and 42. He was saying that listening to God's Word was more important than preparing a meal for the very Son of God and He refused to tell Mary to help Martha. In verse 42 He said, "Mary has chosen the good part, which shall not be taken away from her." Note that this is directly in line with yesterday's scripture Matthew 6:31–34: "Seek first the Kingdom of God." This is more important than our worldly preparations, even when our worldly preparations are for a good cause. Are you more concerned with worldly activities than with studying God's Word and/or fellowshipping with like-minded believers? Try to balance your time so that you are giving proper attention to your God.

Father, I know that doing good works is something we all should be diligently practicing while on this earth. However, today's scripture has shown me that even doing good works could be a problem if the results of doing so much for others causes me to be distracted from Your Word. I can get so busy doing good works that I can neglect my fellowship time with You Jesus, and that can cause me not to be able to hear Your voice even though I am spending my time doing godly works. Help me by the power of Your Holy Spirit to be able to discern how much time I should spend doing works and how much time I should spend seeking Your face. In Your name, Jesus, I pray. Amen.

Nutrition Thought for the Day.

The next mineral is very important in our diet but is also somewhat controversial. That mineral is fluoride (chemical symbol is F). You probably know of fluoride as the mineral that can help prevent tooth decay and you probably are aware that fluoride is added to some toothpaste for this purpose. The question that many ask is fluoride effective and is it safe? I cannot give you definitive answers for either of these, but I can tell you what the research is showing presently. There is a thin layer of enamel that covers your teeth and makes the teeth hard. This enamel requires fluoride in order to be hard and the harder it is the more resistant it is to tooth decay. Ideally, fluoride needs to be added to the diet when the enamel is forming for the most effective results.

Day 353
Be a Fruit Bearer

"My Father is glorified by this, that you bear much fruit, and so prove to be My disciples." (John 15:8)

How can we glorify our heavenly Father? One way your heavenly Father is glorified is by you bearing much fruit. If you bear fruit for your Father, you are also proving yourself to be Jesus's disciple. So how do we reconcile the differences between yesterday's scripture that says not to be obsessed with doing works? One helps the other. Bearing fruit can be done in a number ways. The first thing we think of is leading someone to Christ, and that is certainly being fruitful. But as mentioned yesterday, doing good works for those in need is also being fruitful. Leading someone to Christ is also certainly good works. The key is there is a balance in being a witness for your faith by doing good works but also by studying God's Word to learn to be a better witness. The more you seek your God and the closer you get to Him, the more you should learn about how to be a witness for Him. Being a witness could be one-on-one with someone, teaching Sunday school, or just being godly in your workplace and every-day contact with your peers—including those that you may be working with on your healthy lifestyle program. You see one leads to another in that the more you learn, the more you have to teach, the greater the witness you can be and the more fruit you produce. Look for examples today how you might be a witness with your life as well as with your words.

Father, I ask for You and the Holy Spirit to guide me so that I will know how to be a witness for You in my everyday walk through the world while balancing that with studying Your Word and spending time with You in prayer and worship. I have worldly obligations that I need to complete to be a witness. If I do not complete my worldly obligations, people will see me as someone that is slack and that would not be a good witness as a Christian. At the same time, within the laws of the land, I need to learn how to be a better witness while I fulfill my worldly obligations. I need to balance that with time spent in Your Word and quiet time, talking to You and worshipping You. I ask for guidance to complete this balance in the name of Jesus. Amen.

Nutrition Thought for the Day.

In addition to making teeth hard, fluoride is also necessary to make bones hard and is needed for proper bone formation. Some research indicates that sodium fluoride taken in larger doses in conjunction with calcium supplements appears to stimulate bone production. However, the dose of fluoride used in the research was too large for me to recommend and the research is still too sketchy. Fluoride added to drinking water at the rate of one part per million (1ppm) is enough to prevent tooth decay. Many states require fluoride to be in the drinking water, but many do not. It has been my experience as a nutrition teacher that those students who were raised in an area where fluoride was added to the drinking water experienced very few or no cavities by the time they were in my class (20 to 22 years of age). Those that were raised where there was no fluoridation of the drinking water had large numbers of cavities. Granted that is not a scientific analysis, but this is generally what the research shows.

Day 354
Do Not Look for a Sign but Look to the Lord

For they all saw Him and were terrified. But immediately He spoke with them and said to them, "Take courage; it is I, do not be afraid." (Mark 6:50)

This story took place when Jesus walked on water to meet His disciples while they were trying to row against the wind in a storm. When they first saw Him, they thought He was a ghost and they were terrified until He spoke to them: "Take courage; it is I, do not be afraid." The next verse tells us He got into the boat with them and the wind stopped. They were utterly astonished. Verse 52 of Mark 6 tells us that they were fearful because their hearts were hardened since they did not gain any insight from the incident of the loaves and fishes (just before this Jesus performed the miracle of feeding the 5000 men with just a few loaves and fishes). So how could the men of God that were walking with Jesus and watching Him perform miracles have their hearts hardened? Doesn't it seem like only habitual sinners would have hardened hearts? This shows us that it does not take an extreme sinful nature to cause our hearts to be hardened but we can be seeking God, even walking with Him as the apostles literally were, and still have hard hearts. The apostles' hearts were hardened because they did not receive the miracle Jesus did with the loaves and fishes. Are there works in the Bible that you do not receive? Are there parts of the Bible that seem to be too outrageous for you to set your faith on? Consider today what you believe and what you do not believe and set your hearts on everything the Bible says and has for you. Guard your hearts and do not let them be hardened.

Father, I can see in the Bible that it is not really that difficult to get our hard hearts. It does not take a lot of sin, but disbelief and lack of faith can cause me to have a hardened heart. I want to have a soft, pliable heart that You can work for Your glory. I resolve this day to be attentive to Your Word and ask that You lead me in the way of obedience when I begin to doubt or drift apart from Your Word. I want to guard my heart against ever becoming hard because of my actions or my disbelief. In Jesus's name, I pray. Amen.

Nutrition Thought for the Day.

Fluoride occurs naturally in water and many different foods, but most foods are very low in fluoride. As you know, fluoride is also found in toothpaste, mouth rinses, gels, and various kinds of tooth varnish and fluoride treatments. Research shows fluoride to be effective when combined with a healthy diet and good oral hygiene. The use of fluoride toothpaste or mouth rinses once a day is probably not going to be a sufficient effective oral hygiene. Brushing more frequently and flossing is important. The fluoride in supplements and toothpaste encourage the re-mineralization and strengthening of weak areas on the teeth—that is the spots that are beginning to have cavity formation.

Day 355
In Fearful Times Look to the Lord

When I am afraid, I will put my trust in You. (Psalm 56:3)

In case you think to be a strong Christian you must never have fearful moments, know that is not true. We all have fear from time to time. However, we have not been given a spirit of fear but a spirit of power, love, and a sound mind (2 Timothy 1:7). Each of us has several opportunities a day to give into a spirit of fear. Even when we are walking in the Word and are solid in our beliefs, the devil will still try to hit us with fear. Frequently this will happen at night when we are trying to sleep. The devil loves darkness. Do not feel like something is wrong with you, that you are not a good Christian if fearful, or anxious thoughts run through your head. Remember that you do not have to give in to any such thoughts and you can rebuke them in the name of Jesus and think on the righteous things of the Bible. Always trust in God when fear comes and talk to Him. Remember His promises and recall all the good things that He has done for you in the past. Our God is a God of completion, and He will complete the work that He started in you long ago. You cannot stop fearful thoughts from running through your mind, but you can avoid giving into the spirit of fear by allowing them to stay.

Lord Jesus, I know that I have not been given a spirit of fear but a spirit of power and love. I know that my mind is sound and that I can control my thought life (2 Corinthians 10:5). Although fearful thoughts may come to my head from time to time, I do not have to give in to them, and I choose this day to rebuke them in the name of Jesus. I know that any fearful thought that comes to me is not of You but from the evil one and I refuse to entertain them and allow them to stay in my mind. I declare this in the name of Jesus. Amen.

Nutrition Thought for the Day.

There are no RDA established for fluoride due to insufficient research but intakes of 4 and 3mg per day for males and females respectively are considered adequate. As mentioned, 1 ppm in drinking water is all that is necessary to be effective in preventing tooth decay. An important factor in preventing tooth decay is the amount of sugar and sugary drinks that we take in, particularly what we allow children to have. Excessive sugar and sticky sugary foods (such as gumdrops, licorice, anything that will stick to the teeth including raisins) can cause cavities to begin. Plaque building up on the teeth, due to a lack of brushing and flossing, houses the bacteria that feed on the sugar that ruins our teeth.

Day 356
Continually Offer up Praise

Through Him then, let us continually offer up a sacrifice of praise to God, that is, the fruit of lips that give thanks to His name. (Hebrews 13:15)

Lucifer was originally created to be the leader of worship in the heavens. He was also called star of the morning and the son of the dawn. He rebelled against God because he wanted to receive all the worship for himself. He was thrown out of heaven and cast down to earth because of this and became Satan (Isaiah 14:12). We were originally created to fellowship with our God and to give Him glory. Satan hates for us to worship God because he still wants to receive the worship for himself, hence his constant temptations trying to get us to turn away from our God. When we praise our God, it causes Satan to be angry and to leave our presence because he cannot stand to see us worshipping God. Praise drives out Satan and drives out fear. If fear begins to close in on you from all the worries and cares that you face every day, you can overcome by actively rebuking the temptations and the devil, and you can continually offer up a sacrifice of praise to your God. What comes from your lips should be fruitful and bring praise to His name; your words should be for the glory of your God. At the beginning of your day you can offer it up as a praise offering to your God—everything you do can be done in an attitude of praise if you do it for the glory of God with a heart full of love for Him. Why don't you start your day today by offering everything you do today for the glory of your God and offer the day up as a sacrifice of praise?

Father, I want to praise You continually from my lips, but also I want everything I do to be done in such a godly manner that it will bring praise to You. You alone are worthy of all praise and honor and glory. I desire to be a praise offering to You. I know that the devil cannot stand to see me praise You and when temptations come I ask for Your Holy Spirit to bring to my mind a song of praise, even if it is one I just sing to myself under my breath, I will sing it for Your glory. In Jesus's name, I pray. Amen.

Nutrition Thought for the Day.
Iodine (chemical symbol is I) is required in very small amounts but is extremely important. Our thyroid gland is located in our throat area and lies across the trachea in a symmetrical formation with parts of the thyroid gland on each side of the trachea. If the outline of it was visible, its shape would look similar to a butterfly. The thyroid gland produces a hormone called thyroxine and requires iodine. This hormone regulates our basal metabolic rate. If the thyroid gland is overactive and produces too much thyroxine, this causes a high basal metabolic rate and a very active high-energy person that will probably never gain extra weight. On the other hand, if the thyroid gland produces too little thyroxine, the person will have a low basal metabolic rate and will be very sluggish and gain weight very easily. If you follow a low-calorie diet and exercise program to the letter and you do not lose weight, it would be good to have your thyroxine level checked.

Day 357
Faith is Believing What You Cannot See

And He got up and rebuked the wind and said to the sea, "Hush, be still." And the wind died down and it became perfectly calm. And He said to them, "Why are you afraid? Do you still have no faith?" (Mark 4:39–40)

Jesus was teaching along the coast of the Sea of Galilee and related several parables to the people and His apostles. Later Jesus and the apostles got into a boat and started for the other side of the sea. While Jesus was asleep in the stern of the boat a violent storm came up, and the waves were breaking over the boat so that the boat was filling up with water. The apostles, being very fearful, woke Him up and asked Him if He did not even care that they were all perishing. Jesus got up, rebuked the wind and sea, and commanded it to be still. Jesus asked His apostles why they were afraid and asked them if they still did not have faith. The apostles had been with Jesus for some time now and were witnesses to several miracles. Having seen the miracles that Jesus performed, they should have had their faith strengthened and believed that Jesus would not let them perish. If you were in the boat with Jesus, where would your faith be? No, you have not walked with Jesus as the apostles did, and you have not seen firsthand the many miracles He performed; but you have the scriptures to show you everything that He did and all the miracles performed in His name since then.

When Jesus first appeared to His apostles after His resurrection, Thomas was not with them. When they told Thomas they had seen the Lord, he did not believe them. Later Jesus appeared to them again and Thomas was there. Jesus had Thomas stick his fingers in His wounds so he could believe it was really Him. Then He told Thomas: "Because you have seen Me, have you believed? Blessed are they who did not see, and yet believed" (John 20:29). You are one of those who is blessed because you have not walked with Jesus yet you believe in His Word. Jesus expects you to believe His Word but declares that you are blessed because of it. Be blessed today and encourage yourself with the Words of Jesus.

Lord Jesus, I have not had the privilege of walking side-by-side with You through the streets of Jerusalem, nor have I had the pleasure of watching You perform the awesome miracles recorded in Your Word. However, I have had the privilege of reading Your Word and imagining how the people must have felt when they saw You raise people from the dead. I have also seen testimonies of people who have received miracles in my time, and I know that miracles are still true today. I resolve to believe everything in Your Word and look forward to seeing miracles done today in Your name. It is in Your name that I pray. Amen.

Nutrition Thought for the Day.
So what does iodine have to do with the thyroid gland and the hormone thyroxine? Thyroxine has no function without its cofactor iodine. A deficiency of iodine causes a condition known as goiter, in which case the thyroid gland becomes enlarged and could get to be the size of a softball underneath a person's chin. If the thyroid gland stops producing thyroxine, it can be supplemented by medication. The requirement for thyroxine is only 150 µg per day for men and women. In the United States, the average normal intake should be well over this amount.

Day 358
You Have Been Given the Kingdom

"Do not be afraid, little flock, for your Father has chosen gladly to give you the kingdom." (Luke 12:32)

This is the Luke version of Matthew 6:31–34 in which Jesus told us not to worry about food or clothing but to seek first the Kingdom of God and all these things would be given unto us as well. Earlier in chapter 12 of Luke Jesus tells us the same thing, not to worry about food or clothing but to seek first His Kingdom and these things will be added to us. Then in verse 32, He tells us not to be afraid because our heavenly Father has gladly chosen to give us the Kingdom. If we read the scriptures every day as a duty or just as something we need to do for a checkoff list, we may never stop to meditate on what we are reading, and we may not fully understand this scripture. Jesus tells us that our heavenly Father has gladly chosen to give us the Kingdom! The Kingdom that He is talking about is, of course, the Kingdom of heaven. If we meditate on this, we can see how awesome this statement is. We have waiting for us a heavenly Kingdom where there is no pain, suffering, poverty, and no worry about our weight. This ought to help us get through our trials on this earth if we walk every day meditating on this fact—we are kids of the Kingdom of God, and our mansion awaits us in heaven! Think of this as you go through your day and receive the hope that the scripture has for us.

Father God, I never cease to be amazed at the absolutely good news in Your Word. My time on this earth is temporary and is but a passing vapor compared to eternity. That being said, I have a royal Kingdom waiting for me after this life that is not just a vapor but is a thick silver lined glowing cloud that will last for all eternity. I have this waiting for me not based on what I have done but based on what Jesus has done for me on the cross. I choose to give You, Lord Jesus, all the glory, honor, and praise for what You have done for me. In Your name, Jesus, I make this statement. Amen.

Nutrition Thought for the Day.

One of the best sources of iodine is seafood. The concentration of iodine in plants varies a great deal since it depends upon the concentration of iodine in the soil. Many years ago there was a considerable deficiency of iodine in the central part of our country because of the inability to ship seafood that far inland. When researchers realized what was causing the deficiency they decided to add iodine to something that everyone uses every day, and that is salt. Today salt is iodized and a low salt intake should provide the iodine necessary. A problem with iodine is that some people are allergic to it and have to take in minimal amounts. Because of this, you can also buy salt that is iodine free, but you need to read the label.

Day 359
Do Not Let Your Heart Get Weighed Down

"Be on guard, so that your hearts will not be weighted down with dissipation and drunkenness and the worries of life, and that day will not come on you suddenly like a trap." (Luke 21:34)

If you do not remember to relax and meditate on God's Word for an answer to your problems as they arise, you will also be weighed down as today's scripture warns. You should be on guard so that your hearts are not weighed down with dissipation and drunkenness in the worries of life. You can substitute all kinds of words for drunkenness since this is not just referring to drinking alcohol but gluttony, lustfulness, pride, etc. All of these are distractions and ways of life that you want to avoid. The worries of life mentioned in the scripture could also be a multitude of things such as financial worries, worry about illnesses, safety, and provision for your family in general. All these are included in the worries of life, and if you pay too much attention to them you will find yourself drifting away from God's Word, and suddenly you will be in a trap. If you are walking steadily in God's Word, it is not likely that Satan will come at you with extreme fear all at once. He will gradually bring fearful situations into your mind a little at a time. If you do not deal with the little temptations and distractions as they arise, then they will get bigger and bigger, and you will find yourself in the trap mentioned above. Being that you are on a new program that promotes a healthy lifestyle, it gives place for you to be weighed down with dissipation and worries about not meeting your healthy goals. Do not let the devil come at you with those kinds of worries. Put your progress at the foot of the cross and ask for Jesus's guidance and strength for your own resolve to be successful and you will be.

Father, I thank You that I have Your Word and the Holy Spirit's guidance to help keep me on a direct path to Your Kingdom. I know that the devil will try to distract me and get me off that path with little distractions. If I give in and follow those detours, I will eventually find myself so far off the path that I will be lost. If I find myself in such a situation, I know that I can always turn back to You and Your Word. I trust that the Holy Spirit will guide me off such a path to the path of glory in Your Word. I thank You in the name of Jesus. Amen.

Nutrition Thought for the Day.
Manganese (chemical symbol is Mn) is found in numerous enzymes and functions either as an activator of enzymes or as a cofactor for enzymes. While it is important in many enzyme systems, it is common in a wide variety of foods with legumes being the best sources (beans and peas). Manganese deficiencies are rare and usually do not develop in humans unless it is purposely kept out of the diet. Therefore manganese supplements probably do not need to be added to vitamin supplements, but it is included in most vitamin-mineral supplements.

Day 360
Put Great Value on Discernment

When you lie down, you will not be afraid; when you lie down, your sleep will be sweet. (Proverbs 3:24)

This scripture is in the middle of five verses found in Proverbs 3:21–26. Because of the length of the five scriptures, I only listed one here, but I will tell you that verses 21 and 22 tells us to seek wisdom and discretion and not to let them out of our sight. They will give us direction and guidance and protect us at night when we sleep. We will not be fearful. We will walk with confidence and will not stumble because our God will keep our feet from stumbling. We get wisdom and discernment by reading God's Word and by asking for wisdom and discernment. We should not become legalistic with having to read the Word for a certain length of time each day but, at the same time, the more we read God's Word, the wiser we become, and discernment comes a lot easier. Whenever you get into a tight spot or a situation where you need to come up with an answer to solve some dilemma, whether it be at work, at home, or with your healthy lifestyle, you would do well to follow this advice. Be calm and relax. From your knowledge of the Word, see if you can think of a biblical situation that covers the question you are facing. Ask God to remind you of anything in His Word that pertains to your situation. Ask Him for wisdom and then meditate for a few minutes on what comes through your mind. This does not mean that every single problem that comes up will be easily settled, but if you take the steps, you will be walking in faith and trusting in your God for direction. If you do this regularly, He will guide you.

Father, so many times when a question or problem arises in my life, my immediate reaction is to try to figure it out on my own. Sometimes that may work to my advantage but sometimes not. If I stop and clear my head and think of Your Word and seek Your wisdom, I have a much better chance of solving the problem that is facing me. I ask for Your Holy Spirit to give me direction, guidance, and wisdom for every problem, conflict, or dilemma that I may face today, and I know that I will receive help from You. I thank You in advance in the name of Jesus. Amen.

Nutrition Thought for the Day.
Molybdenum (chemical symbol is Mb) is another mineral that is widespread among all foods, but like selenium and iodine, its concentration in plants is dependent upon its concentration in the soil. It is important as a cofactor of oxidation-reduction enzymes, but a deficiency of molybdenum in humans is rare. The requirement is only 45 µg per day for men and for women. Molybdenum supplementation is not necessary.

WAYNE E. BILLON, PH.D., RDN, LDN

Day 361
Your Struggle is Not against Flesh and Blood

For our struggle is not against flesh and blood, but against the rulers, against the powers, against the world forces of darkness, against the spiritual *forces* of wickedness in the heavenly *places*. (Ephesians 6:12)

Today's scripture and the next four days will be Ephesians 6:12–18. In chapter 6, Paul is telling the Ephesians how to respect one another and how they should treat each other. In verse 12 he tells them who their real enemy is. Note it is not flesh and blood (our family, friends, or those that would do us harm) but it is against the powers of darkness in heavenly places. This scripture clearly tells us our fight is spiritual and not physical. This requires a different kind of warfare. In verses 13–18, Paul relates the best way, the only way, to be successful in fighting spiritual battles. This does not mean that those that come against you, accuse you, or criticize you, perhaps at home or at work, are of the devil. They may even be born again believers, but they could be deceived or influenced by the spiritual forces of evil in heavenly places. Sometimes the people that hurt us the most are the ones that are closest to us. Realize that it is not their flesh and blood we are fighting, it is the demonic powers that influence heavenly places. Do not hate the sinner, hate the sin and the source of the sin which is the devil. God did not create anything bad. He created everything good, and it became bad due to bad influence. The next few days will tell you how to handle this evil influence.

Father God, I now realize that my battles on this earth are not against flesh and blood but against the powers and forces of darkness that lurk in heavenly places. I do not understand everything I should about spiritual warfare but I know that the devil is behind the powers of darkness and would love to see us fall from grace. I ask for the Holy Spirit to shine a light on these powers of darkness so that I can see the truth. I intend to use Your Word to fight the good fight against these evil forces. In the name of Jesus, I pray. Amen.

Nutrition Thought for the Day.

There are six minerals that are considered to be ultra-trace minerals which means they are needed in extremely small amounts for normal metabolism—if they are needed at all. You may be surprised at some of the minerals that are included on this list. Arsenic (chemical symbol is As) is found in the body in trace amounts. Yes, the same arsenic that is toxic and can kill humans. Some research has shown that it is necessary for proper growth in some animals. Human requirements are not known. Boron (chemical symbol is B) is essential for plants to survive but has been found to be toxic to humans. However in the 1980s it was found to possibly be required for animals. Its role in human nutrition, if it has one, is not known.

Day 362
Stand Firm I

Therefore, take up the full armor of God, so that you will be able to resist in the evil day, and having done everything, to stand firm. (Ephesians 6:13)

The only way to defeat the devil and all of his schemes is with the armor of God. There are several parts to the armor and each will be discussed over the next few days. Once you have employed all the armor available to you the Scripture tells you to stand firm. The first three words of verse 12 say, "Stand firm therefore." So when you are under attack by the forces of evil, no matter how the attack comes (by way of your thought life, an abuse from another person, an unfavorable incident, etc.), you are to stand firm. You may not see results immediately in which case you stand firm. Remember James 4:7–8 says to submit yourself to God, resist the devil, and he will flee from you. This is your formula: submit yourself to God, put on the full armor of God, resist the devil, and stand firm. Follow these steps and see if you are not victorious in all of your battles.

Father God, I choose this day to submit totally to You, put on the full armor You have provided as spelled out in Ephesians 6, resist the devil, and stand firm in Your Word. When I have done everything as stated in Your Word, I will remain to stand firm. I know that by following this formula and responding to the lead of the Holy Spirit I will be successful. I declare this in the name of Jesus. Amen.

Nutrition Thought for the Day.
Nickel (chemical symbol is Ni) is another mineral that is found to be essential in the development of some animals but its role in human nutrition is not known. In animals it may function in enzyme activity. Silicon (chemical symbol is Si), otherwise known as sand, may play a role in the hardening of bones. When human bones are analyzed they contain some trace amounts of silicon. Is silicon there because it is required or is it there because it is a contaminant? Definitive answers still need to be determined.

WAYNE E. BILLON, PH.D., RDN, LDN

Day 363
Stand Firm II

Stand firm therefore, having girded your loins with truth, and having put on the breastplate of righteousness, and having shod your feet with the preparation of the Gospel of peace. (Ephesians 6:14 15)

The first step in putting on the armor of God is girding your loins with truth. In the days this was written men wore long robes as a part of their normal attire. If they tried to run or fight with those long robes, they would trip, so they tied their robes up around their loins to prepare for battle. This is symbolic of going into spiritual battle with the truth. The truth is God's Word and what it says about you, such as you are a world overcomer, more than a conqueror, a child of God and coheir with Jesus. Put on the spiritual breastplate of righteousness which you received when you accepted Jesus as your Lord and Savior. Next, you shod your spiritual feet with the Gospel of peace. The Gospel teaches peace; it is the handbook for peace, the peace that surpasses all understanding. This is knowing who you are in Christ and what authority you have over the devil. All of this also refers to you going into battle based on the merit of Jesus and not your own merit. Remember that the battles you face today are fought by the power of God's Word and not by your own power. Do not lose sight of who you are and you will be victorious.

Father God, You have equipped me for battle, and You have prepared me to be a winner in every conflict I may encounter by Your Word and the robe of righteousness given to me at salvation. I choose to receive what You have done for me through Your Son Jesus, and I will fight my battles based on Your Word and the direction of the Holy Spirit. I know that by Your Word I will be victorious and I intend to stand firm on Your Word, in Jesus's name. Amen.

Nutrition Thought for the Day.

Vanadium (chemical symbol is V) is found in a variety of foods but the concentration is very low. Research has shown several possible pharmacological effects but requirements have not been established for humans. Some research shows that it may have a role in treating diabetes but so little is known about the dose necessary to help, if it helps at all. Its effectiveness is still to be determined and I cannot recommend it. There are so many drugs that effectively treat diabetes that I believe we should stay with well-researched medications. The last element is cobalt (chemical symbol is Co). Cobalt is not a requirement per se but vitamin B12, which is not synthesized in our body, has cobalt as a part of its structure. When we take vitamin B12 into our bodies, cobalt is already there. It is necessary for the function of vitamin B12 but it is not a mineral that performs a specific function in our bodies on its own.

Day 364
Stand Firm III

In addition to all, taking up the shield of faith with which you will be able to extinguish all the flaming arrows of the evil one. And take the helmet of Salvation, and the sword of the Spirit, which is the word of God. (Ephesians 6:16–17)

Your faith is like a spiritual shield that can extinguish all of the lies the devil can shoot at you like flaming arrows. The biggest weapon the devil has is lies. He tries to get you to believe that you are a lowly creature who cannot accomplish anything. He will use any slight misfortune or slip-up to try to convince you of that. He will use a bad week in your healthy lifestyle program to try to make you look like a loser. Your faith is stronger than that. You know what God's Word says and you know who you are in Christ. Tell the devil who you are and that you refuse to listen to his lies. The scripture also tells you to use your Salvation as a helmet to protect your head—knowing what you have as a result of your Salvation should help you to keep your head clear and think through things with God's Word as a filter. Use the sword of the Spirit, which is the spoken Word of God, to directly speak to the devil and command him to be gone from you. Most, if not all, of these things you probably have been doing but you may not have realized the power you have through God's Word. As you walk through today be ready to use Ephesians 6 as your defense against any attack the enemy may throw at you. Note that there is no armor for your back. Do not turn your back to the enemy and run but face him head on and be victorious.

Father God, I am glad that, through Your Word, You have equipped me with everything I need to defend myself against the lies of the enemy. Ephesians 6 is an awesome chapter and has the battle plan I need to be victorious. By the power of Your Holy Spirit continuously remind me of the armor I have when I go into battle. I know that if I use the armor as You intended for me that I will be victorious. Holy Spirit I thank You for Your guidance and for leading me into battle. I thank You in the mighty name of Jesus. Amen.

Nutrition Thought for the Day.

One nutrient that we have not spent any time on but is extremely important is water. About 60% of the water that we take into our bodies comes from ingested liquids; approximately 30% comes from ingested foods, and approximately 10% is formed from metabolism in our bodies. The old adage of eight glasses of water a day is probably not enough for most people. If a cup is 8 ounces, and we drank 8 cups a day, that would be 64 ounces or very close to 2 liters. Most adult males need over 3 liters a day, and adult females need almost 3 liters a day. It would be good if the liquids you drank did not contain caffeine or alcohol. Until recently it was recommended that none of your daily liquids contain caffeine because caffeine acts as a diuretic and causes you to lose more liquids through urination. Some of the fluid you take in could be caffeinated, but I do not suggest that you take in a lot of caffeine.

WAYNE E. BILLON, PH.D., RDN, LDN

Day 365
Stand Firm IV

With all prayer and petition pray at all times in the Spirit, and with this in view, be on the alert with all perseverance and petition for all the saints. (Ephesians 6:18)

The final act is to pray. Prayer is not necessarily asking God for something. The dictionary sums up several possibilities for prayer: a devout petition, a spiritual communion with God as in supplication, thanksgiving, adoration, or confession. One might add praising God as an act of worship. Basically, it is fellowshipping with God but not always asking Him for something. Note Ephesians 6:18 says, "with prayer and petition." It separates prayer from petition so there is a difference. The prayer part could be agreeing with God's Word that you have the armor it says you have, it could be praising Him for giving you His Word to fight the devil, or thanking Him for your Salvation. The scripture adds a few more instructions and that is to pray at all times and in the Spirit. In an earlier devotion it was mentioned you could make your entire day an act of praise to your God. This could be one way to pray at all times, understanding that prayer is more than a petition. You can talk to God while you are in the shower, while driving, walking across the parking lot, etc. The scripture also says to pray in the Spirit. For a Spirit filled Christian this is praying in tongues. Reference to this can be found in Romans 8:26–27, 1 Corinthians 14:14, 1 Corinthians 14:39, and Jude 20. If you are Spirit-filled you can pray in the Spirit in all of the circumstances mentioned above. If you do not believe in tongues, you can still pray with your understanding. In either case you can pray in a low whisper or pray in your mind if people are around you. The important thing is to continuously be in communion with your God.

> Father God, I now understand that prayer is more involved than most people think. Too many times my prayers to You have been no more than me asking for something and not for just wanting to communicate to You as a child to his Father. I am sorry that I have not been more talkative with You as my Father. I want to have a conversation with You each day that does not include just petitions but is for fellowship. Help me by Your Holy Spirit's guidance to be ready to talk to You throughout my day. In Jesus's name, I pray. Amen.

Nutrition Thought for the Day.

To maintain hydration during workouts, you should weigh yourself before you work out (any activity this can cause you to perspire a great deal, whether it be working with weights or aerobic exercise) and weigh yourself again immediately after exercise. For every pound you lose during exercise, you can assume the loss is due to water and not fat. To replace the water you lose, the rule of thumb for post-exercise rehydration is about 2 to 3 cups of fluid for every pound of weight loss. A good water replacement would be one of the many replacement drinks available but research it first to make sure it is reputable. Vitamin waters are not recommended for this. Maintaining hydration is extremely important to your health and losing water to lose weight is going to have a detrimental effect on your health.

May God richly bless you and provide you much success with your healthy lifestyle regimen and in everything else you attempt. If you genuinely believe in your heart what it says in John 3:16 ("For God so loved the world, that He gave His only begotten Son, that whoever believes in Him shall not perish, but have eternal life."), and you confess that with your mouth (Romans 10:9, "for with the heart a person believes, resulting in righteousness, and with the mouth he confesses, resulting in salvation"), you will have eternal life in heaven and you will be what is called a believer or saved.

If you have not asked Jesus to be your Lord and Savior and you want to, say aloud, loud enough for your own ears to hear, this prayer: *Lord Jesus, I believe You came to earth as a man, born of a virgin, and died for my sins. I believe that You were buried, rose from the grave, and ascended into heaven and You sit on the throne at the right hand of our Father God, interceding for me. I believe that You did all this for me and I confess to You that I am a sinner and ask You to forgive me of my sins and to come into my heart and be my Lord and Savior. I thank You, Jesus, for saving me.*

That is all it takes. If you said this prayer, and you believe it in your heart, you are now a believer. If you received Jesus as your Savior in the past but want to rededicate your life just say, *Lord Jesus, I have asked You to be my Lord and Savior but I know I have turned my back on You and did things I should not have. I ask for forgiveness even though I know I am already forgiven for I know You have never left me and that You are still in my heart. Continue to show me Your love and guidance. Amen.*

If you said either of these prayers anytime while reading this book, please use the email address here and share your good news with me. If this book has blessed you in any other way, please email me and let me know that too.

healthydevotional@gmail.com.

CPSIA information can be obtained
at www.ICGtesting.com
Printed in the USA
BVHW030241190819
556172BV00001BA/14/P

9 781733 402811